timely
.tions.'
'ormer
;socia-

forces
of the
lation.
ch the
cussed

under-
econ-
actors.
:xperts
,rovide

eoreti-
lations
ing for
those interested in comparative industrial relations as well as political
economy.'
—*Jimmy Donaghey, University of Warwick, United Kingdom*

'The most enduring and valuable book in the field of international
and comparative employment relations in the last 30 years, the sixth
edition covers advanced and emerging economies with insightful theoretical implications from a comparative perspective.'
—*Dong-One Kim, Korea University; President, ILERA*

'The most comprehensive and authoritative comparative analysis of
employment relations . . . especially welcomed because it provides
excellent comparisons of how employment systems in different countries responded to the effects of the post-2007 "Great Recession". By

doing so, this stellar group of authors and editors provide new insights on the adaptability of labor market institutions across the globe.'
—*Thomas Kochan, Massachusetts Institute of Technology, United States; former president, ILERA*

'By far the best and most widely used comparative industrial relations book.'
—*Sarosh Kuruvilla, Cornell University, United States*

'This latest edition is another major contribution by a group of eminent scholars in the field. It serves to promote the study of comparative employment relations in the current context of globalisation, which is also of topical interest to the International Labour Organization (ILO).'
—*Guy Ryder, Director-General, ILO*

'[The book] is state of the art. It is broad in its scope, and sophisticated in its consideration of national context and history. It gives a sense of where countries are headed, but also is replete with micro-level detail drawn from credible primary sources.'
—*Anthony Gould, Université Laval, Canada, in* Relations Industrielles/ Industrial Relations

**Praise for the fifth edition**

'For those of us who present employment relations in scholarly forums and in lecture halls, but also for policymakers and practitioners, *International and Comparative Employment Relations* . . . is an indispensable foundation text'
—*Chris Leggett, James Cook University, Australia, in* Journal of Industrial Relations

'The subject matter is important to a broad group of scholars. Overall, a useful introduction to national systems.'
—*R.L. Hogler, Colorado State University, United States, in* Choice

# INTERNATIONAL AND COMPARATIVE EMPLOYMENT RELATIONS

## NATIONAL REGULATION, GLOBAL CHANGES

Sixth Edition

Edited by

Greg J. Bamber, Russell D. Lansbury,
Nick Wailes and Chris F. Wright

**SAGE**

Los Angeles | London | New Delhi
Singapore | Washington DC

Los Angeles | London | New Delhi
Singapore | Washington DC

SAGE Publications Ltd
1 Oliver's Yard
55 City Road
London EC1Y 1SP

SAGE Publications Inc.
2455 Teller Road
Thousand Oaks
California 91320

SAGE Publications India Pvt Ltd
B 1/I 1 Mohan Cooperative Industrial Area
Mathura Road
New Delhi 110 044

SAGE Publications Asia-Pacific Pte Ltd
3 Church Street
#10-04 Samsung Hub
Singapore 049483

Cover design by Julia Eim
Cover photograph © iStock.com/
Rawpixel Ltd
Index by Puddingburn Publishing Services
Set in 10.5/13 pt Garamond by
Midland Typesetters, Australia
Printed in China at Everbest Printing Co.

**Library of Congress Control Number:
2015945016**

**British Library Cataloguing in
Publication data**

A catalogue record for this book is available
from the British Library

ISBN 978-1-47391-154-3
ISBN 978-1-47391-155-0 (pbk)

# Foreword

Changing the ending is a good way to improve a story. Even better is adding an ending that unites the sub-plots. In a notable advance on its predecessors, this latest edition of a widely respected book adds to the separate studies of different countries a concluding overview of international developments. The result breaks new ground as an integrated account of the forces shaping employment relations in the world economy.

The importance of this ending would be hard to exaggerate. The individual chapters, on twelve carefully selected countries, provide expert analysis of the national regulation of labour for more than half the world's population. It is crucial for this analysis to be up to date, because all these countries have seen substantial changes in the five years since the previous edition was published. From a wider perspective, in the time since the first edition—more than a quarter of a century—the change has been immense. Back in the 1980s, unions played a dominant role in employment relations in developed economies. But by the 2010s, their role in market sectors has withered to become, at least in some countries, almost insignificant. The driving forces behind this change have been international—in trade, in ownership, in finance and in technology. It is only by placing national developments within this international context that we can understand them and their implications for employment standards.

The collapse of the self-described communist world since the first edition of this book has led to a growing appreciation that there are many different ways of running market economies, with varying degrees of labour market coordination and intervention by the state. This has profound implications, not only for employment relations but for countries' broader political processes. The book's Introduction sets out a theoretical framework within which the salient institutional characteristics of the different countries discussed in the following chapters can be appreciated and compared.

However, the concluding chapter argues that this is not enough. It is true that there are common patterns emerging within countries. One example is the displacement of traditional employment with less stable and more crudely commercial relationships. Another example is the growing diversity of employment conditions *within* countries. But many of the underlying forces transcend the nation state. And here this chapter sketches the characters in a new story. Multinational enterprises have their own dynamics, and so have the increasingly complex global supply chains on which they rely. For five of the countries covered here, the European Union has been an important external influence of labour regulation. The scope of the International Labour Organization deserves renewed attention, as it approaches its centenary after languishing in benign impotence. For big corporations, the dependence of global products on brand-name recognition is increasing their exposure to reputational risk. Unions and other pressure groups are learning to exploit this in attempts to protect the labour standards of workers scattered globally across the supply chains. The new front line of employment relations is truly international.

This is the front line that will shape the careers of many of the readers of this book. It is where future employment conditions will be improved, defended or degraded. It is good that the authorship of this valuable collection of studies is moving to a younger generation of scholars. Their research and understanding of the limits of national regulation, and of the scope for international cooperation, will do much to shape the future story of employment.

*William Brown*
*Emeritus Professor of Industrial Relations and former Master*
*of Darwin College, University of Cambridge, United Kingdom;*
*former President, British Universities Industrial Relations*
*Association; former Director, Industrial Relations Research Unit*
*at the University of Warwick and foundation member of the*
*Low Pay Commission, which sets the United Kingdom's National*
*Minimum Wage*

# Contents

# Contributors

## EDITORS

**Greg J. Bamber** is a Professor at Monash University, Melbourne, Australia. His publications include more than 100 refereed articles and such jointly authored publications as *Up in the Air: How Airlines Can Improve Performance by Engaging Their Employees* (with J. Gittell, T. Kochan and A. von Nordenflytch, Cornell University Press, 2009) and 'Regulating Employment Relations, Work and Labour Laws: International comparisons between key countries', *Bulletin of Comparative Labour Relations*, 74 (with P. Pochet and others, Kluwer, 2010). He is a Visiting Professor at Newcastle University in the United Kingdom and a Guest Faculty Member at Harvard University in the United States. <www.gregbamber.com>

**Russell D. Lansbury** is Emeritus Professor of Work and Organisational Studies in the Business School at the University of Sydney, Australia. He is former President of the International Labour and Employment Relations Association and of the Australian Labour and Employment Relations Association. He is former joint editor of the *Journal of Industrial Relations*. His recent research has focused on the impact of management strategies in multinational enterprises on employment relations and labour practices. <http://sydney.edu.au/business/staff/Lansbury>

**Nick Wailes** is Associate Dean (Digital and Innovation) and a Professor at the UNSW Business School, Sydney, Australia. His areas of research interest include international and comparative employment relations and technology-related organisational change. <https://au.linkedin.com/in/nickwailes>

**Chris F. Wright** is a Research Fellow in the Discipline of Work and Organisational Studies, University of Sydney, Australia. He received his PhD from the University of Cambridge in the United Kingdom in 2011. Chris's research covers various issues relating to the intersection of employment, globalisation and public policy. He has a particular interest in labour market regulation, immigration and supply chains. <http://sydney.edu.au/business/staff/chriswr>

## CONTRIBUTORS

**Søren Kaj Andersen** is Associate Professor and Director of FAOS, Employment Relations Research Centre, Department of Sociology, University of Copenhagen, Denmark. He is also Visiting Associate Professor at the International Centre for Business and Politics, Copenhagen Business School.

**Lucio Baccaro** is Professor of Sociology at the University of Geneva, Switzerland. He previously taught at Case Western Reserve University and at MIT in the United States. He also held senior research positions at the International Labour Organization.

**Alexander J.S. Colvin** is the Martin F. Scheinman Professor of Conflict Resolution at the ILR School, Cornell University, Ithaca, in the United States. His recent publications include *Labor in a Globalizing World: An Introduction Focused on Emerging Countries* (with H. Katz and T. Kochan, Cornell University Press, 2015) and 'Convergence in industrial relations institutions: The emerging Anglo-American model?' *ILR Review*, 66(5): 1047–77 (with O. Darbishire, 2013). <www.ilr.cornell.edu/directory/ajc22>

**Fang Lee Cooke** is Professor of Human Resource Management and Asia Studies, Monash Business School, Monash University, Melbourne, Australia. Her research interests are in the area of employment relations, gender studies, diversity management, strategic human resource management, knowledge management and innovation, outsourcing, Chinese outward foreign direct investment and the employment of

Chinese migrants. Fang is the author of *HRM, Work and Employment in China* (Routledge, 2005), *Competition, Strategy and Management in China* (Palgrave Macmillan, 2008) and *Human Resource Management in China: New Trends and Practices* (Routledge, 2012). <www.buseco. monash.edu.au/about/staff/profile.php?cn=fang-cooke>

**Jesper Due** is a Professor at the FAOS Employment Relations Research Centre, Department of Sociology, University of Copenhagen, Denmark.

**Harry C. Katz** is the Interim Provost and Jack Sheinkman Professor of Collective Bargaining at Cornell University, Ithaca, in the United States. His major publications include *Labor Relations in a Globalizing World: An Introduction Focused on Emerging Countries* (with T. Kochan and A. Colvin, Cornell University Press, 2015), *Converging Divergences: Worldwide Changes in Employment Systems* (with O. Darbishire, Cornell University Press, 2002) and *The Transformation of American Industrial Relations* (with T. Kochan and R. McKersie, 2nd ed., Cornell University Press, 1993).

**Berndt K. Keller** is Professor Emeritus of Employment Relations at the University of Konstanz, Germany. He is the author of numerous articles and several books on German and European employment relations, including most recently *Einführung in die Arbeitspolitik* (7th ed., Odenbourg, 2008), *Arbeitspolitik im öffentlichen Dienst* (Edition Sigma, 2010) and *Atypische Beschäftigung zwischen Prekarität und Normalität* (with H. Seifert, Edition Sigma, 2013). He was co-editor of *Industrielle Beziehungen: The German Journal of Industrial Relations*, and was a member of the Executive Committee of the International Labour and Employment Relations Association. <http://www. uni-konstanz.de/keller>

**Anja Kirsch** is a Research Fellow at Freie Universität Berlin, Germany. She received her PhD from the University of Sydney, Australia, in 2008. Her current research focuses on women on corporate boards in Europe and on institutional approaches to employment relations. Recent publications include 'Employment relations in liberal market economies' in *The Oxford Handbook of Employment Relations* (with G. Jackson, Oxford University Press, 2014) and 'Executive board and supervisory board members in Germany's large corporations remain predominantly male', *DIW Economic Bulletin*, 4, pp. 35–47 (with E. Holst, 2015). <www.wiwiss.fu-berlin.de/fachbereich/bwl/management/jackson/team/ akirsch/index.html>

**Katsuyuki Kubo** is a Professor in the School of Commerce at Waseda University, Tokyo, Japan. His papers include 'The relationship between financial incentives for company presidents and firm performance in Japan', *Japanese Economic Review*, 59(4): 401–18. <www.f.waseda.jp/kkubo>

**Patrice Laroche** is a Professor of Human Resource Studies and Labour Relations at the ESCP Europe Business School in Paris, France. His research activity is mainly devoted to the study of industrial and labour relations, with particular emphasis on the analysis of the impact of unions on firm performance. His articles have appeared in *Industrial Relations: A journal of economy and society*, the *European Journal of Industrial Relations*, *Advances in Industrial and Labor Relations* and *Labor History*, among others. <www.escpeurope.eu/nc/faculty-research/the-escp-europe-faculty/professor/name/laroche–1/-/biography>

**Byoung-Hoon Lee** is Professor in the Department of Sociology, Chung-Ang University, Seoul, South Korea. He is the President of the Policy Research Institute for the Korea Government Employee Union and a public-interest representative of the Tripartite Commission. His research has focused on labour market segmentation and non-standard employment, and revitalisation of labour union movements and labour relations of public sectors.

**Jørgen Steen Madsen** is a Professor at the FAOS Employment Relations Research Centre, Department of Sociology, University of Copenhagen, Denmark.

**Kazuya Ogura** is an Associate Professor in the School of Commerce at Waseda University, Tokyo, Japan. He worked for the Japan Institute for Labour Policy and Training in Tokyo from 1993 to 2011. His publications include *Seishain no Kenkyu* (A Study of Regular Employees) (Nikkei).

**Valeria Pulignano** is Professor of Sociology of Labour and Industrial Relations at the University of Leuven, Belgium. She taught at the University of Warwick in the United Kingdom, where she is currently an Associate Fellow. She is also a co-researcher at the Interuniversity Research Center on Globalisation and Work (CRIMT) at the University of Montréal, Canada. <www.kuleuven.be/wieiswie/nl/person/00049644>

**Shyam Sundar** is a Professor in the Human Resources Management area, Xavier Labour Relations Institute, Xavier School of Management, Jamshedpur, India. He teaches Industrial Relations and Principles of Labour Administration. His research interests cover industrial relations issues and labour regulation and laws, and he has written extensively on these issues pertaining mostly to India.

**Hiromasa Suzuki** is an Emeritus Professor in the School of Commerce at Waseda University, Tokyo, Japan. He was formerly at the International Labour Organization in Geneva, Switzerland. His publications include a chapter in *Korekarano Koyou Senryaku* (Towards a Future Employment Strategy) (Japan Institute for Labour Policy and Training, 2007).

**Daphne G. Taras** is Dean of the Edwards School of Business at the University of Saskatchewan, Saskatoon, Canada. Her research investigates non-union forms of employee representation. She also publishes in public policy, and labour and employment law fields. Her publications include *Perspectives on Disability and Accommodation* (with K. Williams-Whitt, National Institute for Disability Management and Research, 2011) and *Canadian Labour and Employment Relations: Understanding union–management challenges and choices* (with M. Gunderson, Pearson, 2005). <www.edwards.usask.ca/faculty/Daphne%20Taras/index.aspx>

**Anil Verma** is Director of the Centre for Industrial Relations & Human Resources and Professor at the Rotman School of Management, University of Toronto, Canada. His work has been on immigrant labour market experience, the minimum wage, non-standard employment and public policies for employment growth. He served as Chair of Ontario Minimum Wage Panel, a Member of the Statistics Canada Advisory Committee on Labour and Income Statistics and a Member of the Board of Directors of COSTI Immigration Services. For a list of publications, see <www.rotman.utoronto.ca/~verma>.

**Jeremy Waddington** is Professor of Industrial Relations at the University of Manchester, United Kingdom, and Project Coordinator for the European Trade Union Institute, Brussels, Belgium. He has written extensively on topics associated with trade union membership, structure and organisation, and European works councils. His most recent book is *European Works Councils: A Transnational Industrial Relations Institution in the Making* (Routledge, 2010). Currently, he is working on board-level employee representation in Europe.

**Scott Walsworth** is an Associate Professor in the Edwards School of Business at the University of Saskatchewan, Saskatoon, Canada. His research interests include the effect of unions on firm performance and the integration of skilled immigrants into the Canadian labour market. <www.edwards.usask.ca/faculty/Scott%20Walsworth/index.aspx>

# Figures, tables and boxes

## FIGURES

## TABLES

## BOXES

# Abbreviations

| | |
|---|---|
| AC | Akademikernes (Confederation of Professional Associations) (Denmark) |
| ACAS | Advisory, Conciliation and Arbitration Service (UK) |
| ACCI | Australian Chamber of Commerce and Industry |
| ACFIC | All-China Federation of Industry and Commerce |
| ACFTU | All-China Federation of Trade Unions |
| ACTU | Australian Council of Trade Unions |
| AFL-CIO | American Federation of Labor-Congress of Industrial Organizations (US) |
| AGIRC | Association générale des institutions de retraite des cadres (French pension plan for senior management) |
| AICCTU | All India Central Council of Trade Unions |
| AiG | Australian Industry Group |
| AIOE | All India Organisation of Employers |
| AIRC | Australian Industrial Relations Commission |
| AITUC | All India Trade Union Congress |
| AMG | Army Military Government (Korea) |
| AMMA | Australian Mines and Metals Association |
| ANI | Accord national interprofessionnel (National Inter-professional Agreement) (France) |
| ARAN | Agenzia per la rappresentanza negoziale delle pubbliche amministrazioni (Agency for Bargaining in the Public Administration) (Italy) |

| | |
|---|---|
| ARPE | Early Retirement for Jobs Scheme |
| ASEAN | Association of Southeast Asian Nations |
| Assédic | Association pour l'emploi dans l'industrie et le commerce (Association for Employment in Industry and Trade) (France) |
| AWA | Australian Workplace Agreement |
| BCA | Business Council of Australia |
| BDA | Bundesvereinigung der Deutschen Arbeitgeberverbände (Confederation of German Employers' Associations) |
| BIS | Department for Business, Innovation and Skills (UK) |
| BJP | Bharatiya Janata Party (India) |
| BMS | Bharatiya Mazdoor Sangh (India) |
| CAI | Confederation of Australian Industry |
| CANSIM | Canadian Socio-Economic Information Management (Statistics Canada) |
| CBI | Confederation of British Industry (UK) |
| CCP | Chinese Communist Party |
| CDU | Christian Democratic Union (Germany) |
| CEC | China Enterprise Confederation |
| CEDA | China Enterprise Directors Association |
| CFDT | Confédération Française démocratique du travail (French Democratic Confederation of Labour) |
| CFE-CGC | Confédération Française de l'encadrement-Confédération générale des cadres (French Confederation of Management-General Confederation of Executives) |
| CFTC | Confédération Française des travailleurs chrétiens (French Confederation of Christian Workers) |
| CGB | Christlicher Gewerkschaftsbund (Confederation of Christian Unions) (Germany) |
| CGIL | Confederazione generale Italiana del lavoro (Italian General Confederation of Labour) |
| CGPME | Confédération générale des petites et moyennes entreprises (General Confederation of Small and Medium Enterprises) (France) |
| CGT | Confédération générale du travail (General Confederation of Labour) (France) |
| CGT-FO | Confédération générale du travail-Force ouvrière (General Confederation of Labour-Workers' Force) (France) |

| | |
|---|---|
| CHSCT | *Comité d'hygiène, de sécurité et des conditions de travail* (Health, Safety and Improvement of Working Conditions Committee) (France) |
| CIE | Council of Indian Employers |
| CIO | Congress of Industrial Organizations (US) |
| CISL | Confederazione Italiana sindacati dei lavoratori (Italian Confederation of Workers' Unions) |
| CITU | Centre of Indian Trade Unions |
| CLC | Canadian Labour Congress |
| CME | Coordinated market economy |
| CNPF | Conseil national du patronat Français (National Council of French Employers) |
| CO-industri | Central Organisation of Industrial Employees in Denmark (Centralorganisationen af industriansatte i Danmark) |
| CPI | Communist Party of India |
| CPI(M) | Communist Party of India (Marxist) |
| CSN | Confédération des syndicats nationaux (Confederation of National Trade Unions) (Canada) |
| CSU | Christian Social Union (Germany) |
| CTUM | Christian Trade Union Movement (Denmark) |
| CTUO | Central Trade Union Organisation (India) |
| CTW | Change to Win (US) |
| CWA | Communications Workers of America |
| DA | Dansk arbejdsgiverforening (Danish Employers' Confederation) |
| DARES | Direction de l'Animation de la Recherche, des études et des statistiques (French Ministry of Labour department of research, studies and statistics) |
| DBB | Deutscher Beamtenbund (German Civil Service Association) |
| DGB | Deutscher Gewerkschaftsbund (German Trade Union Federation) |
| DI | Confederation of Industry (Denmark) |
| DPJ | Democratic Party of Japan |
| EEA | European Economic Area |
| EEC | European Economic Community |
| EFI | Employers' Federation of India |
| EIP | Employee involvement and participation |
| ERISA | *Employee Retirement Income Security Act* (US) |
| ETUC | European Trade Union Confederation |

| | |
|---|---|
| EU | European Union |
| FA | Finansektorens arbejdsgiverforening (Employers' Association for the Financial Sector) (Denmark) |
| FDP | Free Democratic Party (Germany) |
| FIE | Foreign invested enterprise |
| FIOM | Federazione impiegati e operai metallurgici (Federation of Metalworkers) (Italy) |
| FKTU | Federation of Korean Trade Unions |
| FO | Force ouvriére (a French union confederation) |
| FRG | Federal Republic of Germany (West Germany) |
| FTF | Confederation of Professionals in Denmark |
| FWC | Fair Work Commission (Australia) |
| GDNP | Gross domestic national product |
| GDP | Gross domestic product |
| GDR | German Democratic Republic (East Germany) |
| GHQ | General Headquarters (Allied Powers in Japan) |
| GSC | Global supply chain |
| GUF | Global union federation |
| HR | Human resources |
| HRM | Human resource management |
| IAM | International Association of Machinists and Aerospace Workers (US) |
| IFA | International framework agreement |
| ILO | International Labour Organization |
| IMF | International Monetary Fund |
| INC | Indian National Conference |
| INTUC | Indian National Trade Union Congress |
| IOE | International Organisation of Employers |
| IR | Industrial relations |
| IT | Information technology |
| ITUC | International Trade Union Confederation |
| JCC | Joint consultative committee |
| JLMC | Joint labour–management committee |
| JSP | Japan Socialist Party |
| KCCI | Korean Chamber of Commerce and Industry |
| KCTU | Korean Confederation of Trade Unions |
| KEF | Korea Employers Federation |
| KFIU | Korea Finance Industry Union |
| KHMWU | Korea Health and Medical Workers Union |
| KL | Local Government Denmark |
| KLUC | Korean Labor Union Confederation |
| KMWU | Korea Metal Workers Union |
| LDP | Liberal Democratic Party (Japan) |

| LH | Ledernes hovedorganisation (Organisation of Managerial and Executive Staff) (Denmark) |
| LMC | Labour–Management Council (Korea) |
| LME | Liberal market economy |
| LO | Landsorganisationen i Danmark (Danish Confederation of Trade Unions) |
| LPF | Labour Progressive Federation (India) |
| LPG | Liberalisation, privatisation and globalisation |
| MEDEF | Mouvement des entreprises de France (Movement of the Enterprises of France) |
| MNE | Multinational enterprise |
| NAFTA | North American Free Trade Agreement |
| NCEUS | National Commission on Enterprises in the Unorganised Sector (India) |
| NCL | National Commission on Labour (India) |
| NDP | New Democratic Party (Canada) |
| NES | National Employment Standards (Australia) |
| NGO | Non-government organisation |
| NLRA | *National Labor Relations Act* (US) |
| NLRB | National Labor Relations Board (US) |
| NMW | National minimum wage |
| NSSO | National Sample Survey Office (India) |
| OECD | Organisation for Economic Cooperation and Development |
| ONS | Office for National Statistics (UK) |
| PCF | Parti communiste Français (French Communist Party) |
| PCIRR | Presidential Commission on Industrial Relations Reform (Korea) |
| PPP | Purchasing power parity |
| PS | Parti socialiste (Socialist Party) (France) |
| RSA | *Rappresentanze sindacali aziendali* (workplace representation structures of individual workers' groups) (Italy) |
| RSU | *Rappresentanze sindacale unitaria* (workplace representation structures of all workers) (Italy) |
| SEIU | Service Employees International Union (US) |
| SEWA | Self Employed Women's Association (India) |
| SEZ | Special economic zone |
| SME | Small and medium-sized enterprises |
| SOE | State-owned enterprise |
| SPD | Sozialdemokratische Partei Deutschlands (Social Democratic Party of Germany) |

| | |
|---|---|
| TLC | Trades and Labour Congress (Canada) |
| TUC | Trades Union Congress (UK) |
| TUCC | Trade Union Coordination Committee (India) |
| TULRAA | *Trade Union and Labour Relations Adjustment Act* (Korea) |
| UAW | United Automotive Workers (US) |
| UFCW | United Food and Commercial Workers (US) |
| UIL | Unione Italiana dei lavoratori (Italian Union of Labour) |
| UMP | Union pour un mouvement populaire (Union for a Popular Movement) (France) |
| UNEDIC-ASSEDIC | Union nationale interprofessionnelle pour l'emploi dans l'industrie et le commerce—Association pour l'emploi dans l'industrie et le commerce (French unemployment insurance plan) |
| UNIRS | Union Nationale de Interprofessionnelle de retraite des salaries (French benefits plan for non-management employees) |
| UNSA | Union nationale des syndicats autonomes (National Association of Autonomous Unions) (France) |
| UPA | Union professionnelle artisanale (Artisanal Professional Association) (France) |
| USW | United Steelworkers (US) |
| UTUC | United Trade Union Congress (India) |
| VoC | Varieties of Capitalism |
| VW | Volkswagen |
| WDL | Working days lost |
| WERS | Workplace Employment Relations Survey (UK) |
| WTO | World Trade Organization |

# Preface

The changes taking place in the economy have far-reaching implications for the world of work, and are renewing interest in the field of international and comparative employment relations. This book examines patterns and issues in employment relations in twelve significant economies: the United Kingdom, the United States, Canada, Australia, Italy, France, Germany, Denmark, Japan, South Korea, China and India, providing interested readers with the background and understanding necessary for them to compare employment relations policies and practices across countries.

This sixth edition of the book is fully revised and updated, and includes a new Introduction, which discusses the field of international and comparative employment relations and reviews some of the main debates in the field.

Acknowledged experts have written the country chapters. Each analyses employment relations traditions and issues using a similar format, with an examination of context—economic, historical, political, legal and social—and the characteristics of the major interest groups—employers, employees, unions and governments. This is followed by a concise summary of the main process of employment relations in that country. Each chapter concludes with a discussion of contemporary issues and challenges, and a chronology of key events.

In this edition, there is a greater emphasis on the Varieties of Capitalism (VoC) approach as a framework for understanding the similarities and differences in employment relations between countries. The first chapter introduces the VoC approach and considers its application to international and comparative employment relations. The book contains several chapters about countries from each of the main varieties of capitalism. This enables readers to compare employment relations policies and practices within and across different varieties. It also provides a basis for considering how to characterise those countries that may not fit in the VoC framework.

The first four editions of the book included an appendix with comparative statistics and commentary on employment relations and relevant economics data. Instead of this, in subsequent editions we are pleased to have included chapters on the large re-emerging economies of China and India. This was a more appropriate use of space because China and India are so important and interesting. Moreover, recent statistical data has become available on the internet. Examples of such sources are noted in relation to Figure 1.1.

We are indebted to the large number of colleagues from many countries who have kindly provided us with feedback on how they have used previous editions in their courses and have made constructive suggestions. The improvements in this edition reflect the feedback received. For example, the publishers have allowed us to extend the book to include a concluding chapter. Furthermore, at the end of each chapter, this edition lists further reading and useful websites. In addition, there is also a more extensive website hosted by Allen & Unwin and Sage, which includes supplementary information, including discussion questions, that will help readers when reflecting on each chapter.

In the new concluding chapter we reassess the VoC framework in light of the evidence presented in the twelve country-specific chapters. While these provide evidence that supports aspects of the VoC approach, they also identify some of the limitations of this framework. We also examine evidence of increased diversity within national patterns of employment relations focusing on indicators of this trend, including the growth in non-standard employment, differences in employer preferences for coordinating pay determination and other employment relations processes, and the growth of outsourcing and offshoring. In conclusion, we discuss some of the ways in which international institutions and dimensions influence national patterns of employment relations—for example, global supply chains (GSCs), multinational enterprises (MNEs), global labour activism, international framework agreements (IFAs) and the Decent Work Agenda of the International Labour Organization (ILO). The concluding chapter also considers influences of the European Union (EU) and of United Nations agencies, including the ILO and the World Trade Organization (WTO).

We have learnt a great deal from our readers, and recognise the important role they have played in helping us to refine and improve this book. We always welcome more feedback—for instance, on how you use the book—which we can then share on the website.

Earlier English-language editions and the subsequent Japanese, Korean and Chinese editions were repeatedly reprinted and have been read widely around the world since the first edition was published in 1987. This book is adopted in courses at universities all over the world. We hope that this new edition will continue to meet the needs of scholars, teachers, students, practitioners and policy-makers who have an interest in this exciting field.

Compiling a book like this is a challenge. We are obliged to Rawya Mansour for her significant assistance. Despite the challenges of working across different languages and cultures, the contributors have helpfully met our requests for revisions. We are extremely grateful to them. Most of them also contributed to earlier editions, but we also welcome several new contributors to this edition.

We also thank the many colleagues who read drafts of the chapters and provided helpful suggestions. For this edition, these include Frank Burchill, Giuseppe Casale, Gary Chaison, Lorenzo Frangi, Michael Gillan, Rafael Gomez, Joe Isaac, Jeff Keefe, Dong-One Kim, Herman Knudsen, Chris Leggett, Mingwei Liu, Miguel Martinez Lucio, T.S. Papola, E.A. Ramaswamy, Tom Redman, Joe Rose, Gordon Stewart and Jorg Sydow.

We acknowledge several good colleagues who have made kind comments at the front of the book, including Willy Brown for his inspiration and for contributing the Foreword.

Thanks too for the continued support and encouragement of our excellent publishers, represented by Patrick Gallagher, Elizabeth Weiss, Kathryn Knight and Sue Jarvis of Allen & Unwin in Australia and Kirsty Smy of Sage in the United Kingdom. Allen & Unwin and Sage are again co-publishers of this edition. Our greatest debt, however, is owed to our families, to whom this book is dedicated.

*— Greg J. Bamber*
*Department of Management, Monash Business School,*
*Monash University, Melbourne, Australia*
*Email: GregBamber@gmail.com*
*— Russell D. Lansbury and Chris F. Wright*
*Work and Organisational Studies, School of Business,*
*University of Sydney, Sydney, Australia*
*Email: russell.lansbury@sydney.edu.au,*
*chris.f.wright@sydney.edu.au*
*— Nick Wailes*
*UNSW Business School,*
*University of New South Wales, Sydney, Australia*
*Email: n.wailes@unsw.edu.au*

# CHAPTER 1

# Introduction: An internationally comparative approach to employment relations

## Nick Wailes, Chris F. Wright, Greg J. Bamber and Russell D. Lansbury

We live in a period in which national economies have increasingly become interconnected. This is a form of *globalisation*. At least since the 1990s, international employment relations scholars have focused on how globalisation is reshaping employment relations across companies, sectors and countries. Events since the post-2007 global financial crisis have given a more urgent focus to this issue.

Historically, there have been significant differences in employment relations from country to country. These include differences in what it means to be an employee, how employees and employers are organised, how wages and conditions are set, the role of the state in structuring employment relationships, and who benefits—and who is excluded—from employment protections. Changes in the international economy have raised questions about whether such national differences are continuing or fundamentally changing.

Increased competition, often from emerging economies, has placed pressure on the traditional protections and benefits that employees in many developed economies have enjoyed. As the work of Thomas Piketty (2014) shows, the period since the 1980s has seen rising income inequality within countries as well as between countries. Some have argued that the erosion of employment protections, labour market institutions and trade unions in many countries has contributed to these outcomes (Kochan 2013; Jacobs & Meyers 2014). The rise of income inequality has been more acute in countries, such as

1

the United States (Chapter 3) and the United Kingdom (Chapter 2), where employment protections have been weakened to a greater extent. There has also been a dramatic growth of inequality in China (Chapter 12). Countries that have maintained stronger labour market protections, such as Denmark (Chapter 9) and Sweden, have also seen widening disparity in incomes since the 1980s, but have been relatively more successful in containing this trend (OECD 2011).[1]

These developments might suggest that national employment relations institutions continue to play an important role in producing different outcomes between countries. However, the growing size and significance of international business institutions such as multinational enterprises (MNEs) and standardised production systems, often operating across national borders, have led some to conclude that the scope for national differences in how work is organised and governed has been eroded. Meanwhile, as the events of the post-2007 global financial crisis demonstrated, the increasing importance and interconnectedness of global financial markets have placed new and common pressures on governments and firms across countries.

These developments raise important questions. Are traditional forms of labour market regulation sustainable? Is it still possible for labour markets to produce equity and efficiency at the same time? Will unions continue to play an important role in helping to protect the interests of workers? Are new forms of representation developing, and will they be as effective? Will emerging economies develop similar employment relations institutions and outcomes to those that exist in developed economies? Do national institutions, actors and policy-makers still have the most important roles in shaping employment relations outcomes?

This book aims to provide readers with the background information and some of the conceptual tools they need to help answer these and many of the other employment relations–related questions raised by globalisation. The following chapters, written by leading experts on each country, provide a concise overview of employment relations in twelve countries. The book includes chapters on four English-speaking countries: the United Kingdom, the United States, Canada and Australia. It also has chapters on four Continental European countries—Italy, France, Germany and Denmark—and four Asian countries—Japan, South Korea, the People's Republic of China and India. China and India are the world's most populous countries, and in recent years they have come to play an increasingly important role in the international economy.

This chapter provides an introduction to the study of international and comparative employment relations. It discusses some of the benefits and the challenges of adopting an internationally comparative approach. It also provides an overview of a conceptual framework known as the Varieties of Capitalism (VoC) approach, which has become increasingly influential across a number of fields of comparative research, including employment relations. The VoC approach provides a useful starting point for the international and comparative analysis of the impact of globalisation on employment relations.

## WHY STUDY INTERNATIONAL AND COMPARATIVE EMPLOYMENT RELATIONS?

In this book, we are interested in the broad range of factors that shape the relationship between employers and employees, and the similarities and differences in these relationships over time and across countries. As Heery et al. (2008: 2) note, industrial relations (IR) scholarship traditionally has tended to focus on three aspects of the employment relationship: the parties to the employment relationship, the processes through which the employment relationship is governed, and the outcomes of these processes. IR has therefore concentrated on the formal and informal *institutions* of job regulation, including collective bargaining, unions, employers' associations and labour tribunals. Human resource management (HRM), on the other hand, has been focused more at the level of employing organisations, and is concerned with 'the effective overall management of an organisation's workforce in order to contribute to the achievement of desired objectives and goals' (Nankervis et al. 2011: 11). HRM has thus tended to concentrate on issues such as recruitment, selection, pay, performance and human resource (HR) development. Both perspectives are valuable for understanding the factors that shape the relationship between employers and employees, and therefore we adopt the term *employment relations* to encompass both IR and HRM. Where they are appropriate, however, the terms IR and HRM are also used in this book.

Although the study of employment relations focuses on the regulation of work, it must also take account of the wider economic and social influences on the relative power of capital and labour, and the interactions between employers, employees, their collective organisations and the state. A full understanding of employment relations requires an interdisciplinary approach that uses analytical tools drawn from several academic fields, including accounting, economics, history, law, politics, psychology, sociology and other elements of management studies.

Adopting an *internationally comparative approach* to employment relations requires not only insights from several disciplines, but also knowledge of different national contexts. Some scholars

3

distinguish between *comparative* and *international* studies in this field. Comparative employment relations may involve describing and systematically analysing institutions, processes and outcomes in two or more countries. By contrast, international employment relations involves exploring institutions and phenomena that cross national boundaries, such as the labour market roles and behaviour of inter-governmental organisations, MNEs and unions (Bean 1994). This is a useful distinction, but again we incline towards a broader perspective whereby *international* and *comparative* employment relations includes a range of studies that traverse boundaries between countries. This book therefore emphasises an internationally comparative approach, combining comparative and international approaches to the subject.

There are several reasons why it is beneficial to study internation-ally comparative employment relations. First, this area can contribute to our knowledge of employment relations in different countries. One of the consequences of globalisation, with increased levels of cross-border trade and investment, is that IR and HR professionals often need knowl-edge about employment relations practices in more than one country (Strauss 1998).

A second benefit of the internationally comparative study of employment relations is that other countries may provide models for policy-makers, managers and workers. At various times over the past 50 years, aspects of employment relations in the United States, Sweden, Japan and Germany have been seen as models to emulate. One reason for including Denmark in this book is that its system of *flexicurity* has been seen by some as a potential model for other developed market economies. The relevance of different national models to policy-makers explains why other disciplines have taken an interest in employment relations. For example, political scientists have long been interested in the ways in which employers and employees are organised, which are widely seen as relevant for national politics and policy outcomes (Locke & Thelen 1995; Thelen 2014). Some economists have focused on the role that labour market institutions play in explaining differ-ences in aggregate economic performance (Freeman 2008: 640).

The third, and perhaps the most important, reason for the interna-tionally comparative study of employment relations is its potential to provide theoretical insight into the factors and variables that shape the relationships between employers and employees (Bean 1994). Both IR and HRM, as fields of study, can be criticised as overly descriptive and for their apparent inability to develop causal explanations of relevant phenomena (e.g. see Barbash & Barbash 1989; Sisson 1994; Kelly

1998). This view was expressed in John Dunlop's (1958: vi) famous observation that

> the field of industrial relations today may best be described in the words of Julian Huxley: 'Mountains of facts have been piled on the plains of human ignorance . . . the result is a glut of new material. Great piles of facts are lying around unutilised, or utilised only in an occasional and partial manner'. Facts have outrun ideas. Integrating theory has lagged far behind expanding experience. The many worlds of industrial relations have been changing more rapidly than the ideas to interpret, to explain and determine them.

While this tendency towards description has also been noted in comparative employment relations (Clark et al. 1999; Schuler et al. 2002), comparative research offers significant potential for theoretical development by helping us to establish causal inferences (Shalev 1980; Bean 1994; Strauss 1998). This is because comparison requires the abstraction of concepts from particular contexts. As Kochan (1998: 41) puts it:

> Each national system carries with it certain historical patterns of development and features that restrict the range of variation on critical variables such as culture, ideology, and institutional structures which affect how individual actors respond to similar changes in their external environments. Taking an international perspective broadens the range of comparisons available on these and other variables and increases the chances of discovering the systematic variations needed to produce new theoretical insights and explanations.

## WHAT AND HOW TO COMPARE

While an internationally comparative approach may provide the basis for establishing causal inferences in employment relations research, the act of comparison itself does not necessarily ensure this outcome. One of the challenges of comparative studies is the choice of 'what' and 'how' to compare.

The lack of a common language and terminology may create confusion in comparative analysis. As Blanpain (2014: 17) points out, 'identical words in different languages may have different meanings, while the corresponding terms may embrace wholly different realities'. He notes, for example, that the term 'arbitration' (or *arbitrage* in French), which usually means a binding decision by an impartial third party, can also signify a recommendation by a government conciliator to the conflicting parties. In India, the term 'adjudication' is used for a compulsory form of arbitration, while the term 'arbitration' is used only to refer to a voluntary form of arbitration (see Chapter 13).

There can also be difficulties in distinguishing between the law and the actual practice. For example, while Australia formally practised 'compulsory arbitration' from the beginning of the twentieth century until at least the mid-1990s, there was relatively little 'compulsion' in practice, and the arbitration tribunals have relied mainly on advice and persuasion (see Chapter 5).

The collection of comparative data also poses challenges for those studying this field. For example, definitions of industrial disputes differ significantly between countries. Conflicts of *rights* concern the interpretation of an *existing* contract or award, such as which pay grade applies to a particular individual or group of workers. However, conflicts of *interests* arise during collective bargaining about an apparently *new* demand or claim, such as for a general pay increase or a reduction in working hours. In practice, conflicts about interests are usually collective disputes. In the United States, Sweden and elsewhere, this distinction is important. In France, Italy and certain other countries, conflicts about rights are further divided into *individual* and *collective* disputes. The general intention is that different settlement procedures will apply to different types of disputes. In some countries, only conflicts of interests can lead to lawful strikes or other forms of sanctions, but conflicts of rights should be settled by a binding decision of a labour court or similar tribunal (Sheldon et al. 2014).

International agencies attempt to compile data, which can be helpful in terms of conducting comparative analysis. For example, Figure 1.1 offers an interesting comparison of levels of union density and collective bargaining coverage between economies, including most of those on which this book focuses. This gives an indication of broad differences between countries. However, as shown in the following chapters and summarised in Chapter 14, there is much diversity within national patterns of employment relations.

We should be cautious in interpreting comparative data such as that presented in Figure 1.1, since data validity, reliability, collection methods and definitions (e.g. of unions and collective bargaining) may vary between countries (see Bamber et al. 2004). It is difficult to collect genuinely comparable cross-national employment relations measures. Hence the contribution of comparative research based on empirical datasets and large-scale national surveys is limited. Whitfield and Strauss (1998) note the particular difficulties associated with the use of large national surveys in comparative research.

**Figure 1.1  Comparative union density and collective bargaining coverage**

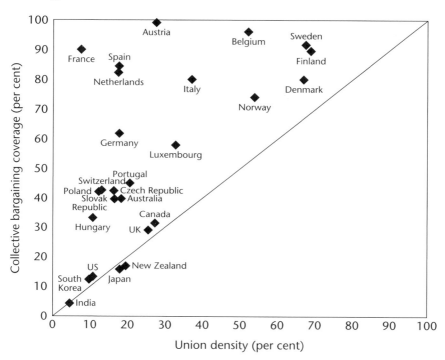

*Sources*: Data from OECD (2014) and Eurofound (2014), except India is estimated.[2]

Many of the problems associated with comparative analysis relate to the difficulties of establishing *conceptual equivalence* when operationalising comparative research. Linden (1998) distinguishes between *phenomenal equivalence*—where identical measures are used for the same concept regardless of context—and *conceptual equivalence*—where different measures are used for the same concept to reflect differences in contexts. He argues that comparative analysis can proceed effectively only on the basis of conceptual equivalence.

In a similar vein, Locke and Thelen (1995: 340) suggest that there are problems associated with comparative analyses, which focus on the same issue across countries, because these studies 'often assume that the same practice has the same meaning or valence across the various countries'. They argue instead for the use of *contextualised* comparisons that focus on different national 'sticking points' between employers and employees across countries. Thus, for example, they show that whereas unions in the United States resisted the introduction of more flexible work arrangements during the 1980s and 1990s, German unions embraced work reorganisation because they saw it as a way of increasing skills. Locke and Thelen (1995) argue that this difference reflects the greater significance of job control for union power in the United States (see Chapter 3). For German unions, they argue, issues of working time and wage flexibility—particularly in the context of German reunification—were much more salient and became a source of contention between employers and employees (see Chapter 8).

Effective comparison therefore generally requires a good understanding of each different national context. Strauss (1998) draws attention to advantages to be gained from studying close pairs of countries with similar economies, cultures and historic traditions. This permits researchers to hold many characteristics constant and examine those that vary between countries. We can identify two different research designs that enhance the likelihood of establishing causal inferences from comparative research (Przeworski & Teune 1970; Skopcol & Somers 1980). The first, alluded to by Strauss (1980), is known as a *most similar case* research design, and involves the comparison of two or more cases that share common features but differ in certain key respects. There are a number of comparative employment relations studies that exploit similarities between countries to identify potential sources of variation. Rose and Chaison (2001), for example, examine differences in the pattern of union decline in the United States and Canada. Despite significant similarities between the countries, union decline has been more rapid and dramatic in the United States than in Canada. Rose and Chaison argue that this difference can be accounted for by differences in the legal systems, which make it easier for US employers to avoid unions, and by closer affiliation between unions and a left-of-centre political party in Canada. McLaughlin (2009) examines the relationship between national minimum wages (NMWs) and productivity in Denmark and New Zealand. While these are both small developed economies with relatively high national pay minima, there are significant institutional differences between the two. McLaughlin (343) shows that the productivity-enhancing effects of an NMW in Denmark are closely related to 'high levels of government funding for training . . . [and] that coordination mechanisms between employers and unions at various levels of the economy play a pivotal role'. By contrast, the absence of equivalent funding and coordination mechanisms in New Zealand helps explain their limited contribution to productivity enhancement there. Thus, by focusing on two countries that share similar policies but have experienced different outcomes, McLaughlin's analysis highlights the causal significance of institutional and bargaining arrangements in shaping the relationship between minimum pay and productivity.

A second comparative research design is known as *most different case* comparison. As its name implies, this approach involves comparison of countries that differ in a number of important ways except for the phenomenon under study. While less common, most different case comparisons are just as likely to produce theoretical insights as most similar case comparisons. Doellgast (2008), for example, examines company-level variations in outcomes of collective negotiations over outsourcing. She does this by analysing the processes and outcomes of bargaining over outsourcing in six telecommunications companies—three in Germany and three in the United States. Her findings show that, despite differences in national employment relations institutions, there is considerable variation in outcomes within each country and that the success of unions in limiting the scale and scope of outsourcing depends largely on their ability to mobilise critical bargaining resources. In the United States, this involves mobilising external community and political support, while in Germany success rests on the ability of the union to establish effective internal coordination. Doellgast's (285) conclusion is that, despite the national context, 'unions can gain an independent voice in restructuring decisions through using traditional forms of bargaining power in innovative ways'. However, doing so requires 'considerable effort, [and] creative and organised political action'. Thus, despite significant differences between the two countries, she was able to identify a common factor (the ability of unions to mobilise bargaining resources) that helped explain differences in outcomes of negotiations about outsourcing within the two countries. Each of the country chapters provides an introduction to key features of employment relations that can help form the basis for this type of detailed comparison.

## CONVERGENCE AND DIVERGENCE IN NATIONAL PATTERNS OF EMPLOYMENT RELATIONS

Since at least the 1960s, there has been debate about the extent to which national patterns of employment relations are either converging (becoming more similar) or diverging (moving further apart). The current debates about globalisation and employment relations echo previous ones.

The original *convergence* hypothesis was developed by Kerr and colleagues in their book *Industrialism and Industrial Man* (1960). Their core proposition is that there is a universal tendency for technological and market forces associated with industrialisation to push national employment relations systems towards uniformity, or convergence. This conclusion is based on the view that there is a *logic of industrialism*, and that as more societies adopted industrial forms of production and organisation, this logic would create 'common characteristics and imperatives' across these societies. To accommodate these imperatives, Kerr et al. (1960: 384–92) assert that industrial societies had to develop a means of fostering consensus. It was argued that employment relations systems that embodied the 'principles of pluralistic industrialism' played a central role in establishing this consensus.

The convergence hypothesis, based on the logic of industrialism, was widely criticised. Some argued that this approach was *ideological* and *prescriptive*. *Industrialism and Industrial Man* was one of several books, including Daniel Bell's (1962) *The End of Ideology* and W.W. Rostow's (1960) *The Stages of Economic Growth*, written during the Cold War, that presented the American social, political and economic system as superior to Soviet communism and as a model for other countries to emulate. To this extent, the links drawn between industrialism and a particular set of social and political institutions were prescriptive. The implication was that countries needed to adopt social and political institutions like those of the United States to be able to benefit from modernisation and industrialism (Goldthorpe 1984).

Others accused Kerr and colleagues (1960) of *technological determinism*, arguing that even though there may have been strong pressures associated with industrialism and modernisation, this did not necessarily imply that there would be convergence on a single set of societal institutions (Cochrane 1976; Doeringer 1981; Piore 1981; Berger 1996: 2–4).

The criticisms of the convergence thesis were largely borne out by the empirical evidence. In the aftermath of the publication of Kerr et al.'s (1960) work, there was an increase in research that aimed to test the extent of convergence in employment relations systems. While some claimed to show evidence of convergence, as Katz and Darbishire (2000: 8) note:

> the thrust of . . . much of the comparative industrial relations literature . . . was that there was wide and persistent variation in industrial relations across countries in part due to the influence of nationally specific institutional factors.

In the late 1970s and early 1980s, research suggested that, rather than converging, national patterns of employment relations were increasingly *diverging*. In an influential analysis, Goldthorpe (1984) identifies the development of two distinct national patterns of employment relations during this period. He argues that some countries—such as Norway,

Austria, Germany and Sweden—attempted to increase economic growth and reduce inflation through *corporatist* policies that involved centralised negotiations between employers, unions and, in some cases, the state. In countries like the United Kingdom and the United States, by contrast, the labour market institutions (e.g. collective bargaining) were being undermined in an effort to eliminate perceived rigidities in the market. Goldthorpe (1984) argued that this was producing a *dualism* in employment relations in these countries, with the workforce separated into core and peripheral employees. The former may remain unionised and within the collective bargaining framework—albeit in a more decentralised mode—while the latter were employed under more individualistic work arrangements characterised by contractual forms of control.

The contemporary debate about globalisation and employment relations does not predict convergence on universal adoption of enterprise unions or widespread collective bargaining, as did Kerr et al. (1960). Rather, it suggests the erosion of these types of practices and a convergence on deregulated labour markets in the face of increased international competition (Baccaro & Howell 2011; Tilly 1995). Nonetheless, there are similarities in the logic that underpins the two arguments, and the same types of criticisms can be levelled at predictions of convergence based on globalisation. As some scholars have noted, there is a strongly *ideological* and *prescriptive* dimension to the contemporary depictions of globalisation. They have shown that the extent to which globalisation has created a completely integrated global market has been greatly exaggerated. In general, analyses of changes in the international economy suggest that, while the current form of globalisation is distinct and has significant impacts for national economies, there is little evidence to suggest that the global economy resembles the completely entwined and undifferentiated free market depicted by Friedman (2006), Fukuyama (1992) and others (e.g. Hirst & Thompson 1996; Wade 1996; Perraton et al. 1997).

Similarly, to the extent that globalisation has created common pressures, there is little evidence to suggest that governments, employers or employees have no alternatives available regarding how they choose to respond, as certain globalisation theorists imply (Garrett 1998). Evans (1997) argues that, rather than spelling the demise of the nation state, globalisation enhances the significance and importance of the nation state in creating and maintaining national competitiveness. Comparative employment relations research provides evidence of divergent responses to globalisation. Thelen (2014), for example, holds that the system of embedded flexibilisation that has emerged in Scandinavian countries has made it easier for their employment relations systems to adjust to the pressures of globalisation compared with other countries. For instance, in Denmark the state and the employment relations actors have responded to economic change by gradually adapting the pay regulation system from a centralised model to an encompassing set of local, industry and national bargaining structures (see Chapter 9). Thelen (2014) claims that this process has allowed core elements of the Danish employment relations model to survive, albeit in a modernised form, to a greater degree than in other countries such as Germany and the United States. Other employment relations research has highlighted the significance of national-level *institutional* variables in shaping how international economic pressures impact employment relations policies and outcomes (Godard 2004; Lansbury et al. 2006).

## THE VARIETIES OF CAPITALISM APPROACH

Research suggests that there is a pattern to the diversity in responses to international economic change. We can identify similarities between groups of countries in terms of how they are impacted by changes in the international economy and distinguish between different types or varieties of market economies. These findings have produced what are broadly called *theories of capitalist diversity*.

As Deeg and Jackson (2007: 151–2) note, despite differences in how they classify diversity, these arguments share some features. First, they are based on the idea that the context within which economic actors operate impacts their decisions, and therefore the national institutional framework is important. Similarities in institutional frameworks across countries are likely to produce similarities in economic outcomes. Second, these theories accept that different forms of organising the economy will produce different forms of competitive advantages. Thus, for example, countries that lack institutions that encourage skill acquisition are unlikely to be able to be very competitive in sectors that require a consistent supply of highly skilled workers. Third, theories of capitalist diversity do not focus on particular institutions in isolation, but rather focus on how different aspects of the economy interact and complement each other.

The most influential and clearly articulated theory of capitalist diversity is Hall and Soskice's (2001) VoC approach, and this is the one mainly used in this book. In this section, we sketch the key features of this approach and then proceed to discuss its application to the comparative analysis of employment relations. In response to predictions that globalisation would produce similar outcomes in different countries, Hall and Soskice reject the notion that there is one best way to organise a market society, and point to the role of institutional arrangements in shaping how market societies function. Hall and Soskice (2001: 6–9) argue that, in market economies, firms are faced with a series of coordination problems, both internally and externally. They focus on five spheres of coordination that firms must address:

- IR
- vocational training and education
- corporate governance
- inter-firm relations, and
- relations with their own employees.

Hall and Soskice identify two institutional equilibria ('ideal types') that resolve these coordination problems and produce superior economic outcomes. The first variety they call *liberal market economies* (LMEs). LMEs are characterised by institutional arrangements that encourage firms to resolve coordination problems through the use of market mechanisms and hierarchies. LMEs are therefore more likely to be characterised by, among other things:

- well-developed capital markets
- 'outsider' forms of corporate governance[3]
- market-based forms of employment relations, with limited long-term commitments by employers to workers, and
- the use of market mechanisms and contracts to coordinate their relations with supplier and buyer firms.

The United States is the prime exemplar of an LME, but the literature also often includes the United Kingdom, Australia, New Zealand, Canada and Ireland in this category.

The second variety of capitalism that Hall and Soskice identify, *coordinated market economies* (CMEs), includes countries in which the institutional matrix allows firms to make greater use of non-market mechanisms to resolve coordination problems. Compared with LMEs, CMEs are more likely to be characterised by:

- 'patient' forms of capital or investments
- 'insider' forms of corporate governance[4]
- employment relations systems based on bargaining, and which reflect a longer term commitment to employees, and
- the use of non-market mechanisms, such as industry associations, to coordinate relations between firms within and across industries and sectors.

Germany is seen as the prime exemplar of a CME, but the literature also often includes other European countries such as Austria, Sweden and Denmark, as well as Japan and sometimes South Korea, in this category.

Central to Hall and Soskice's (2001) argument, and the identification of distinct varieties of capitalism, is the concept of *institutional complementarities*. In the VoC model, institutional complementary refers to two related but separate effects. First, institutions are complementary to the extent that one enhances the effectiveness of another. Thus, for example, a cohesive industry association may enhance the economic efficiency of industry-wide collective bargaining. In this sense, institutional complementarity helps explain why two contrasting institutional configurations, LMEs and CMEs, are both able to produce good economic outcomes.

The idea of institutional complementarity also relates to the tendency of institutional arrangements to converge on one or other institutional equilibrium over time. Hall and Soskice (2001: 18) argue that 'nations with a particular type of coordination in one sphere in the economy should tend to develop complementary practices in other spheres as well' (see also Amable 2003: 54–66). For instance, the VoC model suggests that, in countries characterised by well-developed capital markets and outsider forms of corporate governance, it is difficult to sustain employment relations practices that imply a long-term commitment to employees. In due course, there are likely to be pressures for the adoption of more market-based forms of employment relations to align practices with the more short-term interests of owners. Gospel and Pendleton (2005) demonstrate that there appear to be close relationships between forms of firm financing and labour management practices.

There is some evidence to support this notion of institutional complementarity, particularly in relation to the link between corporate governance and employment relations. Hall and Gingerich (2009), for example, estimate the impact of complementarities in employment relations and corporate governance on economic growth, drawing on measures of shareholder power, dispersion of control, size of the stock market, level and degree of wage coordination and labour turnover. Their results not only suggest that there is a strong degree of institutional congruence across countries (the higher the level of coordination in corporate governance factors, the higher the level of coordination in employment relations factors), but also provide strong empirical support to the notion that institutional alignment produces complementarities (each raises the returns to the other) (Höpner 2005).

The VoC framework is influential in comparative employment relations analysis. It has been used to help explain cross-national similarities and differences in, among other things, the gendered nature of labour markets, employee participation, job quality, vocational training systems and links between labour markets and immigration policies, collective bargaining and union membership density (Martin & Bamber 2004; Frege & Kelly 2004; Estevez-Abe 2006; Harcourt & Wood 2007; Lansbury & Wailes 2008; Bamber et al. 2010; Goergen et al. 2012; Wright 2012; Frege & Godard 2014). For instance, Figure 1.1 illustrates how levels of union density and collective bargaining coverage are generally lower in LMEs than in CMEs.

As Hamann and Kelly (2008) show, the VoC approach builds on a long tradition of employment relations scholarship that distinguishes between different groups or types of countries, but at the same time goes beyond this tradition to provide a clear explanation for why outcomes may differ in one set of countries compared with others.

There are features of the VoC approach that provide a useful framework for the internationally comparative analysis of employment relations in general, and an understanding of the impact of globalisation on national systems in particular. First, many of the coordination problems identified by scholars using the VoC framework relate to variables and issues that have long been a concern of employment relations scholars, including IR, skill development and relations between employers and employees.

Second, the VoC approach suggests that it is not possible to understand employment relations issues in isolation, and that comparative analysis should put changes in employment relations in a broader context. Consistent with comparative research traditions, the VoC approach has the added advantage of specifying a limited number of relevant variables. While some argue that the range of factors in the VoC approach is too limited (which is addressed below), one of the advantages of this approach is that it focuses comparative analysis on a few important issues.

One of the main implications of the VoC approach is that globalisation is likely to have different impacts on employment relations processes and outcomes in different varieties of capitalism (Hamann & Kelly 2008). Increased international competition is likely to create incentives for enterprises in LMEs to adopt more market-based employment relations practices, including decentralisation and individualisation of bargaining, individualised pay systems and more contingent forms of employment. Nonetheless, the institutional dynamics of CMEs suggest that increased international competition may reinforce, rather than undermine, the usual national forms of coordination between employers and employees. Thelen (2001, 2014), for example, argues that the pressures associated with globalisation have reinforced rather than undermined the commitment of German manufacturing employers to industry-wide bargaining and works councils; however, this commitment is much weaker among employers in the emerging services sector.

The VoC approach also suggests that pursuing a neo-liberal employment relations agenda in CMEs has the potential to diminish, rather than enhance, economic competitiveness. For instance, Harcourt and Wood (2007) show how the erosion of employment protections in CMEs has undermined the effectiveness of the vocational training systems that play such an important role in making these economies internationally competitive.

It is also important to acknowledge some of the potential limitations and weaknesses of the VoC approach. These criticisms suggest that the approach needs to be modified if it is to provide a suitable framework for the comparative analysis of employment relations. One of the main criticisms of the VoC approach is that it does not contain enough variety (Allen 2004). The VoC focus is on only two varieties of capitalism—CMEs and LMEs—which has limitations. First, it narrows the range of countries to which the model can be applied. Hall and Soskice (2001: 21) acknowledge that at least six European countries—France, Italy, Spain, Portugal, Greece and Turkey—are difficult to accommodate in either the LME or the CME category, and they raise the prospect of a Mediterranean variety of capitalism. However, they do not fully develop this idea.

Second, the CME and LME categories are so large that the framework has the potential to ignore important differences between countries in the same variety. As the contributions to two books edited by Streeck and Yamamura (2001, 2003) demonstrate, while Japan and Germany are classified as examples of CMEs, there are important differences between them that are overlooked in the VoC approach. Jackson (2001), for example, shows that even though German and Japanese corporate governance arrangements produce similar outcomes, they differ in terms of both the institutional foundations on which they are based and the historical forces that shaped them. Thus, for example, in comparison with LMEs, employees in Japan and Germany have a greater role in corporate governance. However, in the German case, employees' corporate governance rights are contained in legislation, which is not the case in Japan.

If the VoC approach is to be more helpful for comparative analysis of employment relations, it is important to increase the number of varieties of capitalism to capture differences in the social organisation of market economies. Other comparative scholars have developed models that include more varieties of capitalism. Schmidt (2002), for example, adds a third variety of capitalism to accommodate the statist tradition in France. Rhodes et al. (2007) argue for four varieties of capitalism, which they suggest make it possible to extend the model to Central and Eastern European countries. Wailes (2007) introduces the notion of an Asian market economy variety to capture some of the distinctive elements of the social organisation of capitalism—for instance, in Japan and South Korea. China and India have also followed their own distinct paths, which allow for a bigger role for the state in employment relations in comparison with developed economies. While China and India have sought to encourage high growth rates by liberalising economic policies, they have maintained a strong role for the state in social policy and to a large degree in employment relations policy.

A second feature of the VoC framework that has elicited criticism and debate relates to its apparent *determinism*. This is nicely captured by Crouch (2005: 1):

> The main emphasis of the [VoC approach] . . . was that there was no single form of capitalism . . . But I was increasingly struck by the paradoxical determinism behind this ostensibly liberating message: There were two but only two viable forms of capitalism. Nation states possessed one of the other of these two, the institutions appropriate to which extended in a coherent way across a wide range of economic, political and social areas, determining their economic capacities over most products and types of production. And once a country had a particular set of such institutions, there was very little it could do to change it.

As Howell (2003) and others argue, the VoC approach leaves very little scope for agency, policy and conflict to shape social outcomes. This determinism, and the related difficulty that the VoC approach has in accounting for change, can partly be explained, since the VoC approach is based on *comparative statics*—the comparison of two cases at the same time—but it can also reflect assumptions about the path-dependent nature of social action that underpin the model (Deeg & Jackson 2007). This aspect of the VoC model is particularly problematic in the field of employment relations, where at different times conflict and change are very prevalent and play such an important role in shaping outcomes.

A third set of criticisms of the VoC approach focuses on the relative lack of attention the model gives to international factors. As Rhodes et al. (2007: 7) note, the VoC approach has a tendency to treat 'nation-states as "hermetically sealed" and [to] neglect the linkages between them'. Hall and Soskice's (2001) original VoC model seems to infer that economies are relatively closed, so that institutions have homogeneous effects within national boundaries. As a result, the VoC approach tends to downplay or ignore the role played by international factors, other than the competitive pressures associated with economic globalisation. The role of international factors such as international institutions and MNEs in shaping national employment relations outcomes is exemplified in several of the following chapters, and analysed in Chapter 14.

## COMPARING NATIONAL EMPLOYMENT RELATIONS SYSTEMS

As mentioned at the beginning of the chapter, globalisation is having a profound influence on the way work is regulated around the world. In this chapter, we have argued that, if properly designed and conducted, comparative analysis has the potential not only to enhance our understanding of the world around us, but also to generate insights into the factors that shape employment relations outcomes in our own work situations, countries and regions. The following chapters provide some of the background information necessary for readers to start comparing employment relations across countries. They aim to facilitate comparison between similar countries and also comparisons between different types of economies.

While mindful of its limitations, we argue that the VoC approach provides a promising framework for the internationally comparative study of employment relations. The VoC approach—which examines the broader institutional context within which patterns of employment relations develop—can be used to help us to account for similarities and differences in national patterns of employment relations. The following chapters provide introductions to employment relations across a number of different varieties of capitalist economies. The countries included represent different forms of market economy (as shown in Table 1.1). Four (the United Kingdom, the United States, Canada and Australia) are LMEs and three (Germany, Denmark and Japan) can be seen as CMEs. There are chapters on five European economies, including two (Italy and France) that do not fit easily into either the LMEs or CMEs category. There are also chapters on four prominent Asian economies (Japan, South Korea, China and India). The range of countries considered should allow interested readers to assess whether there are systematic differences in employment relations patterns and outcomes across varieties of capitalism and the potential drivers of these outcomes. In the concluding chapter, we revisit the VoC approach in light of the evidence provided by the country chapters and re-examine the question of how globalisation is reshaping the world of work.

**Table 1.1 Categories of economies included in this book**

| Liberal market economies | Coordinated market economies | European developed economies | Asian developed economies | Asian emerging economies |
|---|---|---|---|---|
| United States | Germany | United Kingdom | Japan | China |
| United Kingdom | Denmark | Italy | South Korea | India |
| Canada | Japan | France | | |
| Australia | | Germany | | |
| | | Denmark | | |

## FURTHER READING

Barbash, J. & Barbash, K. (eds) (1989) *Theories and Concepts in Comparative Industrial Relations*. Columbia, SC: University of South Carolina Press.

Hall, P.A. & Soskice, D. (eds) (2001) *Varieties of Capitalism: The Institutional Foundations of Comparative Advantage*. New York: Oxford University Press.

Katz, H.C. & Darbishire, O. (2000) *Converging Divergences: Worldwide Changes in Employment Systems*. Ithaca, NY: Cornell University Press.

Kerr, C., Dunlop, J.T., Harbison, F.H. & Myers, C.A. (1960) *Industrialism and Industrial Man: The Problems of Labour and Management in Economic Growth*. Harmondsworth: Penguin.

Thelen, K.A. (2014) *Varieties of Liberalization and the New Politics of Social Solidarity*. New York: Cambridge University Press.

## USEFUL WEBSITES

European Foundation for the Improvement of Living and Working Conditions (Eurofound): <http://eurofound.europa.eu/about>.

European Industrial Relations Dictionary: <http://eurofound.europa.eu/observatories/eurwork/industrial-relations-dictionary>.

European Observatory of Working Life: Industrial relations country profiles: <http://eurofound.europa.eu/observatories/eurwork/comparative-information/industrial-relations-country-profiles>.

ILO: <www.ilo.org/global/lang--en/index.htm>.

ILO's resources for researchers: <www.ilo.org/global/statistics-and-databases/research-and-databases/lang--en/index.htm>.

International Labour and Employment Relations Association: <www.ilo.org/public/english/iira>.

OECD work on inequality: <www.oecd.org/inequality.htm>.

# CHAPTER 2

# Employment relations in the United Kingdom

## Jeremy Waddington[1]

In the terms used in this book's Introduction, the United Kingdom[2] approximates to a liberal market economy (LME), characterised by deregulation of many features of the labour market complemented by stringent regulation of union activity. Although claims are made for the 'trickle-down' effects of growth within neo-liberal economics, UK rates of inequality soared after 1980 to reach levels exceeded among industrialised economies only by those in the United States (Piketty 2014: 304–35; see also Krugman 2012; Stiglitz 2013). To assess such developments, this chapter first traces changes in the composition of the labour force before examining their impact on the parties to employment relations and key employment relations processes. Then it examines two themes: fairness at work and the consequences of European Union (EU) membership.

## THE LABOUR FORCE IN CONTEXT

The United Kingdom has a total population of 62 million people and an employment rate among those aged 16–64 of 72 per cent, with the male employment rate at 77 per cent and that among women at 67 per cent (ONS 2014).[3] While most men work full time (87 per cent), the proportion of women working part time is high, at 42 per cent, and is significantly higher than the EU average. Temporary employment has grown marginally since the early 1980s, and constitutes 6.2 per cent of all employees. The rate of people classifying themselves as self-employed (14 per cent) is more than double that of the late 1970s, and accounts for much of the recent growth in employment. While estimates vary, recent

Office of National Statistics (ONS) data suggest that there are about 1.3 million jobs on 'zero-hours' contracts. Between 1998 and 2014, the number of people working from home rose from 11 to 14 per cent of those in work. Home working is concentrated among those with above-average earnings, the self-employed and older workers. These figures should be treated with caution, however, as they include those who work from home occasionally, as well as regular workers from home.

Migration from outside the European Economic Area (EEA) rose during the late 1990s, followed by an increase in the EEA migrant population after the enlargements of the EU in 2004 and 2006. Employment rates for the UK (native-born) population remain substantially higher (72 per cent) than for non-EEA migrants (60 per cent), as many of the latter come to the United Kingdom to accompany another migrant or as a family member. Employment rates for the UK (native-born) population, however, are slightly lower than the employment rates for migrants from the EEA (77 per cent) (Home Office/BIS 2014).

As well as compositional shifts in the labour force, there have also been major shifts in the sectoral distribution of workers. In 2013, there were 32.35 million jobs in the United Kingdom, of which 365,000 were in agriculture, which is a smaller proportion in agriculture than any other Organisation for Economic Cooperation and Development (OECD) country; 2.57 million were in manufacturing, a smaller proportion than found in the United Kingdom's major European competitors; and almost 27 million were in services. There has been a greater decline in the United Kingdom's 'industry' category since 1970 than in any other OECD country. In spite of the relative growth of services, there was a steep rise in unemployment, from 1.2 per cent of the working population in 1965 to nearly 12 per cent by 1986; then, the United Kingdom had a higher unemployment rate than any of the other countries discussed in earlier editions of this book. Unemployment fell during the 1990s and the early part of this century, but rose following the post-2007 global financial crisis; the rate in 2014 was more than 7 per cent.

In terms of gross domestic product (GDP) per capita—an approximate indicator of labour output—the United Kingdom ranks in the lower half of developed market economies. The rate of inflation has been steady for much of the period since the mid-1990s, at around 2–3 per cent, but following the post-2007 global financial crisis, this rose to over 5 per cent—largely due to higher energy prices—but declined thereafter to reach 1.6 per cent by the end of 2013. Since 2009, prices have increased at a faster rate than earnings, with the consequence that living standards have declined.

Since 1945, two political parties have dominated the British polity. The Conservative Party's support is strongest among the business and rural communities, whereas the Labour Party's support is traditionally strongest in urban working-class communities, although this has broadened. In May 2010, a Conservative–Liberal Democrat coalition government resulted from the election. As part of the agreement to form a coalition government, the parties agreed to a five-year fixed-term parliament for the first time in the United Kingdom. There are several other political parties, including nationalist parties in Scotland and Wales and other parties representing the different communities of Northern Ireland. Increased devolution of powers to Scotland and Wales modified certain provisions in these countries. The Scottish electorate voted to remain as part of the United Kingdom in a referendum in September 2014. As a consequence of the debate associated with this referendum, and the concessions made by the Westminster parties to encourage a 'no' to separation vote, it is likely that the highly centralised system of governance in the United Kingdom will be subject to more decentralisation.

There has been much change in employment relations in the United Kingdom since the 1980s. Successive Conservative governments over the period 1979–97 set the tone with a radical step-by-step reform of employment relations law, focused on restrictions on the capacity of unions to act; labour market deregulation, consistent with an LME; and attempts to foster a competitive 'enterprise culture' and reduce the 'burden on business'. New Labour governments from 1997 to 2010 continued to promote increased private sector involvement in the public sector through various initiatives, with significant implications for employment relations. As with other broader socio-economic trends, however, this changed in 2008 and substantial state support was provided for the banking sector.

The coalition government elected in 2010 has introduced further labour market deregulation, notably with the privatisation of the Royal Mail and the promotion of further private sector involvement in the provision of public services. The coalition government, however, has retained the terms of the *Employment Relations Act 1999* on union recognition introduced by the earlier Labour government.

## THE EMPLOYMENT RELATIONS PARTIES

### Unions

The United Kingdom was the first country to industrialise. Certain unions can thus trace their roots back to before the mid-nineteenth century. The earliest enduring unions were formed exclusively by and for skilled craft workers. Widespread unionisation of semi-skilled, unskilled and women manual workers began in the late-nineteenth century. Before World War II, most unionised white-collar workers were employed in the public sector. It was only after about 1960 that substantial numbers of private sector white-collar workers were union- ised. There were 1348 UK unions in 1920. By 2013, however—mainly as the result of mergers—there were only 167 unions, though new unions continue to enter the Certification Officer list (Ross 2013). Union membership is concentrated: the thirteen unions with more than 100,000 members account for 84 per cent of the total member- ship and the three largest unions represent almost 48 per cent of the total membership (Certification Officer 2013).

British unions established the Labour Party in 1906. They saw party political activity as a necessary complement to the industrial activities of the unions, particularly after a series of adverse legal judgments meant that new legislation was required to re-establish union rights. For much of the twentieth century, the Labour Party–trade union alliance was contentious, but remained robust, as both wings of the alliance secured benefits that were otherwise unobtainable (Minkin 1991). Indi- vidual unions may affiliate to the Labour Party, contributing to its funds through a 'political levy' on members, from which individuals may 'opt out' if they wish. Since the mid-1980s, the Labour Party leadership has increasingly 'distanced' the party from the unions, the voting power of unions at the annual party conference has been reduced and victories secured by the unions against the party leadership at conferences have been ignored. This distancing from the unions by the Labour Party coincided with a greater proportion of party funds being secured from other sources, including business. The future character of this relation- ship remains to be seen, as funding for the Labour Party from business is in decline and the party is more reliant than in the recent past on funding from unions. At the time of writing, there is a further review of the funding arrangements of the Labour Party underway.

The level and density of unionisation have fluctuated since World War II. Three broad post-war phases can be identified. Between 1948 and 1968, membership grew from 9.3 million to 10.2 million, but tended to lag behind employment growth. During this period, union density fluctuated between 42 and 45 per cent (Price & Bain 1983: 46–7). Membership grew markedly in the 1970s, as workers— particularly those in white-collar occupations—were attracted into unions. Membership grew from 9.7 million in 1968 to an all-time high of 12.6 million in 1979, when density peaked at almost 56 per cent

(Waddington 1992). The onset of the third phase, in 1979, coincided with the election of a Conservative government led by Margaret Thatcher, the policies of which accelerated the decline of employment in manufacturing and prompted the then deepest post-war economic recession, in the early 1980s. The rise in unemployment also accelerated membership decline. Union membership continued to fall, however—albeit at a lower rate—during periods of employment growth in the 1990s and early 2000s. In part, this was because employment growth was concentrated in private sector services where unions found it difficult to organise. Union density declined during the 1980s and 1990s. Between 1979 and 2013, union membership fell by more than 5 million members to 7.2 million (Certification Officer 2013), and between 1979 and 2012, density fell from almost 56 per cent to about 23 per cent (BIS 2013).

Within the labour force, there are variations in union density. Non-manual workers have constituted an increasing proportion of total union membership, and in the early twenty-first century are more likely to be unionised than manual workers. By 2012, union density was about 56 per cent in the public sector, where almost 58 per cent of all union members were employed. Union density in the private sector as a whole was only about 14 per cent, though it was 19 per cent in manufacturing. For the thirteenth consecutive year, union density among women (27 per cent) was higher than among men (20 per cent). Full-time workers were more likely to be unionised (27 per cent) than their part-time counterparts (21 per cent), permanent workers (27 per cent) were more likely to be unionised than temporary workers (15 per cent) and workers over the age of 50 were more likely to be members (33 per cent) than workers aged under 25 years (8 per cent) (BIS 2013).

Although there is no agreement regarding the relative effects of the forces that promoted the decline in unionisation, it is generally accepted that external influences such as macro-economic context, the changing composition of the labour force, management resistance, workplace practices and state policy all had adverse effects on unionisation (Mason & Bain 1993; Metcalf 1991). In addition, issues internal to unionism have contributed to the decline. Included among internal issues are inadequate recruitment programs, whether inadequacy is measured in terms of resources allocated or practices implemented (Voos 1984; Kelly 1990), union failure to deliver benefits effectively for employees (Bryson & Gomez 2005; Metcalf 2005), the commitment of senior officers to reform (Undy et al. 1981) and the failure to reform union policy, practices and government to 'fit' with the interests of potential members (Hyman 1999; Dølvik & Waddington 2005). The election of the Labour government in 1997 was not associated with a significant boost in unionisation. The terms of its recognition procedure in the *Employment Relations Act* were seen as enabling managers to resist unionisation (Gall 2004a, 2004b; Ewing et al. 2003). Although more recent data suggest that the number of new recognition agreements is increasing, they tend to be concentrated in areas where unions are established and barely outnumber de-recognition cases (Gall 2007; Blanden et al. 2006).

Concurrent with the decline in unionisation was a decline in strike activity. From a peak of 3906 strikes resulting in almost 11 million working days lost in 1970, the number of strikes had fallen to 122 with only 410,000 working days lost in 2013 (ONS 2014). Associated with the decline in strike activity, there was a shift in the reasons for strikes, with 'defensive' strikes assuming a greater prominence throughout the 1990s. Pay-related issues, however, still underpinned more than half of all strikes after 1999. The decline in strike activity in the United Kingdom was steeper than in many other countries, due to the restrictive legislation enacted by the Conservative governments during the 1980s (Elgar & Simpson 1993), which was not repealed by subsequent Labour governments.

The United Kingdom has one main union confederation: the Trades Union Congress (TUC), which was established in 1868. In 2013, 54 unions representing almost 5.85 million union members were affiliated to the TUC. The TUC has never had a direct role in collective bargaining, and has little constitutional authority over affiliated unions. In 2012, the TUC elected Frances O'Grady to the post of general secretary—the first woman to occupy the position.

Historically, the TUC has had three primary purposes: the lobbying of governments, the provision of services to affiliated unions and the adjudication of disputes between affiliated unions. The scope of the TUC as a lobbying organisation increased during and after World War II, when the political influence of the TUC increased and it convened union representation on many tripartite institutions and quasi-governmental agencies (Goodman 1994). After 1979, however, most tripartite institutions were dismantled and the TUC was effectively excluded from the 'corridors of power', so its influence diminished to its lowest level since the 1930s. The return of a Labour government in 1997 precipitated a more distant relationship between the TUC and the government than under previous Labour governments, as the government sought to establish a closer alliance with business than its Labour predecessors (Waddington 2003). The TUC has regenerated aspects of its lobbying role in relation to the EU. The TUC still provides a wide range of services to affiliated unions, although many of the larger affiliates are no longer reliant on services from the TUC, and tend to provide them in house. The role of the TUC in adjudicating disputes between affiliated unions has also diminished as the number of disputes has declined.

The loss of political influence combined with the lack of constitutional authority over affiliated unions led to a major review of TUC activities in 1994. The outcome was that the TUC jettisoned much of its committee structure with the intention of becoming more of a campaigning organisation (Heery 1998). A wide range of campaigning initiatives has resulted, two of which are prominent. The first centres on the establishment of the Organising Academy, at which representatives from affiliated unions are trained in organising techniques (Heery et al. 2003). The purpose of the Organising Academy is to encourage a wider range of unions to pursue organising campaigns to try to reverse the membership decline. The range of initiatives taken and techniques employed under the rubric of organising is vast (Simms et al. 2013). While there have been some notable successes arising from organising, they are barely sufficient to match membership losses sustained elsewhere. Nevertheless, many unions are investing considerable resources into organising campaigns. A second prominent campaign highlights the establishment of partnerships with 'good' employers. Partnership initiatives are intended to exploit mutual interest between employees and employers on a range of issues and assume union concessions on work flexibility in return for commitments from employers on job security. Relatively few companies have signed partnership agreements in the complete form envisaged by the TUC, and many of those that have were in the throes of restructuring (Heery 2002; Martinez Lucio & Stuart 2005).

## Management, employers and their associations

The Confederation of British Industry (CBI), formed in 1965, is the peak employer's body in the United Kingdom. It is an important lobbyist of the British government and EU agencies but, like the TUC, it does not participate in collective bargaining. It claims to represent the views of 200,000 employers covering approximately half the workforce in the United Kingdom (Marchington & Wilkinson 2012). Although the smaller Institute of Directors grew in influence during the 1980s, it is no longer significant in terms of employment relations activities.

Historically, associations of employers played an important part in shaping the British voluntarist system of employment relations (Rollinson & Dundon 2007). Initially at the local level and then (more importantly) at the national level, they acted as representatives for employers within industries, reaching agreements with unions about recognition, disputes procedures and the substantive terms and conditions across member employers. They offered forms of mutual defence against union campaigns and, to some extent, took wages 'out of competition' among British employers competing in the same product market (Sisson 1987). There were many signs in the 1950s and 1960s that the agreements to which employers' associations were signatories were losing their regulatory effectiveness. The growth of workplace-based incentive payments and job evaluation systems, the escalation of overtime working and the broadened scope of joint regulation into what notionally were areas of management prerogative were led by workplace-based union shop stewards.

The number of employers' associations declined from more than 1350 in 1968 to only 100 in 2012 (Certification Officer 2013).[4] Employers' associations tend to offer one or more sets of services to their members—for example, collective bargaining (typically little more than the setting of frameworks which the parties at local level then add to in order to address their own specific problems and issues); assisting with dispute resolution by providing, along with recognised unions, an independent role in trying to resolve 'failures to agree' at company level; providing specialist advice about new legislation and answering queries about workplace matters; and representing members' views, either at employment tribunals or to government and the EU. Although there are some exceptions—principally in the public sector—compared to most other parts of Western Europe, employers' associations in the United Kingdom have moved to the periphery of employment relations, offering little more than legal, advisory, training and other services. Today, unlike their counterparts elsewhere in Western Europe, most employers' associations in the British private sector do not directly engage in collective bargaining, although they are available as a source of advice to their members.

The period since the 1980s has witnessed greatly enhanced employer power and freedom of action, driven by higher levels of competition in product markets and restrictions on unionism. While employer objectives in the labour field continue to focus on control, productivity improvement and cost reduction, the mix of strategies and balance of methods is diverse—not surprising given the relative lack of influence employers' associations have in LMEs. Many could be described as using pragmatic/opportunist management styles (Purcell & Sisson 1983), strongly influenced by attempts to cut costs and remain in business; this is especially characteristic of small employers or those whose employment relations style is largely determined by the power of 'lead' firms in sectors such as food retailing or vehicle manufacture (Edwards & Ram 2006). Not all employers use a strictly cost-driven strategy, especially those that compete on the basis of product or service quality, and rely on human capital to achieve competitive advantage (Marchington & Wilkinson 2012). In addition, there are marked variations in the use of human resource management (HRM) practices within sectors (Wood & Bryson 2009).

Managements have aimed for greater levels of flexibility, yet debates on how flexibility might be achieved have tended to polarise. One strand of argument focuses on the extent to which HRM techniques have been adopted as a means to manage labour, while a second strand emphasises employee insecurity, exemplified by the growth in 'zero-hours' and minimum-hours contracts as the chosen route to workplace flexibility.

The vast majority of employment relations managers do not have a job title that indicates they specialise in HRM, employment relations or personnel. In most workplaces (78 per cent), these specialisations are the responsibility of the owner or a general manager. If an employment relations specialist is defined as someone who spends at least half of their time on employment relations matters, irrespective of their job title, 22 per cent of workplaces with five or more employees had such a manager in 2011 (van Wanrooy et al. 2013: 51) compared to 28 per cent of all workplaces with ten or more employees in 2004 (Kersley et al. 2006: 39). Not surprisingly, the likelihood of the presence of an employment relations specialist rises with the size of the workplace: only 15 per cent of workplaces with five to nineteen employees had an employment relations specialist in 2011 compared to 71 per cent of workplaces with at least 100 employees (van Wanrooy et al. 2013: 51). The increasing specialisation of personnel noted for the period 1998–2004 (Kersley et al. 2006: 39) appears to have stopped after 2004 (van Wanrooy et al. 2013: 51).

The likely future pattern of development of the employment relations function is not clear. There is a threat to the future of the function from line managers and from specialist consultancy firms, outsourcing and shared service operations. In many enterprises, line managers undertake a substantial range of HRM activities (Purcell & Hutchinson 2007), and in some cases this has led to the break-up of specialist internal functions (Reilly et al. 2007; Marchington & Wilkinson 2012). The fragmentation of management support for employment relations is likely to accelerate as employers face sustained pressures to reduce costs, focus on their core business and increase contracting out to other firms (Marchington et al. 2005). In contrast, the degree of autonomy allowed to workplace managers on employment relations has increased in recent years, particularly regarding appraisals, health and safety, grievance handling and equal opportunities in the private services sector (van Wanrooy et al. 2013: 52–3).

## The role of the state

Employment relations researchers traditionally have characterised the UK tradition as 'voluntarism' because of its comparatively low level of legal regulation of employment. But that characterisation is less applicable than in the past, as labour law has been subject to greater influence from the EU and employment relations have become more juridified. Historically, 'the British state has been a central actor in the construction, maintenance, and reconstruction of industrial relations institutions' (Howell 2005: 3). The Conservative governments of 1979–97 instigated a major change to the character of state intervention, which is still applicable.

### *Legal reforms of employment relations*

The Industrial Revolution in the United Kingdom laid the groundwork for a drive on the part of workers towards unionisation and, starting with the Combination Acts of 1799 (Orth 1991), a heavy-handed response to unionisation by the state. At the start of the twentieth century, the voluntarist approach began to take shape. Rather than affirming positive rights for employees, the state opted for a system of immunities for unions from various areas of criminal and civil law. This process was consolidated by the 1906 *Trade Disputes Act* (Wedderburn 1986), which served as the foundation of union law until the 1980s.

The principal features of voluntarism included non-legally binding collective agreements; voluntary union recognition by employers; a relatively low level of formalisation of employment relations structures; and a light, voluntary framework of state-provided supplementary dispute resolution facilities, with no governmental powers to order the suspension of industrial action or impose cooling-off periods. The laissez-faire approach to regulation was supported by unions and employers, although the specific terms of its implementation were contested.

From the post-1945 period through the 1970s, unionisation increased while, concurrently, the United Kingdom's economic performance weakened. In an attempt to reverse the decline, employment relations reform was high on the political agenda. Although the Donovan

Commission had argued for a continuation of voluntary reform in its report (Donovan 1968), in subsequent years successive governments resorted to legislation. An example was the Conservatives' 1971 *Industrial Relations Act*, which sought to dampen the ability of workers to strike (Rideout 1971). Following the US model, this ill-fated Act also aimed to make collective agreements legally enforceable contracts. The unions boycotted much of the Act and few employers used it, thereby rendering it largely ineffective. Apart from the unfair dismissal provision, Labour repealed most of the legislation in 1974.

Prime Minister Thatcher's Conservative government swept to power in 1979 with the intention of severely restricting union power and activity. Fairbrother (2002) highlights this date as signalling a transition away from traditional voluntarism and towards a neo-liberal interventionist state. Among the reforms implemented during successive Conservative governments was legislation aimed at limiting the ability of unions to organise lawful industrial action, narrowing traditional union immunities from legal action, outlawing secondary strike action, imposing a secret ballot of union members before they take industrial action, prohibiting the 'closed shop' and removing statutory procedures to facilitate union recognition, thus making it much more difficult for unions to consolidate and extend union membership. In addition, the new laws intervened prescriptively in internal union governance.

The post-1997 Labour governments did not change the main framework of employment relations law introduced by the Conservatives, although they eased some details—such as the introduction of a new mechanism for unions to secure recognition by employers (Simpson 2000; Gall 2007) and a national minimum wage (NMW) to tackle low pay in 1999. In addition to these initiatives, Prime Minister Blair's opt-in to the Maastricht Social Protocol strengthened statutory employment rights to some degree, in relation to representative participation structures, working time regulations, equal opportunities, non-discrimination, redundancy protection and health and safety provisions, among other areas in which EU directives have been transposed into British labour law (Deakin & Morris 2005). The public policy preferences of New Labour did not return to an advocacy of collective bargaining as the means to address employment relations matters. Instead, preference was afforded to individualised methods of regulating the employment relationship.

The post-2010 coalition government has not altered the basic approach of its predecessors. New Employment Tribunal Rules of Procedure were implemented together with the introduction of fees in the employment tribunal, while the *Enterprise and Regulatory Reform Act 2013* lowered the maximum award available for unfair dismissal, and required 'whistleblowing' to be in the 'public interest' before it attracted legal protection. These are not fundamental reforms, but they limit the capacity of the individual to seek legal redress (Tuck et al. 2013). Further, the coalition government has commissioned an independent review of the tactics used by some unions during disputes. Initiated in response to the 'leverage' tactics deployed by UNITE during the dispute at Grangemouth oil refinery, the terms of reference of the review include consideration of the effectiveness of the legal framework to prevent inappropriate or intimidatory actions during a dispute. There are also discussions in the Conservative Party regarding the introduction of a minimum threshold of voters taking part in a strike ballot to make the ballot lawful. It remains to be seen whether such a threshold will be introduced and, if so, at what level.

### Economic policies

The British state has changed its economic policies dramatically. Immediately following World War II, demand-side economics, based on state-directed income redistribution and a commitment to full employment, were the general orthodoxy. This Keynesian consensus ended with the election of the Conservatives in 1979. The new government mainly opted for supply-side solutions to managing the economy, by adopting both monetarist policies and fiscal restraint and by exerting more control over public sector pay. These reforms were accompanied by selected deregulation of the economy and more labour market flexibility. The defeat of inflation became the dominant priority rather than limiting the rate of unemployment, which then remained relatively high.

In 1997, the election of Labour led to policy changes (Dickens & Hall 2010), but the Conservatives' earlier preoccupation with inflation was central to Prime Minister Blair's, and later Prime Minister Brown's, economic policies. For a decade, inflation rates in the United Kingdom remained comparatively low. The Labour government devolved the ability to set interest rates to the independent Bank of England and set an annual target of no more than 2.5 per cent (later 2 per cent). Inflation, however, breached 3 per cent in 2007, just as financial markets and the broader economic outlook in the United Kingdom began to deteriorate. The following year, a global crisis with its origins in the finance sector generated a deep recession.

After its election in 2010, the coalition government successfully persuaded much of the electorate that the crisis was the result of New Labour profligacy, rather than a failure of banking regulation. It implemented a rigorous 'austerity' program, which included tight fiscal controls, intended to reduce the deficit, privatisation of further public services—notably the Royal Mail—and the more wide-ranging exposure of public services to private provision, particularly in health, where the *Health and Social Care Act 2012* has opened the door to private provision on a scale hitherto unknown. Although rates of economic growth in the United Kingdom are higher than those in the eurozone at the time of writing, three consequences of the 'austerity' program are widely debated. First, as a result of widespread low pay, there are more people in poverty who are working than are jobless, thereby requiring the taxpayer to subsidise low pay through tax credits and/or benefits. Second, with the reduction in the share of national income taken by wages, demand has weakened. Before 2008, demand was sustained by increases in household debt. An impact of the financial crisis was that households became more debt averse, a tendency that strengthened as real wages declined. Recovery from the crisis has thus been slowed by weak demand. Third, relatively high rates of unemployment and the weakening of employment protections have resulted in the availability of cheap, insecure labour, with the consequence that there is little incentive for employers to invest when demand rises because they can employ more workers and subsequently dismiss them cheaply if demand declines.

## Dispute settlement

The British state has provided conciliation and arbitration services as a supplement to voluntary collective bargaining and disputes procedures since the end of World War II. These services were initially offered in 1945 by the Personnel Management Advisory Service (later the Industrial Relations Service) in the Ministry of Labour (Kessler & Purcell 1994), but in 1975 the Wilson government established the independent Advisory, Conciliation and Arbitration Service (ACAS) by means of the *Employment Protection Act*. Since then, a tripartite council has governed ACAS, comprising employer and union nominees with a balance of independent members. Thanks to ACAS, successive governments have sought to distance themselves from the direct settlement of particular industrial disputes, although the government's influence as an interested party in the public sector is still important.

ACAS services are publicly financed and include conciliation in complaints by individuals over alleged breaches of statutory employment rights (its principal and much expanded activity) as well as in collective disputes. It also offers information on employment matters, provides advice to the different parties on all aspects of employment relations and policies, and acts as a means for employers and unions to network. ACAS officials carry out individual and collective conciliation and advisory work, but they appoint independent experts (e.g. academics) to act as ad hoc mediators and arbitrators. Unlike the position in some other countries, arbitration is neither compulsory nor legally binding. ACAS was established by the Labour government. It continued under the Conservatives, although they did curtail the use of arbitration in the public sector, cut ACAS's role in conducting inquiries and removed its earlier responsibility to promote the growth and reform of collective bargaining (Goodman 2000).

ACAS received 871 requests for collective conciliation, of which 93 per cent were resolved, in the year to December 2012 (ACAS 2013: 32). During that same year, the ACAS national helpline received 928,995 telephone inquiries and staff made 3664 'advisory visits and in-depth phone calls' (33). During the period, more than 155,000 cases were submitted to ACAS for conciliation by the Employment Tribunal Service, of which 37,598 concerned unfair dismissal, 24,269 the *Wages Act*, 23,849 breaches of contract and 19,807 working time, including annual leave (34). In addition to conciliation and arbitration, ACAS also produces its own research on employee relations and offers training and development programs for managers and employee representatives. ACAS thus plays an important role in injecting an element of 'fairness' into worker–employer relations in the United Kingdom.

## The public sector

The state plays an important role as a direct or indirect employer for a substantial proportion of the labour force. In 2009, for example, 22 per cent of all employees in the United Kingdom were employed in the public sector, a proportion that had fallen to just below 20 per cent by September 2013 (ONS 2014). The state has also sought influence as an exemplar to other employers. Throughout much of the twentieth century, the government aimed to be a 'good' or 'model' employer by encouraging union membership and more secure employment compared to the private sector. The election of the Conservative government in 1979 again marked an important turning point.

Between 1979 and 1997, the public sector was transformed as successive Conservative governments sought to limit public expenditure and reduce both the role and size of the state. The most dramatic change was the privatisation of corporations formerly owned by the public (telecommunications, airlines, coal, steel and the railways) as well as the utilities. In principle, the aim of privatisation was to inject competition into these industries with the intention of improving efficiency and productivity. An obvious effect was a reduction in public sector employment from 30 to 22 per cent of the labour force (Winchester & Bach 1995). Furthermore, strict cash limits and projected efficiency gains were built into forward budgets to restrain public sector pay settlements to lower than inflation rates in many cases (Beaumont 1987). Public sector strikes (e.g. the steelworkers in 1980 and the coal miners in 1984) were resisted and access to arbitration was withdrawn or constrained.

The Conservatives also deregulated many areas—for example, in public transport, local authorities and the health service. Many civil service functions were reorganised into more autonomous and accountable executive agencies, and other areas were subjected to substantial reductions in employment and 'market testing' (Stewart & Walsh 1992). Local authorities were required, under 'best value' provisions, to put some services out to tender with the private sector. Subsequently, public–private partnerships were introduced into local governments and the health service, with major implications for employment relations (Rubery et al. 2002; Grimshaw et al. 2002). This process was meant to institute private sector values and practices into the public sector. In practice, it resulted in a fragmentation of work across organisational boundaries (Marchington et al. 2005).

As with legal reforms and economic policies, between 1997 and 2010 Labour governments and the coalition government have broadly retained many of the earlier Conservative initiatives to transform public sector employment relations by continuing to push for an injection of competition and 'prudent' fiscal policies. Furthermore, to deliver on election promises of improved public sector performance, there has been a push for the introduction of performance-related pay, especially in teaching and health care. An element of the post-2010 coalition government's austerity program promoted more widespread private provision of what are ostensibly public services.

## EMPLOYMENT RELATIONS PROCESSES

The means of regulating pay, working time, methods of working and procedures for resolving differences between workers and employers are central to the employment relationship. These means can be established in various ways, including legal enactment, management decisions—with or without employee consultation—and collective bargaining between unions and employers. Collective bargaining has diminished in coverage and scope, and in many cases managements now set terms and conditions unilaterally, rather than bargaining with unions. Towers (1997) refers to the vacuum left by the contraction of collective bargaining (and the general absence of a mandatory system of employee consultation) as the 'representation gap'.

## Collective bargaining

Collective bargaining has a long history in the United Kingdom. Industrial-level bargaining developed in several industries in the late nineteenth century and in others through 'joint industrial councils' soon after World War I. By the early 1920s, multi-employer bargaining was well established for manual workers, and successive governments encouraged industry-level negotiations as a means of establishing 'orderly' employment relations. Although there were exceptions, centralised negotiations across entire industries generally left little room for workplace bargaining.

In several industries during World War II and afterwards, shop stewards increasingly became involved as workplace bargainers, supplementing the industry-wide negotiations conducted between national union officials and representatives of employers' associations. This development occurred because centralised agreements could not specify workplace rules in sufficient detail; the power of shop stewards increased as labour markets tightened, and resulted in what became known as *wages drift*; and managers were poorly trained and equipped, with the result that they often made short-term concessions to sustain output with little concern for the medium or long term. The Donovan Commission, set up in 1965 to examine the so-called 'industrial relations problem', argued for workplace bargaining to be formalised, as this would weaken the influence of multi-employer, national negotiations and at the same time remove the supposed disorder created by uncoordinated workplace agreements (Donovan 1968). To the extent that employers and unions took this advice, single-employer bargaining received a significant boost and, from the mid-1970s, the coverage of industry-wide collective bargaining in the private sector contracted.

Managers' recognition of unions for the purposes of negotiating pay and conditions is a broad indicator of preparedness to engage with unions. Union recognition declined in the 1980s and 1990s, albeit at slower rates during the late 1990s. Between 1998 and 2004, the fall in union recognition in workplaces with 25 or more employees was not statistically significant, although the fall was significant at smaller workplaces with between ten and 24 employees (Kersley et al. 2006: 122). There were substantial falls in applications to the Central Arbitration Committee for union recognition and in the number of new voluntary recognition agreements (Moore 2013). These falls have not been accompanied by a decline in the proportion of workplaces at which a union is recognised, which remained constant at 22 per cent between 2004 and 2011 (van Wanrooy et al. 2013: 59). Unions are more likely to be recognised at larger workplaces and in the public sector. It remains to be seen whether moves by employers to curtail facility time for union representatives at workplaces where unions are recognised further hinder the capacity of unions to act.

In 1970, collective bargaining covered approximately 70 per cent of the workforce, but it has since declined to around 23 per cent. Between 2004 and 2011, the coverage of collective bargaining in the private sector remained constant at 11 per cent—the first period for more than a quarter of a century in which a decline has not been recorded (van Wanrooy et al. 2013: 79). Nonetheless, the scope of collective bargaining continued to contract during the same period. Even where unions were formally recognised for negotiation, for example, employers negotiated about pay at only 56 per cent of private sector workplaces. The contraction in the coverage and the scope of collective bargaining since the early 1980s have led some to suggest that union involvement in the regulation of workplace employment relations had been 'marginalised', and that many collective bargaining arrangements were 'hollow shells' as managers refuse to negotiate with their union counterparts (Marchington & Parker 1990; Millward et al. 2000).

Multi-employer bargaining in 2011 covered 7 per cent of all workplaces with five or more employees, compared to 9 per cent in 2004. Not surprisingly, multi-employer bargaining is concentrated in the public sector, where 43 per cent of all workplaces with five or more employees were covered in 2011, compared to 2 per cent in the private sector. The coverage of multi-employer bargaining in the public sector declined from 58 per cent in 2004. In the private sector, nine out of every ten employees worked in workplaces where management unilaterally set the pay for at least some employees in both 2004 and 2011 (van Wanrooy et al. 2013: 82–3). Although the stance of the Labour Party towards the restoration of earlier levels of coverage of collective bargaining remains uncertain, trade unionists have recently emphasised the deleterious effects of low collective bargaining coverage rates, and argued for the extension of coverage (Ewing & Hendy 2013).

## Employee involvement and participation

Interest in employee involvement and participation (EIP) has waxed and waned over the past century, with surges of activity at times when employers feel they are under threat from labour and a loss of impetus when this threat recedes (Ramsay 1977). This is illustrated by a growth in participation through profit-sharing in the late nineteenth century, in joint consultation during and just after World Wars I and II (1917–1920, 1940s) and in worker directors through the TUC and the Bullock Committee of Inquiry during the 1970s. The most recent growth of interest and activity has occurred under the EIP label since the 1980s, and it differs substantially from earlier variants. It tends to be individualist and direct (as opposed to collective and through representatives), it tends to be initiated unilaterally by management, and it is directed at securing greater employee commitment to, and identification with, the employing organisation. EIP has grown without much pressure from employees or unions, but with some legislative support for employee share ownership, profit-related pay, and information and consultation.

The growth in EIP is apparent from successive Workplace Employment Relations Surveys (WERS). Millward et al. (1992: 166) note that 'management initiatives to increase EIP were made with rising frequency throughout the 1980s', a trend that continued throughout the 1990s. Cully et al. (1999) indicate that four of the top five 'new management practices and [EIP] schemes' were forms of direct EIP. By 2004, team briefings were used in 60 per cent of workplaces; this had risen to 66 per cent by 2011. In contrast, joint consultative committees (JCCs) have become less widely used, and were present in only 8 per cent of workplaces in 2011, down from 20 per cent in 1998. There was less of a decline in JCCs beyond the workplace, from 58 per cent of branch sites in 2004 to 46 per cent by 2011 (van Wanrooy et al. 2013: 61–4). This picture is reinforced by case study data (Marchington & Cox 2007), and some now argue that direct EIP is more effective than union-based and indirect EIP (Bryson 2004).

Direct EIP takes several distinct forms: downward communication from managers to employees using techniques such as team briefing and employees reports; upward problem-solving designed to tap into employees' knowledge and opinions through practices such as quality circles and suggestion schemes; and task participation, in which individual employees are encouraged or expected to extend the range and types of tasks undertaken at work, using practices such as job rotation, job enrichment and teamworking (Kelly 1982; Appelbaum et al. 2000). There is also financial involvement, which aims to link part of an individual's rewards to their own performance and/or that of the unit or enterprise as a whole. These include profit-sharing and various employee share ownership schemes; the 2004 WERS estimated that 19 per cent of workplaces had one of these schemes, a number that had fallen to 10 per cent by 2010 (van Wanrooy et al. 2013: 96).

Other estimates, however, suggest that the recession encouraged employers to introduce financial participation schemes in the form of either profit-related pay or employee share ownership as a means to encourage employees' efforts and/or to ensure that risk was shared between employers and employees (Pendleton et al. 2009).

Although direct EIP has grown since the 1980s, representative participation has not disappeared. While JCCs were unlikely to survive the development of strong shop steward workplace organisation in the 1960s, they re-emerged during the 1970s before declining after the 1980s (van Wanrooy et al. 2013: 60–3). They remain more extensive in the public sector than in the private, in larger workplaces than in smaller, and where unions are recognised than where they are not. Their decline was influenced by the changing structural and sectoral composition of workplaces—in particular by the falling number of larger establishments. WERS panel data (Millward et al. 2000: 111) suggest that JCCs were rarely introduced as an alternative to unions; direct EIP was equally likely to be found in workplaces where management actively encouraged unions as in those where it did not. The TUC has launched an initiative favouring the introduction of board-level employee representation (TUC 2013). While this initiative avoids stating any specific proposals, it alludes to support from both Liberal Democrats and Labour Party spokespeople and highlights the coverage of board-level employee representation throughout Member States of the EU. The position of affiliated unions to this initiative remains to be seen.

## CURRENT AND FUTURE ISSUES

### Fairness at work

An increasingly important topic in employment relations is the idea of fairness at work. A broad definition of fairness includes absolute and relative pay, fair treatment of immigrants, gender equality in the workplace and bullying and harassment. Each of these topics can be subsumed under the larger debates surrounding dignity at work (Hodson 2001), as can questions about worker voice. It should be acknowledged that what is deemed 'fair' is contested (Hyman & Brough 1975: 1–29), with the principal political parties tending to emphasise different aspects of and approaches to fairness.

The issue of low pay in the United Kingdom has been rising in prominence, especially since the Conservative government abolished wages councils in 1993 in the name of promoting labour market flexibility. The incoming Labour government in 1997 established the Low Pay Commission, which resulted in the introduction of an NMW in 1999. The coalition government elected in 2010 retained the Low Pay Commission. One of the key aims in implementing the NMW was to 'make a positive contribution to fairness' (Grimshaw 2009). Although the NMW directly covers only about 10 per cent of the workforce, it has limited the extent of 'collapsing bottom' inequality (ILO 2008: 26; Machin 2011: 162) without imposing labour market rigidities (Grimshaw 2009). Over its first ten years, the NMW rose by almost 65 per cent, thereby exceeding the rates of increase in price inflation and average earnings, although the rate of increase declined thereafter as an element of the coalition government's austerity program. Evidence suggests that the introduction of the NMW has had no adverse effects on employment, contrary to the expectations of those who opposed its introduction. More recently, debate has shifted to the question of whether the NMW wage constitutes a living wage.[5] Calculation of the living wage suggests that low pay is widespread, and may cover as much as a quarter of the workforce (Savage 2011).

Income inequality increased considerably under the prime ministerships of Thatcher, Major and Blair (Sefton & Sutherland 2005; Brewer et al. 2007), and has continued to rise during the term of office of the coalition government. Although the NMW restricted the impact on income inequality from the 'collapsing bottom', the primary source of rising income inequality in the United Kingdom, as in most other industrialised economies, is the 'flying top' (ILO 2008: 26), characterised by substantial increases in income for those in the higher reaches of the earnings distribution (Machin 2011). While these increases are most notable in the private sector, where chief executives of FTSE 100 companies doubled their bonuses between 2002 and 2010 and increased base salaries by more than 60 per cent (High Pay Commission 2011: 26), income inequality in the public sector was institutionalised under the post-1997 Labour government by the implementation of performance-related pay in the public sector. At a micro level, performance-related pay leverages structured inequality to promote productivity (Armstrong 2002). The extent of income inequality clearly brings into question the 'trickle-down' effect arguments of the neo-liberal position, and has also promoted debate on the issue of 'fair pay' (Toynbee & Walker 2008) and the relationship between rising executive pay and company performance (High Pay Commission 2011).

Women, young people and migrant workers tend to be concentrated in the lower reaches of the earnings distribution, and have been hard hit by the impact of the austerity program of the coalition government. Gender pay equity was accentuated as a political target by the *Equal Pay Act 1970*, but since then progress has been slow. Although the implementation of the NMW had a limited impact on closing the gender gap (Grimshaw 2009), the concentration of women in low-paid part-time jobs, the under-valuing of work where women are over-represented, the degree of sex segregation in workplaces and the absence of women in senior executive positions (Dean & Liff 2010; Forth & Millward 2000) have resulted in women in the private sector being paid between 14.4 per cent (data adjusted for 'observable characteristics') and 28 per cent (unadjusted data) less than men in the United Kingdom (Drolet & Mumford 2012). Issues concerning implementation and the subsequent effects of the financial crisis qualified the impact of the 2006 Women and Work Commission's report (Grimshaw & Rubery 2010). In light of these continuing inequalities and gendered hierarchies, it is no surprise that arguments to 'mainstream' feminist approaches in employment relations in order to capture more accurately the complexities of employment beyond social class remain prominent (Wacjman & Edwards 2005; Holgate et al. 2006).

A further aspect of debates on fairness at work concerns the impact of immigration, the political profile of which increased after the EU enlargements of 2004 and 2006. Estimates suggest that no fewer than 500,000 migrants from the new EU Member States[6] entered the United Kingdom between May 2004 and late 2006 (Blanchflower et al. 2007). A significant proportion of these migrants were economic and temporary (Dustmann & Weiss 2007). The rate of immigration declined and the number of migrants returning to their home country increased when the extent of the financial crisis became apparent. Massive and rapid demographic changes, however, pose new challenges for employment relations institutions. Although unions have responded to these challenges through the implementation of a variety of inclusion policies, shortfalls remain regarding sensitivity to the varied needs and demands of different social groups and addressing challenges of self-organisation (Martinez Lucio & Perrett 2009). The election results for the European Parliament in 2014 also show that immigration is an issue with a high political profile. The United Kingdom Independence Party campaigned on a platform to implement policies to reduce immigration and secured 27.5 per cent—the single largest share—of the national vote. How such results will impact on the policies of the other main political parties remains to be seen.

Of growing importance in the context of the emerging fairness at work debate in the United Kingdom is the issue of workplace bullying and harassment (Hoel & Beale 2006). This topic intersects with low pay and inequities in reward structures (inasmuch as they generate disparate power relations), the fair treatment of immigrants (since they are often the targets of abuse) and gender inequalities (because women are often subjected to sexism in the workplace). The sources of bullying include co-workers (Vartia & Hyyti 2002), customers (Bishop et al. 2005) and managers (Hoel & Beale 2006). Though the issue of bullying is often perceived in relation to physical violence, it has a psychological component as well. Future research in the area of bullying and harassment is justified not only by a moral imperative, but also by the idea that respect in the workplace is good for productivity (Appelbaum 2008).

## Employment relations consequences of EU membership

When the United Kingdom joined the then European Economic Community (EEC) in 1973, employers, led by the CBI, were generally in favour of UK entry, whereas many of the unions were opposed. Since 1973, most employers' organisations have supported the economic aspects of European integration in the form of the development of the Single European Market, although there is no uniform position among employers towards the adoption of the euro. In contrast, the extension of the European social policy agenda has been resisted by most employers' organisations.

There was a change in the United Kingdom in views about the EEC after the address by the president of the European Commission Jacques Delors to the congress of the TUC in 1988. After this address, the majority position in the unions was in favour of deeper European economic integration coupled with a more wide-ranging social dimension. Positions towards the EEC had shifted among the unions after 1979. The policies of the post-1979 Conservative governments influenced the shift in the union position on two counts. First, the exclusion of unionists from engagement with government and the restrictive legislation enacted by the Conservatives limited the political room for manoeuvre for unionists. Second, the growing social agenda of the EU offered employment relations opportunities that were not available domestically, though the opt-out from the Social Protocol of the Maastricht Treaty (Social Chapter) by the Conservative government in 1992 threatened to exclude unionists from many of these benefits. The shift in position among unionists was driven, then, by the aim of gaining access to the benefits of social policy measures that might override the absence of domestic measures.

The post-1997 Labour government reversed the UK opt-out from the Social Chapter, thereby committing the United Kingdom to a range of social policies including the directive on European works councils (94/45/EC). More generally, however, the Labour government sought to retain the competitive advantages it saw arising from the form of regulation enacted by the previous Conservative government, particularly regarding labour flexibility. To this end, the Labour government, supported by employers' organisations, campaigned against the adoption of the directive on information and consultation (2002/14/EC), withdrawing its opposition only when other Member States withdrew from the blocking minority; it also introduced a wide range of exceptions and derogations to the working time regulations, and did not favour a revision of the directive on European works councils that included more specific definitions of information and consultation.

The subsequent faltering progress of European social policy and the increasing prominence of neo-liberal policy objectives within the European Commission (Hyman 2005) has also led many British unionists to reassess their position towards the EU. Among the events that have led to this questioning are the neo-liberal proposals advanced in the Bolkestein directive on the liberalisation of services, the limited social components of the Europe 2020 proposals (Vanhercke 2011) and the decisions from the European Court of Justice that assert the primacy of economic rights over fundamental rights, including respect for national employment relations legislation and collective bargaining (Ghailani 2009).

In addition to legislation on a wide spectrum of health and safety matters, recent legislation from the EU that impinges on UK labour law and employment relations is concentrated in two broad fields: individual employment rights, and information and consultation rights.

The voluntarist approach informed much employment relations practice before the 1960s. While this tradition was weakened by legislation that restricted managerial authority in areas such as recruitment, equality, job termination, redundancy payments and unfair dismissal during the 1960s and 1970s (Anderman 1986), its impact remains evident insofar as the scope of individual employment rights in the United Kingdom is narrow in relation to other Western European countries. Since the reversal of the UK opt-out from the Social Chapter in 1997, a range of new rights have originated from the EU, including those covering the regulation of working time, a right to urgent family leave, a right to parental leave, a right to equal treatment for part-time workers and protection for fixed-term contract workers. The last pair of rights resulted from framework agreements concluded between the social partners at European level. The floor of individual employment rights is thus being extended as a consequence of EU membership and the Social Chapter. The extension of this floor of rights is among the reasons cited by Prime Minister Cameron as underpinning his preference for a repatriation of legislative prerogative in a renegotiation of EU treaties. It remains to be seen whether such a repatriation is possible in negotiation with other Member States, but the Conservative government elected in 2015 has promised a so-called 'in–out' referendum before December 2017. There is therefore a possibility that the United Kingdom may withdraw from the EU. The implications of withdrawal would be wide ranging for employment relations, and are beyond the scope of this chapter, but would encompass economic performance, migration, the legislative regime and the capacity of unions to influence multinational companies.

A second area where EU legislation has impinged on UK employment relations practices is information and consultation. The directives on European works councils (94/45/EC), extended specifically to cover the United Kingdom by directive 97/74/EC and recast in the form of directive 2009/38/EC, on information and consultation (2002/14/EC), and on the European company statute (Regulation No. 2157/2001) and its accompanying directive on the involvement of employees in European companies (2001/86/EC) constitute a wide-ranging network of provisions that operate at national and international levels. Initially, the opt-out from the Social Chapter excluded United Kingdom–based companies from a requirement to comply with the directive on European works councils. The voluntary option allowed by the provisions of the directive for the two years from 1994 was sufficiently attractive for many United Kingdom–based companies to establish European works councils. At the time of writing, however, no United Kingdom–based companies had adopted European company status. Similarly, the response to the information and consultation regulations (the UK transposition of the directive on information and consultation) has been muted among employers, unions and employees (Hall & Purcell 2012). The most recent WERS data, for example, indicate that the impact of the information and consultation regulations in promoting information and consultation arrangements in the form of JCCs 'has been very limited' (van Wanrooy et al. 2013: 61), even though 'voice' systems that combine direct forms of involvement with indirect voice through representative institutions are strongly associated with higher levels of organisational commitment (Purcell & Georgiades 2007). The shift from a single channel to a dual system of representation in the United Kingdom made possible by the directive may be something for the future (Davies & Kilpatrick 2004).

## CONCLUSIONS

Since the 1970s, the system of employment relations in the United Kingdom has been subject to substantial change, with profound implications for the roles of the state, employers and unions. In essence, the United Kingdom adopted more features of an LME in transforming the relationship between state and market, and jettisoning any pretence to social market relations.

Since 1980, the state has overseen the increased juridification of employment relations, characterised by the strong regulation of unionism, the establishment of more individual, rather than collective, labour rights and the deregulation of many aspects of the labour market—notably the diminution of employment protections. While some of these developments were influenced by EU legislation—particularly the provision of individual employment rights—the post-1979 Conservative government led the radical policy changes. Reductions in tax and cuts in public spending underpinned extensive privatisation programs, which sharply reduced the size of and employment levels in the public sector. What remains of the public sector has been exposed to ever-greater market influence. The intention of these policies was to shift the balance of power towards employers. Although the Labour governments of 1997–2010 maintained the principal elements of the policies of the preceding Conservative governments, they introduced an NMW, reversed the opt-out from EU social policy and introduced a union-recognition procedure.

Employers responded to the opportunities provided to them by government policy by withdrawing from some collective bargaining, refusing to recognise unions for collective bargaining at new sites and reducing the scope of bargaining where it remained. Unilateral management decision-making on employment relations issues is thus widespread. There is no evidence to suggest that alternative 'voice' mechanisms have increased in coverage to fill the representation gap left by the contraction of collective bargaining, though there has been a growth of performance pay systems. Employers have also introduced arrangements to increase numerical flexibility, particularly in the form of outsourcing and offshoring, and in the use of self-employed workers.

At workplaces, the evidence is contradictory. Some employers use a wide range of HRM practices intended to generate employee commitment to the goals of the enterprise, which may be accompanied by appraisal systems, training opportunities and sophisticated recruitment and selection. In contrast, and driven by the regulatory framework created by the state, other employers emphasise cost-cutting measures in seeking to maximise the return on capital, rather than developing either organisational or employee capacity. The contrast between 'contract or status' (Streeck 1987) or 'high road versus low road' (Sisson & Purcell 2010) models as a means to improved economic performance divides employers.

The decline of unionism since 1979 has been greater in the United Kingdom than elsewhere in Western Europe. Unions were unable to resist the regulatory assault launched by the Conservative governments after 1979, with the result that union density and the level of industrial action were both much diminished. Although unions have seen organising as a means to reverse this decline, membership density is not increasing. It remains to be seen whether the considerable resources invested by unions yield medium- or long-term rewards in terms of membership and more workplace representatives. While there is not a direct relationship, the declines in density and industrial action have been accompanied by declines in power and influence. The Conservatives effectively dismantled the main tripartite structures after 1979, and unions were unable to resist employer initiatives to withdraw from bargaining or to force new companies to establish collective bargaining. In addition, relations between unions and the Labour Party have been difficult, with the party distancing itself from unionism in many policy areas. The continuing reliance of the Labour Party on unions for finance remains the principal source of influence for unions. The union position on Europe remains ambiguous. The TUC is pro-EU, although there are policy issues where it has concerns. Among its affiliated unions, the position is more complex because the impact of policies of deregulation and the limited scope of social market policies have generated concerns about the contemporary EU.

## FURTHER READING

Farnham, D. (2015) *The Changing Faces of Employment Relations*. London: Palgrave Macmillan.

Gamble, A. (2014) *Crisis without End?* Houndsmills: Palgrave Macmillan.

Tett, G. (2009) *Fool's Gold*. London: Little Brown.

Toynbee, P. & Walker, D. (2008) *Unjust Reward: Exposing Greed and Inequality in Britain Today*. London: Granta Books.

Van Wanrooy, B., Bewley, H., Bryson, A., Forth, J., Freeth, S., Stokes, L. & Wood, S. (2013) *Employment Relations in the Shadow of the Recession*. Houndsmills: Palgrave Macmillan.

## USEFUL WEBSITES

ACAS: <www.acas.org.uk/index.aspx?articleid=1461>.
CBI: <http://news.cbi.org.uk>.
Chartered Institute of Personnel and Development: <www.cipd.co.uk>.
TUC: <www.tuc.org.uk>.
UK government: <www.gov.uk/government/topics/employment employment>.
WERS: <www.gov.uk/government/publications/the–2011-workplace-
    employment-relations-study-wers>.

## A CHRONOLOGY OF UK EMPLOYMENT RELATIONS

1780–1840   Period of primary industrialisation.

1799–1800   Combination Acts provide additional penalties against worker 'combinations'.

1811–14   'Luddites' begin smashing machines.

1824–25   Repeal of Combination Acts.

1834   'Tolpuddle martyrs' transported to Australia for taking a union oath.

1868   First meeting of TUC.

1871   *Trade Union Act* gives unions legal status.

1891   Fair Wages Resolution of the House of Commons.

1899   TUC sets up Labour Representation Committee, which becomes the Labour Party in 1906.

1906   *Trades Disputes Act* gives unions immunity from such liability, if acting 'in contemplation or furtherance of a trade dispute'.

1913   *Trade Union Act* legalises unions' political expenditure if they set up a separate fund, with individuals able to 'contract out'.

1926   General strike and nine-month miners' strike.

1927   Subsequent legislation restricts picketing and introduces criminal liabilities for political strikes.

1945–51   Election of Labour government leads to repeal of 1927 Act; nationalisation of the Bank of England, fuel, power, inland transport, health, steel etc.

1968   Donovan Commission report advocates voluntary reform of IR.

1971   *Industrial Relations Act* legislates for reform; most unions refuse to comply. It also introduces the concept of unfair dismissal.

1974   A miners' strike precipitates the fall of the Conservative government.

1974   *Trade Union and Labour Relations Act* replaces the 1971 Act, but retains the unfair dismissal concept, sets up ACAS and signals a new Social Contract.

1974   *Health and Safety at Work Act.*

1975   *Employment Protection Act* extends the rights of workers and unions; *Equal Pay Act* implemented.

1976   *Race Relations Act.*

1979   'Winter of discontent' followed by election of Conservative government led by Margaret Thatcher.

1980–92   Employment Acts restrict union rights to enforce closed shops, picket and strike; weaken rights of individual employees.

1984   *Trade Union Act* requires regular secret ballots for the election of officials, before strikes and to approve the continuance of political funds.

47

| 1984–85 | Miners' strike. |
|---------|-----------------|
| 1988–90 | Employment Acts remove all legal support for closed shops, and further restrict unions and their scope for invoking industrial action. |
| 1991 | United Kingdom opts out of Social Chapter of Treaty of Maastricht. |
| 1993 | EU establishes a single European market. |
| 1997 | Labour government, led by Tony Blair, elected with a large majority; Labour re-elected in 2001 and 2005. |
| 1998–99 | NMW introduced and *Employment Relations Act* introduces new union-recognition provisions. |
| 2005 | Information and consultation regulations come into force. |
| 2007 | Equality and Human Rights Commission established (combines roles of Commission for Racial Equality, Disability Rights Commission and Equal Opportunities Commission). |
| 2010 | A Coalition government results from the general election and sets a fixed-term parliament. |
| 2014 | Consultation process on zero-hours contracts. |
| 2014 | Scottish electorate votes to remain as a part of the United Kingdom. |
| 2015 | General election scheduled for May. If the Conservative Party forms the government after the general election, the United Kingdom will be committed to an in–out referendum on EU membership in 2017. |

# CHAPTER 3

# Employment relations in the United States

Harry C. Katz and Alexander J.S. Colvin[1]

In the terms used in this book's Introduction, the United States can be seen as the archetypal liberal market economy (LME). In accord with the relatively strong role that market forces have played in US economic history, the United States has long been noted for a high degree of diversity in the conditions under which employees work. Yet, in recent years, the amount of labour market diversity has increased markedly, spurred in part by the share of the labour force represented by unions continuing to decline (from a peak of 35 per cent in the early 1950s to 20 per cent in 1983 and to 11 per cent in the early twenty-first century) (Bureau of Labor Statistics 2014a).

While union representation declined, the American labour movement engaged in revitalisation. Thus, although facing continuing difficulties in organising new members, the American labour movement has been engaged in innovation and experimentation. Diversity was also apparent in collective bargaining outcomes as, although many workers and unions lost devastating strikes or were forced into severe concessions, at least some other unions were winning significant contractual gains—at times as a result of innovative collective bargaining strategies.

The United States has a labour force of more than 156 million people (Bureau of Labor Statistics 2014b). It has a gross domestic product (GDP) of more than US$17 trillion (Bureau of Economic Analysis 2014), which makes it the world's largest economy.[2] Reflecting the size of its economy and its important role in global political affairs, the United States has long been influential in the development of other national systems.

## THE HISTORICAL CONTEXT

American skilled craftsmen started to form unions even before industrialisation, which began in the 1790s. The skilled nature, practical goals and economic strategy of these early, pre-factory unions had a lasting legacy in American unions (Sturmthal 1973).

The establishment of the factory system in the 1850s and 1860s brought into the industrial system large numbers of rural women and children, and many immigrants from Ireland, Britain, Germany and elsewhere. These early factory workers did not unionise. This may have partly been because their pay was generally comparable to American farm earnings and higher than that of factory workers in Europe. It may also have been that the high rate of worker mobility to other jobs, and considerable social mobility, hindered the development of the solidarity among workers that would have facilitated widespread organisation of unions (Lebergott 1984: 373, 386–7; Wheeler 1985). In addition, as often occurred later in US history, vigorous repression of unionisation by employers—both directly and through government action—inhibited unionisation (Sexton 1991).

In spite of these difficulties, skilled craftsmen did form national unions in the 1860s. These pragmatic 'business' unions quickly drove competitors from the field, and in 1886 the craft unions organised on a national basis into a central organisation, the American Federation of Labor (Taft 1964).

Around 1900, building on a large home market made accessible by an improved transport system, large corporations achieved dominance in American industrial life. These complex, impersonal organisations required systematic strategies for managing their workers. Responding to this need, Frederick Taylor, the father of 'scientific management', and his industrial engineer disciples gained a powerful influence on the ideology and practice of management in the United States (Hession & Sardy 1969: 546–7). These ideas became widely accepted before they became influential in Europe and other parts of the world. By declaring 'scientific' principles for the design of work and pay, the Taylorists undermined the rationale for determining these matters by power-based bargaining by unions. Added to this difficulty for the unions was the continuing vigorous opposition of the capitalists, who had enormous power and high prestige (Sexton 1991).

The craft unions survived and prospered in the early part of the twentieth century, partly because of cooperative mechanisms put into place during World War I and their patriotic support of the war. Yet, by the 1920s, there was a powerful alignment of the influence of Taylorism,

50

employer use of company-dominated unions as a union-substitution device, tough employer action in collective bargaining, widespread use of anti-union propaganda by employers' groups and a hostile legal environment. This alignment had reduced even the proud and once-powerful craft unions to a very weak position, though unions in a few industries such as printing and railroads (helped by the passage of the *Railway Labor Act* of 1926) continued to have some success.

It was not until the 1930s, during the Great Depression, that US unions could be seen as a broadly influential and seemingly permanent force. Then, for the first time, unions penetrated the mass-production industry, organising large numbers of factory workers. A conjunction of circumstances led to this: working conditions and pay had deteriorated, there was a changed political environment with the election of Franklin D. Roosevelt as president in 1932, a wave of strikes (many of which were successful) took place in 1933–34, and the *National Labor Relations Act* (NLRA) of 1935 (commonly known as the *Wagner Act*) gave most workers a federally guaranteed right to organise and strike for the first time. Under these conditions, the strategy of mass campaigns by unions was organised not by *craft*, but by *industry* (United Automobile Workers, United Mine Workers, United Steelworkers, or USW). Such unions combined in a new central organisation: the Congress of Industrial Organizations (CIO). This facilitated increasing unionisation of car manufacturing, steel, rubber, coal and other industries (Bernstein 1970; Wheeler 1985).

In the 1940s and 1950s, the unions continued to grow, though federal legislation of this period restricted and regulated them. It was during these decades that they developed the collective bargaining system, with the support of the War Labor Board. This system institutionalised collective bargaining and related dispute resolution mechanisms, due to the need for wage (and price) stabilisation and uninterrupted war production. The post–World War II period saw general prosperity and an improving standard of living accompanied by relative industrial peace. Union automatic wage increases (cost of living clauses) in major industries contributed to this rise in living standards. A wave of organising in the 1960s and 1970s, led by school-teachers, transformed government employment in many parts of the country into a sector with strong unions.

At the same time, US employers throughout the twentieth century often used mobile capital to avoid high labour costs and, in some situations, strong unions. Initially, they accessed less unionised parts of the United States (e.g. the South). They subsequently engaged in offshoring (Cowie 1999). High capital mobility, relatively weak government regulation of employment conditions and decentralised collective bargaining, then, helped make the US industrial relations (IR) system part of an archetypal LME in the view of those who adopt a Varieties of Capitalism (VoC) paradigm.

## THE MAJOR PARTIES

In the United States, all the participants in the employment relations system retain some influence. However, it is the employers that generally have been the most powerful actors and, as will be argued below, they are becoming increasingly dominant.

### Employers and their organisations

As large corporations expanded in the United States in the twentieth century, structured and bureaucratic 'internal labour markets' appeared within those 'primary sector' enterprises. This included well-defined job progressions and formal pay and fringe benefit policies (Doeringer & Piore 1971; Jacoby 1985). Jobs found in the union sector—even in industries, such as construction, that faced substantial cyclical economic volatility—led the way in developing structured and well-paid employment practices.

Yet the United States also retained more unstructured employment practices—often in smaller or rural firms, where pay was lower and administered in a less formal manner. Furthermore, job progressions, dispute resolution procedures and other employment practices were also relatively informal and of lower quality in these 'secondary sector' enterprises, especially when compared to the work practices found in large private or public sector employers.

Employers' organisations are relatively unimportant in the United States (Adams 1980: 4). In contrast to many other countries, there have never been national employers' confederations engaging in the full range of IR activities. In a few industries, such as steel and coal mining, some employers' associations engaged in multi-employer bargaining during the mid-twentieth century period of relative union strength. These multi-employer bargaining structures weakened and mostly disappeared during the 1970s and 1980s, with a few exceptions such as the construction and long-shoring industries. However, there have long been employers' organisations that have the mission of avoiding the unionisation of their members' employees. The National Association of Manufacturers was formed for this purpose in the nineteenth century. In addition, many regional Chambers of Commerce include union avoidance in their activities. The National Right to Work Foundation is an important organisation involved in litigation and lobbying in support of 'right-to-work laws', which prohibit unions from charging dues to workers whom they represent whom are not union members. These employers' groups and others engage in anti-union litigation, lobbying and publicity campaigns.

In contrast to the relative weakness of employers' organisations, management consultants and law firms that represent employers play important roles in the United States. Management consultants are active in advising employers on human resource policies. For example, in wage-setting, employers commonly rely on consulting firms to supply information from pay surveys. Management consultants, along with management-oriented law firms, also engage in the lucrative business of educating employers in techniques of union avoidance.

## The unions

The US labour movement generally is considered an exceptional case because of its apolitical business unionism ideology, focusing rather narrowly on benefits to existing members. The most convincing explanations for this are historical (Kassalow 1974). First, there is no feudal tradition in the United States, which has made the distinctions among classes less obvious than in much of Europe. Second, US capitalism developed in a form that allowed fairly widespread prosperity. Third, the diversity of the population, divided particularly along racial and ethnic lines, has hampered the organisation of a broad-based working-class movement. Fourth, the early establishment of voting rights and free universal public education eliminated those potential working-class issues in the nineteenth century. Fifth, social mobility from the working class to the entrepreneurial class blurred class lines, creating a basis for the widely held belief in the 'log cabin to White House' myth. In consequence, the labour movement has seldom defined itself in class terms. Additionally, the historic experience of unionists was that class-conscious unions (i.e. those that assumed the 'burden of socialism') tended to be repressed by the strong forces of US capitalism (Sexton 1991).

American unions have relied upon collective bargaining, accompanied by the strike threat, as their main weapon. This strategy has influenced the other characteristics of the labour movement. It has provided the basis for an effective role on the shop floor, as the day-to-day work of administering the collective bargaining agreement requires this. It has required unions to be solvent financially so they could make a credible strike threat. It has resulted in an organisational structure in which the power in the union is placed where it can best be used for collective bargaining: the national, the regional or the local union, depending on the locus of collective bargaining (Barbash 1967: 69).

Centralisation of power over strike funds in the national union has been a crucial source of union ability to develop common rules and to strike effectively. It has facilitated, and perhaps even required, an independence from political parties that might be tempted to subordinate the economic to the political. It is one reason why there is a relatively low total union density, as collective bargaining organisations need to have a concern about density only as it pertains to their individual economic territories.

Although unions have emphasised collective bargaining, they have also engaged in politics. For the most part, their political action has taken the form of rewarding friends and punishing enemies among politicians and lobbying for legislation. They have avoided being involved in the formation of a labour party. The American Federation of Labor-Congress of Industrial Organizations' (AFL-CIO) Committee on Political Education and similar union political agencies are major financial contributors to political campaigns, most frequently in support of Democratic Party candidates. The goals of such political activity have often been closely related to unions' economic goals, being aimed at making collective bargaining more effective. However, the labour movement has also been a major proponent of progressive political causes such as laws on civil rights, minimum wages, plant-closing notice, social security and other subjects of benefit to citizens generally.

The structure of the labour movement is rather loose compared with those of many other Western union movements, as the national unions have never been willing to cede power over the function of collective bargaining to the AFL-CIO. The AFL-CIO is a federation of national unions that includes a substantial share of union members. The AFL-CIO serves as a national-level political and public relations voice for the labour movement, resolves jurisdictional disputes among its members, enforces codes of ethical practices and policies against racial and sex discrimination, and is US labour's main link to the international labour movement.

Two major changes have occurred in the AFL-CIO in recent years. In 1995, there was an unprecedented election challenge for the federation's presidency. The president of the Service Employees International Union (SEIU) successfully organised a coalition of union leaders within the AFL-CIO's member unions and defeated the chosen successor of the previous president, who had retired as a result of the challenge.

In an effort to address the decline in union density, the new administration of the AFL-CIO emphasised recruiting members through a variety of new initiatives. Although the new administration began as a reform movement, divisions continued among the national unions around issues such as political and organising strategies. These divisions came to a head in 2005 when a group of major national unions withdrew from the AFL-CIO and formed a new union federation called 'Change to Win' (CTW). We will return to this split in the labour movement and the formation of CTW later.

In the labour movement, the national unions have been described as occupying the 'king pin' position (Barbash 1967: 69). They maintain power over the important function of collective bargaining, in large part through their control of strike funds. The national unions can establish and disestablish local unions. They can also withdraw from national federations if they wish, as happened with the formation of CTW.

Continuing a trend that began in the early 1980s, several mergers and proposals for mergers among national unions have occurred. Recent examples of mergers include the combination of the two largest textile unions. In addition, many small independent unions have begun to choose to be absorbed into national unions, further consolidating the union structure of US unionism (McClendon et al. 1995).

The local unions perform the day-to-day work of the labour movement. They usually conduct bargaining over the terms of new agreements and conduct strikes, although in some industries national unions do this. They administer the agreement, performing the important function of enforcing the complex set of rights created by the collective bargaining agreement. Social activities among union members take place at the local level, where there is a union culture (Barbash 1967: 26–41).

Public sector unions have become an increasingly important component of the American labour movement due to the much higher density of public sector union membership compared with the private sector in the United States. As of 2013, approximately half of all union members in the United States were in the public sector (Bureau of Labor Statistics 2014a).

Beyond the unions of the traditional labour movement, an increasingly diverse array of organisations has arisen, representing American workers in different settings and aspects of their employment. Worker Centers have become an important structure for representing workers outside traditional union membership (Fine 2006). Many of these Worker Centers focus on representing low-wage workers in immigrant communities. These community-based Worker Centers help workers access government services, enforce their employment rights and organise around issues of concern to these communities.

## Government

The rapid increase in public sector unionisation in the 1960s and 1970s was probably the most important development in the US labour movement since the 1930s. Teachers led the way as they successfully protested about declines in their salaries and benefits relative to those of other workers. Rapid expansion in public sector union membership and militancy followed.

In the mid-1970s, a taxpayers' revolt emerged and slowed the gains of public employees' unions, although union representation, as a share of the total public sector workforce, held steady. Then, in the mid-1980s, teachers and other public employees' groups benefited from public concerns over the inadequacy of public services and saw their bargaining power rebound. In the 1990s, calls to reinvent the public sector led to diverse strategies that ranged from downsizing and privatisation to efforts to bring empowerment and a quality focus to public service provision. A politicised attack on public sector unions surfaced in 2011 (discussed later).

Federal, state and local government employees are excluded from coverage under the *Wagner Act*. Separate legal regulations govern collective bargaining in each of these sectors. Federal employees received the rights to unionise and to negotiate over employment conditions other than pay or fringe benefits through Executive Order 10988, signed by President Kennedy in 1962. In 1970, as part of its effort to reform the postal service, Congress provided postal employees the right to engage in collective bargaining about pay, hours and working conditions. Then, in 1978, Congress replaced the executive orders of President Kennedy (and a related order of President Nixon) with the first comprehensive federal law providing collective bargaining rights to federal employees. Subsequently, collective bargaining in the federal sector is regulated by the Federal Labor Relations Authority. Responsibility for dispute resolution is vested in the Federal Services Impasse Panel. The panel may use mediation, fact-finding or arbitration to resolve disputes. The right to strike is prohibited.

As of 2006, all but nine states had legislation that provided at least some of their state or local government employees with the rights to organise and to bargain collectively. Twenty-four states have passed comprehensive laws that cover a range of occupational groups; the others that have not yet enacted public sector bargaining laws are primarily in the South. With the help of favourable state laws, the public sector became the most heavily unionised sector, with almost 39 per cent of public sector workers represented by unions (Bureau of Labor Statistics 2014a).

In 2011, a series of newly elected Republican administrations at the state level sought to weaken collective bargaining rights for state and local public employees (Lewin et al. 2012; Katz 2013). In Wisconsin, historically a union stronghold, this took the form of restricting the subjects of bargaining to wages and benefits, and requiring unions to seek re-certification of majority membership support every year. Widespread protests in Wisconsin failed to defeat these limitations on unions in that state. By contrast, a 2011 law that placed similar limitations on public sector union bargaining in the state of Ohio was overturned that same year through a popular referendum initiative supported by the labour movement. It is unclear what long-term effects the recent limitations imposed on public sector collective bargaining and union rights in several states will have on public sector union membership. In recent years, public sector union membership nationally has declined only slightly, yet large membership declines have occurred in Wisconsin (Katz 2013).

In addition to its role as an employer, the US government has two other main roles in employment relations: the direct regulation of terms and conditions of employment and the regulation of the way in which organised labour and management relate to each other. The direct regulation of terms and conditions of employment is limited to the areas of employment discrimination, worker safety, unemployment compensation, minimum wages and maximum hours, and retirement (Ledvinka & Scarpello 1991). In 1964, the government prohibited discrimination in employment on the grounds of race, colour, sex, religion or national origin. This law was subsequently strengthened and additional laws passed to prohibit discrimination against older workers and disabled workers.

Unusually, compared with other developed market economies, disputes involving employment laws are resolved through the general court system in the United States, rather than through specialised labour courts or employment tribunals. This means that employment law enforcement in the United States reflects the adversarial nature of American litigation, being a system with relatively high procedural complexity and requiring long periods of time for dispute resolution, yet also produces awards that are at times remarkably large in comparison to those of other countries. The combination of high process costs, great variability in outcomes and potential for major damage awards results in employment litigation being a major concern for employers in the United States (Colvin 2006).

From the 1980s onwards, there was a great deal of legislative activity in the broad field of employment relations, in part to fill gaps created by the weakening influence of unions. Legislative initiatives in the areas of minimum wages, termination of employment, pensions, health and safety, plant closing, drug testing, race and sex discrimination, discrimination against disabled workers, polygraphs (lie-detector machines), and family and medical leave have all attracted attention and produced a plethora of new laws. At the same time, the general rule of employment in the United States continues to be that of 'employment at will', meaning there is no requirement for just cause for dismissal or any general entitlement to reasonable notice or severance pay on dismissal.

Unemployment benefits are provided for on a state-by-state basis, but with some federal control and funding. The system involves payments to persons who have become involuntarily unemployed and are seeking work. The duration of payments is shorter than in most other developed economies. Federal and state wage and hour laws provide for a minimum level of pay and a premium pay rate for overtime work, although many workers are excluded from the coverage of these laws.

Retirement benefits are regulated in two main ways. First, through the social security system, employers and employees are required to pay a proportion of wages into a government fund. Pensions are paid from this fund by the government to eligible retired employees (*Social Security Act*). The second way in which government controls pensions is by regulation of the private pension funds that are set up voluntarily by employers. The *Employee Retirement Income Security Act* (ERISA) of 1974 requires retirement plans to be financially secure, and insures these plans. It also mandates that employees become permanently vested in their retirement rights after a certain period. In recent years, the provisions of the ERISA focusing on defined benefit retirement plans have increasingly been bypassed due to the growth of defined contribution plans, which are subject to less regulation (Salisbury 2001).

Unlike in most other advanced industrialised countries, health insurance in the United States is mostly provided through employer benefit plans. These employer health plans are subject to government regulations, which were expanded by the 2009 *Affordable Care Act*, overhauling the US health-care system. Although this Act introduced major changes to the health-care system, it maintained the predominantly employer-based system of insurance provision, ensuring that this will continue to be a major issue in US collective bargaining (discussed later).

Government regulation of the private sector labour–management relationship consists largely of a set of rules through which these actors establish, and work out the terms of, their relationship. Through the NLRA of 1935, as amended in 1947 and 1958, government provides a structure of rules that establishes certain employee rights with respect to collective action.

The process and rules established by law for union certification and bargaining in the private sector represent one of the more unusual features of US labour–management relations. The NLRA specifies a multi-step organising process ordinarily culminating in a secret-ballot election by employees to determine whether they want union certification. The objective of the law regulating union representation elections is to ensure employees have a free choice. To achieve this objective, the National Labor Relations Board (NLRB) determines the appropriate voting unit, conducts the secret-ballot election, certifies the union as the exclusive bargaining agent for the unit when the union achieves a majority of the votes cast, and rules on allegations of unfair labour practices such as employer retribution against employees who support the union. When the union is victorious in the election, the NLRB issues a certification that requires the employer to bargain in good faith with the union. The union has the same obligation.

Much controversy has focused on whether or not the election process is working in accordance with the original legislative intent. This has led to a continuing debate over the adequacy of laws protecting worker rights to form and join unions. The Commission on the Future of Worker–Management Relations (Dunlop Commission), reporting in 1994, reached the conclusion that the labour laws should be changed to facilitate union organising (Commission on the Future of Worker–Management Relations, 1994). Little has yet come from this and other related recommendations to reform US labour laws, however—partly since most employers remain reasonably satisfied with the outcomes of the present legal framework.

The 2008 return to Democratic Party control of Congress and the presidency raised the prospect of renewed attention to labour law reforms, such as the proposed *Employee Free Choice Act* designed to remove barriers to union organising; however, these reforms were defeated in Congress. In the absence of statutory reforms, greater attention has focused on administrative agency action, with the NLRB proposing a series of rule changes to expedite the representation election process. In addition, in the absence of labour law reform, unions are increasingly turning to non-NLRB election-based organising strategies such as employer neutrality and card check recognition agreements.

The government plays only a limited role in the collective bargaining process in the private sector. Although it requires 'good-faith' bargaining efforts, government generally takes a 'hands-off' position—with the notable exception of the railroad and airline industries, which are covered by separate legislation—in influencing contract outcomes achieved between labour and employers in private sector collective bargaining.

Although private sector labour–management relations are primarily regulated by the federal government, states are able to pass 'right-to-work' laws, under which states can prohibit collective bargaining agreements from containing clauses that require all employees (whether union members or not) to pay fees for the representation services they receive from the union. Right-to-work laws tend to reduce the financial resources available for unions to represent workers and are commonly taken as a symbol of the anti-union orientation of the state. Some 24 states, mostly in the South and Prairie or Mountain regions, have passed right-to-work laws. The most recent states to adopt right-to-work laws were Indiana and Michigan, both in 2012.

## THE MAIN PROCESSES OF EMPLOYMENT RELATIONS

In the *non-union sector*, employers have devised a set of management practices to determine pay and conditions of work systematically. In terms of pay, a combination of job evaluation and individual perfor-mance evaluation systems is widespread. The range of possible pay rates to be paid to workers in, say, a clerk's job are determined by an assessment of the worth of the job to the firm (i.e. job evaluation). A particular employee is assigned a pay rate within this range depending upon seniority, performance and other factors. In addition to pay, other benefits such as health insurance, pensions, vacations and holidays are determined by company policy. All of this is done with an eye to the external labour market, with total benefits having to be adequate to attract and keep needed workers (Gomez-Mejia et al. 1995).

In the *union sector*, the structure of collective bargaining is frag-mented, and this fragmentation is increasing. As is the case in many other developed economies, trends discussed below suggest that the locus of collective bargaining is further decentralising towards the enterprise or workplace level (Katz 1993). Single-company or single-workplace agree-ments are the norm in manufacturing. Most collective bargaining takes place at such levels. Even where there are company-wide agreements, as in car manufacturing, substantial scope is left for local variation.

While the government plays only a very limited role in determin-ing collective bargaining agreements in the private sector, mediators employed by the national government through the Federal Mediation and Conciliation Service are active in the negotiation of new agreements, and their work is generally popular with the parties. In negotiations involving government employees, some state laws provide for binding arbitration of unresolved disputes about the terms of a new agreement. This is especially common where the government employees involved, such as firefighters or police officers, are considered to be 'essential', such that a work stoppage involving those employees would do substantial harm to the public. Interest arbitration of the terms of a new agreement is rare in the private sector.

Although there is considerable variety in collective bargaining agreements (contracts), the majority share certain features. Most are very detailed. Agreements generally cover pay, hours of work, holidays, pensions, health insurance, life insurance, union recognition, management rights, the role of seniority in determining promotions and layoffs, paid time off and the handling and arbitration of grievances. Most agreements have traditionally had a limited duration—usually of one to three years. However, there is a recent trend towards agreements of longer duration—for example, Spirit Aerosystems and the relevant union entered into a ten-year agreement in 2010 and the National Basketball Association similarly agreed to a ten-year contract with the union representing its players in 2011.

In both the private and public sectors, nearly all agreements provide a formal multi-step grievance procedure that culminates in rights arbitration. The formal procedure specifies a series of steps through which the parties can settle disagreements about the application and interpretation of an existing collective bargaining agreement. The procedures are almost always capped by the provision for an independent arbitrator to be selected jointly by the union and the employer. Compared with most developed economies, the emphasis on formal grievance arbitration represents one of the more unusual features of employment relations in the United States. A substantial body of private 'law' has grown up through arbitral decisions, providing employment relations with a set of norms that are often used in the non-union sector, as well as the union sector. Decisions of arbitrators have historically been treated by the courts as final, binding and not appealable (Feuille & Wheeler 1981: 270–81).

In 1991, through its decision in the Gilmer case (*Gilmer v Interstate/Johnson Lane Corp.*, 500 US 20, 1991), the Supreme Court allowed statutory employment rights claims to be resolved in arbitration. This spurred the spread of 'alternative dispute resolution' procedures—particularly in the non-union sector—to settle disputes over matters such as dismissals or racial discrimination. In 2001, further impetus to so-called employment arbitration was provided by the Supreme Court's Circuit City decision (*Circuit City Stores Inc. v Adams*, 532 US 105, 2001). Some analysts observed that the replacement of court procedures with private justice violates employee rights (Stone 1996). Employment arbitration has proved attractive for many employers because it allows them to avoid the uncertainties and risk of large awards in the litigation system. Employment arbitration procedures probably cover more employees in the United States than are represented by unions (Colvin 2007; Lewin 2008). It is less clear whether employment arbitration will serve as a substitute for litigation or will represent a more substantial change in the nature of employment relations in non-union workplaces in the United States.

## The twenty-first century: Growing pressures on employment relations

The 2000s saw a combination of growing pressures on the US employment relations system, yet relatively limited changes in response to these pressures. Polarisation in both incomes and collective bargaining continued to intensify. Growing cost pressures on health-care and retirement benefits dominated many collective bargaining relationships. Pressures from globalisation became particularly acute, even though exports of goods constitute only 12 per cent of US GDP—smaller than any other Organisation for Economic Cooperation and Development (OECD) country (*Economic Report of the President*, 2001). The relative unimportance of exports to the economy reflects the large US home market, which creates a considerable potential for self-sufficiency. However, international trade and investments have become increasingly important to US-based multinational enterprises (MNEs). The wage and other cost control pressures resulting from increased international competition have led to more aggressive management behaviour towards unions. Regional trade pacts—particularly the North American Free Trade Agreement (NAFTA)—have helped spur further globalisation.

Benefit issues have emerged as an increasingly important topic for collective bargaining. Due to the US system, in which most working-age employees and retirees under 65 years of age receive health insurance through employer-provided plans, health insurance is a major labour cost item for many employers. As health-care costs grew rapidly in the 1990s and 2000s, significantly outpacing inflation, this put increasing pressure on employer cost structures. Employers sought to control cost increases through measures such as requiring employees and retirees to pay larger portions of premiums, reducing benefits and increasing co-pays. Whereas these changes could be introduced unilaterally for non-union employees, employers' attempts to negotiate similar measures for unionised employees often produced major tensions in collective bargaining.

Retirement benefits were also a major issue in collective bargaining—particularly for industries such as car manufacturing and steel that had sizeable retiree 'legacy' costs dating from earlier decades, when they supported much larger workforces. In the car industry, the efforts of General Motors to lower its retiree health-care costs led to a major strike in 2007 and eventually led to an agreement whereby General Motors, Ford and Chrysler transferred their retiree health insurance obligations to a union-run Voluntary Employee Benefit Association (Bureau of National Affairs 2007). The United Automotive Workers (UAW) later agreed to the introduction of a lower tier of pay for newly hired workers in the face of further pressure to reduce benefit (and pay) costs when General Motors and Chrysler received federal 'bail-out' funds in late 2008 in an effort to forestall their bankruptcies. The UAW has vowed to eliminate, or at least reduce, the pay differential between lower- and upper-tier car workers. It remains to be seen how the UAW makes use of the increased bargaining leverage this union has gained due to the car sales recovery, and also how any tensions between lower- and upper-tier members affect union solidarity and internal affairs.

Globalisation continues to be a major force affecting the US economy. The trade deficit is very high. Outsourcing is a growing concern in employment relations—particularly in the service sector, which previously was more insulated from international competition. For example, in 2004 two major service sector unions, the SEIU and UNITE HERE, launched a joint plan to address outsourcing of service work through organising outsourcing firms and creating alliances with unions in other countries. In 2006, the Communications Workers of America (CWA) negotiated an agreement with AT&T to bring back offshored technical service support jobs (Katz et al. 2007: 395). At the political level, organised labour has been active in lobbying for the inclusion of labour rights provisions in trade agreements.

The US employment relations system has remained relatively stagnant. In the absence of legislative action, labour law reform attention turned to prospects for administrative agency action. Most notably, a set of rule changes was proposed by the NLRB with the goal of reducing delays in representation elections. The importance of administrative agency actions was also illustrated by the 2012 controversy that developed over Boeing's relocation of a production line from its heavily unionised facilities in Washington state to its non-union facility in South Carolina.

Although employers in the United States are generally free to make plant location decisions without government involvement, Boeing's chief executive had made comments in a media interview indicating that the motive for relocating production was a response to strike activity by the union representing Boeing workers in Washington. This led to a complaint being filed with the NLRB alleging an unfair labour practice of interference with the protected activity of striking. Despite not having reached the stage of adjudication by the board, this complaint engendered intense political controversy over allegations of government interference with free-market business decisions.

Eventually, the legal issue was resolved when the union withdrew its complaint as part of a settlement of outstanding bargaining issues with Boeing management. However, labour–management relations at Boeing continue to be tense. In 2013, serious conflict erupted over management demands to reopen the collective agreement to reduce labour costs in return for agreeing to locate production of the company's next generation version of its 777 airliner in Washington state. After local union members initially rejected the management's proposal, the national International Association of Machinists and Aerospace Workers (IAM) union stepped in to renegotiate the proposed deal and put it to a second vote of the union membership, where it narrowly passed.

## CHANGING EMPLOYMENT RELATIONS

The non-union sector has continued to grow in the private sector as management has aggressively resisted union organisation and taken advantage of new technologies and relatively lax enforcement of labour laws to shift work within or outside the United States, or rely on outsourcing or 'contingent labour' to meet competitive pressures and union organising efforts.

### Union revitalisation

Faced with a growing non-union sector, since the mid-1990s the labour movement has initiated innovative efforts to stimulate new organising. Union organisers have been elected to leadership positions in several unions. National unions and the AFL-CIO have begun to spend more on organising, and innovative organising tactics, including efforts to organise on a community or regional basis outside the NLRB procedures, have been launched (Turner et al. 2001).

One of the purposes of the AFL-CIO organising initiatives is to diffuse throughout the labour movement some of the successful organising strategies used by affiliated unions. Unions such as UNITE HERE and the SEIU have had above-average success in their organising. The campaigns of these unions use young, well-educated organisers and involve extensive direct communication with prospective members and links to community groups such as churches.

This approach to organising has been labelled a 'rank-and-file' style, and contrasts with more top-down traditional organising that relied on appointed organisers and formal communication strategies. Rank-and-file organising also tries to modernise and broaden the issues around which employees are attracted to unions by confronting child care, equal pay and other issues that are of concern to the current workforce. Research suggests that this method of union organising has been more successful than traditional methods in the private sector (Bronfenbrenner 1997). However, during the 1990s and 2000s, there was little evidence of any widespread effect from these new organising initiatives, as union density rates continued to decline, reaching a low of about 11 per cent in 2014 (Bureau of Labor Statistics, 2015).

## Division in the AFL-CIO and the formation of the CTW Coalition

With declining union membership, there have been divisions in the labour movement about how best to rebuild union strength. In 1995, John Sweeney was elected president of the AFL-CIO on a reform platform, challenging the existing direction and leadership of the AFL-CIO. A decade later, a new group of union leaders emerged to challenge the Sweeney administration leadership of the AFL-CIO and proposed a new direction for the labour movement.

During 2005, conflicts about the future direction of the AFL-CIO came to a head. Four major unions—the SEIU, UNITE HERE, the Teamsters and the Laborers—issued a joint proposal for reforms of the AFL-CIO. The executive committee of the AFL-CIO rejected the proposed reforms and instead adopted a counter-proposal offered by President Sweeney. In June 2005, the four dissenting unions, along with the United Food and Commercial Workers (UFCW), announced the formation of a new organisation, to be called the Change to Win Coalition. In addition to its initial five members, the CTW Coalition was also joined by the Carpenters Union and the United Farm Workers. Together, the seven unions in the CTW Coalition represented some 6 million workers, compared with the nearly 9 million workers represented by unions that were still members of the AFL-CIO.

Developments in the period since the 2005 split suggest that the formation of the CTW Coalition did not have the positive impact for which its supporters had hoped. The evidence suggests that although the CTW Coalition included some of the more successful organising unions in the labour movement, there was no significant increase in either the union organising success rate or the numbers of workers organised by CTW unions following the formation of the new coalition (Aleks 2015). Some of the leadership issues that may have prompted the split also disappeared as both Sweeney and Andy Stern, the President of the SEIU who had been a key leader of CTW, retired from their leadership positions. Sweeney was succeeded in 2009 as leader of the AFL-CIO by Richard Trumka, the former leader of the United Mine Workers, who pursued policies encouraging reconciliation between the members of the two federations. This approach has brought success, with a number of members of the CTW Coalition rejoining the AFL-CIO, including UNITE HERE in 2009, the Laborers in 2010 and the UFCW in 2013. With the CTW Coalition now shrunk to only three member unions, the Teamsters, the SEIU and the relatively small United Farm Workers, it appears that the US labour movement is on track to full reunification.

## Variation in employment practices

Economic pressures have induced a substantial increase in the amount and nature of the variation in employment practices. Some of the increased variation has been spurred by a decline in unionisation and the differences between the union and non-union sectors. Even within the union and non-union sectors, variation has been increasing through the spread of a diverse array of employment practices. Another divergent aspect of collective bargaining is that union representation is much more substantial in the public sector, where the unionisation rate was more than 35 per cent, compared with less than 7 per cent in the private sector in 2013 (Bureau of Labor Statistics 2014a).

The level of unionisation in the United States has never approached the higher levels found in many other countries. As a result of a lower level of unionisation, and the limited influence of other constraints on managerial behaviour, the United States generally has had a relatively large low-wage employment sector. Nevertheless, there were other non-union firms that chose to pay more, often as part of employment strategies that followed either bureaucratic, human resource management (HRM) or Japanese-oriented employment patterns.

The downward trend in unionisation increased the variation in employment conditions, given that where it existed, unionisation brought a high degree of standardisation in employment conditions. Job-control unionism put a high premium on contractual rules and pattern bargaining, linking contractual settlements within and between industries (Katz 1985: 38–46). In contrast, a common feature of non-union employment systems has been procedures that relate pay and other employment terms to individual traits and organisational goals. The result has been much higher variation in employment practices across individuals, companies and industries, compared with union employment systems. This variation in employment practices is a major driver of another key feature of the US economy: its high level of economic inequality.

## Economic inequality and unemployment issues and debates

Among developed economies, the United States has relatively high levels of income inequality, indicated by its above-average Gini coefficient compared with other OECD countries (OECD 2013). Research by Picketty and Saez (2003) using tax return data shows that in recent years income inequality levels in the United States have returned to heights not seen since the 1920s (also see Levy & Murname 1992: 1333). There is accumulating evidence that a mixture of market and institutional factors—most importantly the low level of unionisation and the decentralised structure of collective bargaining—has caused income inequality to rise, and helps explain why the rise in inequality is so large in the United States (Blau & Kahn 1996).

Another related labour market problem that has received much attention is the slow reduction that has occurred in the US unemployment rate during the post-2007 global financial crisis recovery and the particularly high share of long-term unemployed. Debate has followed regarding whether that unemployment is 'structural' (i.e. long term) or 'cyclical' in nature (Rothstein 2012). Structural factors that might have contributed to the high unemployment rate include intensified global competition (and the expansion in global labour supply), 'skill-biased' technological change, the weakening of governmental labour market protections and the decline in unionisation. It is noteworthy that there is significant overlap between potential causes and the debates concerning income inequality and high unemployment.

## Collective bargaining initiatives

Unions have struggled in recent years to extend their membership and maintain their influence in unionised settings. In response, unions have made significant changes in the process and outcomes of collective bargaining, including corporate campaigns and the linking of collective bargaining to organising and political strategies. While corporate campaigns historically had been used sporadically by the US labour movement, the use and intensity of these campaigns increased after the 1990s as unions struggled to find ways to counteract the power advantages management had gained through factors such as the availability of outsourcing, globalisation and the use of permanent striker replacements (Block et al. 2006).

Corporate campaigns are characterised by the use of media, political, financial, community and regulatory pressures to build bargaining power. The USW has been particularly aggressive in developing these tactics, and successfully used corporate campaigns in disputes with the Ravenswood Aluminum Corporation (Juravich & Bronfenbrenner 1999) and, after their merger with the United Rubber Workers, in the Bridgestone dispute (settled in 1996). Unions painfully learnt through lost strikes at Phelps Dodge (Rosenblum 1995) and International Paper (Getman 1998) that, to succeed, corporate campaigns had to be well developed and started early.

The revitalisation efforts of the CWA highlight the advantages of a triangular agenda linking organising, politics and collective bargaining (Katz et al. 2003). In such a triangulation strategy, union activities in any one of these three spheres interact with and complement activities in another sphere. It was, for example, through novel language won in collective bargaining agreements in the telecommunications industry (with the Regional Bell phone companies) that the CWA gained card check recognition and employer neutrality in representation elections, key parts of the union's organising initiative. Similarly, the CWA has linked political actions towards public agencies that regulated pricing and access in the telecommunications industry with efforts to strengthen the union's strike leverage (and win more in collective bargaining).

Given several Supreme Court cases against agency shop–type union fee arrangements and NLRB appointments, it is possible that the court will reverse the long-standing allowance for card check recognition procedures. Since unions such as the SEIU and UNITE HERE rely heavily on card check and related neutrality agreements to gain members, this sort of court action could further diminish union organising.

The US labour movement also will have to find ways to respond to the internationalisation of product and labour markets. The expansion of international trade and the expansion of MNEs extend markets internationally. John R. Commons (1909) explained, in his classic analysis of early union formation among American shoemakers, that as the extent of the market expanded, to counteract 'competitive menaces' and retain bargaining power, unions at the beginning of the twentieth century shifted to a national structure. This provided a structure of worker representation that paralleled the emerging national structure of product markets.

The problem confronting labour movements all over the globe is that they face the need for cross-national unionism, but their efforts to create such unionism come up against substantial barriers, including divergent interests (i.e. each labour movement wants the employment) and national differences in language, culture, law and union structure. Yet unions will need to find an international parallel to the sort of domestic sphere linkages being pursued by the CWA.

There are some recent signs of increased international activity among US unions. Several cases where American unions have engaged in cross-national pressure campaigns involve NAFTA provisions (Katz et al. 2007: 390–1). The USW, which has significant membership in Canada as well as the United States, has formed an alliance called 'Workers Uniting' with the largest British private sector union, Unite, partly in response to the increasing dominance of the steel industry by MNEs. However, union gains on this and related fronts in the United States are limited, and the barriers remain daunting.

The continuing challenges to American unions were illustrated by the 2014 defeat of a UAW organising drive at the Volkswagen (VW) assembly plant in Chattanooga, Tennessee. The UAW has long sought to organise the plants operated in the United States by international auto makers such as Honda, Toyota, Nissan, BMW and Mercedes. These plants are mostly located in right-to-work states in the American South and to date all are non-union. For its organising drive at the Chattanooga plant, the UAW used its connections with the powerful German union IG Metall to help win a commitment from VW to stay neutral in the organising drive, with the plan that a local works council, similar to those existing in other non-US VW plants, would be established along with union representation. However, although VW management stayed neutral in the organising drive, local politicians and anti-union lobbying groups launched a vigorous campaign against the UAW, including suggestions that tax subsidies that had been used to entice VW to locate in Tennessee would be withdrawn if the plant unionised.

The campaign against the union was successful as a narrow majority of workers voted against UAW representation in the election held by the NLRB. Nevertheless, the UAW has vowed to continue to carry out organising campaigns at non-union car manufacturers and suppliers. Discussion is also underway at the VW plant, with the UAW's approval, for the possible introduction of some form of (non-union) works council at the plant to facilitate labour and management dialogue regarding workplace issues.

Another important union organising development is the effort to organise college athletes. In 2014, the regional director of the NLRB ruled that scholarship athletes (football players) at Northwestern University were employees under the NLRA and directed a secret-ballot union representation election in response to a petition to become the players' bargaining agent by the College Athletes Association. The NLRB in April 2014 granted Northwestern University's request to review the regional director's decision. Consequently, the representation ballots cast by Northwestern University's 85 football players were impounded pending a decision by the NLRB as to whether college athletes had the right to unionise and collectively bargain.

## CONCLUSIONS

Diversity in employment relations is growing as a reflection of the growth in non-union employment and the variety of union and non-union employment practices. The breakdown of pattern bargaining across enterprises and industries in the union sector, and the spread of contingent forms of pay and associated greater reliance on individualised rewards, are all contributing to increased variation in work rules and pay. The changes in pay practices have contributed to the exceptionally large increases in income inequality in the United States.

While team systems have spread and operate as a critical part of the employment systems in some firms, more traditional forms of work organisation continue in other firms. Decentralisation, more direct management–employee communication and increased employee (and union) involvement in business decisions are also part of the increasing divergence in practices.

There is also wide variation in the tenor of collective bargaining. In some cases, heightened conflict has appeared, while in others, partnerships have been forged. While some workers have suffered greatly as management took advantage of a power imbalance provided by globalisation and the growth of non-unionised enterprises, in other contexts, unions used innovative bargaining or traditional strike leverage to make gains.

Unions have shown a willingness to cooperate with workplace changes that attempt to increase productivity and product/service quality where the innovations also include attention to the union's goals. As such, consistent with US business unionism, the collective bargaining process has shown flexibility in responding to competitive pressures. The challenge faced by the labour movement is to find ways to combine collective bargaining successes and revitalisation efforts to further promote high-end employment outcomes and limit the growth of low-pay employment patterns and income inequality.

## FURTHER READING

Freeman, R.B. & Medoff, J.L. (1984) *What Do Unions Do?* New York: Basic Books.

Jacoby, S.M. (2004) *Employing Bureaucracy: Managers, Unions, and the Transformation of Work in the 20th Century*, rev. ed. Mahwah, NJ: Lawrence Erlbaum.

Katz, H.C. & Darbishire, O. (2000) *Converging Divergences: Worldwide Changes in Employment Systems.* Ithaca, NY: ILR Press.

Kochan, T.A., Katz, H.C. & McKersie, R.B. (1994) *The Transformation of American Industrial Relations*, 2nd ed. Ithaca, NY: ILR Press.

Milkman, R. (2006) *LA Story: Immigrant Workers and the Future of the U.S. Labor Movement*. New York: Russell Sage Foundation.

## USEFUL WEBSITES

AFL-CIO: <www.aflcio.org>.
Alternative dispute resolution guide: <www.hg.org/adr.html>.
ILR School, Cornell University: <www.ilr.cornell.edu>.
NLRA: <www.nlrb.gov>.
Triangle Shirtwaist factory fire: <www.history.com/topics/triangle-shirtwaist-fire>.

## A CHRONOLOGY OF US EMPLOYMENT RELATIONS

| | |
|---|---|
| 1794 | Federal Society of Cordwainers founded in Philadelphia—first permanent US union. |
| 1828 | Working Men's Party founded. |
| 1834 | National Trades Union founded—first national labour organisation. |
| 1866 | National Labor Union formed—first national 'reformist' union. |
| 1869 | Knights of Labor founded—a 'reformist' organisation dedicated to changing society; it was involved in strikes for higher wages and improved conditions. |
| 1886 | Formation of the American Federation of Labor, a loose confederation of unions with largely 'bread-and-butter' goals. Peak of membership of the Knights of Labor (700,000 members), which then began to decline. |
| 1905 | Formation of the Industrial Workers of the World, the 'Wobblies', an anarcho-syndicalist union. |
| 1914–22 | Repression of radical unions because of their opposition to war, and during the 'Red-scare' after the Russian Revolution. |
| 1915 | Establishment of the first company-dominated union, Ludlow, in Colorado. |
| 1920s | Decline and retrenchment of the US labour movement. |
| 1932 | Election of Franklin D. Roosevelt as president —a 'New Deal' for unions. |
| 1935 | NLRA *(Wagner Act)* gave employees a federally protected right to organise and bargain collectively. Also, formation of CIO, a federation of industrial unions. |
| 1935–39 | Rapid growth of unions covering major mass-production industries. |
| 1941–45 | Growth of unions and development of the collective bargaining system during the war. |
| 1946 | Massive post-war strike wave in major industries. |
| 1947 | Enactment of *Taft-Hartley Act*, which prohibited unions from certain organising and bargaining practices. |
| 1955 | Merger of American Federation of Labor and CIO to form the AFL-CIO. |
| 1959 | *Landrum-Griffin Act*, regulating the internal operations of unions. |
| 1960 | New York City teachers' strike—the beginning of mass organisation of public employees. |
| 1960–80 | Growth of unionism of public employees. Decline in union density in the manufacturing sector. |
| 1962 | Adoption of Executive Order 10988 by President John F. Kennedy, providing for limited collective bargaining by federal government employees. |

| | |
|---|---|
| 1977–78 | Defeat of Labor Law Reform Bill in Congress, as employers' movement in opposition to unions gained strength. |
| 1980 | Election of President Ronald Reagan—new federal policies generally averse to organised labour. |
| 1981 | Economic recession. |
| 1988–89 | Federal legislation on drugs, lie detectors, plant closing, minimum wages. Court decisions on drug testing and termination of employment. |
| 1991 | Federal legislation prohibiting discrimination against disabled workers. Federal legislation strengthening employment discrimination laws. |
| 1991 | Through the Gilmer case and related decisions, the Supreme Court allows statutory employment rights disputes to be resolved through (private) arbitration. Alternative dispute resolution then spreads, particularly in the non-union sector. |
| 1991–92 | Extended economic recession. |
| 1992 | Election of President Bill Clinton. A more labour-friendly national administration comes to power. |
| 1992–2000 | Sustained economic growth with low unemployment, low inflation and limited real wage growth. |
| 1994 | The Commission on the Future of Worker–Management Relations (Dunlop Commission) recommends that a number of changes be made in the nation's labour laws, but these recommendations are ignored by the US Congress. |
| 1994 | Republicans win Congressional elections. A very conservative Congress comes into being. |
| 1994 | NAFTA removes tariff and other trade barriers among the United States, Canada and Mexico. |
| 1995 | Increases in the NMW voted by Congress. |
| 1995 | John Sweeney elected president of the AFL-CIO, spurring accelerated union revitalisation. |
| 2000 | George W. Bush elected president in an extremely close election. Republicans subsequently gain control of the Senate and House. |
| 2001 | Economic recession; 9/11 attacks. |
| 2002–07 | Slow economic recovery with limited real wage and job growth. |
| 2005 | The CTW Coalition splits from the AFL-CIO. |
| 2006 | Democrats win Congressional elections. |
| 2008 | Barack Obama elected president. Democrats expand majorities in Congress. |
| 2009–13 | Three CTW unions (UNITE HERE, LIUNA, UFCW) rejoin the AFL-CIO. |
| 2010 | Republicans win control of House of Representatives. |
| 2011–12 | Restrictions on public sector bargaining and unions imposed in Wisconsin and a number of other states. |

2014      In the *Harris v Quinn* case (134 S.Ct. 2618, 2014) the US Supreme Court rules that agency shop-type union fees are illegal for non-union homecare workers, and raises doubts about the constitutionality of other agency fee arrangements. In the *N.L.R.B. v Noel Canning* case (134 S.Ct. 2550, 2014), the Supreme Court rules that recess appointments to the NLRB made by President Obama were invalid and thereby set aside numerous NLRB decisions.

# CHAPTER 4

# Employment relations in Canada

## Daphne G. Taras and Scott Walsworth[1]

Employment relations in Canada rest on several fundamental characteristics. A large proportion of the labour force is either directly or indirectly subject to the influence of collective bargaining, and there is strong legal protection for this form of bargaining. There are traditions of adversarialism and moderate levels of strike activity. The structures of employment relations are less centralised than in many other nations. While Canada has incorporated employer, union and public policies that originated in the United States, it has a distinctive employment relations system.

On a comparative basis, Canada is a liberal market economy (LME), and its employment relations display the characteristics of that model. Firms rely on hierarchies and markets, bargaining structures are decentralised, and unions are not generally key participants in economic and labour policy-making.

## THE HISTORICAL, POLITICAL AND SOCIO-ECONOMIC CONTEXT

Canada's federal system of government is one of the most decentralised in the world, vesting authority for most employment matters in the ten Canadian provinces. Federal authority is mostly limited to regulation of the federal civil service and employment in nationwide industries, such as inter-provincial transport. Approximately 6 per cent of Canadian workers are in this domain (Human Resources and Skills Development Canada 2008). Although this decentralisation has led to public policy experimentation, all jurisdictions have similar labour legislation.

Into this already complex mix is added the history and traditions of French Canada, with the province of Quebec having social, economic and legal traditions that are distinct from those of the rest of North America. Quebec is the second most populous province in Canada, after the neighbouring Ontario. The strong nationalism of many Quebec residents (Quebecois) has reinforced the already powerful decentralising forces within Canada. Canada is well known as a bilingual and bicultural nation; however, the country is regionally fractured into the primarily French-speaking province of Quebec and parts of adjacent provinces, and the primarily English-speaking provinces known colloquially as the 'Rest of Canada'.

Immigration continues to be important. Immigrants have accounted for 80 per cent of labour market growth in recent years, and almost 20 per cent of all Canadians are immigrants. By 2031, Statistics Canada (2011) estimates that a third of the labour force will be foreign born and a third will be visible minorities. After World War II, Europe—especially the United Kingdom—was the biggest source of immigrants. From the 1960s onwards, the pattern of immigration shifted to developing countries, especially (South-East) Asian nations. By 2006, China (including Hong Kong) was the largest source of immigrants. Recent immigrants lack the tradition of industrial working-class activism displayed by earlier European immigrants; however, many have strong cultural collectivist experiences; this has created challenges and opportunities for Canadian unions. In recent years, rapidly changing workplace demographics have caused organising and representation challenges for the Canadian labour movement—for instance, workplaces, especially in large urban centres such as Toronto, Montreal and Vancouver, are increasingly populated by visible minorities with varying degrees of English/French proficiency.

Simultaneously, the relatively conservative political tradition of the United States has been a powerful model for Canadians. These influences, along with a Westminster parliamentary political system (and its acceptance of minor political parties), have combined to produce a value system that incorporates US-style individualism in an LME with some of the traditions of collectivism found in European coordinated market economies (CMEs). Firms in Canada pursue growth and profits in a competitive liberal market—perhaps not as independently as they do in the United States, but without the same level of government interference or coordination found in Scandinavia or Germany.

Politically, Canada has a multi-party system reflecting regional interests. For decades, the country was dominated by a rivalry between two parties—the Liberals and the Conservatives—with a third party, the New Democratic Party (NDP), able to achieve some of its left-of-centre agenda when it occasionally held the balance of power. Since the 1930s, the

Liberals have dominated federal politics, occasionally forming a minority government or yielding power to the Conservatives. The Liberals are a pragmatic and reformist party, with a traditional base of support in Quebec and Ontario. The Conservatives are a right-of-centre party, usually drawing votes from the eastern and western regions. The Conservatives won large majorities in 1984 and 1988, and formed minority governments in 2006 and 2008. While they had a market orientation and a preference for small government, the Conservative governments did not embrace the social and economic policies of either the Thatcher government in the United Kingdom or the Reagan Administration in the United States. After the 2011 election, the Conservative Party formed a majority government and, for the first time, the pro-labour NDP won the status of official opposition. With their majority, the Conservatives have taken moderate steps to shift the balance of power further away from unions, citing a 'business-friendly' agenda. The same rise of popular conservatism has been witnessed in many of the provinces, including Saskatchewan, Alberta, New Brunswick, and Newfoundland and Labrador.

As the provinces have exclusive jurisdiction over labour relations for more than 90 per cent of the labour force, provincial politics are significant. Each province has a distinct political culture, reflecting regional differences in the various economies of Canada, immigration patterns and political attitudes. None of the federal parties is strong in all the provinces, and solely provincial parties have governed in three provinces: Quebec, Saskatchewan and British Columbia. While the NDP has never gained the power to govern in the federal arena, it has won elections in four provinces. However, it has almost no support in Quebec's provincial elections, where a pro-independence Parti Quebecois takes similar positions on social and economic issues.

The labour movement receives more favourable treatment when a pro-labour party wins provincial government, even if the party seldom achieves majority status. As of 2014, the NDP was in power only in Manitoba while the Parti Quebecois governed Quebec until early 2014.

While Canada has a standard of living equal to the more prosperous nations in Western Europe, it depends heavily on the production and export of raw materials and semi-processed products—petroleum, minerals, food grains and forest products. Although Canada enjoys a comparative advantage in the production of most of these commodities, their markets are unstable, and primary industries do not generate substantial direct employment. There is a large manufacturing sector in Ontario and Quebec; however, manufacturing accounts for less than 11 per cent of the gross domestic product (GDP) and has experienced sharp declines in recent years (Statistics Canada 2014). Due to

Canada's lack of a large domestic market, it signed a free-trade agreement with the United States in 1988 and the North American Free Trade Agreement (NAFTA) with Mexico and the United States in 1994. The immediate impact of free trade was to accelerate the integration of the manufacturing sector into a larger North American economy. Levels of employment in traditional industries, such as textiles and furniture, fell substantially and caused the elimination of thousands of unionised jobs, while other sectors, such as car manufacturing and chemicals, initially expanded until the 2008 economic destabilisation.

Canada exports approximately one-third of its gross national product and imports slightly more, resulting in a negative balance of payments of –$3.5 billion in 2013 (Industry Canada 2013). The United States accounts for approximately 76 per cent of Canada's exports, China accounts for less than 5 per cent, while the European Union (EU) accounts for less than 7 per cent (Foreign Affairs, Trade and Development 2013). Apart from proximity and a natural complementarity of the two economies, Canadian–US trade relations are encouraged by extensive US ownership in many primary and secondary industries, as well as the free-trade agreements.

Canada has a mixed economy, with active roles for the public and private sectors, often in the same industries. Public enterprises typically emerged for pragmatic reasons—provision of an essential service, development of natural resources or preservation of jobs. Thus Canadian federal and provincial governments once owned many public utilities, transport and communications companies. When privatisation of public assets became a trend in the mid-1980s, federal and provincial governments disposed of natural resources, transport and infrastructure companies, in addition to smaller holdings. Subsequently, the trend abated—although some provinces enter partnerships with private firms to build and operate new facilities. Over the past three decades, the highly unionised public sector has not grown as fast as the private sector.

From 2000 to late 2008, the Canadian economy performed well. Canada achieved a 32-year low in unemployment in 2007, with a rate of less than 6 per cent. A boom in natural resources after 2000 contributed to falling rates of unemployment. The development of 'unconventional' oil (extracted from sand and shale by techniques similar to mining) in the province of Alberta was a major factor in Canada's economic performance. Furthermore, rising commodity prices (mostly grain) as well as increases in demand for potash and uranium (mostly from China) made the western provinces relatively rich compared with the eastern provinces, such as Ontario and Quebec, which were affected by the decline of the manufacturing industry. As a result, there is on ongoing internal westbound migration of workers from the eastern provinces. The relatively labour-intensive technology and the remote location of the resource-extraction industries in the west attracted workers from other regions, reducing unemployment rates nationally. Canada weathered the post-2007 global financial crisis better than most developed economies, partly because its banking system is regulated to avoid over-exposure to risk. Canada escaped much of the economic contraction seen in the United States. Unemployment numbers rose slightly, but still remain relatively low, as shown in Table 4.1.

While economic growth did not cause an increase in inflation, income differentials among Canadians were wider than in preceding decades. Comparatively, Canadian income differentials are higher than in Europe and lower than in the United States, partly as a result of government income transfers. One of the levers of government policy is the exchange rate. A high Canadian dollar increases citizens' purchasing power for foreign goods, but a low Canadian dollar reduces the unemployment rate. The Canadian dollar has fluctuated sharply in recent years. It fell to a low of approximately 63 cents to the US dollar in 2003 and then fluctuated between 79 and 104 cents to the US dollar thereafter.

During the inflationary periods of the 1970s, governments intervened directly to reduce pressure on prices. Between 1975 and 1978, the federal government and nine of the ten Canadian provinces imposed an anti-inflation program, which fell most heavily on public sector workers and their unions. Although opinions differ about the impact of the program, the rate of inflation declined during this three-year period and the rate of wage increases fell even more sharply. Labour and management resented the restrictions in the program, and therefore it was not extended; however, almost 30 years later (2009), the federal government and most of the provinces implemented pay controls in response to growing budget deficits.

During the recession of 1982, federal and provincial governments had imposed temporary public sector pay controls to reduce government spending. In the following decade, Canada experienced slow economic growth. After 2000, Canada's inflation rate of less than 2.5 per cent was among the lowest of any developed economy, and the Bank of Canada has aimed for a 2 per cent inflation rate, giving credence to the government's efforts to suppress pay.

Government efforts to deal with economic problems are restricted by the nation's political structure. Like Australia, Canada is a confederation with a parliamentary government. To a greater extent than in contemporary Australia, however, the Canadian provinces still hold substantial powers over employment relations, with only a few

**Table 4.1  Union density and unemployment rate by gender, age and province (%)**

| | Union density[a] | | | Unemployment rate[b] | | |
|---|---|---|---|---|---|---|
| | 2009 | 2011 | 2013 | 2009 | 2011 | 2013 |
| National | 29 | 29 | 29 | 8.3 | 7.4 | 7.1 |
| *By gender* | | | | | | |
| Male | 28 | 28 | 28 | 9.4 | 7.8 | 7.5 |
| Female | 31 | 30 | 31 | 7 | 7 | 6.6 |
| *By age* | | | | | | |
| 15–24 | 145 | 14 | 13 | 15.2 | 14.2 | 13.7 |
| 25–44[c] | 30 | 30 | 30 | 7.4 | 6.5 | 6 |
| 45–64 | 6.6 | 6 | 5.9 | 6.6 | 6 | 5.9 |
| 65+ | 4.3 | 4.8 | 4.3 | 4.3 | 4.8 | 4.3 |
| *By province (listed from east to west)* | | | | | | |
| Newfound. and Lab. | 37 | 37 | 38 | 15.5 | 12.7 | 11.4 |
| Prince Edward Island | 31 | 30 | 33 | 12.1 | 11.3 | 11.5 |
| Nova Scotia | 29 | 30 | 29 | 9.2 | 8.8 | 9 |
| New Brunswick | 28 | 28 | 28 | 8.8 | 9.5 | 10.4 |
| Quebec | 36 | 36 | 36 | 8.5 | 7.8 | 7.6 |
| Ontario | 26 | 26 | 26 | 9 | 7.8 | 7.5 |
| Manitoba | 34.5 | 34 | 34 | 5.2 | 5.4 | 5.4 |
| Saskatchewan | 34 | 34 | 33 | 4.8 | 5 | 4 |
| Alberta | 23 | 22 | 21 | 6.6 | 5.5 | 4.6 |
| British Columbia | 30 | 30 | 30 | 7.7 | 7.5 | 6.6 |

*Notes:*
(a) CANSIM Table 282–0223.
(b) CANSIM Table 282–0002.
(c) Authors' calculations. Some numbers rounded.

*Source:* Statistics Canada (2013).

industries—principally transport and communications—under federal authority. The provinces, often led by Quebec, have not only resisted any efforts to expand federal powers, but have gradually gained greater powers at the expense of the federal authorities.

A fundamental change in Canadian political life occurred in 1982. The Liberal government produced the nation's first written Constitution, which included a Charter of Rights and Freedoms. The charter guarantees certain fundamental freedoms, including freedom of association, thought, belief, opinion and expression. The charter applies to federal and provincial governments and most public organisations. It does not, however, apply to the private sector—including private employers.

Initially, the charter had little impact on employment relations. The courts ruled that it did not apply to the parties in private sector employment relations, even if they operated under a legal regime to protect collective bargaining. In a dramatic reversal of earlier decisions, the Supreme Court of Canada ruled in 2007 that the charter protected collective bargaining as an institution, and courts should be guided by international standards in interpreting that right. This decision is discussed in greater detail in Box 4.2 later in the chapter. This decision, known in Canada as 'BC Health', is the most significant development in the legal regime affecting employment relations.

## THE PARTIES IN EMPLOYMENT RELATIONS

### Unions

The Canadian labour movement has grown since the 1930s, despite long-standing patterns of disunity. The number of employees covered by union bargaining arrangements was more than 4 million at the start of the twenty-first century—that is, more than 29 per cent of paid employees in 2013 (Statistics Canada 2014). While absolute numbers of employees represented by unions continued to grow, increases in the labour force occurred more rapidly, so union density has declined only moderately since 1984, in contrast to other countries such as the United Kingdom, the United States and Australia. Union membership is divided between two national centres and a large number of unaffiliated unions. The Canadian density figure reflects growth in female union members and a high union density rate in the public sector. Other than the public sector, the greatest penetration of unionism is in primary industries, construction, transport and manufacturing. In the late nineteenth and early twentieth centuries, Canadian unions were established first in construction and transport—mostly on a craft basis. During the 1930s and 1940s, industrial unionism spread to manufacturing and primary industries, not including white-collar workers in the private sector. Since the late 1960s, the major source of union growth has been the public sector. First, public servants, then health and education workers, joined unions. Professionals—notably teachers and nurses—had long been members of their own associations, and these transformed themselves into unions as their members' interest in collective bargaining grew. Public sector employees are almost four times more likely to belong to unions as private sector workers. In 2013, more than 18 per cent of Canadian workers were classified as belonging to the public sector. Table 4.2 shows the relative density of unionisation by industry, sector and job permanency.

**Table 4.2   Union density by industry, sector and job permanency (%)**

| | Union density | | |
|---|---|---|---|
| | *2009* | *2011* | *2013* |
| National[a] | 29 | 29 | 29 |
| *By industry*[b] | | | |
| Education | 68 | 67 | 69 |
| Public administration | 67 | 67 | 67 |
| Utilities | 62 | 63 | 61 |
| Health care and social assistance | 54 | 52 | 53 |
| Transportation and warehousing | 40 | 40 | 39 |
| Construction | 30 | 30 | 31 |
| Manufacturing | 25 | 25 | 25 |
| Natural resources | 22 | 20 | 19 |
| Management, administration and support | 14 | 15 | 14 |
| Accommodation and food | 6.9 | 7 | 6.7 |
| Professional, scientific and technical | 4.2 | 4.1 | 4.6 |
| *By sector*[a] | | | |
| Public | 71 | 71 | 72 |
| Private | 16 | 16 | 16 |
| *By job permanency*[b] | | | |
| Full-time | 33 | 33 | 33 |
| Part-time | 25 | 24 | 25 |

*Notes:*
(a) CANSIM Table 282–0223.
(b) CANSIM Table 282–0224.
Numbers rounded.

*Source:* Statistics Canada (2013).

There are approximately 500 unions in Canada, ranging in size from fewer than 100 members to almost half a million members. Two-thirds are affiliated with one of the central confederations, with the remainder—mainly in the public sector—independent of any national centre or in Quebec. The fifteen largest unions contain 59 per cent of all members. Mergers have created 'mega-unions', concentrating union membership in fewer and larger organisations—for instance, two large unions joined forces in 2013 to form the largest private sector union in Canada (see Box 4.1).

Unions in Canada have a variety of approaches. Some are restricted to a business unionism approach while others play a social and political role. Most of the old craft groups still espouse a US-style apolitical business unionism model, restricting activities to collective bargaining for pay, benefits and job security. A larger number of unions see themselves fulfilling a broader role, and actively support the NDP and various social causes. A few groups—particularly in Quebec—are highly politicised and occasionally criticise the prevailing economic system from a socialist perspective. Rhetoric aside, though, the major function of all unions is collective bargaining.

The role of United States–based 'international' unions is a special feature of the Canadian labour movement. Most of the oldest labour organisations in Canada began as part of American unions—hence the term 'international'. Geographic, cultural and economic ties between the two countries encouraged the union connection, while the greater size and earlier development of US unions attracted Canadian workers to them. For many years, the majority of Canadian union members belonged to such international unions, which often exerted close control over their Canadian locals. But the spread of unionism in the public sector during the 1960s and 1970s brought national unions to the fore, as internationals were seldom active among public employees. Since the 1970s, many Canadian unions have seceded from internationals. This reflected a perception of inattention to Canadian workers' needs, the protectionism of American unions and a wave of Canadian nationalism. Hence, the proportion of international union membership declined from more than 70 per cent in the mid-1960s to its current level of less than 25 per cent. The Canadian experience illustrates the difficulties unions face in exerting effective transnational action.

Despite this cross-border history, there is one area in which Canadian unions enjoy a distinct advantage over their United States–based counterparts. The majority of Canadians who are represented by unions are required to pay union dues, whether they want to be members of unions or not. This prevention of free riding is required by

---

## BOX 4.1 TWO BIG UNIONS JOIN TO FORM THE LARGEST NATIONAL PRIVATE SECTOR UNION

In August 2013, the Canadian Auto Workers Union and the Communications, Energy and Paperworkers Union of Canada merged to form a new union called Unifor, which became Canada's largest private sector union. Jerry Dias, Unifor's first president, says the new union will be a powerful force to influence change in Canadian labour relations:

> 'Unifor is here because it's time to stop playing defence and it's time we started to play offence,' said Dias in his fiery inaugural address at Unifor's founding convention in Toronto. 'It's time to stop reacting and it's time to start setting the agenda.'

Dias seems to be especially focused on labour relations with the federal government, even though most of Unifor's members are under provincial jurisdiction, because the provinces often follow the lead of the federal government.

> 'The Conservative government has decided to challenge our democratic right to organize and collect dues. They are singling out unions. They're attacking our finances. They're attacking our ability to represent our members,' said Dias.

Furthermore, Dias said he would uphold Unifor's promise to dedicate 10 per cent of its revenues to organising workplaces and adding new members. He also said that Unifor would welcome workers traditionally excluded from collective bargaining and would seek other ambitious and creative ways to expand membership. The union will initially represent more than 300,000 workers across roughly 20 sectors of the economy, primarily in manufacturing, communications and transportation. It will also represent some public sector employees in the health, education and transit sectors. Officials have said the switch to a non-traditional name—one that goes beyond simply listing occupations or industries—signals the union is looking to branch out.

*Source:* Quotations from <www.ctvnews.ca/canada/caw-s-jerry-dias-first-president-of-unifor-merger-of-caw-and-cep–1.1435200>.

labour statutes in most Canadian jurisdictions under an arrangement popularly known as the 'Rand Formula'. Hence, there is no equivalent of the 'right-to-work' movement that has greatly weakened the ability of US unions to organise and function (see Chapter 3). However, at the time of writing, the Alberta, Saskatchewan and federal governments were discussing the possibility of weakening union security protections through amendments to legislation. As more and more northern states in the United States adopt right-to-work legislation, it becomes easier for business-friendly governments concerned with Canadian competitiveness to make the case against 'mandatory dues'.

The most important central confederation is the Canadian Labour Congress (CLC), representing almost 70 per cent of all union members belonging to 98 national and international union affiliates. Members of CLC affiliates are in all regions and most industries. It is the principal political spokesperson for Canadian labour, but it is weaker than confederations in many other countries. It has no role in bargaining, for instance; nor does it have any substantial powers over its affiliates—unlike confederations in Germany and Scandinavia. The CLC's political role is further limited by the constitutionally weak position of the federal government (its obvious contact point) in many areas that the labour movement regards as important, such as labour legislation, regulation of industry and human rights. In national politics, the CLC has supported the NDP. The poor electoral record of the NDP federally further weakens the CLC's political role. The CLC has chartered federations in each province to which locals of affiliated unions belong. Some of these federations wield considerable influence in their provinces.

The second-largest congress is the Confédération des syndicats nationaux (CSN, or Confederation of National Trade Unions), representing more than 6 per cent of all union members—most of them located in Quebec. It began early in the twentieth century under the sponsorship of the Catholic Church as a conservative French-language alternative to the predominantly English-language secular unions operating elsewhere in Canada and in Quebec. As Quebec industrialised during and after World War I, members of the Catholic unions grew impatient with their lack of militancy and unwillingness to confront a conservative provincial government. As part of a rapid change to a secular society, the Catholic unions severed their ties to the Catholic Church, abandoned their former conservatism and moved into the vanguard of rapid social change in Quebec. Since then, competition has prevailed in the Quebec labour movement, and the CSN has become probably the most radical and politicised labour organisation in North America. It has supported Quebec independence and adopted left-wing political positions. Reflecting the union's history, current political posture and the large provincial public sector in Quebec, CSN membership is concentrated heavily among public employees.

## Management

The majority of unionised firms grudgingly accept the role of unions, and open attacks on incumbent unions are rare. In industries with a long history of unionism—for example, manufacturing or transport—unionism is accepted as a normal part of the business environment. However, non-union enterprises energetically strive to retain that status, some by matching the wages and working conditions in the unionised sector, others by combinations of paternalism and coercion. Some enterprises have union-substitution policies, which replicate many of the forms of a unionised work environment, with grievance procedures or mechanisms for consultation. Management-influenced forms of employee representation for non-union workers are not illegal, as they are in the United States. Almost 20 per cent of Canadian non-union workers have a formal non-union employee representation plan at their workplace, and of those workers, more than half—some 10 per cent of all workers—are covered by such a representation plan. Thus, although the number of workers represented by unions is slightly more than 29 per cent, the number of workers who experience some form of collective representation is considerably higher.

The high degree of foreign ownership in the Canadian economy affects the economy generally, but seldom affects employment relations directly. About 25 per cent of the assets of all business enterprises are foreign owned, chiefly by multinational enterprises (MNEs). About 75 per cent of foreign investment comes from American MNEs. Foreign ownership affects strategic managerial decisions, such as product lines or major investments. But there appears to be little impact by non-Canadians on employment relations decisions in unionised sectors. Foreign owners prefer to remain in Canada's mainstream of employment relations for their industries, rather than imposing their corporate policies.

Most employers do not rely on employers' associations for employment relations functions, although the role of employers' associations varies among regions. No national employers' association participates directly in employment relations; rather, several employers' associations present management viewpoints to government or the public. Since most employment relations law is in provincial jurisdictions, no industries have national bargaining structures under provincial legislation. In two provinces, Quebec and British Columbia, local conditions and public policy have encouraged bargaining by employers' associations formed specifically for that purpose. Elsewhere, single-plant bargaining with a single union predominates, except in a few industries with many small and medium-sized enterprises (SMEs), such as construction, docking or trucking, where multi-employer bargaining is common.

Canadian employers favour limited roles for government in the economy, including deregulation of their own activities. They generally prefer unilateral control over the employment relationship and accept unions grudgingly. After 2000, a wave of corporate acquisitions changed the face of the Canadian economy. Foreign firms, including MNEs based in developing nations, purchased dozens of large Canadian companies, including iconic unionised firms.

## Government

The government in Canada has a dual role in employment relations: it regulates the actors' conduct and employs about 19 per cent of the labour force, both directly and indirectly.

There is extensive government regulation of union–management relations, though it rests on an assumption of voluntarism. Each province, as well as the federal government, has at least one Act covering employment relations and employment standards in the industries under its jurisdiction. Employment standards legislation generally sets minima for such areas as pay or holidays, reflecting the LME in Canada. Enforcement of these laws often is weak, relying much more on resolution of complaints rather than a proactive system of inspections and fines for non-compliance.

Although the details vary considerably, employment relations legislation combines many features of the US *National Labor Relations Act* (*Wagner Act*) and an older Canadian pattern of reliance on conciliation of labour disputes. Each statute establishes and protects the right of most employees to form unions and sets out a procedure by which a union may demonstrate majority support from a group of employees to obtain the right of exclusive representation for them. Unionisation typically occurs at the level of the workplace, reinforcing the decentralised structure of Canadian employment relations. The employer is required to bargain with a certified union. A quasi-judicial labour relations board administers this process and enforces the statute, although the legislation often specifies the procedural requirements in detail.

Legislation imposes few requirements on the substance of a collective agreement, although the exceptions are significant and expanding. Canadian laws prohibit strikes during the term of a collective agreement, while also requiring that each agreement contain a grievance procedure and a mechanism for the settlement of mid-contract disputes that relies on a neutral third party. Despite these restrictions, about 15 per cent of all stoppages occur while a collective agreement is in force. Most of these stoppages are brief, and seldom attract legal action.

There is separate legislation federally and in most provinces for the public sector. These statutes may apply to government employees and to quasi-government employees, such as teachers or hospital workers. They are patterned after private sector employment relations Acts except for two broad areas. The scope of bargaining is restricted by previous civil service personnel practices and broader public policy consider-ations. In a majority of provinces, there are restrictions on the right to strike of at least some public employees. Police and firefighters are the most typical categories affected by such limits, but there is no other common pattern of restrictions. Employees' groups without the right to strike have access to a system of compulsory arbitration. While a statute requires arbitration, the parties normally can determine the procedures to be followed and choose the arbitrator. As Canada continues to ride a wave of political conservatism, it is expected that new essential service legislation may be developed to limit the ability of public sector workers to go on strike. For instance, Saskatchewan has enacted aggressive new legislation that is before the Supreme Court of Canada to determine whether it infringes on the constitutionally protected freedom to associ-ate. The precedent of the BC Health case (see Box 4.2) led to the 2015 decision to constitutionalise the right to strike in Saskatchewan. In a 5 to 2 ruling, the majority wrote, 'The ability to engage in the collective withdrawal of services in the process of the negotiation of a collective agreement is, and has historically been, the irreducible minimum of the freedom to associate in Canadian labour relations.' Thorny issues involving essential service dispute resolution alternatives to the strike, such as interest arbitration, remain on the labour policy agenda in the coming years.

## THE PROCESSES OF EMPLOYMENT RELATIONS

The major formal process of Canadian employment relations is collec-tive bargaining, with union power based on the ability to strike. Joint consultation is sporadic. Health and safety legislation in all jurisdic-tions requires joint consultation on those subjects for all but the smallest employers. The parties have initiated consultation outside any legislative framework in about a quarter of employing enterprises, covering such subjects as product quality, technological change and performance. Other formal systems of worker participation in management are rare. Nonetheless, in a period in which employee involvement arrangements have become popular, more collective agreements have included novel clauses reflecting this thrust, including some relaxation of strict work rules, multi-skilling and cross-crafting, and pay for education and training. Arbitration of interest disputes is largely confined to the public sector.

## Collective bargaining

Collective bargaining is decentralised. The most common negotiating unit is a single establishment–single union, followed by multi-establishment–single union. Taken together, these categories account for almost 90 per cent of all bargaining units and more than 80 per cent of all employees. Enterprise-wide bargaining is common in the federal jurisdiction—for instance, in railways, airlines and telecommunications—and in provincially regulated industries concentrated in a single province, such as logging or car manufacturing.

Despite the decentralised structure of negotiations, bargaining often follows regional patterns. National patterns in bargaining are rare; instead, one or two key industries in each region usually influence provincial negotiations. In larger provinces, such as Ontario and Quebec, heavy industry patterns from steel, paper or cars often predominate.

The results of bargaining are detailed, complex collective bargaining agreements. Few of the terms are the result of the law; negotiated provisions typically include pay, union security, hours of work and holidays, layoff provisions and miscellaneous fringe benefits. Grievance procedures are legal requirements, and invariably conclude with binding arbitration. In addition, there are often supplementary agreements covering work rules for specific situations or work areas. Seniority provisions are prominent features in almost all collective agreements, covering layoffs, promotions or transfers, with varying weight given to length of service or ability.

Given the detail in collective agreements and the parties' preference for litigation, rights arbitrations are frequent and legalistic. In turn, this emphasis on precise written contracts often permeates employment relationships.

## Strikes and settlement methods

Another outcome of collective bargaining is labour stoppages, the most controversial feature of Canadian industrial relations (IR). In most years, Canada has lost more working days due to industrial disputes than any other developed country in this book. Canada's strike rate tends to be the highest in the Organisation for Economic Cooperation and Development (OECD); however, strike frequency and duration are declining in Canada. There have been frequent allegations—although no proof—that labour unrest has hindered the nation's economic growth. Like other developed countries, Canada experienced a steady decline in strikes during the 1990s. Although the number of working days lost is high compared with most other countries, it represents less than 0.1 per cent of total time worked.

Historically, strike levels have moved in cycles. There was a wave of unrest early in the twentieth century, another around World War I, a third beginning in the late 1930s and a fourth in the 1970s. The latest wave abated in 1983, and most measures of disputes have fallen sharply since then. From an internationally comparative perspective, the two salient characteristics of Canadian strikes are their length and the concentration of time lost in a few disputes (see Table 4.3). Involvement is medium to low (3–10 per cent of union members annually), and the size of strikes is not especially large (150–297 workers per strike on average). The largest five or six strikes typically account for 35 per cent of all days lost. Over recent years, the frequency of labour disputes has decreased significantly from a high of 297 in 2004 to 151 in 2013. The average number of workers involved in a dispute and the duration of the average strike follow a similar trend. From 2004 to 2008 they decrease and then increase until 2013. We cannot predict whether these increases will continue and change the earlier trend of declining labour disputes in Canada. The number of lost days to a labour dispute has not approached the very high levels of 2004 and 2005, with the exception of the most recent year. It is too early to tell whether this reversal will continue, and change the trend of declining labour disputes in Canada.

Conciliation and mediation efforts have long been features of Canadian collective bargaining. There are two models: a tripartite board may be appointed and given authority to report publicly on a dispute; alternatively, there may be single mediators without the power to issue a report. In most jurisdictions, participation in some form of mediation is a precondition for a legal strike. The vast majority of all collective agreements are achieved without third-party intervention.

Apart from the public sector, compulsory arbitration of interest disputes is rare. However, there may be special legislation to end particular disputes in public sector or essential services disputes. Back-to-work laws (where the neutral government labour board orders striking workers to return to work) are unpopular with the labour movement,

**Table 4.3  Working days lost to labour disputes**

| Year | Number of strikes | Number of workers involved | Average duration (days) | Total lost days (000s) | Change in lost days over previous year[a] |
|------|-------------------|----------------------------|-------------------------|------------------------|-------------------------------------------|
| 2004 | 297 | 259,229 | 41.8 | 3,218,224 | NA |
| 2005 | 260 | 199,007 | 36.4 | 1,883,402 | −70.9 |
| 2006 | 151 | 42,314 | 50.3 | 321,388 | −486.0 |
| 2007 | 206 | 65,552 | 40.8 | 550,951 | 41.7 |
| 2008 | 188 | 41,331 | 45.4 | 352,768 | −56.2 |
| 2009 | 157 | 67,313 | 60.8 | 642,543 | 45.1 |
| 2010 | 174 | 57,725 | 51.7 | 519,283 | −23.7 |
| 2011 | 148 | 91,139 | 49.8 | 671,731 | 22.6 |
| 2012 | 281 | 137,398 | 23.9 | 922,751 | 27.2 |
| 2013 | 151 | 207,414 | 88.4 | 2,768,645 | 66.6 |

*Notes:*
(a) Authors' calculations. Some numbers rounded. Retrieved 20 November 2014 from <www.labour.gc.ca/eng/resources/info/datas/work_stoppages/work_stoppages_year_sector.shtml>.

*Source:* Strategic Policy, Analysis, and Workplace Information Directorate, Labour Program, Employment and Social Development Canada. Released 7 February 2014.

and have contributed to the politicisation of employment relations in some areas. In the public sector, interest arbitration is common. Arbitrators are usually chosen on an ad hoc basis from among judges or professional arbitrators, who are usually lawyers or academics. The process is legalistic without the use of sophisticated economic data. When collective bargaining first developed in the public sector, there were concerns that compulsory arbitration would cause bargaining to atrophy. Experience has demonstrated that collective bargaining and compulsory arbitration can coexist successfully, though the availability of arbitration does reduce the incidence of negotiated settlements.

## CURRENT AND FUTURE ISSUES

The future of collective bargaining is being questioned in many developed economies. Such debates include the ability of unions to retain, or even expand, their traditional bases of strength in heavy industry and manual occupations. Though union density in these arenas has fallen in Canada, it has not declined in absolute numbers, and is still twice as high as that of the United States, for instance. However, Canadian unions have had difficulties similar to their counterparts elsewhere in extending their membership base into the more rapidly growing areas of the service sector and technologically advanced industries. As employment shifts from the goods-producing sectors to services, the historic base of collective bargaining gradually shrinks as a proportion of the labour force. For example, from 1976 to 2013 the proportion of Canadians employed in the bastion of traditional unionism, the manufacturing sector, fell from 32 per cent to less than 19 per cent (Statistics Canada 2014). Compared with the non-union employers, the unionised elements of the labour force have played a leading role in the expansion of employee rights and improvements in pay and conditions of employment. If collective bargaining is confined to declining sectors of the economy, this leading role will diminish as well—although, since union density in Canada has not declined in this period (1976–2013), it appears that the labour movement has been successful in replacing members in the manufacturing sector with new members, perhaps in growing industries such as the service sector.

Since the 1930s, the leading private sector unions in Canada have been based in manufacturing. These organisations produced innovations in terms and conditions of employment, were heavily involved in politics and constituted a large percentage of provincial federations. It is unlikely that they will be able to retain their influence in the face of the continuing economic changes—for example, sharp declines in Canadian manufacturing employment provoked by the post-2007 global financial crisis. Thousands of jobs in that sector—especially in car manufacturing—disappeared when US auto makers cut production. Such changes have not yet been fully explored.

Well before the post-2007 crisis, collective bargaining was under pressure from foreign competition and deregulation, as in other developed economies. Canada has long relied heavily on foreign trade, so foreign competition is not new. Tariff barriers were reduced slowly in the 1960s and 1970s, and more rapidly after the free-trade agreement took effect in 1989. The Canadian manufacturing sector, aided by a depreciating currency, responded well to these challenges. The decentralised structure of collective bargaining seems to have facilitated adaptation to economic change. Exports rose steadily, while manufacturing employment was stagnant. These developments were sources of stress for employment relations institutions, but the changes were incremental.

What was the impact of deregulation? Governments deregulated product markets in most of the transport and communications sectors in the 1980s and 1990s. In addition, several public enterprises in these sectors were privatised. Employment in the unionised firms in these industries shrank, while new competitors were largely non-union. These developments took place gradually and generally did not provoke disputes.

The future of collective bargaining will be a function of the actions of governments and managers in the face of unions' economic and political power. Federal and provincial governments continue to respect the legitimacy of collective bargaining and an active labour movement; however, some recent government initiatives regarding union security clauses, such as mandatory dues, have caused considerable concern for the labour movement. Nevertheless, for the most part, legislation and other public policies reflect the general acceptance of unions and collective bargaining, even when the most right-of-centre political parties govern. Occasional efforts by right-wing governments to change the legal framework of collective bargaining have failed to upset the basic features of the system.

On balance, it appears that the legislative support for collective bargaining will not change markedly across Canada. However, there is little political support for reform that would appreciably strengthen union power. Given Canada's tilt towards a more right-wing agenda in governments, in marked contrast to the Supreme Court's activism, it is likely that we will see a testing of unions' newfound legal victories, with the outcome impossible to determine.

## Public sector employment relations

The public sector is the area of Canadian employment relations most subject to change, especially in areas that are seen as providing essential services. From the mid-1960s through the 1980s, mature systems of collective bargaining developed in all provinces and the federal government. Beginning with the 1982 recession, governments in several jurisdictions addressed budgetary shortfalls by restricting public sector pay levels. In general, governments dealt with their fiscal problems by legislation rather than bargaining. By 1987, legal restraints had been removed. In 1991, the federal government led another round of restrictions on public sector bargaining and pay. By 1995, a majority of all provinces had imposed restrictions on public sector bargaining as part of their programs of fiscal restraint. Over the preceding ten years, legislation was relaxed, but it was renewed after the post-2007 global financial crisis. While Canada's economy then fared better than most OECD economies, there is often a high degree of support for reducing unions' ability to increase the costs of government by raising pay.

One of the harshest examples of policies directed against public sector workers and their unions was in British Columbia in 2001. A newly elected right-wing government (misnamed 'Liberal') removed many provisions from public sector collective agreements, mandating the contracting out of health-sector jobs and the layoff of more than 10,000 employees. The provincial government made no effort to consult with the unions affected by these changes, and passed the enabling legislation quickly. Union members demonstrated to no avail. Similar, though less severe, legislation applied to teachers in the public school system.

The health-care unions launched a challenge to the law under the Charter of Rights and Freedoms. In a 2007 decision, the Supreme Court of Canada held that the government had violated the charter, reversing an earlier line of cases (see Box 4.2). The legislation in question was not eliminated, but the court extended the protections of the charter to collective bargaining and stated that the principles in International Labour Organzation (ILO) standards should govern the application of this protection in the future. Years will pass before the full implications of this decision are known. But at this stage the court has barred the more severe legislation affecting collective bargaining in the public sector.

Apart from legislative action, the practice of free collective bargaining at the level of the federal and provincial governments has been undermined substantially. The frequency of back-to-work legislation in the 1990s through the mid-2000s put unions on notice that they could not defy government fiscal policies at the bargaining table. A pattern developed whereby governments made offers, normally consistent with the economic climate, and then imposed these terms on public sector unions. An even more aggressive model was thwarted by the Supreme Court in 2015 whereby the province tried to craft legislation that allowed public sector employers (government) to unilaterally determine the number of workers permitted to go on strike, thereby eliminating the union's ability to conduct a meaningful strike. Thus, the Supreme Court has blocked the more egregious unilateralism of management, and there likely will be legal challenges by unions to the use of back-to-work orders.

## Political role of the labour movement

Although many unions and union leaders are active in partisan politics, the labour movement has been unable to define a political role for itself. Officially, the CLC supports the NDP, but this alliance has presented problems. Federally, in the 1990s and until the 2001 election, the NDP

## BOX 4.2   BC HEALTH SERVICES: SUPREME COURT OF CANADA 2007 DECISION

### Background
The province of British Columbia described itself as being in a 'crisis of sustainability' in its health-care system. Health costs were rising at three times the rate of growth of the province's economy from 1991 to 2001. The province passed an Act, *Bill 29*, to reduce costs and force reorganisation to enhance management's ability to restructure service delivery. There was no meaningful consultation with the many affected unions, and litigation commenced.

### Case analysis
In a six to one majority decision, the Supreme Court summarised as follows (with numbers indicating the paragraph at which the concepts may be found):

> The constitutional right to collective bargaining concerns the protection of the ability of workers to engage in associational activities, and their capacity to act in common to reach shared goals related to workplace issues and terms of employment. Section 2(*d*) of the *Charter* ['freedom of association'] does not guarantee the particular objectives sought through this associational activity but rather the process through which those goals are pursued. It means that employees have the right to unite, to present demands to government employers collectively and to engage in discussions in an attempt to achieve workplace related goals. Section 2(*d*) imposes corresponding duties on government employers to agree to meet and discuss with them. It also puts constraints on the exercise of legislative powers in respect of the right to collective bargaining. However, s. 2(*d*) does not protect all aspects of the associational activity of collective bargaining. It protects only against 'substantial interference' with associational activity. [89–90] [92]
>
> Determining whether a government measure affecting the protected process of collective bargaining amounts to substantial interference involves two inquiries: (1) the importance of the matter affected to the process of collective bargaining and, more specifically, the capacity of the union members to come together and pursue collective goals in concert; and (2) the manner in which the measure impacts on the collective right to good faith negotiation and consultation. [93–94] [109]

A basic element of the duty to bargain in good faith is the obligation to actually meet and to commit time to the process. The parties have a duty to engage in meaningful dialogue, to exchange and explain their positions and to make a reasonable effort to arrive at an acceptable contract. However, the duty to bargain in good faith does not impose on the parties an obligation to conclude a collective agreement, nor does it include a duty to accept any particular contractual provisions. In considering whether the legislative provisions impinge on the collective right to good faith negotiations and consultation, regard must be had for the circumstances surrounding their adoption. Situations of exigency and urgency may affect the content and the modalities of the duty to bargain in good faith. Different situations may demand different processes and timelines. Moreover, failure to comply with the duty to consult and bargain in good faith should not be lightly found, and should be clearly supported on the record. [100–101] [103] [107]

## Summary

The Supreme Court explicitly reversed its previous precedents. Cases decided on associational rights prior to 2007 no longer inform Canadian disputes. Collective bargaining is consistent with freedom of association, both in an analysis of Canadian history and in international law. British Columbia's government engaged in substantial interference with collective bargaining, and parts of its Act were declared unconstitutional.

*Source: Health Services and Support—Facilities Subsector Bargaining Assn v British Columbia* [2007] 2 SCR 391, 2007 SCC 27.

was unsuccessful in raising its share of the popular vote (and legislative seats) beyond about 20 per cent, and the labour movement has been unable to deliver large blocs of votes to the federal NDP. However, in the 2011 federal election, the NDP won a record 36 per cent of the popular vote; this influence has not stopped the trend towards anti-union legislation in Canada.

The LME model, with limited use of consultation with labour on economic and social policies, is more firmly entrenched in Canada than before. Federally, the political role for labour is limited and shows no signs of expanding. Future gains in the status of labour may come through the courts. Provincially, the situation is different. The NDP has governed in Ontario and three western provinces, and labour's political role is better defined when the NDP is a viable option provincially. However, the labour movement's partisan position provincially risks making labour issues more political and subject to sharp variation after changes of government. Quebec unions have supported independence for the province, and have enjoyed great political influence when pro-separatist parties have governed Quebec. Politically, labour has a role in policy deliberations in Quebec, which resembles a CME to a greater extent than other parts of Canada.

The state of employment relations is affected by a trend in Canadian society to individualise worker responsibilities and risks. Canada is not unique in this regard. The Canadian tendency is one of a series of small actions, driven by the same objectives found in other countries. Many employers prefer labour to be a commodity—flexible, already trained but easily disposable. Long-term employment relationships are no longer an expectation of the labour market, and employees are instructed to manage their own careers. Employment systems have increasingly used performance-based pay, and pension plans have changed from defined benefit plans to defined contribution plans. Hours of work have been increased, and the pay premium for unionised workers has been reduced. Pay has been put into competition where production can be moved. When labour shortages appeared after 2000, federal and provincial governments established programs to import thousands of temporary and vulnerable migrant workers from developing countries rather than allowing market forces to raise the pay of domestic workers substantially. These initiatives intensified after the post-2007 global financial crisis. Employers use technology to monitor the behaviour of individual employees more closely. Within several sectors, including parts of construction, meat packing, trucking and logging, de-unionisation has been effected through contracting out, decentralisation of bargaining and deregulation. Service sector employers with multiple branches prevent union inroads by matching negotiated conditions.

Governments have not increased statutory rights for workers in any major way for more than a decade. Enforcement of employment standards is weak at best, and employers face little risk of being charged or punished for evading the law. Even in policy areas where there has been a tradition of labour involvement, such as apprenticeships and health and safety, governments do not highly value the role of organised labour.

Such policies—public and private—have undermined the strength of the labour movement. By 2013, Canadian income differentials were greater than at any time since the 1920s. Neither of the major federal parties—the Liberals and the Conservatives—even pretends to advocate for labour rights. The NDP has been able to exercise only limited influence in opposing these tendencies, mostly at the provincial level. Few Canadians look to unions as an effective agent that might address problems in the Canadian society or economy.

## CONCLUSIONS

A major change in the trajectory of Canadian employment relations is unlikely. The employment relations system displays few of the overt signs of structural changes seen in other developed economies. Unlike in the United States, employers have not subjected unionism and collective bargaining to continual attacks. By contrast with the United Kingdom, it is rare—although not unheard of—for governments to undertake sustained anti-union campaigns. The labour movement has legitimacy in Canada. It has forged ties with the women's movement, and with environmental, youth and consumer groups, for instance. The labour movement is recognised as the spokesperson for workers in economic and social consultations. But the status of organised labour as a factor of production or a major consideration in public policy has been undermined. The most noteworthy changes are arriving via Supreme Court decisions.

Canada's record of moderate economic growth, punctuated by commodity-based booms and busts, provides scant support for politicians or employers who wish to blame collective bargaining or unionism for the economy's performance. The collective bargaining system has responded successfully to most of the changes in economic conditions. There is not much evidence of renewed militancy among Canadian workers, but this might change if circumstances were to change. The lack of perceptions of crisis in employment relations has stifled debate over the broader questions of worker representation outside the traditional strongholds of unions. The post-2007 global financial crisis did not create a direct assault on the stability of the Canadian labour market; therefore, the recent pattern of incremental adaptation seems destined to continue.

### FURTHER READING

Camfield, D. (2011) *Canadian Labour in Crisis: Reinventing the Workers' Movement*. Halifax: Fernwood.

Doorey, D. (ed.) (2011) *Labour and Employment Law: Cases, Materials, and Commentary*. Toronto: Irwin Law.

Gunderson, M. & Taras, D.G. (2009) *Canadian Labour and Employment Relations*, 6th ed. Toronto: Pearson.

Heron, C. (2012) *The Canadian Labour Movement: A Short History*, 3rd ed. Toronto: James Lorimer.

Kumar, P. & Schenk, C. (eds) (2005) *Paths to Union Renewal: Canadian Experiences*. Peterborough: Broadview Press.

## USEFUL WEBSITES

Canadian labour law blog, by Professor David Doorey: <http://lawofwork.ca>.

Centre for Industrial Relations and Human Resources, University of Toronto: <www.cirhr.utoronto.ca>.

Lancaster House, labour, employment and human rights law resource: <http://lancasterhouse.com>.

*Perry Work Report*, weekly labour newsletter: <http://cirhr.library.utoronto.ca/perry-work-reports-home>.

Statistics Canada: <www.statcan.gc.ca/start-debut-eng.html>.

Unifor, the largest Canadian private sector union: <www.unifor.org>.

## A CHRONOLOGY OF CANADIAN EMPLOYMENT RELATIONS

| | |
|---|---|
| 1825 | Strike by carpenters in Lachine, Quebec, for higher wages. |
| 1825–60 | Numerous isolated local unions developed. |
| 1867 | Confederation—Canada became an independent nation. |
| 1872 | Unions exempted from criminal and civil liabilities imposed by British law. |
| 1873 | Local trade assemblies formed the Canadian Labour Union, the first national labour central. |
| 1886 | TLC formed by 'international' craft unions. |
| 1900 | Department of Labour established under the *Conciliation Act*. William Lyon Mackenzie King became first deputy minister. First issue of *Labour Gazette* published. |
| 1902 | 'Berlin Declaration'; TLC shunned unions not affiliated to international unions. |
| 1906 | Canadian chapter of Industrial Workers of the World founded. |
| 1907 | *Canadian Industrial Dispute Investigation Act*—first national labour legislation, emphasised conciliation. |
| 1908 | Under the *Government Annuities Act*, the federal Department of Labour administers a plan to help individual Canadians provide for their old age. |
| 1909 | *Labour Department Act* creates a separate labour portfolio in the federal government. William Lyon Mackenzie King becomes the first minister of labour. |
| 1919 | Winnipeg General Strike—most complete general strike in North American history. ILO established with Canada a founding member. |
| 1921 | Canadian and Catholic Confederation of Labour formed; Quebec federation of Catholic unions. |
| 1927 | All-Canadian Congress of Labour founded. |
| 1930 | *Fair Wages and Eight-Hour Day Act* for workers in the federal jurisdiction; Great Depression leads to the passage of the *Unemployment Relief Act* for a system of relief payments to provinces and municipalities. |
| 1935 | Following the NLRA (*Wagner Act*) in the United States, there are demands for similar Canadian legislation. |
| 1937 | Auto workers' strike at General Motors, Oshawa, Ontario, establishes industrial unionism in Canada. |
| 1939 | TLC expels Canadian affiliates of US CIO. |
| 1940 | CIO affiliates join All-Canadian Congress of Labour to form the Canadian Congress of Labour; Unemployment Insurance Commission comes under the direction of the federal Department of Labour. |
| 1944 | Order-in-Council PC 1003 guarantees unions' right to organise (combining principles of the US *Wagner Act* with compulsory conciliation). Imposes a legal obligation upon |

the employers' and the employees' bargaining agents to negotiate in good faith; many provinces begin extending PC 1003 to their own jurisdictions or drafting similar legislation between the late 1930s and mid-1940s.

| | |
|---|---|
| 1948 | *Industrial Relations and Disputes Investigation Act.* Collective bargaining rights are firmly established in law; Canada Labour Relations Board created in the federal jurisdiction. |
| 1949 | Miners in Asbestos, Quebec, strike in defence of law, initiating a 'quiet revolution' in Quebec. |
| 1956 | Merger of TLC and Canadian Congress of Labour to form the CLC. |
| 1958 | Full-time workers in the federal jurisdiction are guaranteed two weeks of paid vacation per year under the *Annual Vacation Act.* |
| 1960 | Canadian and Catholic Confederation of Labour severs ties with the Catholic Church to become the Confederation of National Trade Unions. |
| 1965 | Canada Labour (Standards) Code establishes minimum standards for hours of work, pay, vacations and statutory holidays for workers in the federal jurisdiction. |
| 1967 | Federal government gives its employees bargaining rights; other jurisdictions follow suit. |
| 1975 | Federal government imposes first peacetime wage and price controls. |
| 1977 | *Canadian Human Rights Act* is passed, forbidding discrimination against certain groups. |
| 1982 | Federal government enacts Charter of Rights and Freedoms. |
| 1984 | Protection from sexual harassment is added to the Canada Labour Code. |
| 1986 | Joint employer–employee safety and health committees in the workplace are required under the Canada Labour Code; *Employment Equity Act* passed to deal with issues of discrimination. |
| 1987 | Charter of Rights and Freedoms (enacted in 1982) takes effect. |
| 1991 | Legislated pay freeze imposed on federal government employees. |
| 1994 | North American Agreement on Labour Cooperation between Canada, United States and Mexico. Commits countries to protection of labour standards and enforcement of their own labour laws. |
| 2001 | Government of British Columbia removes major sections of collective agreements in the health sector, causing thousands of layoffs. |
| 2007 | Supreme Court of Canada declares collective bargaining by public employees protected by the Constitution by overturning actions of the British Columbia government in 2001. |

| | |
|---|---|
| 2008 | Government of Saskatchewan enacts the *Public Sector Essential Service Act*, which gives the employer the unilateral ability to determine the size of a strike. |
| 2013 | Unifor, the largest private sector union, is created when the Canadian Auto Workers and the Communications and Energy and Paperworkers Union merge. |
| 2015 | The Supreme Court of Canada strikes down Saskatchewan's 2008 essential services legislation and affirms that the right to strike is essential to collective bargaining. |

# CHAPTER 5

# Employment relations in Australia

## Chris F. Wright and Russell D. Lansbury[1]

Australia was colonised by the British in the late eighteenth century, has a wealth of mineral and energy resources and, except along the eastern coastal belt, is sparsely populated. In 2013, Australia had a population of 23 million people and gross domestic product (GDP) of over US$1.5 trillion and was the twelfth-largest economy in the world. Out of its total civilian workforce of approximately 11.4 million people, 77 per cent are employed in services and 18 per cent in manufacturing and construction. Australia's economy remains highly dependent on export earnings from mining and agriculture, which employ only 5 per cent of the total workforce. However, a recent decline in general economic activity and a reduction in manufacturing employment have underlined Australia's dependence on mining, which is subject to periods of boom and bust.

Although Australia has experienced minor periods of recession (most recently in 1990–91), over the past two decades it has enjoyed steady economic growth and emerged relatively unscathed from the post-2007 global financial crisis. By 2013, Australia was experiencing an annual growth rate of 3.5 per cent (equal to the average of the past 50 years), inflation was less than 3 per cent and unemployment was at 5.6 per cent. Australia has a labour force participation rate of around 82 per cent for males and 70 per cent for females.

Australia is widely regarded as a liberal market economy (LME) with a relatively flexible labour market (Hall & Soskice 2001: 19). However, these features have emerged only in recent decades. Since the early 1990s, there has been a shift away from the centralised system of compulsory arbitration that characterised Australian employment relations for much of the twentieth century towards a decentralised and more individualised regulatory framework. The continued existence of a (weakened) system of occupational and industrial awards allows for some coordination in the determination of wages and conditions and a stronger safety net for workers than other LMEs such as the United States. The structure of employment has changed radically in recent years, with a decline in full-time permanent work, expansion of various kinds of non-standard forms of employment, such as casual and temporary jobs, and increased use of outsourcing and labour market intermediaries.

This chapter examines the main features of the Australian employment relations system. After outlining the key aspects of the regulatory and institutional framework, it looks at the changing roles and functions of the main actors and processes. The chapter then explores three significant issues in the contemporary employment relations landscape: workplace productivity, gender equality and precarious work. Finally, the likely future directions of the Australian system are considered.

## THE LEGAL, ECONOMIC AND POLITICAL BACKGROUND

Australia achieved federation in 1901. When the former colonial governments agreed to establish the Commonwealth of Australia, the new federal government was given a limited jurisdiction over employment relations. Under the Constitution of the Commonwealth of Australia (1901), the federal government was empowered to make industrial laws only with respect to 'conciliation and arbitration for the prevention and settlement of industrial disputes extending beyond the limits of any one State' (Section 51, para. xxxv). However, the scope of federal powers over employment relations and other matters gradually expanded, particularly after World War II.

During the 1990s, there were major changes to the Australian system. The 1993 *Industrial Relations Reform Act*, introduced by the Keating Labor government, made it possible to certify non-union collective agreements in the federal jurisdiction, which had not been permitted previously (Bennett 1995). Furthermore, in line with Australia's obligations under International Labour Organization (ILO) Conventions 87 and 98, for the first time this Act incorporated a right to limited industrial action during the designated collective 'bargaining period', and thus introduced the distinction between disputes of 'interest' and 'rights'.

The election of a Liberal–National Coalition government in 1996 under the leadership of John Howard (in office 1996–2007) heralded further changes to the employment relations system. The *Workplace Relations Act 1996* attempted to limit the power of the Australian Industrial Relations Commission (AIRC), and for the first time made it possible to register individual (non-union) contracts, known as Australian Workplace Agreements (AWAs), giving them primacy over collective agreements (McCallum 1997; Pittard 1997). Despite attempts by the Howard government to further decentralise and de-collectivise employment relations, a hostile Senate (upper house) blocked further legislative reform until the government was returned with a majority in the Senate in 2005. This allowed the government to implement its Work Choices legislation, which introduced fundamental changes to the Australian employment relations system. Key objectives of the reform package included the creation of a single national system for labour market regulation, expansion of AWAs that could replace awards, increased restrictions on union activities and a reduced role for the AIRC. Work Choices provided exemption from unfair dismissal laws for small- to medium-sized businesses with fewer than 100 employees, introduced five minimum employment conditions and removed the no-disadvantage test whereby workplace agreements could previously only be certified if employees were no worse off 'overall' compared with a relevant award.

Work Choices proved to be highly controversial, and contributed to the loss of government by the Coalition parties at the 2007 federal election. The union movement launched a high-profile campaign called 'Your Rights at Work', which included television and newspaper advertising and online petitions. The unions gathered strong support from church and community leaders, who also spoke out strongly against the 'excesses' of the government's new workplace laws (Cooper & Ellem 2008).

One of the most significant aspects of Work Choices was changing the constitutional foundation for federal employment relations legislation from the conciliation and arbitration power to the corporations power. Among other things, this allowed the federal government to directly set minimum terms and conditions of employment without recourse to the making of awards in the settlement of an industrial dispute. Despite challenges from state governments that the law was unconstitutional, the High Court upheld the new law and opened the way for the federal government to exclude state laws, with some specific exceptions.

After Labor's 2007 election victory, the governments of Kevin Rudd and Julia Gillard (in office 2007–13) promised to implement a 'fair and balanced' employment relations policy under the banner of 'Forward with Fairness'. However, as the detail of the policy was revealed, critics argued that it appeared to be 'more a retreat from the excesses of Work Choices than a fundamental recasting of industrial relations'

(Hall 2008: 376). The main features of the *Fair Work Act 2009* were as follows:

- The Fair Work Commission (FWC)[2] was established as the new employment regulator, replacing six existing bodies, including the AIRC. The Office of the Fair Work Ombudsman was established to promote and enforce compliance with the new workplace laws.
- Individual statutory agreements such as AWAs were abolished but individual common law contracts of employment were permitted.
- Ten new National Employment Standards (NES) were established to set minimum conditions for all workers covered by the national system. The NES included provisions for annual leave, personal leave, flexible work arrangements for parents, notice of termination and redundancy pay.
- A new system of 'modern awards' was introduced to provide an additional safety net for most employees.
- Unfair dismissal protection was broadened to cover all workers in enterprises with fewer than fifteen full-time equivalent positions. Employees are excluded only if dismissed during a qualifying period of service.
- Enterprise flexibility clauses were introduced to allow the conditions of employees earning more than $100,000 per year to be governed by arrangements not based on an award.
- Employers and unions are now required to bargain in good faith, although parties are not required to reach an agreement. However, the FWC is permitted to make a workplace determination where a party ignores a good-faith bargaining order.
- The FWC is empowered to settle disputes between parties where there is protracted industrial action that is causing damage to people or the economy.
- No distinction is made between union and non-union agreements, but an agreement now requires the approval of employees. A union that has acted as a bargaining agent during negotiations may apply to the FWC to be covered by the agreement.
- Union officials were given rights to enter workplaces to hold discussions with employees provided that they hold a permit issued by the FWC and they abide by certain conditions of that permit.
- There is limited provision for the making of single- or multi-purpose agreements, subject to obligations to bargain in good faith, and a test that requires each employee to be better off overall than they would be under an applicable award.

In September 2013, the Liberal–National Coalition led by Tony Abbott was elected after promising 'minimal change' to employment relations, despite the urging of some employers and their associations for reforms that would weaken the position of unions and allow individual agreements to be used more easily. Nevertheless, the Abbott government established several inquiries soon after gaining office that are expected to recommend changes to existing aspects of the employment relations systems, such as union governance and bargaining arrangements.

## THE MAJOR PARTIES

### Unions

The establishment of the arbitration system soon after Federation encouraged the rapid growth of unions and employers' associations as required by the objects of the *Commonwealth Conciliation and Arbitration Act 1904*. By 1921, approximately half of the Australian labour force was unionised. Although union membership declined during the Great Depression of the early 1930s, the 1940s witnessed a steady increase in density and a peak of 65 per cent was achieved in 1953. Union density in Australia has been falling steadily over the past three decades, from 49 per cent in 1990 to 17 per cent in 2013, with only 12 per cent of the workforce in the private sector unionised compared with 42 per cent of the public sector workforce (Table 5.1). With the decline of industries in which male blue-collar workers were dominant, the 'union heartland' has become the public sector and certain service industries in which professionals and women are more prevalent (Bailey & Peetz 2014).

The reasons for the long-term decline of union membership are complex and varied, but include changes in the structure of the economy, which has seen contraction of employment in manufacturing—a sector in which unions traditionally have been well organised—and the growth of the private service sector, in which unions have been weaker. A related change has been the falling proportion of full-time employment and the rise of non-standard employment. Yet these phenomena have characterised most advanced industrialised countries, not all of which have experienced as much decline in union membership as Australia. Other factors contributing to the decline of unionism include growing anti-unionism among employers, new laws making it more difficult for unions to organise and the removal of institutional arrangements enshrined under the arbitration system (such as de facto compulsory unionism), which artificially inflated union membership numbers. Hostile policies towards unions by the conservative governments led by John Howard have also contributed

**Table 5.1    Union membership density by selected characteristics (%)**

| Gender | | Industry (continued) | |
|---|---|---|---|
| Females | 18 | Health care and social assistance | 26 |
| Males | 16 | Mining | 16 |
| Age | | Construction | 16 |
| 15–19 | 7 | Manufacturing | 15 |
| 20–24 | 9 | Retail trade | 14 |
| 25–34 | 13 | Information media and telecommunications | 11 |
| 35–44 | 17 | | |
| 45–54 | 23 | Arts and recreation services | 10 |
| 55–59 | 28 | Financial and insurance services | 9 |
| 60–64 | 24 | Other services | 8 |
| 65+ | 18 | Administrative and support services | 6 |
| Employment type | | Accommodation and food services | 5 |
| Full-time | 19 | | |
| Part-time | 14 | Wholesale trade | 4 |
| Employees with paid leave entitlements | 22 | Professional, scientific and technical services | 3 |
| Employees without paid leave entitlements | 7 | Rental, hiring and real estate services | 2 |
| Owner managers of incorporated enterprises | 3 | Agriculture, forestry and fishing | 2 |
| | | Occupation of main job | |
| Sector | | Managers | 7 |
| Public | 42 | Professionals | 24 |
| Private | 12 | Technicians and trades workers | 17 |
| Industry | | Community and personal service workers | 22 |
| Education and training | 37 | | |
| Public administration and safety | 34 | Clerical and administrative workers | 11 |
| Electricity, gas, water and waste services | 29 | Sales workers | 13 |
| | | Machinery operators and drivers | 26 |
| Transport, postal services and warehousing | 28 | Labourers | 16 |

Source: Australian Bureau of Statistics (2014a).

to the decline in union membership. It remains to be seen whether the policies of the incumbent Abbott Coalition government will lead to further union decline (Bailey & Peetz 2014; Peetz 1998).

The Australian Council of Trade Unions (ACTU) is the main confederation for manual and many non-manual unions. It was formed in 1927 and includes around 95 per cent of all unionists. Under the ACTU's direction, strategies aimed at reversing membership decline have been put in place by unions in recent years. During the 1990s, the union movement focused on restructuring and amalgamations, which resulted in the merger of 360 federally registered unions into 20 industry-based 'super unions'. The rationale for the creation of these unions was that it would release resources for improved provision of services to members. While the strategy was successful in changing the structure of Australian unions and reducing their number, it did not halt the decline in membership density.

The strategy adopted by the union movement following the decentralisation of employment relations in the 1990s was to focus on the principles of organising. Unions were encouraged to build workplace activism, develop alliances with the broader community and strengthen their capacity for strategic campaigning. The objective was that unions should redefine themselves as more autonomous and less dependent on the state. In 1994, the ACTU initiated an 'organising works' program, based partly on the experience of US unions, in order to build the organising skills and capacities of Australian unions and to give effect to an 'organising model'. At the ACTU Congress in 2000, a new strategy was launched, Unions@Work, which emphasised the central role of the organising model in building a more inclusive, social movement approach to unionism, and thereby increasing membership (Cooper 2000).

More recently, unions have adopted 'comprehensive campaigning' strategies to broaden their appeal to a wider range of workers and to mobilise union members to influence government policy decisions. Hence, the Australian Services Union mounted a strong public campaign for equal remuneration for social and community service workers, the Transport Workers Union sought to improve wages and work safety in road transport and the Textile Clothing and Footwear Union of Australia successfully campaigned for stronger regulation to protect the conditions of garment manufacturing workers (Bailey & Peetz 2014; Kaine & Wright 2013). However, this approach has not galvanised popular support for the unions; nor has it been adopted by the majority of unions.

The Rudd–Gillard Labor government did not induce union revitalisation, despite the *Fair Work Act 2009*, which contained provisions favourable to workers and their unions. Although the unions welcomed the abolition of AWAs and the strengthening of awards and collective bargaining, there were complaints about continued limitations on the contents of enterprise agreements, restrictions on unions' right of entry to workplaces and the maintenance of penalties for unlawful industrial action. This period has been characterised as unions having 'influence without partnership' with the Labor government (Wright & Lansbury 2014).

Unions face challenges. While they continue to have a strong role in the Labor Party, in terms of both voting rights and financial support, there is discussion about reducing union influence in the party and moving to a more independent relationship, as occurred in the United Kingdom. The internal governance and financial management of unions are also coming under greater scrutiny, as signified by the Abbott government's establishment of a royal commission into these matters, the findings of which may diminish the public image of the broader union movement (Bailey & Peetz 2014).

## Employers' associations

The early growth of unions in Australia encouraged the development of employers' associations and led them to place greater emphasis on employment relations functions than their counterparts in some other countries. Employers' associations have lacked unity for many years, although they appeared to gain greater solidarity over the past decade in support of more decentralised and individualised labour market regulations. This partly reflects the waning influence of manufacturing employers, which have tended to support coordinated wage determination and skills formation and have been more prepared to work with unions, and the growing power of employers in the mining and private service industries that prefer market-oriented and non-union arrangements (Cooney 2010; Wright 2015b).

Numerous employers' associations have a direct role or interest in employment relations (Plowman 1989). However, there is variation in the size and complexity of employers' associations, from small, single-industry bodies to large organisations that attempt to cover all employers within a particular state. In 1977, the Confederation of Australian Industry (CAI) was established as a single national employers' body, almost 50 years after the formation of the ACTU. In 1983, a group of large employers set up the Business Council of Australia (BCA), partly as a result of their dissatisfaction with the ability of the CAI to service the needs of its large and diverse membership. Membership of the BCA comprises the chief executives of Australia's 100 largest corporations, which has given it a high profile and significant authority when making pronouncements on matters such as employment relations. The BCA led the argument for a shift towards enterprise-based bargaining away from a centralised, award-based system of employment relations in an influential report published in 1989, which had a significant influence on subsequent changes towards a more decentralised system (Sheldon & Thornthwaite 1999).

Several large affiliates, such as the Metal Trades Industry Association and the Australian Chamber of Manufacturers, left the CAI in the late 1980s. In 1992, the CAI responded to these developments and sought to attract back former affiliates by merging with the Australian Chamber of Commerce to form a new organisation, the Australian Chamber of Commerce and Industry (ACCI).

There has been a general trend among employers' associations away from an emphasis on providing industrial advocacy towards a broader range of fee-based services for members and greater focus on general economic policy issues. This shift may reflect the decline of the centralised bargaining system, and the need for advocacy on behalf of employers before industrial tribunals. Sheldon and Thornthwaite (1999) claim that increased competition between employers' assocations for members has encouraged their consolidation. Notable among these was the 1998 merger of the Metal Trades Industry Association and the Australian Chamber of Manufacturers to form the Australian Industry Group (AiG).

A key development has been the growing influence of the Australian Mines and Metals Association (AMMA), which casts itself as one of the four leading employers' organisations (Thornthwaite & Sheldon 2014). The rise of AMMA has been due partly to the significance of the mining industry to the national economy but also because the association has adopted a more radical agenda and vigorously supported further decentralisation of the employment relations system, which has become popular within parts of the wider business community.

During the 2007 election campaign, schisms occurred within the ranks of the employers' bodies. ACCI and the BCA strongly defended Work Choices and criticised the policy platform of the Labor Party, arguing that any 'roll-back' of Work Choices would risk an upsurge of industrial disputes and excessive union influence. While a supporter of the Work Choices regime, the AiG declined to contribute funds to the employer advertising campaign led by the BCA and ACCI, and declared that it was a non-partisan employers' organisation. Greater unity between the employers' groups was evident during the federal election of 2013, when they lobbied for changes by the victorious Coalition parties. However, the Abbott government was cautious in its employment relations proposals, due to widespread opposition to the Howard government's earlier radical workplace reforms.

## The state

The powers of the federal government over employment relations, as noted previously, were limited under the Constitution until the High Court's ruling on the corporations power in 2007. The lack of legislative power—particularly over prices and incomes—had frustrated federal governments of all political persuasions over many years. The Howard government's election victory of 2004 represented a turning point for the role of federal governments within the employment relations system. The majorities achieved by the Coalition parties in both houses of the Australian parliament at the election opened the way to the most radical employment relations reforms since 1904. Although the Howard government had advocated 'deregulating' the labour market, Work Choices was a most ambitious attempt to 're-regulate' employment relations. It represented a comprehensive attack on arbitration, unions and collective bargaining that took many employers by surprise.

Despite the unpopularity of Work Choices in the wider electorate, which assisted the Labor Party to victory in the 2007 federal election, the Rudd–Gillard Labor government proceeded very cautiously with changes to the legislation. Neither the union movement nor the employers' bodies were satisfied with the reforms enacted by Labor, but the incumbent Abbott Coalition government also appeared unwilling to make too many changes during its first term in office. This seems to reflect a view on both sides of the political divide that there was general 'reform fatigue' within the electorate in relation to employment relations, despite the advocacy by unions and employers' bodies. Hence, there has appeared to be a preference among governments since 2007 to undertake incremental rather than radical changes to employment relations policy and to achieve these through regulatory rather than legislative means (McCrystal 2014). This is somewhat ironic, given that the Howard government's successful use of the corporations power has given subsequent federal governments greater legislative power in this area.

The role of the federal industrial tribunal has undergone considerable change in the past decade. As indicated above, the FWC is the key employment relations institution and workplace 'umpire'. Although the continuing shift towards a more decentralised system has meant a gradual diminution in its role over time, its functions were revamped by the Rudd–Gillard government to ensure that it would be more effective. The FWC has been modernised and made more accessible by the incumbent president, Iain Ross, but the vision of the tribunal as a 'one-stop shop' for employers and employees has proved difficult to achieve (Stewart 2011). In contrast to pre-1996 legislation, the FWC has limited powers to intervene in disputes unless its services are sought by both parties.

## EMPLOYMENT RELATIONS PROCESSES

### The determination of wages

Historically, the arbitration system led to the development of a relatively centralised framework of wage determination in Australia. This was achieved by increasing the influence of the federal tribunal over key wage issues, despite constitutional limitations. The federal tribunal initially became involved in fixing a minimum wage in 1907 when it described the 'basic wage' as being intended to meet 'the normal needs of an average employee, regarded as a human being living in a civilised community'. The basic (male) wage was set at a level sufficient to cover the minimum needs of a single-income family unit of five, and became the accepted wage for unskilled work. The rate for women workers was set at 54 per cent of the basic wage. The custom of wage differentials ('margins') for skills was formalised in the 1920s, based largely on historical differentials in the metal and engineering trades (Hancock 1984).

The federal tribunal thus began to regulate wages and differentials through decisions on the basic wage and margins at National Wage Case hearings. These were much-publicised rituals, and occurred at regular intervals—usually with one National Wage Decision per year. The employers, unions (through the ACTU) and governments (at federal and state levels) each made submissions to the Commission, which later handed down its decision.

The system of arbitration was compulsory in two senses. First, once engaged, it required the parties in dispute to submit to a mandatory procedure for presenting their arguments. Second, tribunal awards were binding on the parties in dispute. Awards specified minimum standards of pay and conditions, which employers were required to meet or else face legal penalties. However, awards were more flexible in practice than they appeared to be in a formal sense. Unions and employers were free to negotiate above these minimum standards, and there was a considerable amount of workplace negotiation between the parties, generally assisted by conciliation by tribunals. This practice of informal direct bargaining became much more common during the 1970s. It was halted by the federal tribunal's attempts to control a wage explosion through a highly centralised system based on the indexation of wages, and was followed by attempts to foster more collective bargaining within limits set by the arbitration system (Isaac 2012).

To prevent the risks of uncontrollable wage inflation, the Prices and Incomes Accord ('the Accord') was negotiated between the Labor Party and the ACTU prior to the 1983 election. This social compact was renegotiated on seven occasions to accommodate changing economic circumstances, and became the dominant feature of Australian wage determination under the Hawke–Keating Labor governments (in office 1983–96). Under the Accord, the government and the ACTU presented a joint submission to the National Wage Case. For most of this period, with one notable exception in 1991, the AIRC largely accepted these proposals and introduced wage principles designed to give them effect. In its initial stages, the Accord led to the return of centralised wage determination following the collapse of the indexation system in 1982. The Accord began as an essentially voluntary incomes policy in which the ACTU pledged that unions would make no extra claims in wage bargaining in return for wage indexation. For its part, the government pledged—among other things—to strengthen the 'social wage' by introducing compulsory superannuation, universal health coverage and progressive taxation measures. The trend towards greater decentralisation of employment relations processes increased in the early 1990s in response to economic stagnation, greater international competition and growing political pressures. Enterprise-level collective bargaining consequently became the main instrument for regulating wages and conditions, with awards acting as safety nets for workers not covered by enterprise agreements (Wright & Lansbury 2014).

The Howard government's election in 1996 ended the Accord and its role in shaping wage policy. As noted, the *Workplace Relations Act 1996* further decentralised wage determination by retaining the award stream and the mechanism of safety net adjustments, but it reduced the ability of the AIRC to vet outcomes of non-union enterprise agreements and individual contracts. Under Work Choices, responsibility for setting minimum wages passed from the AIRC to another body, the Australian Fair Pay Commission, which had the power to determine its own processes and procedures for setting minima—albeit with less independence than the AIRC. Its decisions focused mainly on macroeconomic considerations rather than the broader social considerations followed by the AIRC.

Following the implementation of the *Fair Work Act 2009*, a Minimum Wages Panel under the FWC, which included three members outside the Commission, replaced the Australian Fair Pay Commission. While the Rudd–Gillard Labor government abandoned individual bargaining in favour of collective bargaining, established a new regulatory agency and restored some of the federal industrial tribunal's powers, there has been no reversion to compulsory arbitration. Notwithstanding the continued emphasis on enterprise-level determination of wages and conditions, awards continue to remain an important regulatory instrument, especially for workers in low-paid and non-unionised sectors such as hospitality (Bray & Macneil 2011).

The decentralisation of wage bargaining over the past two decades has exacerbated wage dispersion in Australia. While the national minimum wage (NMW) was set at 66 per cent of the median wage in 1992, this fell to 53 per cent in 2012, but there has been a moderate compression of pay dispersion since 2008. Pay dispersion and income inequality in Australia have increased at a faster rate than in some Western European economies, but remain at lower levels than in the United Kingdom and the United States.

## The settlement of disputes

One of the principal motivations behind the introduction of compulsory arbitration was to render strikes unnecessary. The 'rule of law' provided under arbitration was supposed to displace the 'barbarous expedient of strike action' (Macintyre & Mitchell 1989). For many years, the *Conciliation and Arbitration Act 1904* contained a provision making strike activity illegal and subject to penalties. Although this provision was removed in 1930, Australian unions whose members were on strike were subject to penal provisions in the federal system. It was not until the passage of the *Industrial Relations Reform Act 1993* that unions were granted a qualified and limited right to strike.

Under the 1993 Act, either party could notify the other of its intention to use industrial action during the designated bargaining period. The AIRC could intervene and make use of its traditional arbitral functions if it believed that the parties were not acting in good faith, if there was little likelihood of an agreement being reached or on the grounds of public interest. In seeking to resolve the dispute, parties engaging in unlawful strikes could be fined as well as have their awards suspended or cancelled. The Howard government maintained a limited right to strike during the designated bargaining period in its *Workplace Relations Act 1996*, strengthened the AIRC's powers to address illegal industrial action, prohibited the payment and acceptance of pay or wages for workers when involved in strike action and restored secondary boycott provisions to the *Trade Practices Act*, with substantial fines for breaches (Lee & Peetz 1998).

The Work Choices reforms further eroded the AIRC's role in dispute settlement by removing its compulsory arbitration powers. Although it might have been expected that a Labor government would restore these powers of the federal industrial tribunal, the capacity of the newly established FWC to intervene in industrial disputes is generally limited to instances where industrial action is causing significant economic harm to the parties.

Another older sanction, used sparingly by tribunals, has been to deregister a union that has acted in defiance of a tribunal order. Since deregistration has tended to be difficult and complex, tribunals have generally hoped that the threat of this sanction would be sufficient. However, threats made little impact on the Builders Labourers Federation, deregistered in 1986; its members were quickly absorbed by other unions, leaving only the shell of a once-powerful union.

As Figure 5.1 indicates, the incidence of working days lost (WDL) through industrial disputes has fallen significantly in recent decades. However, there has been an increase in the use of employer-initiated industrial action to support non-union agreements among private sector employers. Several high-profile disputes have been sparked by employers attempting to introduce non-union agreements in areas such as the mining and maritime industries, which traditionally were strongly unionised. Such employers have been actively seeking to eliminate unions from their operations and activities by the use of lockouts, a tactic that increased significantly under the Howard government (Cooper et al. 2009).

## CURRENT ISSUES

### Workplace productivity

The relationship between labour market regulation and workplace productivity has been at the heart of recent debates over the future of the Australian employment relations system. Employers' associations and business commentators have vigorously promoted the view that further decentralisation and de-collectivism, in the form of a return to individual employment contracts and restrictions on union rights, would help to bolster Australia's national productivity levels, which have waned since the mid-2000s. Soon after its election to office, the

**Figure 5.1    WDL per 1000 employees in industrial disputes**

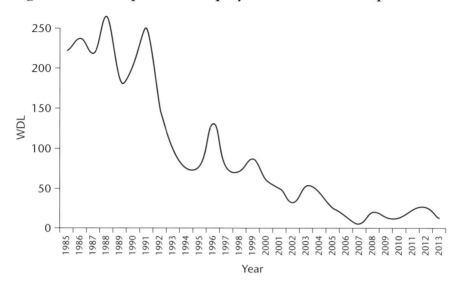

*Source:* Australian Bureau of Statistics (2014b).

Abbott government asked the Productivity Commission to investigate the impact of the *Fair Work Act 2009* on various matters including productivity performance. The Productivity Commission's report, which is due to be published in 2016, is expected to foreshadow future attempts by the Coalition to reform the employment relations system.

Debates over the impact of labour market regulation on productivity are long-standing. In the late 1980s and early 1990s, the advocates of labour market decentralisation anticipated that enterprise-based wage determination would positively impact upon workplace productivity. Among the various studies subsequently conducted, there is wide agreement that labour and multi-factor productivity levels indeed surged in the years following the introduction of enterprise bargaining, but that there is no conclusive causal relationship. A consistent finding of these studies is that the shift to a decentralised regulatory system is just one of a multitude of factors that may have contributed to increased productivity in the 1990s, with extensive micro-economic reforms and greater utilisation of technology also likely to have had significant impacts (Green et al. 2012; Hancock 2012; Peetz 2012).

The recent worsening of Australia's national productivity performance has allowed advocates of further labour market reform to gain traction in public debate. In calling for the return to a more decentralised and individualised regulatory system, proponents claim that the strengthening of workers' collective rights under the *Fair Work Act* has weakened managerial prerogative and undermined workplace flexibility and productivity (*Australian Financial Review* 2012). These claims were rejected by an expert panel that the Gillard Labor government commissioned to evaluate the impact of the *Fair Work Act*, which found that rapid falls in multi-factor productivity across the economy—particularly in the mining sector following an earlier investment boom—largely accounted for the relatively low labour productivity of recent years. The panel rejected the notion that different labour market regulatory frameworks can account for fluctuations in Australia's productivity performance, particularly the view that a more decentralised system would produce an upsurge. In its report, the expert panel noted that 'over the [past] two decades labour productivity growth was slowest under *Work Choices*, which arguably imposed the fewest constraints on management decisions' (McCallum et al. 2012: 72).

Peetz (2012) reaches similar conclusions, finding that labour productivity at the industry level has been higher on average since the introduction of the *Fair Work Act* than under Work Choices. He also notes that the several changes to employment relations policy in recent decades have made little tangible difference to national productivity outcomes. This is supported by Jefferson and Preston (2013: 352), who claim that 'existing analysis suggests that there are a number of contributory causes to Australia's productivity slump that are not directly related to the labour market. There is little evidence that it is specifically related to industrial relations legislation.' Nevertheless, the workplace productivity debate is likely to continue.

## Gender equality at work

The participation rate among women in Australia is higher than the Organisation for Economic Cooperation and Development (OECD) average, and has been increasing at a faster rate over the past decade, but remains lower than the Northern European economies as well as Canada, New Zealand and Switzerland. Women have not fared as well as men in the labour market, as their wages are lower and they are concentrated in industries and occupations defined by low pay and non-standard employment. Furthermore, women are much more likely to be under-employed (10 per cent) than men (6 per cent) and much less likely to be in full-time employment. In 2013, 26 per cent of all female employees were employed on a 'casual' (i.e. non-permanent) basis and 45 per cent on a part-time basis, with women making up

55 per cent and 72 per cent of the casual and part-time workforce respectively (Charlesworth & Macdonald 2014).

The gender pay gap (as measured by full-time average weekly ordinary-time earnings) has also widened in recent years, from 15.5 per cent in 2005 to 17.5 per cent in 2013. There are differences between states and industries, with private sector industries tending to have larger gender pay gaps than those in the public sector (Charlesworth & Macdonald 2014; Todd & Preston 2012). In the past, major advances in achieving pay equity came from test cases in the FWC and its predecessors, where wage increases were achieved through the application of equal pay principles. However, these advances stalled after changes introduced by Work Choices had a negative impact on women, particularly in relation to unfair dismissal, job security and pay (Pocock et al. 2008).

The *Fair Work Act 2009* promised to improve the situation for women at work in several ways. The right to request flexible work arrangements was included as one of the ten NESs. The Act also enabled the FWC to make orders requiring equal remuneration for work of equal or comparable value, which replaced the more limited provision of 'equal remuneration for work of equal value'. Applicants seeking an equal remuneration order would not need to prove that discrimination had caused the gender pay gap. This removed the high threshold of proving that discrimination had occurred, as was required by the *Workplace Relations Act 1996*, which had discouraged any successful equal remuneration case from being conducted at the federal level (Lyons & Smith 2007: 28).

Following an application in 2010 made by unions representing social and community services workers under the equal remuneration provision of the *Fair Work Act*, the FWC determined that these workers experienced pay disparity compared with their counterparts performing comparable work in other industries, and that this was partly due to their gender. The FWC subsequently decided to increase the pay rates of the award covering social and community services workers by between 19 and 41 per cent, to be phased in over eight years, with the then Labor government announcing that it would fund its share of increased costs associated with the higher pay rates (Cortis & Meagher 2012; Todd & Preston 2012). While it is anticipated that similar claims for equal remuneration will be pursued in relation to other groups of underpaid workers, the Abbott Coalition government scrapped several initiatives of its Labor predecessor that had the potential to improve pay equity for aged-care and child-care workers (Charlesworth & Macdonald 2014).

Until recently, Australia was unique among OECD member states (aside from the United States) in lacking a universal and comprehensive paid parental leave scheme. However, the Rudd–Gillard Labor government introduced a scheme that allowed working parents with primary care responsibility for a newborn child to take eighteen weeks of paid leave at the NMW. Increasing female workforce participation by linking the payment of paid parental leave directly to employment, improving gender equity in the home and allowing parents to stay home from work for longer periods after the birth of their child were the three stated objectives of the scheme, which took effect in January 2011. According to Baird and Whitehouse (2012: 185), these objectives 'signal government and public acknowledgment of the much closer interface between home and work in contemporary Australian life', and show that 'the state has a role to play in facilitating work–family transitions and balance'.

The paid parental leave initiative was accompanied by a 'Dad and Partner Pay' extension of the scheme, which from January 2013 granted the partners of primary carers two weeks of paid leave to be used within twelve months of their child's birth or adoption. At the 2013 election, the Abbott-led Coalition pledged to introduce a more generous paid parental leave entitlement, but abandoned this policy in the face of opposition from employers' groups and opposition parties and from within the Coalition parties.

## Precarious employment

While unemployment has been lower in Australia compared with most other advanced economies in recent years, the growth of non-standard contracts and under-employment presents significant challenges. The number of workers engaged on arrangements other than permanent full-time employment increased during the 1990s, and has remained at high levels ever since. In 2010, 23 per cent of the workforce were engaged as casual employees, 13 per cent on a permanent part-time basis and 4 per cent on fixed-term contracts.

The patterns of workers engaged in these forms of non-standard employment are highly gendered. More than half (53 per cent) of all female workers are casual, contract or permanent part-time compared with 28 per cent of male workers, but a growing number of male workers are now also casuals. Younger workers are more likely to be engaged in these forms of employment than older workers. Non-standard employment can potentially allow workers greater work–life balance, which may benefit workers who have significant responsibilities outside work, such as carers and full-time students. Moreover, casual employees in Australia receive certain protections that typically are not available to their counterparts in other countries. These include a loading of 20–25 per cent of the hourly wage to compensate casual employees for not having access to the job security and paid leave entitlements afforded to permanent employees. However, there is evidence that casual employees face significantly greater barriers to skilled training and career development than permanent employees (Richardson & Law 2009; Richardson et al. 2012).

Non-standard employment contracts tend to be concentrated in the industries where unions are weakest, with only 6.5 per cent of casual workers holding union membership in 2013. The growth of casual and other forms of non-standard employment has been one factor accounting for the dramatic fall in union membership over recent decades. Unions have sought to address this problem by developing strategies specifically aimed at improving the position of these workers. For example, in 2012 the ACTU commissioned an inquiry into insecure work in Australia, which highlighted the problems faced by the large number of workers in non-standard employment. Unions have also campaigned for the use of innovative regulations to improve the conditions of workers in non-standard employment arrangements in the transport, cleaning and clothing trades industries (Kaine & Wright 2013).

The prevalence of unemployment and under-employment in some parts of the Australian labour market is another issue of concern. Many workers are employed at levels below their qualifications and skills, and a high proportion of part-time workers want more hours of work, often in order to maintain a basic standard of living. These problems are especially acute among younger workers. In 2013, younger male workers were three times more likely to be unemployed (13 per cent) than the national average, while women workers aged 15–24 years were more than twice as likely to be under-employed (17 per cent) than the national average. While younger workers were more likely to be unemployed or under-employed than other cohorts, around one-third of all unemployed workers aged 55 and over were long-term unemployed, reflecting a pattern identified in other advanced economies (Healy 2014).

Despite the relatively high rates of unemployment and under-employment among certain groups of workers, persistent labour shortages have been a feature of the Australian labour market over the past two decades. Consequently, both Coalition and Labor governments have relaxed skilled visa regulations to allow employers to fill job vacancies quickly, resulting in the intake of migrants on work visas increasing from around 80,000 in 1996 to over 430,000 in 2012 (Wright 2015b).

In contrast to the low-skilled nature of labour immigration prevalent in many European countries, Australian immigration policy is focused primarily on attracting skilled and professional workers, although a large number of young temporary immigrant workers (typically students or working holiday-makers) are a source of labour for various agricultural and service industries. However, there have been ongoing concerns about the impact of the employer-sponsored temporary 457 visa scheme, which has become the largest avenue for skilled immigration.

In 2013, Prime Minister Gillard claimed that the 457 visa was denying opportunities to residents for employment, training and higher wages and leading migrant workers to be exploited. Several unions have made similar criticisms of the 457 visa consistently for the past decade, as have some academic studies (Campbell & Tham 2013). These assertions have been challenged by employers' groups, which have welcomed the shift towards a more liberal skilled visa policy; this view is supported by other studies suggesting that the 457 visa is beneficial for employers and workers alike (Khoo et al. 2007). The Rudd–Gillard Labor government introduced various safeguards to address the concerns of unions. Notwithstanding these controversies over the 457 visa, both major parties remain committed to maintaining a relatively liberal skilled immigration policy as a means of addressing skilled labour shortages in a flexible and responsive manner (Wright 2015b).

## CONCLUSIONS

The past two decades have been a period of frequent regulatory change in the Australian employment relations system, with several major pieces of legislation passed since 1993 and numerous other unsuccessful attempts at reform. There is something of a tendency among Labor and Coalition governments to implement changes favourable to their supporters in the labour movement or business community. According to a former president of the FWC, these oscillations in employment relations policy have generated considerable uncertainty and high transaction costs at the workplace level. Instead, greater emphasis should be placed upon developing a stable policy framework that is likely to be broadly acceptable to employers, employees and their representatives (Giudice 2014). Other prominent analysts claim that the costs of regulatory reform will inevitably create political opportunity costs and workplace adjustment costs that can be expected to greatly exceed the benefits, which in any case are likely to be minimal (Borland 2012). However, with some employers' groups agitating for a return to individual agreements, a curtailment of union rights and a weakening of certain employment conditions, further changes appear to be likely.

The shift towards a more decentralised form of labour market regulation in the 1990s indeed represented a period of significant change in the Australian system. While there is considerable disagreement between unions and employers' groups over issues relating to collective rights and workplace representation, there appears to be little appetite from the major political parties to revert to a more coordinated and centralised regulatory system. While this may exacerbate existing challenges relating to workplace productivity, gender inequality and precarious work, the system of workplace-level determination of wages and conditions is likely to remain as the centrepiece of Australian employment relations for the foreseeable future.

## FURTHER READING

Baird, M., Hancock, K. & Isaac, J. (eds) (2011) *Work and Employment Relations: An Era of Change*. Sydney: Federation Press.

Borland, J. (2012) 'Industrial relations reform: Chasing a pot of gold at the end of the rainbow?' *Australian Economic Review*, 45(3): 269–89.

Cooper, R. & Ellem, B. (2008) 'The neoliberal state, trade unions and collective bargaining in Australia'. *British Journal of Industrial Relations*, 46(3): 532–54.

Peetz, D. (1998) *Unions in a Contrary World: The Future of the Australian Trade Union Movement*. Melbourne: Cambridge University Press.

Sheldon, P. & Thornthwaite, L. (1999). *Employer Associations and Industrial Relations Change: Catalysts or Captives?* Sydney: Allen & Unwin.

## USEFUL WEBSITES

ACTU: <www.actu.org.au>.

AiG: <www.aigroup.com.au>.

Australian Department of Employment: <www.employment.gov.au>.

FWC: <www.fwc.gov.au>.

National Centre for Vocational Education Research: <www.ncver.edu.au>.

## A CHRONOLOGY OF AUSTRALIAN EMPLOYMENT RELATIONS

| | |
|---|---|
| 1788 | European settlers arrive in New South Wales, with separate British colonies established subsequently. |
| 1856 | Building unions win recognition of the eight-hour day. Melbourne Trades Hall Council is formed. |
| 1879 | First Inter-Colonial Trade Union Conference. |
| 1890–94 | Great Strikes. Following defeat by combined employer and colonial government power, unions establish Labor parties in each colony. |
| 1901 | Commonwealth of Australia founded. |
| 1904 | Commonwealth Conciliation and Arbitration Court established under the *Commonwealth Conciliation and Arbitration Act*, with powers of legal enforcement. |
| 1907 | Harvester case establishes the principle of the basic wage, above which the court could award a margin for skill. |
| 1927 | Founding of the ACTU. |
| 1929 | The Conservative government is defeated in a federal election in which proposals to weaken powers of the Conciliation and Arbitration Court are a major issue. |
| 1956 | Following Boilermakers' case, the Arbitration Court is disbanded. Conciliation and Arbitration Commission set up with arbitral functions, and Industrial Court with judicial responsibility. |
| 1972 | A federal Labor government is elected after 23 years of Liberal–National (formerly Country Party) Coalition government. |
| 1975 | Wage indexation introduced; Whitlam Labor government defeated. |
| 1981 | Wage indexation abandoned. |
| 1983 | Hawke Labor government elected. Labor Party–ACTU Prices and Incomes Accord becomes the linchpin of government policy. Return to centralised wage fixation and full wage indexation. Formation of the BCA. |
| 1985 | Report of the Committee of Review of Australian Industrial Relations Law and Systems (the Hancock Report). |
| 1988 | Elaboration of structural efficiency principle; reforms to federal *Industrial Relations Act*. |
| 1989 | Award restructuring; domestic airline pilots' dispute. |
| 1991 | (October) National Wage Case decision condones a shift to more enterprise bargaining |
| 1992 | Further movement towards decentralisation of bargaining, including amendments to the federal *Industrial Relations Act*. |
| 1994 | *Industrial Relations Reform Act 1993* comes into operation and extends the scope of enterprise bargaining. |

| | |
|---|---|
| 1996 | Election of Howard Liberal–National Party Coalition government. |
| 1997 | *Workplace Relations and Other Legislation Amendment Act 1996* is proclaimed. |
| 2006 | *Workplace Relations Amendment (Work Choices) Act 2005* comes into force. |
| 2007 | The Rudd Labor government is elected; employment relations policy features strongly in the election platform. |
| 2009 | The Labor government's *Fair Work Act* comes into effect. |
| 2013 | Election of Liberal–National Coalition government led by Tony Abbott for a three-year term. |

# CHAPTER 6

# Employment relations in Italy

## Lucio Baccaro and Valeria Pulignano[1]

The Italian employment relations system has tended to baffle comparative scholars, who have had a hard time placing it into cross-country classificatory schemes—both those issuing from the literature on corporatism and, more recently, those based on the Varieties of Capitalism (VoC) literature (Hall & Soskice 2001). While the Italian employment relations system appeared to share several features with coordinated market economies (CMEs)—most importantly, a relatively centralised structure of bargaining—the absence of a well-developed apprenticeship system specialising in the production of industry-specific skills and of cooperative institutions at the workplace level—like the German Works Councils—made it a mixed case that did not clearly fall into either the 'liberal' or the 'coordinated' camp (Thelen 2001). Also, Italy's system seemed to lack the institutional and organisational features (e.g. social democratic dominance of government, highly centralised interest associations) that were once considered conducive to corporatist policy-making, yet corporatist agreements were often attempted and sometimes surprisingly agreed upon in this country.

Within Italy, the tone of the academic debate has often been one of engaged critique, if not reproach. Italian employment relations have often appeared to analysts within the country as chaotic, poorly institutionalised and not sufficiently mature in comparison with those of other developed economies. For a long time, the main problem has been perceived to rest with the Italian unions' militancy and political divisions, and their unwillingness to compromise on a much-needed policy of centralised wage moderation. The absence of a clear set of agreed-upon rules has also frequently been singled out as problematic. The failure of national agreements in the early 1980s, and the decentralisation of collective bargaining that ensued, provided empirical support for these critical views.

126

Beginning with the early 1990s, though, the situation of Italian employment relations changed dramatically. With a series of central-ised agreements, governments, unions and to a lesser extent organised employers spearheaded a new era of social pacts and collaborative policy-making in Europe. The architecture of collective bargaining was thoroughly reformed in 1993, and the linkages across bargaining levels became far more institutionalised.

In the 1990s, the Italian employment relations system saw the emergence of a new kind of 'concessionary' corporatism (Rhodes 1996, 2001; Streeck 2000; Baccaro 2007). The unions were involved in all the major policy-making decisions, even though they sometimes disagreed among themselves about the desirability of specific measures. However, centralised negotiations produced few of the redistributive and de-commodifying outcomes that formerly had characterised Scan-dinavian corporatism. Instead, they contributed to mobilise societal support for a market-conforming economic policy based on moderate wage growth and tightly controlled public expenditures. This insti-tutional setting did nothing to stem the erosion of the union's organisational strength or to redress the country's economic woes: stag-nating economic growth, growing inequalities and a widespread sense of economic insecurity. When the post-2007 global financial crisis and the euro crisis hit in 2008–10, the Italian government considered that the kind of macro-concessions it could extract from the unions were insufficient to regain the confidence of international financial markets, and thus Italian corporatism was unceremoniously dismantled.

## THE DEVELOPMENT OF ITALIAN EMPLOYMENT RELATIONS UNTIL 1992

The trajectory of Italian employment relations after World War II was linked to the evolution of the Italian political system as a whole. In 1944, union groups of different ideological orientations (commu-nists, socialists, Catholics and others) joined ranks to establish a unitary union confederation, the Confederazione generale Italiana del lavoro (CGIL). The unions' organisational structures were recon-stituted almost from scratch, and were populated by party personnel who often lacked specific union experience (Romagnoli & Treu 1981; Turone 1992).

With the start of the Cold War, the unity of anti-fascist forces vanished, both at the governmental and the union levels. In 1950, both the Catholic faction and the republican and social democratic factions quit the CGIL to establish independent union confederations: the

Confederazione Italiana sindacati dei lavoratori (CISL) and the Unione Italiana dei lavoratori (UIL) respectively.

In the 1950s, Italian unions were weak and employers dominated employment relations (Locke 1995). Wages lagged below productivity (Salvati 1984). Strikes were rare, and when they occurred their motivation was predominantly political rather than economic (Bordogna & Provasi 1989). Wage moderation and labour quiescence contributed to creating the preconditions for the low-cost, export-oriented strategy of economic growth from which emerged the economic miracle of the late 1950s and early 1960s.

Employment relations changed dramatically in the 1960s. Labour market conditions became much more favourable to labour, especially in the north-western parts of Italy. With the diffusion and consolidation of Fordist models of work organisation in large firms, trade unions began devoting a greater deal of attention and resources to negotiating work conditions at the shop-floor level than had previously been the case.

With the so-called Hot Autumn, a massive wave of strikes in the 1969–72 period, political divisions within the Italian labour movement were overcome from below (Pizzorno et al. 1978; Sabel 1982). In many industrial plants—especially in the metalworking industry—the three union confederations embraced unity of action. In 1972 there was a partial reunification of the Italian labour movement, with the establishment of the Federazione unitaria CGIL-CISL-UIL.

The Hot Autumn introduced a number of innovations in collective bargaining. Campaigns for the unification of blue- and white-collar job classification schemes, the abolition of territorial differences in wage levels, demands for equal wage increases for all workers regardless of skill levels, improvements in health and safety conditions, and reductions in the speed and duration of work were all promoted in these years. The metalworking federations of the CGIL, CISL and UIL, together with the unitary Federazione lavoratori metalmeccanici, acted as vanguards for the whole labour movement (Golden 1988). They consistently practised unity of action and used their power to push for higher wages, limit overtime, regulate layoffs, restrict internal mobility and slow down the pace of work. The Hot Autumn overturned virtually all the social, political and economic patterns established in the post-war period. However, it simultaneously impaired the national strategy of export-led growth by increasing inflation and unit labour costs, and squeezing profits (Barca & Magnani 1989). Italy's competitiveness in international markets deteriorated sharply, and the current balance turned from positive to negative.

In the mid-1970s, a general consensus emerged among Italian political-economic elites that union demands and industrial conflict were imposing unbearable costs on the Italian economy (Lama 1976). With the worsening of Italy's economic crisis in the second half of the 1970s, the three major union confederations, the CGIL, CISL and UIL, embraced a new strategy that became known as the EUR Policy. With it, they accepted to moderate wage demands and limits on industrial conflict in exchange for participation in national policy-making (Lange & Vannicelli 1982).

In 1977, a first tripartite agreement entailing minor labour concessions was negotiated. National-level negotiations continued in the early 1980s. In 1983, a tripartite agreement cut wage indexation (*scala mobile*), imposed a series of wage ceilings on sectoral collective bargaining negotiations, and banned plant-level wage negotiations for eighteen months. In 1984, the government proposed to renew and update the previous tripartite pact by cutting wage indexation again (Carrieri 1985; Regini 1985). However, this government proposal met with union opposition: the CISL and UIL supported it, while the CGIL refused to sign it. Faced with union division, the government implemented the accord through an executive order. One year later, the Communist Party promoted an electoral referendum to abrogate the government's decree. The results of the referendum favoured the pro-government factions, but led to the demise of unity of action among the three union confederations. The Federazione unitaria was dismantled.

The failed agreement of 1985 and the ensuing referendum seriously undermined relationships among the three confederations. The structure of collective bargaining was decentralised again, and industry-level agreements lost much of their previous lustre (Locke 1992). The demise of centralised bargaining was only a temporary phenomenon, however: this type of agreement returned to dominate the scene in the early 1990s. Before analysing these more recent developments, however, the next section examines the actors of the Italian employment relations system.

## THE PARTIES IN EMPLOYMENT RELATIONS

Italy's interest representation system appears remarkably fragmented in comparative perspective, and organisations are divided on both functional and political lines. The most important employers' association is Confindustria. This organisation represents all kinds of enterprise interests. However—also due to a weighted system of voting—the interests of large enterprises predominate (Vatta 2007).

Two different strategic orientations vie for power within Confindustria. On the one hand, there are the interests of large firms, which often face strong and militant unions at the company level, and hence are generally not prejudicially against retaining some form of dialogue with unions at the national level. On the other hand, there are small and medium-sized enterprises (SMEs), which generally face weaker unions at the workplace level, and hence favour a more muscular approach to employment relations and labour market policy. In 2001, the president of Confindustria was elected on a platform emphasising the need to strengthen the voice of SMEs. The result was a shift in the organisation's policy away from national, tripartite negotiations and towards greater support for governmental attempts to introduce flexibility in hiring and firing, including through unilateral measures (Baccaro & Simoni 2004).

Reliable data on representation and density are not available for employers' organisations. In 2002, Confindustria declared that the total number of workers employed by its affiliates was 4,280,085. In the same year, the total number of employees in industry (including construction) and services was 15,398,000. This corresponds to a density of 28 per cent. However, the density would probably be much higher if we were to take into account only the employees of non-craft companies (Vatta 2007).

Aside from Confindustria, there are other specialised employers' organisations in Italy that represent small enterprises, companies operating in the retail and service sectors, craft-based companies (which have a special legal status) and cooperatives. Organisations representing retail and service companies, craft-based companies and cooperatives are divided along party lines, with one organisation being closer to left-of-centre politics and the other leaning towards the right. While these additional employers' associations increasingly participate in national negotiations, their ability to shape the strategy of the employers as a whole in these negotiations is limited, and they generally follow the line of Confindustria.

Turning to the unions, scholars usually have focused on the three major union confederations, the CGIL, CISL and UIL. There are, however, several other organisations that claim to represent workers in particular sectors or skill categories. Data on other organisations' members are sparse and often unreliable; if we were to accept their self-reported membership figures, the union density in Italy would have doubled, at least. Since 2006, union density in Italy has remained relatively stable at about 35 per cent (AIAS 2013).

Figure 6.1 presents aggregate union density rates for the three major confederations against time. It shows that after peaking at about

**Figure 6.1   Union density rate CGIL-CISL-UIL**

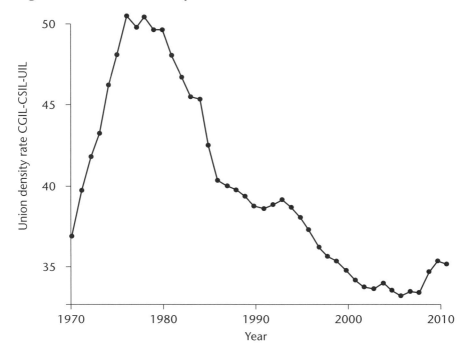

*Source:* AIAS 2013.

50 per cent of the workforce in the late 1970s (after the Hot Autumn mobilisations), union density declined until the late 2000s. During the post-2007 global financial crisis, unionisation increased a little. Much of this can be attributed to the massive fall in employment, particularly in traditionally unionised sectors. Despite falling density rates, union membership has grown constantly, thanks to the steady increase (until 2005) in the number of retired workers affiliated to the three confederations. Unionisation of retired members is favoured by the presence of semi-public institutional arrangements, known as *patronati*, that process the workers' applications for retirement and in exchange persuade workers to join the pensioners' unions.

Self-reported membership data generally over-estimate union density, which is revealed by comparing data based on administrative sources and on labour market surveys for those countries in which both are available.[2] According to survey data, the estimated *total* union density among active workers in Italy in 2008 was less than 30 per cent, including all union organisations, not just the three major confederations. These survey data are based on a representative sample of about 1600 dependent workers aged eighteen and older, and retirees, stratified by labour market status (active/retired), gender and geographical area of residence.[3] The density among retired workers was about 28 per cent. The three main confederations, the CGIL, CISL and UIL, organised about 81 per cent of all union members, so were the most representative organisations.

Union density was estimated to be only 19 per cent in the private sector, based on this survey data. The estimated density was considerably higher in the public sector: 44 per cent. We also estimate that density was only 19 per cent for employees aged between eighteen and 34. This is much lower than the 29 per cent density among employees who were more than 54 years old.

The survey data could include sample errors. However, they are in accord with officially certified data, and thus appear to be reasonably reliable. They paint a picture that is considerably bleaker for unions than those painted by earlier scholarly work, including our own (Baccaro et al. 2003). Unions may not be significant labour market actors in the future. This scenario reflects their density of less than 20 per cent in the private sector, the challenge of organising young workers (also due to the extent of contingent work among these cohorts) and the continuing retirement of older union members.

## ORGANISATIONAL STRUCTURES

The organisational structures of employers' and workers' organisations match each other: both Confindustria and the three confederal unions have both vertical, industry-based organisational structures and horizontal structures. In the case of the CGIL the most important horizontal structure is the local *camera del lavoro* (labour chamber). The other confederations have similar entities. The chamber's jurisdiction approximately corresponds to that of Italian provinces. The unions' vertical structures link the enterprise level, provincial industry organisations and national industry federations. In 2008, thirteen industry federations were affiliated with the CGIL (nineteen in 1985), nineteen with the CISL (seventeen in 1985), and eighteen with the UIL (28 in 1985). As in other countries, over time there has been a tendency towards consolidation of the industry federations through mergers (Ebbinghaus 2003). Aside from this trend, the organisational structure of the unions has remained more or less stable above the workplace level, while it has changed considerably at the workplace level itself. This has been the area in which the most interesting organisational innovations have emerged.

The organisational model of the early post-war years was that of the *commissione interna* (internal commission). Formally, it was not a union body, had no bargaining prerogatives and could not call strikes; rather, it was a small parliament in charge of ensuring smooth relations between workers (union and non-union) and companies. Its functions ranged from consultation to monitoring the implementation of collective agreements signed by external trade unions. However, because in the early post-war years free-trade unions had not yet been established, the internal commissions were in some cases assigned bargaining rights as well.

With the Hot Autumn wave of strikes, the internal commissions were replaced by the *consigli di fabbrica* (factory councils), composed of worker delegates elected by and directly accountable to small homogeneous workers' groups. Simultaneously, a major legislative reform, the Workers' Statute (Law 300) of 1970, authorised the 'most representative' unions to establish workplace representation structures (*rappresentanze sindacali aziendali*, or RSA). The Workers' Statute never defined how exactly 'most representative' was to be determined, and for a long time it was simply presumed that it referred to the three main confederations.

The synthesis between the organisational model embedded in the Workers' Statute and the one emerging from the workers' struggles was reached pragmatically: the three confederations recognised the factory councils as their own and attributed to them the institutional benefits to which they were entitled by virtue of their 'most representative' status under the law. Thus, the factory councils became union structures, but at the same time represented all workers in a workplace.

However, this synthesis had a downside. When in 1984 the three confederations broke up over the issue of wage indexation reform, relationships deteriorated at both the national and the workplace levels. In some cases, the unitary factory councils were dismantled and each organisation established its own RSA. In other cases, factory councils were not renewed for several years, thus jump-starting a heated debate about the lack of union democracy in Italy (Baccaro 2001).

Different reform initiatives were launched in the late 1980s and early 1990s. In 1993, the three union confederations and the employers settled on the *rappresentanze sindacale unitaria* (RSU). Like the factory councils, the RSUs were both union organisations and organs of general worker representation. Unlike the factory councils' delegates, however, RSU members were elected by the workers at large, and no longer by homogeneous groups. To ensure institutional continuity between external unions and internal workplace structures (also at the request of employers), it was established that two-thirds of RSU representatives were to be elected by all workers in a workplace, while one-third were to be appointed by the most representative unions, which would in this way almost certainly be assured control over these structures.

The creation of the RSUs allowed the main union confederations to set worker representation on a more solid and predictable footing (Pulignano 2006). The RSUs became the formal bargaining agents at company and local levels on issues explicitly referred to in national agreements; they were also attributed consultation and information rights, which concurred to identify them as formal bodies of employee participation and therefore an important instrument for union democracy (Carrieri 1995).

The introduction of the RSUs spurred a wave of union elections in Italian workplaces. The CGIL, CIS and UIL obtained close to 95 per cent of the workers' votes in most cases, except in the case of a limited number of well-identified skill groups (e.g. locomotive engineers). In 1997, the RSUs were extended by law to the public sector. The Legge Bassanini mandated the regular election of workplace representatives in the Italian public sector and imposed the official counting of membership data.[4]

The purpose of these dispositions was the measurement of union representation. Those unions that passed a threshold of 5 per cent (calculated as the average between electoral votes and quota of membership cards) were designated as 'representative', and were therefore allowed to participate in collective bargaining in the various public sector compartments (e.g. schools, ministries, municipalities) and sign collective bargaining agreements that were binding for all workers. The official data gathered by the Agenzia per la rappresentanza negoziale delle pubbliche amministrazioni (Agency for Bargaining in the Public Administration, or ARAN), the public agency in charge of public sector employment relations, revealed that the fragmentation of trade union representation was in some cases extreme—for example, in the health-care sector, workers were affiliated with 68 different organisations. Notwithstanding this fragmentation, the CGIL, CISL and UIL together organised 71 per cent of all union members in the public sector. The number of votes that they obtained in the first RSU elections was slightly lower (68 per cent), but still considerable.[5]

Despite several legislative attempts at institutionalising the election of workplace representatives in the private sector as well, the RSUs remained private and voluntary in the private sector. Consequently, from the mid-1990s, the RSUs displayed signs of fatigue (Carrieri 1997). At the core of their difficulties was a lack of unity among the three main confederations, the limited diffusion of company bargaining and non-renewal of the elected representatives. The results of the RSU elections bolstered the confederal unions' claim to general representation of Italian workers and, for some time, contributed to re-legitimatising and re-energising them (Carrieri 1995, 1996). However, as mentioned, they did not prevent a serious erosion of union density.

The post-2007 period has been characterised by a dramatic shift in the employment relations strategy of Fiat Auto, which at some point seemed to foreshadow the possible return to a structure of workplace representation based on the RSA (Cella 2012). The shift was brought about by the 2010 Pomigliano and Mirafiori agreements, which were negotiated under management threats to relocate production from the above-mentioned Italian plants to foreign factories if the unions did not agree to concessions (Pedersini 2012a). These agreements induced Fiat to leave both Confindustria and the metalworking industry agreement, and to introduce a separate company agreement. The goal was to avoid having to deal with the most representative union in the metalworking industry, the Federazione impiegati e operai metallurgici (FIOM), which had refused to agree to the concessions.

In accord with the Workers' Statute (Law 300 of 1970 as modified by a popular referendum in 1995), only unions that are signatories to a collective agreement that is applied in the relevant workplace can set up workplace representation structures. Thus, by exiting from the employers' organisation and terminating all existing collective agreements, Fiat thought it would be able to exclude the FIOM both from collective bargaining and from workplace representation. So far, labour courts have ruled that the exclusion is an unfair labour practice according to the law, and have condemned Fiat's action. Nonetheless, Fiat's initiative was a major blow to the established structure of collective bargaining and union representation. As a result, in June 2011, an inter-sectoral agreement was signed by Confindustria and the CGIL, CISL and UIL to introduce new criteria (based on union representation) for participation in industry-wide bargaining, and for the signing of valid company deals. This agreement has reduced some of the tensions between the CGIL on the one side, and the CISL and UIL on the other (Pedersini 2012a). Nevertheless, long-standing differences remain.

## THE PROCESS OF EMPLOYMENT RELATIONS

### The national level

For years, central neo-corporatist deals have seemed unlikely. This was not for lack of trying, however. From the late 1970s, there had been various attempts at national-level negotiations between the government and the social partners. The crux of the problem seemed to be in the organisational and institutional structure of the Italian employment relations actors, which lacked the centralised organisational capacities needed for corporatism to succeed (Tarantelli 1986; Cella & Treu 1989). One element, in retrospect, was especially important in determining the early failures related to strategy rather than structure: a sizeable portion of the union movement was unwilling (and not just unable) to commit to a policy of pay restraint.

This situation changed dramatically in the early 1990s. Two factors facilitated the re-emergence of centralised bargaining. The first was economic: in the early 1990s, Italy was faced with a serious economic crisis and the Italian currency was not acceptable in the European Monetary System in September 1992 (Vaciago 1993). The second factor was political: the old political party system, which had both shaped and constrained relations among collective actors, disappeared in the space of a few years. The Communist Party changed in 1989. Then it pledged allegiance to parliamentary and reformist methods of action, and applied for membership of the Socialist International—that is, the international association of social democratic parties. In early 1992, Tangentopoli (Bribeville), a wave of corruption scandals, shook all major governmental parties, including the Christian Democrats and the Socialists. Both parties went through a legitimation crisis and were dismantled. Their place was taken by a new coalition of centre-right political parties led by Silvio Berlusconi, a media tycoon.

The concomitance of both political and economic crises provided the union confederations with a major opportunity to impose themselves on the national political sphere as the senior partners of 'emergency' governments. The governments of 1992, 1993 and 1995 were weak, devoid of parliamentary majorities and (as in the case of the 1993 and 1995 executives) composed of independent 'technicians' formally not affiliated with any political party. The range of tasks these governments had to perform was daunting. First, they had to avoid the nominal devaluation of the then currency, the lira, sparking a new inflationary spiral. For this, wage moderation was indispensable. Second, since public finances were disastrous (the public deficit was around 10 per cent of gross domestic product, or GDP, between 1992 and 1993, and public debt reached 125 per cent of GDP in 1994), the government could not use counter-cyclical (Keynesian) policies. Instead, the authorities needed to engage in fiscal consolidation—a set of policies that generally proves unpopular as it involves cuts in public expenditure and/or rises in taxes (in Italy, it involved both)—while trying to preserve social cohesion and peace.

The three confederations were well placed to provide the support and collaboration governments needed. First, unlike other major socio-political actors in Italy (e.g. the employers and the politicians), the confederations emerged from the Tangentopoli scandals almost unscathed. Second, due to the transformations in the political party structure, the unions' political sponsors either had disappeared or were for the first time in Italy's post-war history sitting together as partners in the same centre-left coalition. This political rapprochement contributed to generate close unity of action among the three confederations. Between 1992 and 1998, a series of central bargaining agreements was negotiated by the three confederal unions and the Italian governments, with or without (as in the case of the 1995 pension reform agreement) Confindustria.

In 1992, in an ill-fated attempt to stave off expectations of a forthcoming devaluation of the lira, a tripartite agreement brought about the abolition of wage indexation. In addition, enterprise-level bargaining was also temporarily banned. Another centralised agreement was signed in July 1993. This confirmed the abolition of wage indexation, linked industry-level wage increases to the government's macro-economic targets and introduced a two-tier structure of collective bargaining, at the industry and company levels.

In 1995, the government and unions (but not the employers) negotiated a comprehensive reform of the pension system. This introduced a simulated funded system in the long term (with benefits proportional to paid contribution), but only marginally attacked acquired rights. The 1996 tripartite Pact for Labour introduced a moderate flexibilisation of the rules regulating flexible and contingent forms of labour. In 1998 the Christmas Pact confirmed the structure of collective bargaining on the two levels established in 1993, and introduced a contractual obligation for government to consult with the social partners on all social policy issues and even to devolve decision-making authority to the social partners.

At the end of the 1990s, the newly emerged corporatist system seemed well on its way to institutionalisation, and there was even talk of embedding it in the Italian Constitution (Carrieri 1997). The three main confederations also seemed close to merging into a single organisation. However, this opportunity was missed: the CGIL and CISL, in particular, had different views on key issues such as union democracy (with the CISL opposing widespread use of worker referenda and the CGIL favouring them) and the decentralisation of collective bargaining (with the CISL being much more open than the CGIL). In some cases, these differences led to agreements signed only by the CISL and UIL but not the CGIL, as with the metalworking contract of 2001 and the proposed Pact for Milan in early 2000.

Confindustria became increasingly disenchanted with tripartite negotiations and, on the eve of national elections in 2001, struck a strategic alliance with the centre-right coalition. The new government's labour program emphasised labour market deregulation and criticised concertation as a pompous rite that blocked much-needed structural reform and underscored the need to move from job protection to employability (Biagi et al. 2002). In 2002, another tripartite agreement was signed. This time, however, the union front split. These tripartite negotiations started with the ambitious objective of boosting employment creation with a comprehensive reform of both employment protection legislation and economic shock absorbers. Eventually, however, the scope of the agreement shrank and the proposed text ended up exchanging the promise of tax reductions for a less rigid regulation of individual dismissals. The CGIL refused to sign this agreement, and called for workers to mobilise in opposition. This call was largely heeded and the policy reform stalled. As a result, the government never implemented the new rules on dismissals that it had negotiated.

Corporatist policy-making returned in full splendour in 2007. The opportunity was once again a pension reform. While the reform of 1995 had fundamentally altered the future structure of the system, it had only a limited impact on the transition phase affecting workers who had matured pension rights under the old regime. To prevent a short-term increase in pension expenditures, in 2004 the centre-right government unilaterally increased the minimum age for seniority-based pensions. However, it postponed the introduction of the reform to 2008 in order to avoid political problems with its base. The new centre-left government abolished the unilateral reform and negotiated with the unions a gradual increase of the minimum age for seniority-based retirement. Left-wing parties in the government opposed the agreement and appealed to Italian workers to reject it. As had previously occurred, in both 1993 and 1995, the three confederations organised a massive campaign of information among the workers, followed by a binding referendum. The workers approved the agreement by an overwhelming proportion and thus contributed to bolster both the unions' and the government's credibility.

In 2008, the centre-right coalition returned to power. Strategic divisions among the three confederations resurfaced and the unions split again. The crux of the matter this time was the updating of the 1993 agreement and the reform of collective bargaining structure. This was a topic that had been tabled repeatedly in the past, including during the

1998 negotiations, but had never been dealt with due to the parties' inability to find a mutually agreed solution. The January 2009 agreement confirmed the 1993 articulation of collective bargaining on two levels (industry and company), but introduced some changes to the old regime. All the major employers' organisations signed the agreement, as did the CISL and UIL, but not the CGIL, whose refusal was motivated by the agreement's inadequate protection of the purchasing power of pay.

While the incisiveness of the early pacts was largely gone (Carrieri 2008), the parties continued to negotiate national-level agreements well into the twenty-first century, following what had become a rather predictable pattern: when the centre-left coalition was in power, all three confederations shared responsibility for the final agreement; when the government was in the hands of the centre-right coalition, the CISL and UIL (as well as the other union confederations) signed, while the CGIL dug its heels in. The CGIL seemed to find it difficult to negotiate agreements with a government it did not trust.

Retrospectively, it could be argued that without the centralised agreements of the 1990s, Italy would not have joined the single European currency. Whether economic conditions would be worse than they currently are as a result is impossible to say. However, the resurgence of tripartite negotiations did nothing to prevent continuous erosion of the unions' representation capacity among active workers, especially in the private sector.

After 2009, the financial and economic crisis weakened social concertation at the national level even further. Faced with pressure from financial markets, all governments—Berlusconi (centre-right), Monti (technical), Letta (centre-left) and Renzi (centre-left)—have refused to seriously negotiate with the social partners on crucial government choices concerning the pension system and labour market (deregulation).

## The sector level

Historically, the sector (industry) level contract has had a symbiotic relationship with enterprise-level bargaining, and the two levels have often vied for primacy. After the Hot Autumn, enterprise bargaining (in large firms) became the channel through which the most interesting collective bargaining innovations emerged, and the role of the industry contract was to generalise and diffuse them (Cella & Treu 2009). In the 1980s, there was a trend towards collective bargaining decentralisation, which Italy shared with other developed economies (Katz 1993; Katz & Darbishire 2000), and the industry agreement lost some of its significance (Locke 1992). However, with the tripartite agreement of 1993, it was restored to its prime place (Regalia & Regini 1998).

The 1993 agreement introduced a division of labour across bargaining levels. Something similar had been attempted with the tripartite agreement of 1983, but had been short lived. Collective bargaining was to be conducted at both the industry level (every four years in the case of normative clauses, every two years as far as pay and conditions were concerned) and the enterprise (or territorial) level (every four years). The role of the industry agreement was to homogenise the working conditions of the employees belonging to a specific productive sector. As far as remuneration was concerned, industry-level negotiations had the function of keeping inflation expectations in check by tightly linking wage increases distributed at the industry level with the expected inflation rates decided by the government. Also, they would guarantee purchasing power stability by compensating ex post for any positive difference between anticipated and actual inflation. Even in this case, the adjustment would be net of terms of trade changes.

By its institutional design, the 1993 agreement had the potential to cause a decline of the wage share in Italy. Productivity increases were supposed to be no longer redistributed at the industry level, but only at the enterprise or regional level. Hence, unless the coverage rate of enterprise bargaining increased dramatically, wages would grow less than productivity. To obviate this situation, from 2006 the metalworking contract began to include an additional (small) wage element to be paid to workers to whom only the industry contract applied.

The collective bargaining structure introduced in 1993 represented a delicate equilibrium among different interests and views (Mascini 2000). This made it very difficult to reform it, despite repeated attempts. In principle, the employers were against collective bargaining at two levels, and argued for a single bargaining level. Initially, they favoured the industry contract; however, over time they shifted to the enterprise contract. The unions vocally defended the complementary nature of both the industry and the enterprise level of bargaining, and argued for the need to keep both. When push came to shove, however, the CISL and UIL proved willing to experiment with institutional solutions increasing the weight and importance of decentralised levels, while the CGIL cast itself in the role of defender of the industry contract.

Divisions over the proper role of the industry level did not just pit different organisations against one another, but often also reflected specific sectoral traditions and peculiarities. For example, the chemical sector agreement of May 2006 attributed greater autonomy to company-level bargaining, and even introduced an opt-out clause for companies in distress. The 2008 metalworking contract, which in many ways re-centralised employment relations at the industry level, was very different. A significant innovation was introduced only for craft-based companies in 2004. For these companies, the role of compensating differences between anticipated and actual inflation was moved from the national to the regional level of bargaining. This reduced the importance of the industry agreement.

After years of fruitless discussion and failed negotiations, the 2009 national agreement explicitly set out to reform the architecture of Italian collective bargaining. Hailed as a historic event, it did not fundamentally alter the existing system. Rather, it confirmed the dual structure introduced by the 1993 accord, increased the duration of industry-level agreements from two to three years, linked industry-level wage increases not to Italy's expected inflation but to a European Union (EU)–wide predictive index, reiterated that decentralised bargaining should take place only on issues explicitly delegated by the industry contracts and should not concern topics already negotiated at other levels, and affirmed the need for the government to increase the diffusion of decentralised bargaining by introducing special tax advantages. The largest union confederation (the CGIL) refused to sign it.

In 2010, at the insistence of Fiat, an amendment to the 2009 agreement was added. It contained an explicit opt-out clause, which affected particularly the metalworking sector, as it allowed employers to conclude derogatory company agreements to counter the effects of a company crisis. However, minimum salary levels could not be changed; nor could inalienable worker rights. Unsurprisingly, the FIOM was strongly critical of such initiative while the other unions found it helpful to promote employment and to navigate company crises (Sanz 2011: 10).

## The enterprise level

At the enterprise level, too, the 1993 social protocol was a landmark. It did two things: it established the RSU, a new system of workplace representation that, at least for some time, reinvigorated and re-legitimised the Italian confederal unions; and it introduced, for the first time in Italian history, a series of rules regulating decentralised bargaining. These were contractual rather than legal rules, so institutionalisation was weaker than it could have been. However, compared with the previous situation—in which decentralised bargaining had depended on voluntary recognition and on the balance of power between the parties—the 1993 accord was an important step forward.

As argued above, the 1993 protocol attributed an important role to enterprise-based bargaining, and was in many ways premised on greater diffusion of enterprise bargaining than the status quo ante. Yet the available evidence fails to indicate that the coverage of enterprise bargaining increased. A survey conducted in 1995–96 by the Italian statistical agency, based on a representative sample of private-sector enterprises with at least ten employees, estimated that company bargaining involved only 10 per cent of relevant enterprises and covered 39 per cent of private sector employees (ISTAT 2002). Based on various sources of data, Rossi and Sestito (2000) conclude that enterprise bargaining in 1995–97 was less diffuse than in 1988–89 and approximately as diffuse as in 1985–86.

There was a peak of enterprise-based bargaining in 1996, presumably as a result of the 1993 accord, but it was not sufficient to bring the coverage rate back to previous levels. Overall, the time trend was negative. The propensity to negotiate at the enterprise level was strongly positively correlated with enterprise size (see also Bordogna 1997, 1999) and enterprise-specific union density. Hence, the decline in decentralised bargaining appears to have been due both to a decline in average size and to a decline in union density. This analysis also shows that there was no increase in the relative importance of wage increases negotiated at the enterprise level. Instead, increases decided unilaterally by management became more important. However, the type of wage increases negotiated seem to have changed in the direction indicated by the 1993 agreement. Wage bargaining at the enterprise level concerned mostly the 'variable wage', and was linked to enterprise productivity or profitability (Pulignano 2007). Overall, in those companies in which there were negotiations, enterprise bargaining was used to negotiate more flexible working conditions and to establish workplace partnerships.

A more recent analysis of decentralised bargaining trends confirms the above findings and shows that bargaining declined between 1998 and 2006 for a sample of private enterprises with at least 100 employees. The decline was greater for companies of smaller size (CNEL 2007). Thus, it looks as though the institutionalisation of enterprise negotiations in 1993 did not increase the diffusion of this form of bargaining. Two forces possibly operated at cross-purposes: on the one hand, the 1993 protocol provided unions with a 'right to access' that previously had been unavailable; on the other, due to the decline in their density, unions were increasingly unable to act on such a right.

Since the post-2007 global financial crisis, there have been trends towards firm-level decentralisation. The June 2011 inter-sectoral agreement on representativeness and derogations from industry-wide agreements states that company-level agreements can introduce temporary and experimental modifications to rules set by industry-wide agreements, although in accordance with the limits established by the same industry-wide accords. Relevant in this respect is the introduction of Article 8 of Law 148/2011 on the derogations of both sectoral agreements and legislation by decentralised 'proximity agreements'. Furthermore, the inter-confederal agreement on productivity of November 2012 specifies the derogatory potential of decentralised bargaining and envisages the assignment of 'full autonomy' to second-level agreements on work organisation and working time. Decentralisation at the firm level tends to assume a 'concessionary' connotation, since it often addresses restructuring and reorganisation processes, and it is institutionalised as a means to derogate from collectively agreed or even legislative rules through lower-level collective bargaining (Pedersini & Regini 2013). The derogations are meant to increase company competitiveness and boost employment levels.

## Employment relations in the public sector

The year 1993 was crucial for employment relations in the public sector as well. A 1993 union–government agreement, translated into law (Law 29/1993), introduced the principle of autonomy in collective bargaining. The main goal was to 'privatise' public sector employment relations. In accordance, employment relations in the public sector are currently formally regulated via collective agreements.

The reform created an autonomous agency, ARAN, which is a technical agency with organisational and managerial autonomy, reporting directly to the central government. It is legally responsible for all national collective bargaining in the public sector. It also oversees the equal application of collective employment contracts and, upon request, assists with specific needs of the administration involved.

The impetus for the establishment of an independent agency came from the perceived need to correct some of the unintended consequences of the 1983 reform. This had de facto introduced collective bargaining in the public sector, but had created few incentives for employers to resist union demands. In the public sector, it was argued, there was a situation of 'pluralism without market' (Bordogna 1994), in which the parties were more or less free to negotiate the terms of the employment relationship; however, due to the multiple protections enjoyed by public sector employees and the particular electoral constraints of public sector employers, they had few reasons to settle on reasonable terms.

In the mid- to late 1980s, public sector collective bargaining had contributed to both wage inflation and growing public sector deficits because politicians had been unable to resist the explosive wage demands put forward by small and extremely militant professional unions, the *comitati di base* (grassroots committees)—particularly in the school and railway bargaining units. With the creation of ARAN, public sector collective bargaining was constrained by tight budget limits imposed by the government.

In 1997, another law, the *Legge Bassanini*, integrated the previous legislative reform. It further extended contractualisation by abolishing some remaining constraints to decentralised negotiations. As a result, the structure of public sector collective bargaining is similar to the one that exists in the private sector. Accordingly, decentralised bargaining takes place under the coordination of, and within the limits indicated by, national industry agreements, which are different for the various branches of the public administration (e.g. schools, health-care services, central government). Administrative units are—at least in theory—allowed to use their own funds in second-level negotiations to reward and motivate their personnel. However, the addition of a new layer of decentralised collective bargaining does not seem to have had an appreciable effect on the productivity of the administrations involved or the quality of the services provided (Bordogna 2008).

It is not clear what effects the various reforms have had. The wage spirals that were observed in the late 1980s have disappeared, but this may be due to the fact that the macro-economic situation of the country is now considerably different. Some important progress has been made with regard to the qualitative aspects of negotiations (Ricciardi 1996)—for example, the number of job classifications has been cut, and now wage increases are more strictly tied to tasks and responsibilities, as opposed to being simply linked to automatic career progression. Moreover, new forms of labour flexibility have been introduced, such as part-time, fixed-term contracts and teleworking.

Since 2008, wage moderation for public sector employees has been imposed by legislative interventions. First, wage increases for the 2008–09 bargaining round were set at a level around half of those agreed in 2004–05 and 2006–07. Then, in May 2010, a blockade of the bargaining round was introduced for the years 2010–12, and the blockage was later extended to 2013. Other measures included a substantial restriction of decentralised agreements on pay; a wage freeze for individual salaries (excluding variable pay related to merit and performance) for the 2011–14 period; the blockage of the economic effects of career progression; the freezing of seniority pay increases for public employees not covered by collective bargaining (such as university professors, police and armed forces, diplomats, prefects and partly judges); and the cutting of end-of-service allowances. In addition, wage cuts were introduced on higher salaries. Although the Italian Constitutional Court later repealed this last measure on the grounds of discrimination, clearly the era of largesse has come to an end for Italian public sector workers.

## CONCLUSIONS

The main trend in Italian employment relations has been the emergence since 1992, and the demise in the post–global financial crisis period, of a new type of corporatism. This involves the social partners in economic policy, but produces few—if any—of the redistributive, egalitarian and de-commodifying outcomes of the classic coordinated market economy (CME) Scandinavian corporatism. More controversially, this chapter has suggested that Italian corporatism may have contributed to stagnating growth rates, more disperse wage and income distributions, and a pervasive sense of economic insecurity in the country.

Specifically, this outcome has been the result of the particular way in which the crucial tripartite agreement of 1993, regulating the collective bargaining structure, was implemented. This agreement was a very important and historic event. The new system attributed a new role to the industry-level contract: that of guaranteeing purchasing power stability. It also established that productivity increases should be distributed at the enterprise level. The problem was that most private sector workers were covered (directly or indirectly) only by the industry contract, and the second level of bargaining became less, not more, pervasive over time. In these circumstances, the institutional structure of collective bargaining created a situation in which wages were likely to grow more slowly than productivity.

To illustrate, Figure 6.2 shows wage in efficiency units over time. This is (approximately) a measure of unit labour costs, keeping factor proportions (labour/capital) constant. A growth in the index indicates that wages grow faster than (technologically warranted) labour productivity, and vice versa. Figure 6.2 shows that between 1973 and 1991, the wage in efficiency units first grew and then returned more or less to the same level. From 1992 (i.e. with the abolition of wage indexation and the onset of the new Italian corporatism), there was a sustained period of decline, which was not simply a cyclical phenomenon. In the early 2000s, wages began to grow faster than productivity again. In the recession of 2008–10, labour costs increased while productivity decreased.

**Figure 6.2   Wage in efficiency units (1973 = 100)**

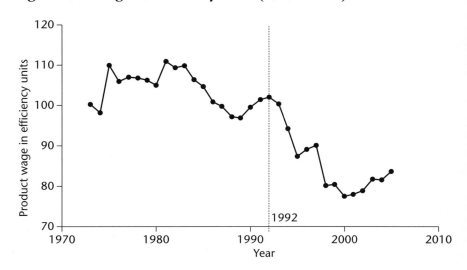

*Source:* AMECO Database of the European Commission, DG ECFIN.

This would suggest a negative impact on the relative competitiveness of the Italian economy. By 2010 productivity growth exceeded labour costs growth only slightly, by 0.3 percentage points (Meager & Speckesser 2011).

Figure 6.3 shows wages as a share of GDP over time for the four largest European economies. In 1992, Italy's wage share was the same as Germany's and larger than France's. Between 1992 and 2000, the wage share in Italy declined much faster than elsewhere. Both figures suggest that something in the Italian system of pay determination developed a gap between wage and productivity dynamics in the 1990s.

Wages that grow less than productivity (i.e. falling unit labour costs) may not necessarily be a bad thing, as this implies improvements in cost competitiveness. Obviously, not all Italian problems stem from the employment relations system. Riccardo Faini and André Sapir (2005) offer an interesting analysis, focusing on comparative advantage and sectoral specialisation. They argue that Italy has been hit by globalisation, which implies greater economic integration with emerging economies—particularly China. Unlike the other three big European countries, Italy specialises in labour-intensive sectors, and thus competes to a greater extent with China and other developing countries.

**Figure 6.3 Wage shares of GDP in large European economies**

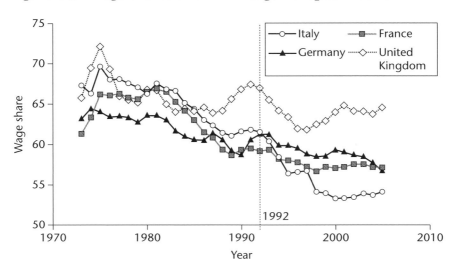

*Source:* AMECO Database of the European Commission, DG ECFIN.

Also, while other European countries upgraded their productive structures in the 1990s and moved towards higher value-added markets, Italy is the only country to have become even more specialised in traditional sectors. This phenomenon points to some historic weaknesses of the Italian economy—for example, low investments in research and development, prevalence of small firms and inefficient public services. However, it also hints at a role that the employment relations system could have played and did not: that of acting as a 'beneficial constraint' (Streeck 1997). If unit labour costs fall dramatically, if the 'low road' is an option, managers and entrepreneurs have fewer incentives to upgrade.

The main challenge for the Italian employment relations system, as well as for the Italian economy as a whole, is that of addressing the current wage emergency and, associated with it, the current sense of insecurity. Addressing this fundamental distributive issue will require a reform of collective bargaining institutions. Current reform initiatives focus on strengthening the second bargaining level. This is unlikely to lead to an equitable distribution of productivity gains short of a dramatic boost in enterprise-level bargaining. However, one of the key determinants of decentralised bargaining is the local strength of the union, and that has been declining for several years. Additional institutional mechanisms will probably be necessary.

There is also the micro-economic problem of rekindling productivity growth. This will require reforms of the educational system, the skill development system and industrial policy. Upgrading the Italian productive structure to enable it to weather the challenges of globalisation is unlikely to happen through the 'invisible hand': it will require the targeting of particular sectors and the deliberate building of capacities.

Employment relations can contribute to this policy mix particularly by addressing inefficiencies in the public sector and by increasing the quality of public services. However, this is not the direction that policy-making has taken. Emergency measures by the Monti, Letta and Renzi governments in 2012–14 have focused on further tightening the pension system, cutting public expenditure and trying to make the labour market more flexible. Governments consider it an accolade if they can say publicly that they were able to circumvent union opposition. A return to tripartite policy-making seems unlikely.

Finally, there is the problem of labour's organisational strength. This has been waning, as reflected in falling union density. The unions still maintain remarkable mobilisation capacities, their density rates are still considerable (especially in comparative perspective), and their legitimacy is bolstered by their generally good performance in workplace elections. Nonetheless, with less than 20 per cent coverage among private sector workers, they may be becoming marginal labour market actors. These trends seem likely to continue in Italy and in most other developed economies. Hence, students of employment relations should be reflecting on what a world without unions would look like. They should also consider which new institutions and social forces may emerge to take up the crucial role—embedding a market economy—historically played by unions.

## FURTHER READING

Lange, P. & Vannicelli, M. (1982) 'Strategy under stress: The Italian union movement and the Italian crisis in developmental perspective', in P. Lange, G. Ross & M. Vannicelli (eds), *Unions, Change, and Crisis*. Boston: Unwin Hyman, pp. 95–206.

Locke, R.M. (1995) *Remaking the Italian Economy*. Ithaca, NY: Cornell University Press.

Regalia, I. & Regini, M. (1998) 'Italy: The dual character of industrial relations', in A. Ferner & R. Hyman (eds), *Changing Industrial Relations in Europe*, 2nd ed. Malden, MA: Blackwell, pp. 459–503.

Regini, M. & Colombo, S. (2011) 'Italy: The rise and decline of social pacts', in S. Avdagic, M. Rhodes & J. Visser (eds), *Social Pacts in Europe*. Oxford: Oxford University Press, pp. 118–46.

Vatta, A. (2007) 'Italy', in F. Traxler & G. Huemer (eds), *Handbook of Business Interest Associations, Firm Size and Governance*. London: Routledge, pp. 204–39.

## USEFUL WEBSITES

CGIL: <www.cgil.it>.
CISL: <www.cisl.it>.
Confindustria: <www.confindustria.it>.
Ministry of Labour and Social Policies: <www.lavoro.gov.it/Pages/default.aspx>.
UIL: <www.uil.it>.

# A CHRONOLOGY OF ITALIAN EMPLOYMENT RELATIONS

| | |
|---|---|
| 1848 | First printing workers' associations. Development of craft unions. |
| 1850s | Mutual aid societies, local unions are the dominant union model. |
| 1861 | Unification of Italy (Il Risorgimento). Growth of unionism. |
| 1868 | First city-wide general strike, in Bologna. |
| 1870s | Class-conscious but local and sectional leagues of resistance supplant mutual aid societies as dominant model. Multi-unionism develops. |
| 1880s | Growth of local and socialist union organisations, particularly in northern agricultural areas. |
| 1891 | First *camera del lavoro* (labour chamber) in Milan (based on French model) as worker- and union-controlled local labour exchange. Horizontal, inclusive, localist unionism. *Rerum Novarum* (papal encyclical) fosters Catholic labour movement activism. |
| 1892 | Formation of Socialist Party of Italy. Federation of labour chambers. |
| 1900 | Industry union of railway workers. |
| 1901 | Socialists active in forming Federterra (Agricultural Workers' Union Federation), Italy's largest union, FIOM, and other important industry unions. |
| 1902 | First local, all-industry employers' federation (Monza). |
| 1906 | CGL, composed of labour chambers and industry unions. |
| 1910 | Confindustria, national employers' confederation. |
| 1918 | Catholic Union Confederation. |
| 1919 | People's Party (Catholic). |
| 1920 | First national industry collective agreement, for gas workers. |
| 1921 | Communist Party of Italy. |
| 1922 | Mussolini and Fascist Party seize power. |
| 1925 | Fascist government abolishes freedom of association, bans non-fascist unions, strikes and other forms of union action. |
| 1943–45 | Liberation of Italy, starting from the south; many strikes in the north against fascist regime and Nazi occupation. Final liberation, 25 April 1945. |
| 1944 | Pact of Rome (anti-fascist forces) to create single, non-party union confederation (CGIL). |
| 1945–48 | Coalition government of anti-fascist parties. |
| 1946 | National referendum abolishes monarchy and creates the republic. |
| 1948 | Constitution guarantees rights to union freedom and to strike. Democrazia Cristiana wins parliamentary majority and excludes Communist and Socialist parties from government. Catholics leave CGIL to form CISL. Start of decades of intense political rivalry among unions and their decline. |

| | |
|---|---|
| 1949 | Social Democrats and Republicans leave CGIL and later form UIL. Subsequently, Communist Party increasingly controls CGIL. |
| 1959 | Law (ergo omnes) allowing extension of collective agreements to the entire sector. |
| 1962 | Protocol between metalworkers' unions, ASAP and Intersind (public sector employers' associations) for enterprise-level collective bargaining. |
| 1968–73 | Long wave of industrial conflict including 1969 Hot Autumn. Unions gain and entrench workplace presence. Factory councils (*consigli di fabbrica*)—novel horizontal forms of workplace representation. Workers' Charter (Statuto dei diritti dei lavoratori) advances protection of employee and union rights. New phase of Italian employment relations: union ascendancy at all levels. Employers on the defensive. |
| 1972 | Unified union federation CGIL–CISL–UIL. |
| 1975 | Economy-wide agreements between Confindustria and CGIL-CISL-UIL on wage indexation (*scala mobile*) favours lower-paid employees. Start of decade of tripartism. |
| 1976–79 | Communist Party supports Christian Democrat government at time of economic crisis and domestic terrorism. |
| 1980 | Fiat dispute. Revolt of Fiat technicians and supervisors against union policy (march of 40,000 people). Metalworking unions vanquished. New phase: employer ascendancy and crisis for unions. |
| 1983 | Tripartite agreement on labour costs and wage indexation. Law formalises collective bargaining in public employment. |
| 1984 | Inconclusive tripartite negotiations on wage indexation lead to collapse of CGIL-CISL-UIL federation. Government decree codifies agreement with CISL and UIL. |
| 1987–89 | Rise of rank-and-file committees challenges leading role of union confederations in the public sector. |
| 1990 | First unfair dismissal legal protection for employees in 'micro-enterprises' (fewer than fifteen employees). Law restricting strikes in public sector essential services. Tripartite agreement abolishes wage indexation. |
| 1992 | Tripartite central agreement reshapes incomes policy, bargaining structure, union workplace representation structures and rights. New phase: more institutionalised employment relations. |
| 1994 | First Berlusconi (right-wing) coalition government elected, but soon collapses. |
| 1996–2001 | Centre-left governments with leading role for the Partito Democratico della Sinistra (formerly the Communist Party). Structural changes and reforms to employment and labour market policies, welfare and collective bargaining via tripartite 'social pacts' that subsequently are legislated. |

| 1998 | Italy enters European monetary union. Christmas Social Pact confirms the 1993 central agreement and new forms of decentralised concertation. |
|------|------|
| 2001 | Berlusconi's right-wing coalition regains power; this government presents a white paper promoting labour market flexibility for employers. |
| 2002 | Pact for Italy on competitiveness and social inclusion, but CGIL refuses to sign. Includes a partial temporary abolition of the application of the Workers' Charter for new hires in smaller firms. |
| 2006 | Narrow electoral victory of the centre-left coalition; new government supported by unsteady coalition of centrist, reformist and radical left parties. |
| 2007 | Tripartite reform of pensions. |
| 2008 | Centre-left government implodes; Berlusconi's right-wing coalition returns to power. |
| 2009 | Reform of collective bargaining and decentralisation. |
| 2010 | Fiat leaves Confindustria. Separate enterprise agreements introduced at Pomigliano and Mirafiori. |
| 2012 | A sovereign debt crisis. Productivity agreement promotes decentralised bargaining on work organisation and working time. Monti government adopts unilateralism in policy decisions. |
| 2013 | Start of the left-right coalition government led by Renzi. |
| 2014 | *Jobs Act*; one of the main aspects is dismissals. Other aspects are temporary contracts, minimum wages and unemployment benefits. |

# CHAPTER 7

# Employment relations in France

## Patrice Laroche[1]

There has been some controversy about whether France is a coordinated market economy (CME) or another distinctive type of capitalism associated with a high level of state intervention (Hall & Soskice 2001). While the French system appears to share some characteristics with CMEs, the absence of stable practices of collective bargaining and cooperation on labour relations issues means that it does not share all of their characteristics. Debates about France have often used the concept of exceptionalism to describe the particularity of French political and social life. According to observers, the specificity of France lies in its lack of a historical compromise between capital and labour during its industrialisation process—unlike Germany, the United Kingdom and the Scandinavian countries. After World War II, employers, state representatives and union leaders favoured the 'battle of production' over any real increase of union influence in workplace management and decision-making.

Shaped by historical, political and economic factors, French exceptionalism is paradoxical. The density of unionisation in France is among the lowest in Organisation for Economic Cooperation and Development (OECD) countries (less than 8 per cent), while the coverage of collective bargaining is among the highest (93 per cent). The first apparent paradox is France's employment relations system, in which unions and employers negotiate not only for specific members, but for all employees in a sector, through the collective agreement extension procedure. The second paradox is that the unions have become indispensable social actors, firmly anchored in French society, while simultaneously seeking social change as if from outside the system. France's low union density does not indicate an absence of union representation for employees: despite their low membership, French unions are present in most of the larger employing organisations and are able to mobilise employees on key issues. Moreover, French unions participate fully in the social system and are present at various levels of the social structure, particularly through their management activities in joint agencies (e.g. those governing unemployment insurance and pension funds). This situation seems paradoxical in light of their strategies, which are often marked by rhetoric of class conflict among their more radical members.

We offer a brief introduction to France's social and political context before examining the development of employment relations. In 2013, more than 10 per cent of the French labour force was unemployed. Unemployment tends to be greater among young people, along with less qualified workers, foreigners and, to a lesser extent, women. The employment situation has also been impacted by major structural changes. Wage-earning has become the dominant form of employment in France, representing almost 90 per cent of all jobs. There are approximately 5.7 million people employed in public services. Employment is above all becoming service based: since the late 1970s, agriculture has represented less than 2 per cent of jobs, while the industrial sector's share was cut in half between 1978 and 2007, dropping from 28 per cent to 14 per cent, thereby transforming France into a post-industrial economy.

The French political landscape has undergone three major developments since the 1980s: a decline in support for the Parti Communiste Français (PCF), a progressive decline in the centrist electorate and a rise in popularity of extreme right-wing parties. An increasing number of people have abstained from voting. Since the 1990s, the two main parties in France have been the Union pour un mouvement populaire (UMP) and the Parti socialiste (PS). The UMP is a centre-right party and a member of the European People's Party. The PS is a centre-left party and a member of the European Socialist Party. Following the outcome of the French presidential elections in 2012, François Hollande (former leader of the PS) was elected president after defeating the outgoing president, Nicolas Sarkozy.

The new president took office on 1 May 2012 and nominated Jean-Marc Ayrault as prime minister. That year, Hollande reached an agreement between the social partners to create the Contrat de génération (Generation Contract), which was designed to create jobs for young people aged 16–25 and keep workers aged over 56 in employment. In early 2013, unions and employers agreed to safeguard career paths by signing an Accord national interprofessionnel (ANI, or national interprofessional agreement). The president used consultation mechanisms to implement these reforms. Under his leadership, a social conference was organised in 2012 and subsequently institutionalised as an annual event. In an effort to gauge the future, President Hollande also implemented a general strategy and forecasting commission, established in April 2013. The commission provides a discussion forum to help prepare for reforms and consider economic and social matters. Following the April 2014 municipal elections, the president nominated Manuel Valls as prime minister and adopted a more social-liberal approach to government policies. Among his other measures, the president put the Pacte de responsabilité (Responsibility Pact) back at the centré of the new government's future policies. This measure, announced by the president on 31 December 2013, provides for a reduction in labour costs, the modernisation of the tax system and greater administrative simplicity for companies in an effort to promote hiring and social dialogue. Some unionists, particularly the communist-leaning Confédération générale du travail (CGT), argue that a reduction in social security contributions to obtain employment is a 'fool's bargain'. This echoes the views of some French economists, who hold that lower taxes have no impact on demand. Others, however, argue that it is appropriate for the government to try to improve the low profit margins of companies.

This was the social context in which the third social conference was held in 2014. The CGT and the Confédération générale du travail-Force ouvrière (CGT-FO) union confederation, joined by the Federation Syndicale Unitaire (FSU)—the main national education federation—soon left the conference, condemning the government's methods. Discontent continued to fester among the unions. In particular, the CGT and CGT-FO have denounced Prime Minister Manuel Valls' concessions to the Mouvement des Entreprises de France (MEDEF) confederation of employers (discussed later in the chapter). The CGT and CGT-FO argue that the government is too sympathetic to employers and their demands. The relationship of Manuel Valls' government with the unions degenerated in this context. The government resorted to a form of corporatism that is typical in France.

## THE INDUSTRIAL RELATIONS ACTORS

The French employment relations system has been described as a 'polarised pluralism' system, in which the role of the social partners is highly politicised and ideologically fragmented (Van Ruysseveldt & Visser 1996). Because unions and employers' organisations have been unable to develop stable practices of collective bargaining and cooperation on labour relations issues, the government has often intervened to regulate the employment relationship. The French state thus plays an important role in the employment relations system.

## The unions

The union movement is characterised by several organisations that have overlapping interests with similar categories of employees. This unusual phenomenon partly explains the fall in the number of union members since the 1970s. Union density dropped from 23 per cent in the 1970s to just 7 per cent in 2014. There are five major national union confederations that are recognised: the CGT, the CGT-FO, the Confédération Française démocratique du travail (CFDT), the Confédération Française des travailleurs chrétiens (CFTC) and the Confédération Française de l'encadrement-confédération générale des cadres (CFE-CGC). Until a law was enacted in 2008, any union belonging to these five major confederations could obtain immediate and automatic recognition in workplaces. After 2008, unions affiliated with the five confederations had to prove their representativeness, particularly through elections.

Apart from Jean-Claude Mailly, who remains at the head of the CGT-FO, every other union and employers' organisation in France replaced its leaders in 2013. Within two years, a new generation of leaders took office. But this new generation appears to have adopted the strategic positions of the previous one.

## CGT

At its founding in 1895, the CGT claimed to belong to the revolutionary movement, with its primary objective being to end the capitalist system. The hard line in the 1906 Charter of Amiens steered the confederation away from any possibility of social dialogue. On the one hand, the charter's references to class struggle equate employment negotiations with the compromise of union actions; on the other, aspirations to transform the state radically make it difficult for unions to build bridges with the state.

At the end of World War II, the CGT became involved in the national reconstruction effort, despite strong opposition in the PCF about the best ways to proceed. The influx of new members along with the rise of communism led to statutory reforms. Reassembling the existing forces resulted in a split. There were violent strikes in 1947, against the backdrop of the emerging Cold War. These strikes were condemned by the union's secretary general, Léon Jouhaux, and his reformist platform. The start of 1948 saw the birth of the CGT-FO, led by Jouhaux. In the mid-1950s, the CGT decided to put its permanent support behind the PCF, to which it delegated all decisions about its future.

There was a renewal of union militancy in the 1960s. During the social disruption of May 1968, the CGT described the student movement as 'bourgeois' and condemned the students. The drafting of the Grenelle Agreements, which provided for the establishment of the délégué syndical (union delegate), was an effort to halt the spread of social movements throughout the working class—but they continued to grow. There was a new development in the 1980s: the beginnings of the CGT asserting its independence from the PCF. Subsequently, the CGT has argued for 'proposal-based unionism', including collective bargaining as a legitimate form of action (Andolfatto & Labbé 2007). The CGT profoundly modified its statutes in 1995 by abandoning its mandate to transform a capitalist society founded on private ownership into a socialist society founded on collective ownership (Article 1 of the CGT statutes).

Since March 2013, Thierry Lepaon has held the post of secretary general of the CGT. His nomination occurred after several months of discord within the CGT. Afterwards, the CGT experienced much internal division, with one radical faction hostile to both the CFDT and the socialist government, and another more reformist faction. Thus Lepaon faces a set of contradictory pressures and has had difficulty defining clear objectives. Furthermore, the CGT is engaged in open competition with the Solidaires unions, as demonstrated by the June 2014 conflict in the Société Nationale des Chemins de Fer Français (SNCF). Lepaon is against any change regarding the rights of employees. He has refused to sign the ANI on the protection of employment, stating that such a law would lead to overriding agreements providing fewer benefits to employees. The CGT claimed 729,000 members in 2014 and remained the largest union confederation in terms of its electoral results and membership.

## CGT-FO

The Force ouvrière (FO) was formed in 1948 following a split within the CGT. In the 1950s, it rapidly began focusing its efforts on contractual policies, which allowed it to build privileged partnerships with governments during the 1960s. From its beginnings, the CGT-FO promoted itself as the heir to the older CGT that had once signed the Charter of Amiens and refused all cooperation with political parties. The CGT-FO argued that the interests of employees differed from those of employers, and so remained wary of participation. Nonetheless, it took part in many negotiations and signed several agreements during the Trente Glorieuses (Glorious Thirty), the years 1945–75, when there was rapid population and economic growth in France. The agreements included a supplementary pension plan for senior management (Association générale des institutions de retraite des cadres, or AGIRC) in 1947, the benefits plan for non-management employees (Union Nationale de Interprofessionnelle de retraite des salaries, or UNIRS) in 1957, and the unemployment insurance plan (Union nationale interprofession-nelle pour l'emploi dans l'industrie et le commerce–Association pour l'emploi dans l'industrie et le commerce, or UNEDIC-ASSEDIC) in 1958. The economic turnaround during the 1970s created difficulties for the FO's contractual policies. The union became less conciliatory and introduced tougher policies towards government and employers, altering the confederation's image in the 1980s and 1990s. In 2004, the CGT-FO began questioning its own future and sought to retain its dwindling membership by adopting a more open approach to discussions. One of the CGT-FO's peculiarities is the difficulty it has experienced in establishing itself in the private sector since its inception. This has deprived the FO of a strong foundation on which to base its stated aim to unite all workers. The CGT-FO claims 800,000 members, a number that is much overstated. According to Andolfatto and Labbé (2007), the FO's membership was closer to 300,000 in 2006.

## CFTC

The CFTC was founded in 1919, after World War I, drawing its inspiration from 'Christian social morality'. It is steadfast in its refusal to see employment relations through a prism of class struggle. In this sense, it does not generally see strikes as a relevant means of union action (though it does not exclude strikes), but instead chooses to promote dialogue and human dignity. Before World War II, the CFTC was fairly well established with employees, but had difficulty establishing its credibility with the working class. It has also been discredited by the CGT. With its close ties to Christian democracy, the CFTC played no part in the Front populaire, although it did participate in a few protests during the spring of 1936. It was not among the signatories of the Matignon Agreements. Another peculiarity of the CFTC is the importance it places on family-oriented policies. It was the CFTC that initiated the March 1932 Landry Act, which promotes family allowances for all employees. The union listed 141,000 members in 2006, but some experts estimate its membership to be closer to 100,000. The reformist stance adopted by the CFTC in the twenty-first century has raised fears that it may soon become marginalised. Nonetheless, the CFTC sees itself as one of France's three main historic reformist unions, alongside the CGT-FO and the CGC.

## CFDT

The CFDT began as a mainstream faction of the CFTC, which decided to abandon any reference to Christian social morality during its 1964 convention. While preserving a few ideas from the old CFTC (e.g. the family as the 'basic unit of society', spiritual requirements), the CFDT's statutes legitimised the role of Marxism in union action. This ambiguity occasionally led the CFDT to engage in extreme behaviour; it drew closer to the CGT during the 1970s. In 1978, its secretary general, Edmond Maire (1971–88), recognised the CFDT's deviation from the CFTC and helped change the CFDT, steering it towards a more reformist position.

Through the CFDT's demands for the right to discuss working conditions, it became the driving force behind the important 1982 Auroux Laws, creating an impetus for collective bargaining in work-places. Simultaneously the CFDT began to steer away from strikes and militant action. In 1992, Nicole Notat (secretary general 1992–2002) implemented a policy that broke away from the traditions of the French labour movement. The CFDT agreed to recognise the legitimacy of employers and began referring to market economies as 'a positive reality', while emphasising the value of negotiations and, consequently, collective agreements. During its 42nd congress, held in 1992, the CFDT confirmed its reformist stance and reconfirmed its position that all union action must be geared primarily towards employment.

During the November–December social movement of 1995, the CFDT supported the intent of the Juppé government's pension plan reforms. This was met with hostility from the CGT and the FO, and to a large extent from the general public; many of them took to the streets. That same reformist stance led CFDT general secretary François Chérèque (2002–2012) to sign a pension agreement with the Raffarin government in May 2003, creating a rift with most of the other unions and especially with the CGT, which contested the agreement. In November 2012, Laurent Berger replaced Chérèque at the head of the CFDT. Unlike changes in personnel at the tension-filled CGT, Berger's nomination was planned long in advance and enjoyed full support within the CFDT. The new leader is in accord with the CFDT's reformist stance. By signing the ANI on employment security, in opposition to the CGT and the CGT-FO, Berger embodies the social reform he seeks to implement. The CFDT has around 650,000 members, though it claims 800,000.

## CFE-CGC

The CFE-CGC is a special case among French unions. For decades, it claimed 'categorical representation' for employees holding management status (*cadres*). In 1944, several management and sales representative unions came together as the Confédération générale des cadres, which was recognised as nationally representative in 1946. The CGC quickly generated many benefits for managers, including a management pension plan, the Association professionnelle pour l'emploi des cadres, collective agreement amendments and a nominating council for managers during workplace elections. In 1987, the CGC became the CFE-CGC to demonstrate its commitment to representing all management personnel, not just *cadres*.

Carole Couvert became the head of the CFE-CGC in 2013. As the union's former secretary general, she was vocal in her opposition to predecessor Bernard Van Craynest's management approach; her election came at the end of a three-year internal conflict within the CFE-CGC, which led to much disagreement among its members. Her presidency makes the CFE-CGC the only union headed by a woman. As the new CFE-CGC president, Couvert brings a new profile and approach to French unionism. Breaking with the outgoing president's practice, she has announced plans to change the union's modes of action, particularly through the principle of participatory democracy.

According to its data, the CFE-CGC had 160,000 members in 2013, down from 398,700 in 1978. While the CFE-CGC remains eager to preserve its categorical role, it must contend with consequences arising from new provisions for union representativeness, provisions that bind it to its electorate. After considering a number of bridge-building projects, particularly with the Union nationale des syndicats autonomes (UNSA) in 2010, the CFE-CGC embraced a possible 'third union route' that would bring together all 'minority' confederations.

Beyond these five nationally recognised confederations, France has unaffiliated unions, referred to as autonomous or independent unions. They distinguish themselves by attracting professional members. The Groupe de dix (Group of Ten) was founded in 1981 and originally brought together ten federations and autonomous unions, seven of which had originated from the split between the CGT and the CGT-FO in 1947. During the 1990s, the Solidaires Unitaires Démocratiques unions joined the Groupe de dix, breathing new life into an organisation that had become more of a think-tank than a union. In 2004, the Groupe de dix changed its name to the Union syndicale Solidaires. In 2009, it listed 45 unions and federations among its members (Pernot 2005). Solidaires has formulated proposals to reform the retirement system, which it deems unjust and inefficient, and has taken part in every strike and protest day held against the 2010 retirement reforms. Solidaires argues that social security contributions should not be increased, and nor should their durations, opting instead to focus on the earned rate of return—that is, dividends—along with other benefits offered to shareholders. During its 2014 congress, Solidaires renewed its national secretariat with the departure of Annick Coupé, who was replaced by two co-spokespersons, Cécile Gondard-Lalanne (Solidaires, Unitaires et Démocratiques—Postes, Télégraphes et Téléphone, or SUD-PTT) and Eric Beynel (Solidaires Douanes). Solidaires has been very critical of François Hollande's policies and has announced plans to hold campaigns on the cost of capital and against the large transatlantic trade agreement.

The UNSA resulted from a 1992 meeting between the Fédération de l'édcation nationale and four other unions that had once belonged to the Groupe de dix but had grown hostile to the Groupe de dix's dissenting approach. This partnership progressed gradually and became a union organisation that enjoys some support from employees, particularly those working in public services.

## The decline of union membership

France's unions have experienced a significant decrease in membership since the mid-1970s. In 50 years, general union density has dropped from approximately 20 per cent to 8 per cent (see Figure 7.1). Union coverage is estimated to be only 5 per cent in the private sector, and approximately 15 per cent in the public sector. Experts have suggested a number of reasons for this—none of which is mutually exclusive.

The drop in union membership can be explained by the economic crisis experienced in the second half of the 1970s. The 'oil shocks' in 1974 and 1979 precipitated a decline of the old union strongholds. Factory closures, layoffs, the rise of precarious employment and stagnant purchasing power created an unfavourable context for union growth. In addition, French society has undergone significant changes. One of these is the larger role of individuals in society. The rise of individualism in workplaces may partly explain a growing dissatisfaction with unions and the devaluation of collective action. This development also explains why unions have difficulty in recruiting young employees, many of whom are better trained and more critical of unions than their elders. Enterprises increasingly have introduced individualised human resource management (HRM) practices (including individual arrangements for pay, training and performance management) in response to a phenomenon that seems to reflect the increasing preference of individuals to differentiate themselves and be treated as people with some autonomy of judgement.

**Figure 7.1   Union membership**

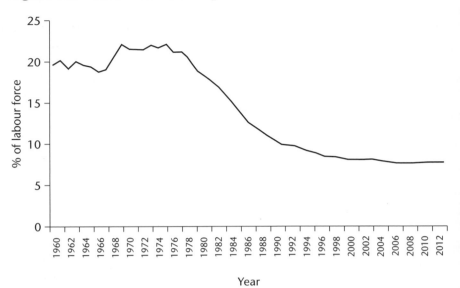

*Source:* OECD (2014a).

Divisions and politicisation in the unions may also help to explain why unionisation is so low in France. Union divisions complicate the way union strategies are perceived. In addition, unions face a decline in the ideologies that once fuelled their actions and overall direction. The collapse of the communist bloc in Europe ruptured the historic link between the CGT and the PCF, but it also dealt a huge blow to the application of communist values and the pursuit of communism's objectives through union action.

There is a tendency among French employees to criticise their union representatives for becoming 'professional' representatives—that is, they spend more and more time working for the union, some of them becoming full-time union representatives. This increases the risk of a disconnect between militant union work inside the union and the work of representing employees. Moreover, one of the most oft-cited reasons for comparatively low unionisation rates compared with other countries is the lack of services provided for union members. Unlike unions in some other countries, particularly those in Scandinavia, French unions do not offer their members specific services. In France, an agreement between a union and employer is applied to all employees, whether or not they are union members.

This may encourage free riders and help to explain France's low rate of union membership.

Nevertheless, French unions are still important actors in the collective bargaining process with governments and employers. For example, in August 2008 the CGT and the CFDT leaned heavily on the government to ratify a law modifying rules of union representation to ensure greater legitimacy for union representatives.

## The representative status of unions

Before the 2008 law, any union affiliated with one of the five nationally recognised confederations could establish a union section within a workplace, regardless of its membership, legal form or objectives. After the 2008 law was ratified, unions were no longer assumed to be representative without first passing an electoral test and winning at least 10 per cent of votes. Expanding on the 2004 Fillon Law, the 2008 law also modified the validity requirements for signed agreements between the social partners. Any agreement made in an employing organisation must be signed by one or more unions, which are deemed representative after obtaining at least 30 per cent of votes during the first round of the previously held workplace elections (for works council and personnel delegates). Further, having obtained the majority of votes during those same elections, no opposition must be voiced by one or more representative unions (for an example, see Box 7.1).

---

**BOX 7.1   NEW RULES OF BARGAINING AT THE WORKPLACE LEVEL**

As an example of the post-2009 law in practice, if five unions put forward lists of candidates to participate in the professional election, three of whom do not meet the 10 per cent threshold defined by the law, several configurations can challenge the right of opposition. Imagine that the CFTC obtains 8 per cent of votes, the CGT-FO 9 per cent, the CFE-CGC 8 per cent, the CFDT 35 per cent and the CGT 40 per cent. The CFDT and CGT could sign collective agreements alone (each has >30 per cent) or together (35 + 40 per cent), but in the latter case no other union could exert its right of opposition. The collective agreement is then valid despite the absence of the right of opposition. These validation rules of collective agreements were enacted in 2009.

---

## The employers

Employer representation is mainly structured around three organisations: the Conseil national du patronat Français (CNPF), which became the MEDEF in 1998, the Confédération générale des petites et moyennes entreprises (CGPME), and the Union professionnelle artisanale (UPA). With a membership of 750,000 employers, MEDEF is the largest of these organisations. The traditional attitude of employers towards social dialogue is broadly hostile. Employers and their organisations have helped to shift the centre of legal gravity towards the sector, with the specific intention of 'neutralising' the company in order to limit union influence in the workplace (Tchobanian 1996). Sector agreements that fail to integrate components linked to work organisation become less constraining to companies. Beyond certain exceptions—for example, a few large corporations like Renault—employers have long regarded social dialogue as prejudicial to their legitimate autonomy in terms of managerial prerogatives.

Nonetheless, MEDEF has embarked on a complete turnaround regarding collective bargaining over the past decade. For that reason, the 'social rebuilding' draft adopted by the CNPF in 1997 represents a fundamental change in the position taken by employers' organisations towards social dialogue in enterprises, and collective bargaining in particular. It seeks to reconsider the link between the law and employment contracts. Its aim is to overturn the hierarchy of norms and to transform a system in which law prevails over employment contracts (top-down) into a system where the employment contract, which includes the consent of both parties, would prevail over other norms (bottom-up). Then the law preserves its role in defining general objectives while maintaining public order.

Regretting France's lack of social pacts, like those found in a range of other European countries (see Chapters 8 and 9), MEDEF has attempted to promote the development of national agreements under the stewardship of its president Laurence Parisot (elected in 2005). MEDEF was also responsible for the common positions reached in 2001 and 2008, which sought to demonstrate its willingness to position itself as a social partner, along with its attempts to reform the legal system that governs employment relations. This partnership strategy came with several conditions. Of particular interest among these are the similarities between its social rebuilding proposals and the legal provisions introduced under the laws of May 2004 and August 2008, in terms of MEDEF's aim to reform union access rules regarding representation. These changes seem to point to a major reversal of attitude by employers' organisations towards the legitimacy of collective bargaining at the workplace level.

In July 2013, Pierre Gattaz succeeded Laurence Parisot as president of MEDEF. Among his first statements, the new president asked for a €100 billion income tax and charge reduction for companies. His election therefore helped MEDEF's liberal fringe to gain ground. There is increasing pressure from MEDEF members who are exasperated by income taxes that are increasing and an economic situation that is not improving. For small entrepreneurs, radical discourse is gaining ground. In mid-2014, a report by the Economic, Social and Environmental Council (Conseil économique, social et environnemental, or CESE), *Social Dialogue, a Vector of Democracy, Social Progress and Competitiveness*, failed to go through due to joint abstention from the CGT and MEDEF. Gattaz does not appear to be especially open to social dialogue; he even refuses to comply with the job-creation commitments under François Hollande's competitiveness pact, which grants financial assistance to employers.

This ill-will on behalf of French employers is part of a wider set of debates and discussions about the representativeness of employers' organisations, which none of the various reports and legislative bills on union representativeness has sought to question. MEDEF remains in a dominant position but, unlike the other employers' organisations (e.g. the CGPME and UPA), it does not gain its legitimacy from any election beyond industrial tribunals, where, for certain councils, alliances between employers' organisations make representativeness difficult to gauge. The representativeness of employers' organisations at the inter-professional level is under the prime minister's mandate, while the representativeness of unions at the sector level is granted after an administrative investigation by the labour minister. Debates about the representativeness of employers' organisations face several issues, including those that involve companies belonging to many organisations (e.g. at the national and local levels), and those that address whether or not representativeness should be measured according to the number of employees, not the number of employers. The Combrexelle Report on employer representativeness, issued in 2013 to the labour minister, suggests using the employers' organisations' own membership criteria as a measure. A membership representativeness threshold of 8 per cent at the sector and national levels appears to satisfy the various employers' organisations involved.

## The state

The state plays a very important role in French social relations (Crouch 1993). In the German co-determination tradition, unions and employers' organisations have a contractual relationship. They prefer to keep the state out of negotiations. In France, it is assumed that the parties are unable to reach agreement. Under such conditions, it would appear necessary to involve the state. The result is a process conducted as if the rights of employees are better protected through public intervention than by agreement between the social partners. This type of reasoning reveals an obvious defiance of a company's main stakeholders. Defiance is a guiding principle underlying the actions of the state.

State intervention in employee–employer relations is not new in France—even if, for many years, the state merely preoccupied itself with enforcing law and order and calling in the army whenever strikes took a turn towards insurgency. State interventionism can be traced back to the very beginnings of unionism and the Waldeck-Rousseau Law (1884). In 1892, work inspectors were commissioned to enforce the first laws that were passed to safeguard against child labour. Nonetheless, it was not until 1906 that Council President Georges Clemenceau appointed the socialist René Viviani as France's first labour minister. The new ministerial position was created when the CGT's influence was growing and there was a turbulent social context. There were 1300 strikes lasting an average of nineteen days in 1906.

During World War I, the Ministry of Labour and Social Security had the challenge of organising the war effort and finding a workforce that could replace workers who had been sent to the front. Greater prominence was also given to the labour minister under the Front populaire government, with the 1936 Matignon Agreements paving the way for major social progress.

The state became a definitive and essential player in employment relations after World War II. The introduction of social security in 1945 marked the beginnings of the welfare state. Earlier, the state had a smaller role, restricted to regulatory functions (e.g. the police, army and justice). The Trente Glorieuses post-1945 period was ripe for social change, not least through new legislation. This had benefits for unions and employers, as they could now wait for the state to settle social questions. More recently, however, the state has aimed to participate in building compromise, rather than imposing decisions. Then, later, the state legislates and provides a legal guarantee. Unions faced a new form of presidential power following the election of Nicolas Sarkozy in 2007. This president placed great pressure on national employment relations negotiations, steering their content while implementing legislation that certain unions criticised as socially regressive (e.g. deregulating the organisation working time and health-care expenses, privatising Gaz de France). In France, then, there was no contractual autonomy for the social partners. However, under François Hollande, the state has displayed more respect for submissions by the social partners than it did under Sarkozy.

## THE PROCESS OF EMPLOYMENT RELATIONS

### Employee representation within enterprises

The employee representation system depends on various roles to ensure the functionality of its grievance process (*délégué du personnel*, or personnel delegate), its information and consultation process (*comité d'entreprise*, or works council), and its claims and negotiations process (*délégué syndical*, or union delegate). Any company in the private sector must hold elections for personnel representatives when it reaches a certain employee threshold. Companies (or establishments) with at least eleven employees must elect personnel delegates, while those with 50 employees or more must assign a works council, along with a *comité d'hygiène, de sécurité et des conditions de travail* (CHSCT, or Health, Safety and Improvement of Working Conditions Committee).

The personnel delegate's principal mandate is to approach the employer with any individual or collective request involving pay, and to monitor the application of the Labour Code, along with all other applicable rules within the company (e.g. internal regulations, labour conventions, collective agreements). The personnel delegate therefore acts as a spokesperson for the company's employees. The personnel delegate must be elected every four years. The required number of personnel delegates is determined by the number of employees working in the company.

A works council must be created for any company employing 50 people or more. Its principal mandate is to consider the collective expression and interests of employees when decisions are made about the company's management, as well as its economic and financial development. To help the works council fulfil its mandate, the employer is obliged to provide a certain amount of economic, financial and social information on a periodic basis, or on certain occasions. The employer is also obliged to consult the works council before making specific economic decisions—for example, about the size and nature of the workforce. For this, the employer must provide works council members with information and hold discussions with them before making major decisions. The employer, however, is not specifically bound by the advice of the works council, and retains sole control over the final decision. The works council must also coordinate, monitor and participate in the employer's social and cultural activities (e.g. restaurant vouchers, sporting activities, holiday camps, holiday gift exchanges). To ensure the proper functioning of the works council, the employer must provide it with an annual subsidy equal to 0.2 per cent of the current year's gross salaries.

The union delegate is the employer's key partner in matters of collective bargaining in workplaces. Since ratification of the August 2008 law, unions are no longer considered representative by default without first passing the electoral test and obtaining at least 10 per cent of the votes. Because the duties of the union delegate are compatible with those of the personnel delegate and members of the works council, a single individual could fulfil a number of roles, particularly in small and medium-sized enterprises (SMEs). The number of union delegates for each union varies according to the number of employees working in the company. Union delegates have many functions within the company. They must represent their union when dealing with employers and act as coordinators for the local company union. They must take part in negotiations and be signatories to collective agreements within companies. All such cases involve an obligation to negotiate, not conclude, agreements with the union. Each year, for example, the employer is obligated to negotiate pay along with the duration and organisation of working hours (Laroche 2009). The presence of union delegates at the workplace level is particularly low in the private sector, especially in small enterprises, whereas union presence is much greater in larger enterprises (see Table 7.1.).

The creation of a CHSCT in enterprises employing at least 50 people has been mandatory since the Auroux Laws were enacted in 1982. The committee's mandate is to monitor employee health and safety in

**Table 7.1   Union delegate presence at the workplace level**

| Number of employees | Public sector (%) | Private sector (%) |
|---------------------|-------------------|--------------------|
| <10                 | 15                | 2.4                |
| 10–49               | 35                | 16                 |
| 50–99               | 65                | 44                 |
| 100–499             | 74                | 65                 |
| >500                | 76                | 79                 |

Note: Numbers rounded.

Source: Adapted from DARES, French Ministry of Labor, 2010.

the workplace. The employer must therefore consult the CHSCT, while the latter may request expert appraisal, at the employer's expense, in the event of an important project that modifies health, safety or working conditions.

## Employee participation and collective bargaining

Collective bargaining in France takes place on three different levels: first, the social partnership or national level; second, the industry or sector level; and third, the workplace, enterprise, company or establishment level. These negotiation levels are not necessarily mutually exclusive.

Social partnership negotiations are at the national level. The actors who intervene at this level represent the union confederations and large employers' organisations (MEDEF, the CGPME and the UPA). National-level negotiations aim to produce framework agreements while preserving the social protection systems put in place after World War II by way of contractual agreement. Such agreements may cover conditions relating to retirement or protection against unemployment. Examples include the 1958 agreement that introduced the Association pour l'emploi dans l'industrie et le commerce (Assédic), which aims to supply replacement income in the event of job loss, and the 1967 agreement promoting supplementary pensions.

National-level negotiations developed in an antagonistic way following the Grenelles Agreements and helped set conditions to ensure both a reduction in the working week in 1968, and a monthly basis for wages in 1970. In the more difficult economic context of the late 1980s, such negotiations allowed the social partners to agree jointly to new rules in accordance with the then current economic constraints on companies. National negotiations also helped establish provisions for 'early retirement and employment' (Early Retirement for Jobs Scheme, or ARPE), revise management conditions for the unemployed, and redefine specific conditions for collective bargaining.

These types of negotiations have led to the 2009 ANI on training and the development of career paths. This agreement is based on the 2008 national agreement on labour market modernisation, and provides major guidelines for training reform. The 2008 ANI on labour market modernisation was implemented in mid-2009. Among other provisions, the agreement provides for a portability system regarding supplementary health coverage. Thus, after termination of a work contract, employees who are entitled to unemployment insurance benefits may continue to benefit from their company's additional health guarantees during their period of unemployment for a maximum of nine months, regardless of the reason for the termination.

While the national negotiation level aims to build a foundation for agreements about employment conditions at the lower echelons, the sector level has long been the centre of collective bargaining in France. This is where negotiations take place for collective agreements that regulate working conditions for employees working in the sector, including minimum pay, job classifications and training. Collective agreements seek to improve the conditions contained in the Labour Code and adapt them to the realities of the sector, and to handle issues that fall beyond the scope of the law. More than 90 per cent of private sector employees are covered by a collective agreement. Collective agreements cover general employment conditions in the sector, while workplace agreements generally focus on more specific aspects.

Negotiations at the workplace level began in the 1980s under the Auroux Laws, particularly the law of 1982, which established mandatory annual negotiation (*négociation annuelle obligatoire*) of pay and working time. Before that time, collective bargaining in workplaces had experienced only limited development due to the absence of

---

**BOX 7.2  SOCIAL DIALOGUE AT GENERALI FRANCE**

Social dialogue at Generali France (an insurance and financial products company) is very dynamic and the HR department has undertaken a dialogue with all the unions, except the CGT-FO (which won 17 per cent of votes in the election). In this company, we can see two forms of unionism. First, the CGT-FO considers that there are competing interests between employers and employees. Second, the CFDT considers that it is important to construct change jointly through dialogue and with full respect for the other party, even if the interests of the parties differ. Some unionists within Generali blame the HR department for fostering the division between the unions. According to the CGT-FO, the HR department speaks only to the CFDT (25 per cent of votes) and to the CFE-CGC (27 per cent); these two together make up the majority, and do not deny that they have privileged access to the employer. They also note that collective bargaining is changing in workplaces. Unions need to become more involved in the broader scope of workplace bargaining, such as training, work organisation, work–life balance and gender issues.

*Source:* Guillot & Rubia (2009).

union representation in workplaces. It was not until 1968 that a legal framework was put into place to provide representative unions with an opportunity to create local unions and designate union delegates in workplaces. More recently, collective bargaining at the workplace Level has developed in an antagonistic way under the 35-hour Aubry Laws. The 1998 and 2000 laws on the reduction of working time, known as the Aubry I and II Laws, led to certain companies negotiating with union delegates or, in their absence, with employees mandated by the unions.

Social dialogue in France is far from anaemic, despite the fact that companies with more than 500 employees have signed more than 21 per cent of agreements by themselves. In 2012, the industrial sector was responsible for 38 per cent of the collective agreements signed in that year, despite employing no more than 19 per cent of the work-force. The service sector represents more than half (57 per cent) of all agreements signed on behalf of 74 per cent of the workforce. However, certain sector collective agreements make up for the scarcity of company negotiations in the more fragmented sectors, such as construction.

## Representative elections

At the workplace level, the population criterion is measured during the Work Council elections or, failing this, during the personnel delegate or works council elections. Unions seeking representativeness recognition in a workplace must obtain at least 10 per cent of votes in the election. The population criterion regarding representativeness at the sector level and at the national level must be measured by aggregating the election results for workplaces in the sector or national level. A union must obtain at least 8 per cent of votes to become representative of the sector or national level. Its territorial implementation must also be balanced at the sector level.

For the 2013–17 period, the five previously recognised unions can maintain their representativeness only by rising above the 8 per cent voting threshold (see Table 7.2). In relative terms, the 'reformist' unions (the CFDT, CGC and CFTC) exceed the 50 per cent threshold, which prevents the other two (the CGT and CGT-FO) from blocking agreements. By exceeding 30 per cent, the CGT is the only union that can sign agreements on its own, unless three other unions, including the CFDT, exercise their right to oppose. The validity of a workplace agreement is subordinate to the signature of one or more representative unions having obtained at least 30 per cent of the vote during the first round of the last workplace elections (works councils, personnel delegates), and in the absence of opposition from one or more

**Table 7.2   Results of national representativeness elections**

| Unions | % of votes cast | Representative | Relative weights (%) |
|---|---|---|---|
| CGT | 27 | Yes | 31 |
| CFDT | 26 | Yes | 30 |
| CGT-FO | 16 | Yes | 18 |
| CFE-CGC | 9.4 | Yes | 10.8 |
| CFTC | 9.3 | Yes | 10.6 |
| UNSA | 4.3 | No | – |
| Solidaires | 3.5 | No | – |
| Other unions (<1%) | 4.4 | No | – |

*Note:* Numbers rounded.
*Source:* Adapted from DARES, French Ministry of Labor, March 2013.

representative unions which have obtained a majority of the vote during the same election.

## Industrial disputes

Strikes have always been the preferred mode of action for unions in France, contributing to the country's reputation for worker unrest. Striking is an element of French social history. The right to strike is enshrined in the Constitution of 1958, which defines it as 'the collective and concerted cessation of work in order to successfully conclude pre-established professional demands that the employer refuses to satisfy'. But the right to strike is not absolute. Statutory or collective bargaining provisions may limit recourse to such methods to specific circumstances. For instance, the principle of public service continuity requires that minimal public services are maintained in France. The concept of minimal services is also found in other developed economies. Similarly, the protection of public health and safety represents a constitutional principle that takes precedence over the right to strike. Also, collective agreements often contain provisions that require prior notice, or even conciliatory procedures, before any strike can be called. Such provisions can often limit a union's ability to strike.

New forms of industrial action, other than strikes, have been deployed since the 1980s, including walkouts, petitions and overtime bans. These have not led to the end of industrial disputes, but to different methods of protest that reflect a changing workforce (Bévort & Jobert 2008). Contemporary industrial disputes can be linked to two phenomena: the decline of strikes as a primary expression of conflict and the simultaneous rise of new forms of protest. Therefore, we look beyond working days lost (WDL) due to industrial disputes as a way to measure this decline. WDL linked to strikes are on the decline. More than 3 million WDL each year were recorded at the end of the 1970s, but since the mid-1990s, this number has been much lower: between 250,000 and 500,000. Significant disparities have also been observed regarding specific sectors: in 2007, 654 WDL were recorded for every 1000 employees working in the transport sector, but a mere seventeen in retail and construction. Union presence in the establishment is an essential determining factor. Strikes are more frequent in the public service, where jobs are protected and unions have a greater presence. This helps to explain France's comparatively high ranking in international comparisons of WDL in industrial disputes.

Conflict therefore continues to be an aspect of employment relations. The use of forms of social dialogue—particularly collective bargaining—is intended to settle the claims of a variety of interests by cooperation. But the willingness of legislators and the social partners to cooperate may not coincide with reality. The dialectic between conflict and negotiation is fuelled by two processes: conflict and collective bargaining. These complement one another. Workplace conflict, then, is not necessarily a failure of negotiation, but may be the route to a settlement (Béroud et al. 2008).

## CURRENT ISSUES

The union membership situation differs from that in most other developed economies. In France, union density—especially in the private sector—is comparatively low, while the rate of collective agreement coverage is comparatively high. In this context, increasing the membership density contributes to several objectives. The first involves making unions more representative of the labour force as a whole. An analysis of France's main unions reveals an over-representation of men over the age of 45, along with employees from the public sector and large corporations (Andolfatto & Labbé 2007). This is reflected in an 'employee representation deficit' in SMEs, which employ more than 40 per cent of the workforce. However, less than a quarter of SMEs (employing fewer than 50 employees) has a union delegate. It is an important challenge to strengthen the link between unions and employees by promoting union membership.

Another objective of increasing union membership is to strengthen the financial autonomy of the unions. French unions are too dependent on the state and employers. Unions would have more demonstrable autonomy if their finances relied to a greater extent on members' subscriptions.

Enterprises should also improve the dissemination of information through less formal channels. The effectiveness of social dialogue depends on the quality of interaction between managers and employees (Laroche 2009). It is also important to consider the criteria for employer representativeness, which has not yet been reformed. Despite the increasing use of sophisticated HR management methods, employees still experience difficulty in obtaining reliable information about the operations of many enterprises. An investigation by the National Association of Human Resources Directors shows that most employees claim to lack information surrounding their company's strategic objectives. Despite the improvement of internal communications, communication is often deemed insufficient.

Comparisons with other developed economies show that dialogue between French employees and employers seems to be less frequent and more conflictual. The lack of trust that characterises employment relations in France hinders the ability of the parties to cooperate. This induces the government to regulate many more aspects of employment relations than in other liberal market economies (LMEs) such as the United States and the United Kingdom.

There is a vicious circle: the poor quality of social dialogue justifies state intervention, but this appears to absolve potential negotiators of responsibility to develop collective agreements autonomously. This contributes to the development of comparatively rigid regulatory laws. Some employers' interests argue that this hinders economic performance by limiting the scope for employers to reallocate employment in the labour market. Reports have identified potential reforms to expand the field of collective bargaining (Chertier 2006; Institut Montaigne 2011); however, such reforms cannot be undertaken without first strengthening the legitimacy of the social partners.

Another path to improving social dialogue in enterprises could involve a greater presence of employee representatives on corporate boards. The June 2013 law which restates the national agreement signed on 11 January 2013 provides for the participation of employee representatives with voting rights in the governing and monitoring councils of large enterprises.

In this context, the social partners succeeded in reaching the ANI on competitiveness and employment security on 11 January 2013.

Employers' organisations (MEDEF, the UPA and the CGPME) and three unions (the CFE-CGC, CFDT and CFTC) agreed to grant new scope for labour market flexibility to enterprises and new rights to employees. The FO and CGT refused to sign, however. The agreement allows employers to employ people on a flexible basis in exchange for an increase in the rights of employees (such as full access to a health-care mutual fund), the strengthening of conditions about the use of precarious employment (e.g. through the taxation of short-term contracts) and an increase in the information provided to employees and personnel representatives regarding the company's strategic choices. The effects of the agreement are difficult to evaluate yet. Among other things, the impact of measures will depend on the way in which they are implemented, as most of the new employee rights will require subsequent negotiations.

## CONCLUSIONS

The development of union strategies, the increasingly neo-liberal orientation of employers' organisations and the continuing central role of the state are important factors. These frame the social dialogue in France, which is shaped by a series of national agreements.

Considering the many challenges facing employers, it is essential that employers involve and recognise employees as key players in the achievement of organisational objectives. A direct relationship between employees and their line managers is essential, but not sufficient. French employers must recognise the importance of social democracy. Collective bargaining is a vital component because it helps resolve conflicts between the interests of employees and employers. For this reason, employers should not see meetings with representatives in terms of their additional costs, but instead as investments that help to ensure the involvement and engagement of the workforce. This requires sustainable forms of negotiation and compromise between employers and employees, and their representatives, in the long term. To this end, the state seeks to strengthen the negotiating skills of the social partners. It is unfortunate for employees and employers if the decentralisation of collective bargaining leads to short-term opportunistic behaviour (e.g. one party trying to take advantage of another party). We should keep in mind that unions can fulfil at least three roles: representing employees' interests, regulating conflict and helping to engage the workforce. These roles can facilitate the efficiency and effectiveness of enterprises.

## FURTHER READING

Jefferys, S. (2003) *Liberté, Égalité and Fraternité at Work: Changing French Employment Relations and Management*. New York: Palgrave Macmillan.

Jenkins, A. (2000) *Employment Relations in France*. New York: Kluwer Academic.

Parsons, N. (2005) *French Industrial Relations in the New World Economy*. New York: Routledge.

Rojot, J. (1989) *The Myth of French Exceptionalism*, in J. Barbash & K. Barbash (eds), *Theories and Concepts in Comparative Industrial Relations*. Columbia, SC: University of South Carolina Press, pp. 76–88.

Visser, J. (2000) 'France', in B. Ebbinghaus & J. Visser (eds), *The Societies of Europe: Trade Unions in Western Europe since 1945*. Basingstoke: Macmillan, pp. 237–77.

## USEFUL WEBSITES

DARES, French Ministry of Labour: <http://travail-emploi.gouv.fr/etudes-recherches-statistiques-de,76/statistiques,78/relations-professionnelles,85>.

ETUC: <www.etuc.org/fr/issue/industrial-policy–0>.

European Foundation for the Improvement of Living and Working Conditions: <www.eurofound.europa.eu/observatories/eurwork/comparative-information/industrial-relations-country-profiles>.

European Trade Union Institute: <www.worker-participation.eu/National-Industrial-Relations/Countries/France/Trade-Unions>.

Federation of European Employers: <www.fedee.com/labour-relations/industrial-relations-across-europe>.

## A CHRONOLOGY OF FRENCH EMPLOYMENT RELATIONS

| | |
|---|---|
| 1791 | The Chapelier Law forbids strikes and unions, but not employers' associations. |
| 1821 | Building industry employers' association is established. |
| 1830s–40s | Many illegal combinations of workers and some collective agreements. |
| 1864 | Abolition of the Chapelier Law. |
| 1871 | Paris Commune. |
| 1884 | Unions entitled to organise on a craft or industry basis, but not at enterprise or plant level. |
| 1895 | CGT established. |
| 1906 | Anarcho-syndicalist Amiens Charter asserts the CGT's independence from political parties. |
| 1919 | CFTC established following the 1891 *Rerum Novarum*, a labour encyclical by Pope Leo XIII. |
| 1919 | First national industrial employers' confederation founded. |
| 1936 | Election of the Front populaire coalition of socialists, communists and radicals. Many strikes and sit-ins. Collective agreements between the employers' association and the reunited CGT. Major social reforms enacted/initiated: paid holidays, bill on collective bargaining, 40-hour legal working week, introduction of workplace employee delegates. |
| 1944 | CGC established. |
| 1946 | CNPF established as the main employers' association. |
| 1948 | Creation of the CGT-FO, following a split within the CGT. |
| 1950 | Law on collective bargaining and establishment of a minimum wage system. |
| 1964 | A majority of CFTC members vote to form the secular CFDT. A minority of members reject this decision and remain within the CFTC. |
| 1968 | Events of May precipitate a general strike; workplace union branches permitted. |
| 1971 | Amendment to 1950 Act to permit workplace-level bargaining. |
| 1976 | New redundancy law enacted. |
| 1981 | President François Mitterrand's (left-wing) socialist–communist coalition forms government. Aroux Laws enacted, including *Employee Participation Act* and *Collective Bargaining Act*. Retirement age reduced from 65 to 60 years. |
| 1987 | New redundancy act repeals the earlier requirement for prior administrative approval; new flexible working hours law introduced. |
| 1988 | Socialist government returns to power after two years' absence. Bill regarding minimum integration income (*revenu minimum d'insertion*). |

| 1993 | Right-wing coalition government takes office under Prime Minister Édouard Balladur. |
| 1995 | Jacques Chirac (right-wing) elected president. Major public sector strikes against policies of Prime Minister Alain Juppé's government. |
| 1997 | Election of left-wing government, headed by Prime Minister Lionel Jospin. |
| 1998 | New laws (the Aubry Law) introduce the 35-hour week. |
| 1999 | The main employers' confederation (CNPF) is replaced by MEDEF. |
| 2000 | IR reform (*refondation sociale*) launched by MEDEF. |
| 2001 | *Social Modernisation Act* strengthens the information rights of works councils on redundancies. |
| 2003 | Reform of the general pension system in both the private and public sectors. |
| 2004 | Government's social cohesion plan, supporting employment, housing and anti-discrimination. |
| 2005 | *Social Cohesion Act*. |
| 2007 | Nicolas Sarkozy (right-wing) elected president. |
| 2008 | New law (20 August 2008 Act) introduces new rules of representation for unions. A union has to obtain at least 10 per cent of electoral votes to be able to negotiate with an employer. |
| 2012 | François Hollande (left-wing) elected president. |
| 2013 | (11 January) ANI on labour market reform contributes to increasing flexibility of the job market. |
| 2014 | François Hollande's Pacte de responsabilité between the government and employers. The government would cut taxes for employers who would commit to creating jobs. |

# CHAPTER 8

# Employment relations in Germany

## Berndt K. Keller and Anja Kirsch

In the Varieties of Capitalism (VoC) approach (Hall & Soskice 2001), Germany is seen as the classic example of a coordinated market economy (CME), where employment relations are characterised by well-organised trade unions and employers' associations that comprehensively regulate working conditions through industry-wide collective bargaining, formalised participation of employees in decision-making to curb managerial prerogative, secure employment and elaborate industry-based training schemes that produce a labour force with high industry-specific and firm-specific skills.

In this chapter, we review the historical development of the actors and processes in employment relations and highlight current practices. We show that, while the formal institutional framework largely corresponds to the way Germany is portrayed in the VoC approach, current practices deviate a great deal from this model.

## THE HISTORICAL, LEGAL AND SOCIO-POLITICAL BACKGROUND

After the destruction caused by World War II, the West German economy recovered so fast that the 1950s and 1960s came to be known as the decades of the 'economic miracle' (*Wirtschaftswunder*). West Germany quickly developed into the strongest economy in Europe, and one of the leading nations in world trade. The high-productivity, high-added-value and high-wage model of production based on a highly skilled workforce lasted until the mid-1970s, when the collapse of the Bretton Woods system of fixed but adjustable exchange rates and two oil crises led to an economic downturn and rising unemployment.

The economy recovered in the 1980s, when West Germany achieved record export surpluses and additional jobs were created in new areas of employment. The German model, with its focus on negotiated compromises between unions and employers' associations, proved successful in mastering the challenge of modernising the economy. However, unemployment remained persistently high.

The Federal Republic of Germany (FRG, or Bundesrepublik Deutschland) and the German Democratic Republic (GDR, or Deutsche Demokratische Republik) were unified in 1990. The integration of the socialist command economy into the capitalist social market economy (*soziale Marktwirtschaft*) has created unique and enduring challenges. In the early 1990s, after the relatively short 'unification boom' in the west, unified Germany experienced high unemployment and the most severe economic crisis since World War II. Between the mid-1990s and the mid-2000s, the rate of economic growth was low and unemployment remained high; Germany was sometimes called 'the sick man of Europe'.

After the post-2007 global financial crisis, there was a loss in gross domestic product (GDP) of more than 5 per cent. In contrast with the majority of European Union (EU) and Organisation for Economic Cooperation and Development (OECD) countries, the economy recovered quickly, unemployment did not rise and employment grew (Möller 2010; Dustmann et al. 2014). Therefore, austerity measures were less urgent than in other EU Member States. Germany is the largest economy in Europe, with a population of more than 81 million, a total labour force of more than 42 million and a GDP of around US\$3.5 trillion in 2013 (OECD 2014b).

West Germany and, since 1990, unified Germany have experienced a relatively high degree of political continuity and stability. Between 1949 and the late 1960s, the conservative Christian Democratic Union (CDU) was in power in coalition with the Christian Social Union (CSU), in most cases in coalition governments with the Free Democratic Party (FDP). In the period between 1969 and 1982, coalition governments forged between the Social Democratic Party (Sozialdemokratische Partei Deutschlands, or SPD) and the FDP ruled the country and changed the system of employment relations in various regards. Between 1982 and 1998, the CDU/CSU was back in power, again in coalition with the FDP, and promoted various measures of labour market flexibility. Since then, the ruling parties have alternated more frequently. An SPD and Green coalition government (1998–2005) was followed by a grand coalition between the CDU/CSU and the SPD (2005–09). Then a CDU/CSU and FDP coalition government (2009–13) preceded another grand coalition between the CDU/CSU and the SPD.

The legal-institutional infrastructure was put in place in the early period of the FRG, although its roots extend from the Weimar Republic (1919–33) (Jacobi et al. 1998). According to the Constitution, the Basic Law (Grundgesetz) of 1949, Germany is a federal polity. The states (*Bundesländer*) have autonomous rights in different fields of public policy (e.g. cultural affairs, education and science). In employment relations, however, the legal foundations are the same for all states, and in this regard Germany differs from other federal systems such as Canada and the United States.

Like other Western European countries, Germany is classified as a conservative welfare state (Esping-Andersen 1990). Regulations date back to late-nineteenth-century Bismarckian reforms, and consist of all-encompassing systems of social protection (including unemployment insurance, health insurance and pension schemes). They are based on occupational status and the insurance principle, and are regulated by law, not by collective bargaining (Leibfried & Wagschal 2000).

## THE EMPLOYMENT RELATIONS PARTIES

### Employers and their associations

As in Switzerland and Scandinavia, employers form various types of interest organisations. The three types are general business or trade associations (*Wirtschafts* or *Unternehmensverbände*), special employers' associations (*Arbeitgeberverbände*) and chambers of industry and commerce (*Industrie- und Handelskammern*) as well as chambers of trades (*Handwerkskammern*) (Schroeder & Weßels 2010). Business or trade associations represent general economic and product market interests vis-a-vis the state, whereas employers' associations are concerned with social policy, labour market interests and employment relations, including collective bargaining. These two types of voluntary organisations cooperate closely; firms are frequently members of several associations. The chambers of industry and commerce or trades, on the other hand, are public entities that perform public and semi-governmental tasks; membership is compulsory.

Employers' associations represent firms by industry and region, and these industry and regional associations are affiliated with the Confederation of German Employers' Associations (Bundesvereinigung der Deutschen Arbeitgeberverbände, or BDA). The industry associations are responsible for collective bargaining (Schroeder & Weßels 2010).

Exact membership density levels are unknown. In the past, member firms were estimated to employ 75–80 per cent of all employees (Visser

& Van Ruysseveldt 1996), but membership has been declining since the late 1980s. Currently, member firms employ about 60 per cent of employees, which is high in comparison with many EU Member States. As is the case in many countries, employers' association density is much higher than union density (Brandl 2013).

Collective bargaining coverage rates depend on the employers' (not the unions') membership density. Legally, all member firms must adhere to the conditions of the collective agreements that their association negotiates with a union. However, employers' associations are finding it increasingly difficult to balance the interests of various member groups. Small and medium-sized enterprises (SMEs, or *Mittelstand*) are frequently dissatisfied with their associations' policies, which they consider to be dominated by the interests of large enterprises, and decide to cancel their membership (Voelkl 2002). These tensions have weakened employers' associations' capacity to exercise discipline and authority over their member companies during collective bargaining and in the implementation of collective agreements.

In response to membership decline, and thus loss of organisational power and financial resources, some employers' associations now allow companies to join and receive membership benefits such as information and legal advice without being bound to collective agreements (membership *ohne Tarifbindung*). Other associations have established separate entities offering *ohne Tarifbindung* membership. This widespread strategy is controversial, and it is unclear whether it solves the problems of declining membership or leads to the rise of a new type of association and the further decline of existing ones—thereby weakening industry-level collective bargaining (Behrens 2011). Recently, it seems that internal tensions have been reduced.

## Unions

Unions were re-established after World War II according to the principles of industrial unionism (*Industriegewerkschaft*) and unitary unionism (*Einheitsgewerkschaft*). The principles mean that, first, all employees in an industry may join the same union, irrespective of their occupation or blue- or white-collar status; and second, that the unions are not closely affiliated with political parties. Traditionally, the industry unions engage in collective bargaining, while the peak federation, the German Trade Union Federation (Deutscher Gewerkschaftsbund, or DGB), is responsible for political activities including lobbying (Schroeder 2014).

More than 80 per cent of union members belong to unions affiliated with the DGB. The remaining 20 per cent belong to unions affiliated to the Confederation of Christian Unions (Christlicher Gewerkschafts-bund, or CGB) or the German Civil Service Association (Deutscher Beamtenbund, or DBB). The CGB has fewer than 300,000 members, while the DBB has about 1.2 million. The DBB organises in the public sector, and its elements have been privatised. The DBB mainly looks after civil servants; it is the only confederation with membership growth since the 1990s (Keller 2010).

As Figure 8.1 shows, the organisational structure of around seven-teen DGB-affiliated industry unions was remarkably stable for more than four decades. While union mergers are common in many countries (Waddington 2005), they were not seen in Germany until the mid-1990s, when shrinking membership, decreasing financial resources and structural changes in the economy—including increased labour market flexibility and deregulation—led to a 'merger mania' that has replaced the system of industrial unionism with only eight unions. Currently, the two biggest unions, IG Metall and ver.di, represent almost 70 per cent of all members of DGB affiliates.

Since the early 2000s, some small professional associations of airline pilots, air traffic controllers, doctors in hospitals and train drivers have become more assertive and have developed into professional unions (Schroeder et al. 2011). They have initiated strikes and engaged in collective bargaining for the special interests of their members. They have managed to conclude collective agreements because their members are in strategic positions in the labour market and are well organised. Thus, these professional unions are challenging the existing system of interest representation in their organisational domains.

Membership density in the DGB unions fluctuated around the 30–35 per cent level from the 1950s to the 1980s (Müller-Jentsch & Ittermann 2000). Figure 8.2 shows that after a short-lived surge in membership following unification in 1990, all unions experienced significant losses. Meanwhile density has fallen to less than 20 per cent. These losses have contributed to the decline in unions' organisational and bargaining power, and to the rise of a major non-union sector, which is novel in Germany. Union density is currently lower than the Western European average (Visser 2006).

Recently, strategies of 'union revitalisation' originating from the United States have been discussed (Behrens et al. 2003; Rehder 2014). Some unions, such as IG Metall and ver.di, have experimented with the 'organising approach', and tried to adapt it to German legal-institutional circumstances. Occasionally, they have managed to initiate the election of works councils or to stop the long-term downward trend of membership.

**Figure 8.1  Mergers among DGB unions**

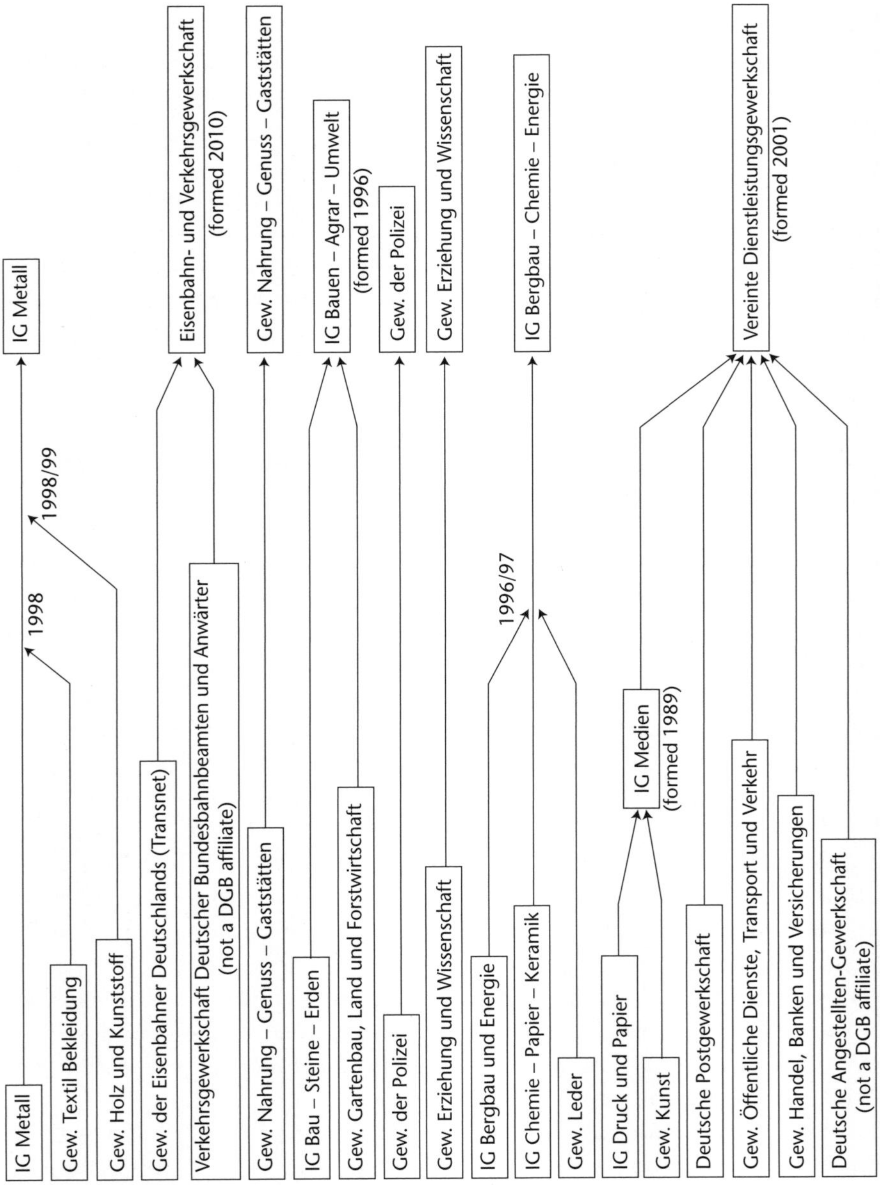

*Source:* Waddington & Hoffmann (2000).

**Figure 8.2  Membership in DGB-affiliated unions**

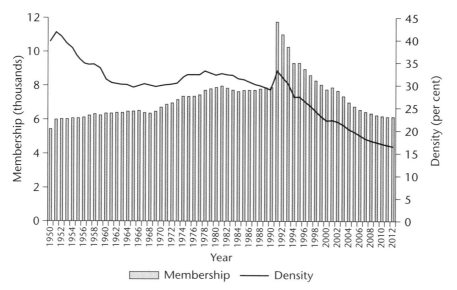

*Source:* Translated from Schroeder & Greef (2014: 130).

The composition of union membership reflects the workforce structure of the 1970s: membership is concentrated among skilled, male, full-time workers in the manufacturing sector and among public sector employees. Changes in the composition of the workforce mean that women, younger employees, highly educated and qualified employees, private service sector employees, foreign workers and workers in atypical employment are under-represented (Ebbinghaus & Göbel 2014). To secure their long-term survival as powerful actors, unions need to organise the unorganised—especially women and white-collar employees (*Angestellte*) in the private service sector, and formulate new policies that appeal to both existing and new membership groups (Kirsch & Blaschke 2014).

## The state

In contrast to the more voluntaristic systems of the liberal market economies (LMEs), German employment relations are characterised by a high degree of juridification (*Verrechtlichung*) (Weiss & Schmidt 2008). The most important laws are the *Works Constitution Act*, the Co-determination Acts, the *Collective Agreement Act* and the *Social Security Act*. There is one major exception to the reliance on codified

185

laws: collective labour disputes are subject to case law (*Richterrecht*), a series of binding decisions from the independent Federal Labour Court as well as the Constitutional Court (Brox et al. 2007). Compared with other countries, there is an independent and specialised system of labour courts at the local, state and national levels.

The Constitution guarantees all individuals the right of freedom of association. Hence, membership of interest associations is voluntary, and union security arrangements such as closed shops and union shops are illegal. Unions, employers and their associations have the right to free collective bargaining (*Tarifautonomie*) as specified in the *Collective Agreement Act* (*Tarifvertragsgesetz*) of 1949, amended in 1969 and 1974. This means that they engage in collective bargaining without any active state interference. Informal and/or public recommendations are the only means of intervention. Collective agreements are binding for both signatory parties and their members. Employers frequently extend the terms of the agreements to all their employees in order not to provide incentives for joining unions. There is a strict peace obligation (*Friedenspflicht*) during the term of an agreement. This rule limits opportunities for industrial action and contributes to the comparatively low levels of industrial conflict.

There are mediation agreements (*Schlichtungsvereinbarungen*) in all major sectors. These procedural arrangements are the results of voluntary negotiations between both sides of industry, and are not determined by legal enactment or any other form of state interference. Compared with other countries, federal and/or state mediation and conciliation services are of little importance.

Until the 1980s, this extensive juridification was criticised as being too restrictive. In the 1990s, it was recognised that the laws stabilise the employment relations system (Jacobi et al. 1998). Recent legal changes have been incremental only, and the institutional framework remains largely intact (Weiss 2013). Within this framework, unions and employers' associations have more freedom to determine their own structures and their dealings with each other (e.g. collective bargaining and dispute resolution) than is the case in countries that generally were characterised by voluntarism, such as the United Kingdom.

Besides providing a legal framework, the state may take an active role through corporatist arrangements as forms of private-interest governance. The late 1960s and 1970s were the heyday of neo-corporatism in several European countries, when governments included unions and employers' associations in processes of socio-economic policy-making in exchange for pay restraint by the unions or for the implementation of a binding income policy.

In Germany, the SPD-FDP coalition governments of the 1970s used tripartite management of the economy and Keynesian economic macro-steering and demand-side economics to pursue the macro-economic goals of price stability, full employment, steady economic growth and a foreign trade balance. The Concerted Action (Konzertierte Aktion, 1967–77) was based on voluntary pay restraint rather than on statutory incomes policy, and has therefore been termed a 'weak form of macro-level coordination' (Iversen 1999: 159). On comparative scales of corporatism (Siaroff 1999; Molina & Rhodes 2002), Germany scores in the middle, between non-integrated pluralism (as in the Anglo-Saxon world) and integrated corporatism (as in Austria and the Scandinavian countries).

Across Europe, centralised, macro-corporatist arrangements lost importance with the decline of Keynesianism and its macro-steering capacities, with the shifting of political preferences towards conservative majorities, and with the rise of neo-liberal ideologies and supply-side economics. Since the mid-1990s, there has been a revival of neo-corporatism in some Western European countries (Avdagic et al. 2011). This 'competitive corporatism' takes non-classical network forms of macro-coordination and intends to increase national competitiveness and employment (Traxler 2004).

In Germany, attempts to introduce such new mechanisms by the conservative CDU-led government in the mid-1990s, as well as by the SPD-led government in the early 2000s, failed. Their Alliance for Jobs, Training and Competitiveness (Bündnis für Arbeit, Ausbildung und Wettbewerbsfähigkeit) sought to achieve a general reorientation of social and fiscal policies, stimulate investment and generate more employment.

## EMPLOYMENT RELATIONS PROCESSES

This section discusses the main processes in the employment relations system: co-determination at the workplace and enterprise levels, collective bargaining and industrial disputes.

### Co-determination

Co-determination is the distinguishing feature of employment relations. This form of employee voice and participation in management is based on the idea of industrial democracy. It originated in the Weimar Republic. Legislation institutionalises labour–management cooperation at both the workplace and enterprise levels.

187

## The workplace level

The *Works Constitution Act (Betriebsverfassungsgesetz)* of 1952, amended in 1972, 1988 and 2001, is the legal basis for co-determination at the workplace level. It gives works councils *(Betriebsräte)* a set of rights relating to specific issues. As Table 8.1 shows, these rights range from the right to receive information, through consultation to binding co-determination and strict veto rights. Generally, these rights are stronger in social matters than in personnel, economic and financial matters. Through these rights, works councils are able to influence issues that remain 'managerial prerogatives' in other countries.

The *Works Constitution Act* does not apply to very small enterprises (those with up to five employees) or to the public sector, which is covered by separate *S*taff Representation Acts (Personalvertretungsgesetze) at the federal and state levels. Furthermore, enterprises that serve political, religious, charitable, educational and scientific aims are only partially covered.

On the basis of these legally guaranteed and enforceable rights, management and works councils negotiate binding works agreements *(Betriebsvereinbarungen)* that regulate enterprise-specific issues such as rostering and redundancies. As works councils and management are obliged to cooperate 'in a spirit of mutual trust for the good of the employees and of the establishment', and as works councils are not allowed to strike, these negotiations are generally not conflictual, and their outcomes are not allowed to contradict the provisions of industry-wide collective agreements (Weiss & Schmidt 2008). Due to the trend of bargaining decentralisation, the number and content of works agreements have increased.

In legal terms, works councils are independent and separate from unions. Co-determination at the workplace and collective bargaining at the industry level are supposedly strictly separate, and works councils are meant to be detached from all 'quantitative' problems of pay and income distribution. In reality, however, many works councillors are active union members, and unions provide important services (e.g. information, training, legal expertise and advice) that facilitate works councils' everyday activities. Unions depend on works councils to recruit new members, monitor the implementation of collective agreements at the enterprise level and informally assist in industrial action. In this regard, works councils show some functional similarities with enterprise unions in other countries. Thus, despite the legal separation, these institutions are often interdependent. Nevertheless, in recent years some works councils have begun to operate more independently of unions.

**Table 8.1** **Works councils' rights of participation**

| Rights (from weak to strong) | Examples |
| --- | --- |
| Right to information | The works council (WC) has the right to meet with management each month. Management must supply the WC with information on the economic and financial situation of the company and on strategic decisions such as changes to the premises and working procedures and operations. It must also inform the WC on present and future human resources needs, vocational training measures and resulting staff movements. |
| Right to inspect documents | The WC must be given access at any time to documentation it may require to carry out its duties. It is entitled to inspect payrolls and personal files. |
| Right of supervision | The WC has the right to ensure that the employer observes and complies with laws, safety regulations, collective agreements and works agreements. |
| Right to make recommendations and give advice | The WC can make recommendations to the employer for action on social matters such as policies on smoking or parking, and regarding manpower planning. |
| Right to be consulted and right to object | The WC must be consulted before every dismissal and informed about who is to be dismissed, why it should take place and when. Dismissals carried out without consulting the WC are null and void. The WC may object to a dismissal if it believes that it is unfair or breaches selection guidelines, or if job transfer, retraining or changes to the job are possible. |
| Right to veto a decision | The employer must inform the WC about every recruitment, classification, reclassification and transfer, explain the consequences of such personnel measures and obtain the WC's consent. The WC can refuse to consent to such decisions for a number of reasons (e.g. if the measure is unlawful or breaches selection guidelines, or if the WC is concerned that the measure will lead to unfair and avoidable disadvantages for employees). The employer may apply to the labour court for a decision in lieu of WC consent. |

| Rights (from weak to strong) | Examples |
| --- | --- |
| Right to initiate and negotiate matters with genuine co-determination between the employer and the WC | The WC has the right to co-determine social matters in the workplace such as the distribution of working hours and breaks; leave schedules; the introduction and use of technical devices for monitoring employee behaviour and performance; when, where and how employees are paid; and how piece rates and other performance-related pay components are determined. The employer and WC may, after negotiation, sign a works agreement on these matters which has a direct and binding effect on all employees. If no agreement can be reached, a conciliation committee decides the matter. If the employer plans to make significant changes to operations such as merging, spinning off, offshoring or closing down parts of a business or changing production methods, the WC must be consulted. The employer and the WC negotiate a Social Compensation Plan that compensates employees for disadvantages that result from such changes. If no agreement can be reached, a conciliation committee decides the matter. |

Source: Page (2006: 14–16).

Although works councils are mandatory, the *Works Constitution Act* does not oblige employers to initiate their election, so they must be formed upon employee initiative. This means that in many enterprises there are no works councils (Artus et al. 2006). Recent data (see Figure 8.3) indicate that only about one-quarter of all eligible enterprises have works councils, and these cover less than 50 per cent of the private sector workforce.

Over half of all private sector employees are not covered by works councils, and this percentage has been rising since the mid-1980s. Employees in eastern Germany, in the private service sector and in SMEs are least likely to be represented, and even some large companies have (more or less actively) prevented the establishment of works councils (Ellguth & Kohaut 2013). Thus, in contrast to widespread assumptions, the majority of private sector employees have no access to shop-floor interest representation and there is a growing 'representation gap'

**Figure 8.3   Coverage rate of works councils**

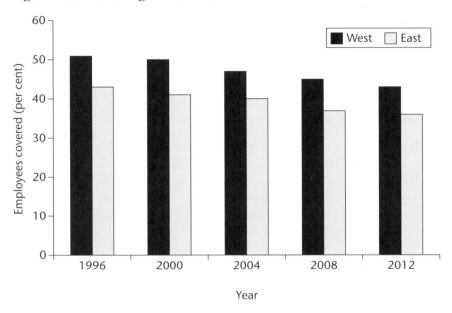

*Sources:* Ellguth & Kohaut (2010, 2013).

despite the legal guarantees. 'Dual interest representation' through unions and works councils is less frequent than often assumed.

Traditionally, co-determination has been justified as a basic political right rather than on grounds of economic efficiency. Since the mid-1990s, the impact of co-determination on indicators such as productivity, profitability, investment, fluctuation and innovation—especially at the shop-floor level—has been discussed, controversially. In contrast to earlier research, recent econometric studies with large samples and sophisticated methodologies find no evidence of detrimental impacts that could justify changes to the current co-determination system (Dilger 2002; Frick 2003; Jirjahn 2011).

Co-determination is not the only form of employee voice at the workplace level. Since the 1990s, there has been a growing trend towards 'alternative representation bodies' such as round tables or staff spokespersons (Ellguth 2009; Hauser-Ditz et al. 2009). These bodies are not established by law, but voluntarily introduced and controlled by management in enterprise-specific arrangements. They often consist of employee *and* management representatives, are particularly prevalent in SMEs and the service sector, and often exist for only a short time. Overall, they cover about 15 per cent of employees in the private sector. By comparison, works councils cover 42 per cent of employees in the private sector (Ellguth & Kohaut 2013). For the time being, it is unclear whether these bodies can supplement works councils or constitute functional equivalents.

## The enterprise level

German companies have a two-tier board structure—in contrast to the one-tier boards in Anglo-Saxon countries. Theoretically, all strategic decisions are made by the supervisory board (*Aufsichtsrat*), which represents the owners and stakeholders. It appoints and controls the members of the smaller management board (*Vorstand*), whose full-time managers implement strategic decisions, and monitor and control everyday affairs. In practice, however, their impact is more encompassing (Gerum 2007).

A specified percentage of members of the supervisory board (from one-third to almost one-half, depending on individual Acts) are employee representatives. Often they are works councillors or union officials. Furthermore, one member of the management board, the labour director (*Arbeitsdirektor*), is supposed to represent employees' interests. In the majority of companies, they are in charge of employment relations and human resource management (HRM).

For historical reasons, there are three Acts on co-determination (*Mitbestimmungsgesetze*) at the enterprise level that differ in the rights granted to employees. The *Co-determination Act* for the coal and steel industries (*Montan-Mitbestimmungsgesetz*) of 1951 (several amendments) established the most far-reaching form of 'full parity' between the representatives of capital and labour on the supervisory board. It is of only minor importance today, due to the decline of these industries—about 30 companies are covered by its provisions. However, it is still of symbolic value to the unions, and constitutes their blueprint for future regulation.

The first version of the *Works Constitution Act* (1952) granted weaker rights to employees: one-third of the seats on the supervisory board. It covered joint stock and limited liability companies with 500 to 2000 employees. In 2004, it was superseded by the *One-Third Participation Act* (*Drittelbeteiligungsgesetz*), which applies to about 1500 enterprises (Bayer 2009).

The *Co-determination Act* of 1976 grants rights close to parity and applies to all limited liability companies with more than 2000 employees. Since the 1990s, the number of covered companies has grown to about 700, due to unification, the splitting of large companies into smaller ones and the privatisation of public enterprises.

These two channels of co-determination, through works councils and employee representatives on supervisory boards, have contributed to the development of cooperation at the workplace and enterprise levels. Therefore, the exchange relations between capital and labour are characterised by the notion of mutual recognition within a social partnership rather than by concepts of class antagonism or 'adversarial' employment relations. However, nowadays only a minority of employees work in companies where their interests are represented by both channels. The majority have no representation at all, and this will surely have an effect on the nature of employment relations in the future.

Despite its institutionalisation, co-determination has always been contested. Initiatives from business and employers' federations have attempted to dismantle existing standards (BDA/BDI 2004). These demands have been refuted by external experts on empirical grounds, have faced fierce opposition from trade unions and other stakeholders, and have not managed to win a political majority.

## Collective bargaining

Unions and employers' associations (or individual employers) engage in collective bargaining in order to regulate pay and other working conditions. The basic procedures are stipulated in the *Collective Agreement Act*. There are three kinds of collective agreement: pay agreements (*Lohn- und Gehaltstarifverträge*) fix the level of pay and periodic increases; framework agreements (*Rahmentarifverträge*) specify payment systems; and 'umbrella' agreements (*Manteltarifverträge*) regulate all other conditions of employment (e.g. working time, overtime, holidays). There are about 68,000 agreements currently in place (Bispinck & WSI-Tarifarchiv 2013), indicating, in contrast to popular assumptions, an enormous heterogeneity and flexibility.

In the majority of industries, collective bargaining takes place at the regional and industry levels—for example, between the regional branches of Gesamtmetall and IG Metall in the engineering industries. These activities have traditionally occurred annually, and more recently every two years. The activities are centrally coordinated by the national unions and employers' associations. This structure has led to pattern bargaining in engineering. Traditionally, pilot agreements concluded in carefully selected bargaining districts are transferred to other districts of the same industry, and they also predetermine the results in other major industries, which results in a high degree of de facto coordination.

International comparative literature has examined the impact of bargaining centralisation on macro-economic performance (e.g. unemployment, inflation and economic growth). Recently, the original 'hump-shaped' relationship (Calmfors & Driffill 1988) was called into question when studies showed that it was not so much bargaining centralisation but coordination that influenced macro-economic performance (Traxler et al. 2001). Germany belongs to the group of countries with intermediate levels of centralisation but comparatively high degrees of bargaining coordination within and between industries.

In the past, this moderately centralised and highly coordinated system meant that pay differentials between individuals and groups of employees, sectors, regions and qualification levels were relatively narrow and working conditions were more standardised than in decentralised bargaining systems. Changes in labour costs were similar for all companies in a particular industry because pay was 'taken out of competition'. However, since the mid-1990s, pay differentials—and thus inequality of living conditions—have been increasing considerably (Schettkat 2006).

Instead of adhering to an industry-wide agreement, some enterprises—particularly SMEs—conclude their own enterprise agreements (single-employer bargaining). Although the number of enterprise-level agreements has increased from about 3000 in the early 1990s to about 10,000 (Bispinck & WSI-Tarifarchiv 2013), their macro-economic impact remains small. Only about 7 per cent of employees in western Germany and 12 per cent in eastern Germany are covered (Ellguth & Kohaut 2013).

The coverage rate of industry-level agreements has decreased to such an extent that its decline is referred to as a 'crisis' of sectoral collective bargaining—sometimes even as the 'erosion of industrial relations' (Hassel 1999). As Figure 8.4 shows, coverage has declined from 70 per cent of all employees in western Germany in the mid-1990s to 53 per cent. In eastern Germany, coverage has declined even more, from 56 to 36 per cent (Ellguth & Kohaut 2013). There is significant variation between sectors. About 40 per cent of employees in western Germany and 50 per cent in eastern Germany work in companies that are not legally bound to any collective agreement; about half of these employees work in companies that provide working conditions similar to those specified in the relevant industry agreements (Ellguth & Kohaut 2013). Overall, compared with other

OECD countries, Germany has only medium collective bargaining coverage rates (Traxler 2003).

Another problem threatening the stability of the collective bargaining system is the 'tacit escape from collective agreements' (*stille Tarifflucht*). This means that some companies maintain their membership of employers' associations but no longer comply with the terms of the industry-wide collective agreement, despite the legal requirement to do so. Most frequently, they deviate from the provisions on working hours, but they do so also on fringe benefits and pay. While works councils and unions generally ensure that individual employers actually implement the standards defined in collective agreements, they may tolerate this non-compliance quietly in order to save scarce jobs in times of high unemployment, prevent offshoring and outsourcing, or increase the productivity of 'their' enterprise. The phenomenon is difficult to quantify, but is more widespread in the east than in the west.

Due to this 'tacit escape', the official collective bargaining coverage rates over-estimate their real scope. Together, this creeping, internal erosion of sectoral bargaining and the membership loss of employers' associations indicate that the viability and legitimacy of collective

**Figure 8.4 Industry bargaining coverage rates**

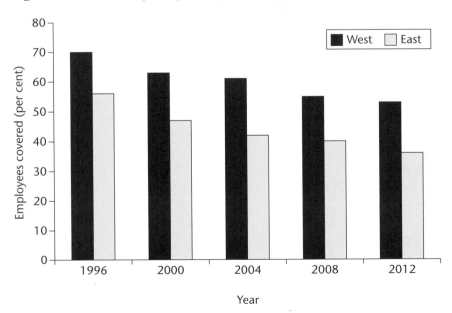

*Source:* Ellguth & Kohaut (2013).

195

bargaining and its key players have been undermined. Collective agreements are no longer able to fulfil their original task of 'taking pay out of competition'. Informal and uncoordinated 'wildcat cooperation' between managers and works councils seems to be widespread, and has grown since the 1990s. Comparative studies have argued that 'the growing variation in employment systems that appears within countries has resulted from a shift in bargaining power in management's favour' (Katz 2005: 275). Germany is a prototypical example of this trend.

Employees' interests are supposed to be represented in a dual system: co-determination at the workplace level as well as collective bargaining at the industry level. However, as we have seen, only a minority of employees actually enjoy these conditions. In fact, less than one-third are covered by a collective agreement *and* represented by a works council. The institutional base of the dual system has gradually been weakened and representation gaps have grown at both levels.

## Industrial disputes

Due to the structure of collective bargaining, industrial disputes are usually industry-wide within a certain region, and are coordinated centrally by unions and employers' associations. According to the Constitution and its guarantee of freedom of association, strikes and lockouts are legal instruments. When unions organise a strike, they conduct membership ballots to ensure the necessary support. These ballots are prescribed by unions' statutes and not by legislation, as in other countries such as Australia. Employers' associations use lockouts to intensify and extend disputes to additional workplaces. Doing so exhausts the unions' resources because they have to provide strike pay to more of their members.

Although there are major disputes occasionally, the level of industrial disputes in Germany is low compared with other countries. Only small countries, such as Switzerland, Austria and the Netherlands, have lower rates (Gumbrell-McCormick & Hyman 2013). Disputes have had only limited aggregate economic impact on a range of indicators (e.g. companies affected, employees involved or working days lost, or WDL, per 1000 employees). Lockouts mainly occurred between the 1950s and early 1980s, and were concentrated in a few industries—primarily engineering and related industries (Schroeder & Silvia 2014). Since then, employers' associations have found it increasingly difficult to organise lockouts as a unified associational policy due to the increasing heterogeneity of their members' interests.

There are several reasons for the low degree of industrial conflict. First, relatively centralised systems of collective bargaining tend to result in less industrial conflict than more decentralised ones. Second, the dual system of employment relations promotes long-term cooperation and mutual trust. Third, there is a clear legal distinction between disputes regarding the interpretation of existing collective agreements and disputes about the terms and conditions of new collective agreements (rights disputes versus interest disputes). For the former, either the existing conciliation committees at the enterprise level operate as efficient grievance machinery, or these disputes are resolved in labour courts. Either way, they are settled by peaceful means (Behrens 2014). Only conflicts about new collective agreements can be the subject of legally sanctioned industrial action. Unions and employers' associations have put mediation agreements in place in case of bargaining impasses.

## CURRENT AND FUTURE ISSUES

This section explores changes to public sector employment relations, the introduction of a statutory minimum wage, the increase in labour market flexibility, growth in atypical employment and the decentralisation of collective bargaining.

### Public sector employment relations

The state is Germany's largest employer, and employment relations in the public sector are characterised by the legal distinction between public employees (*Tarifbeschäftigte*) and civil servants (*Beamte*). While employees enjoy the same rights as in private industry, civil servants are not allowed to bargain collectively or to strike. Instead, their employment conditions are determined by law and their interest associations influence the determination of pay and conditions through lobbying (Keller 2010). For decades, similar or identical pay and working conditions were achieved for both groups. Since the early 2000s, public employers have changed this long-term practice of equal treatment of status groups to the disadvantage of civil servants.

Collective bargaining used to be highly centralised, and took place at the national level for all federal (*Bund*), state (*Bundesländer*) and municipal (*Gemeinden*) employers. In addition, the federal state set working conditions for civil servants at all levels. For a long time, this structure contrasted with the growing decentralisation of public sectors in other countries (Bach et al. 1999; Dell'Aringa et al. 2001).

However, German public employers have recently somewhat decentralised bargaining. Since the mid-2000s, the states have bargained separately from the federal state and the municipalities. Furthermore, since the reform of the federalist system at about the same time, the states have been allowed to set the working conditions of their civil servants (Keller 2010).

Collective disputes are rare—major strikes took place only in 1974, 1992 and 2006. In the 2006 strike, unions tried to resist bargaining decentralisation. In general, differences in labour market strategies between private and public sector employers have been diminishing as both pursue greater flexibility and take advantage of labour market conditions (Keller 2013a).

Public sector employment grew in the early 1990s when the comparatively over-staffed former East German public sector was integrated into the West German system. Since then, employment has decreased by about one-third to about 4.6 million employees (Keller 2013b). This is partly due to the strict stability criteria established for countries participating in the European Monetary Union. In comparison with other OECD countries, Germany has only a medium-sized public sector and constitutes a 'lean state'.

Privatisation has had an impact on employment practices, but it has been less significant than in some other European countries, such as the United Kingdom. Privatisation has taken place mainly at the local level (e.g. rubbish collection), and some state monopolies (e.g. the postal service and railways) have also been privatised.

## Minimum wage

Germany introduced a statutory minimum wage from 1 January 2015, and joined the vast majority of EU and OECD countries that have such legislation. Until the mid-2000s, a statutory minimum wage was considered unnecessary, as collective bargaining coverage was extensive. However, in recent years bargaining coverage has declined substantially. In addition, the mere existence of a collective agreement does not guarantee a sustainable pay level, as unions find themselves unable to secure adequate pay through collective bargaining in industries in which they have few members and little bargaining power.

Recently, the low-pay sector—that is, according to international standards, pay below two-thirds of median pay—has been increasing considerably in comparison with other EU countries and the United States (Kalleberg 2011). The phenomenon of the 'working poor', formerly unknown in Germany, has become an urgent problem not only among atypical and part-time workers but also—although to a lesser degree—among full-time employees (Bosch & Weinkopf 2008).

In the mid-2000s, unions began to favour a general minimum wage, while the majority of employers' associations vehemently opposed it. Successive governments were divided on the issue and unable to reach a decision. The social partners agreed on some sector-specific minimum pay levels in the service sector (Möller 2012). Finally, in 2014 the grand coalition government passed legislation on a statutory minimum wage of €8.50 per hour with some exceptions, such as employees under eighteen years of age and the long-term unemployed in the first six months of employment.

## Labour market flexibility

Since the early 1980s, employers and their associations have demanded more flexibility. The reasons advanced include the changing conditions of labour and product markets, and new patterns of work organisation following the demise of the Taylorist-Fordist age of standardised mass production. We distinguish between temporal flexibility, flexibility of pay and functional flexibility.

*Temporal* or *working-time flexibility* was a key concern in collective bargaining in the 1980s. The unions—principally IG Metall—demanded fewer weekly working hours (i.e. the 35-hour week). After a major industrial dispute in 1984, an agreement was struck that combined the union's goal of reduced working hours with the employers' goal of greater flexibility and differentiation in the allocation of working hours (Seifert 2005). It was with this agreement that bargaining decentralisation and the use of opening clauses allowing the regulation of working conditions at the enterprise level began. Working hours can be arranged flexibly and distributed unevenly across days, weeks or even seasons. Working hours have also been decoupled from the operation time of the enterprise so that production hours have increased, despite fewer working hours for individuals.

Further collective reductions are no longer on the bargaining agenda. Instead, the de-standardisation and individualisation of working hours have become the main focus of attention. In major sectors, individual working-time accounts (*Arbeitszeitkonten*) have been introduced. These arrangements can be used for various purposes, such as extended leave, care for the elderly, further training or early retirement. As their negotiation and implementation are a major concern of works councils (Seifert 2008), concerns arise about declining works councils coverage rates (Berg 2008).

Working time is still a contested terrain. Some enterprises and sectors have successfully reversed the secular trend towards fewer working hours, and managed to conclude collective agreements with extended working hours—at times with only partial compensation or even without additional pay. Today, the average collectively agreed weekly working time is 37.7 hours (Bispinck & WSI-Tarifarchiv 2013). Effective working times are longer, at about 40.3 hours, and are increasing. At the same time, part-time work has significantly increased to about 26 per cent of the labour force, so overall there is a trend towards a polarisation of working time.

*Flexibility of pay* (and other benefits) became a major bargaining topic in the 1990s. Employers argued that cutting labour costs was necessary and that pay levels should correspond with an enterprise's 'ability to pay'. Unions have hardly been able to increase—or sometimes even maintain—real pay. Labour's share of national income has fallen to the level of the early 1970s. Income redistribution—formerly an essential bargaining issue—has declined in importance, and since the mid-1990s income inequality between the low paid and high paid, as well as between blue- and white-collar workers, has increased considerably (Schettkat 2006).

*Functional flexibility* is not a central bargaining concern because the vocational training system—a peculiarity of the German-speaking countries—provides many young people (about two-thirds of labour market entrants) with a broad range of skills. Therefore, the introduction of greater flexibility in work organisation, work rules and production processes has been less controversial than in other countries such as the United States, where job demarcations and seniority rules are prominent.

Apprentices spend part of their working time undertaking general training in specialised vocational schools (*Berufsschulen*), and also acquire specific skills in their workplaces. This system of creating human capital is jointly run by employers, unions and the state, and provides Germany with a competitive advantage over countries with less developed vocational training structures. It creates large pools of qualified labour, fosters a multi-skilled workforce and leads to the continuous supply of employees with standardised theoretical and practical qualifications. It also results in a comparatively low percentage of youth unemployment, because it eases the transition from school to the labour market. However, its structures constantly need to be adapted to changing requirements and conditions of supply and demand on labour markets (Bosch & Charest 2008; Busemeyer 2009).

## Atypical forms of employment

A standard employment relationship (*Normalarbeitsverhältnis*) comprises full-time, continuing employment and inclusion in social insurance schemes (including health care and pensions). As in other countries (Vosko 2010; Kalleberg 2011), non-standard, atypical employment such as part-time work, marginal employment (*Minijobs*), new forms of solo self-employment (Solo-Selbst ständigkeit), fixed-term contracts and agency work has increased since the 1980s (Table 8.2). Currently, over one-third of the workforce is engaged in such non-standard employment. With the only exception being agency work, women are over-represented in all these atypical forms.

The growth of non-standard employment has increased labour market segmentation and the growth of dual labour markets (Jackson & Sorge 2012; Palier & Thelen 2010). We observe a split into a core, unionised and protected segment and a peripheral, unorganised and unprotected segment. Workers in non-standard employment receive lower pay, have less employment security and are less likely to be union members or to be represented by works councils. Most likely, this trend will have negative consequences for the composition of the labour force and also for social cohesion, social equality, including future old-age poverty, and employment-related social insurance schemes, particularly pensions (Keller & Seifert 2013).

## Decentralisation of collective bargaining

There is a trend towards collective bargaining decentralisation in many countries (Traxler et al. 2001). The processes through which decentralisation takes place in Germany have been categorised as 'organised' as opposed to 'disorganised' (Traxler 1995). Since the 1980s, 'opening clauses' have become the major instrument of adaptation. Such clauses are increasingly included in industry-wide collective agreements and allow individual companies to vary or deviate from certain provisions of the agreement in order to adapt it to their specific circumstances. Such variations must be negotiated between employers and works councils at the enterprise level and regulated in a works agreement.

The Pforzheim Agreement (*Pforzheimer Abkommen*), concluded in the engineering and machine-building industry in 2004, is regarded as a milestone of decentralisation. It allows companies to temporarily deviate from any provision of industry-wide agreements in order to secure employment or make specific investments. Many companies have made use of this opportunity. Furthermore, since the late 1990s

**Table 8.2  Development of forms of non-standard employment**

| Year | Employment 000s | Part-time work[a] 000s | Part-time work[a] % of total employment | Marginal employment[b,c] 000s | Marginal employment[b,c] % of total employment | Marginal employment only 000s | Marginal employment only % of total employment | Midijobber[d] Total[g] 000s | Midijobber[d] Total[g] % of total employment | Temporary agency work[b] 000s | Temporary agency work[b] % of total employment | Fixed-term contracts (excluding vocational training) 000s | Fixed-term contracts (excluding vocational training) % of total employment | Solo self-employed[e] 000s | Solo self-employed[e] % total employment[g] | Total[f] atypical employment (%) |
|---|---|---|---|---|---|---|---|---|---|---|---|---|---|---|---|---|
| 1991 | 33,887 | 4736 | 14.0 | | | | | | | 134 | 0.4 | 2431 | 7.5 | 1383 | 4.1 | |
| 1993 | 32,722 | 4901 | 15.0 | | | | | | | 121 | 0.4 | 2221 | 7.1 | 1412 | 4.1 | 19.3 |
| 1995 | 32,230 | 5261 | 16.3 | | | | | | | 176 | 0.5 | 2388 | 7.8 | 1515 | 4.5 | 23.7 |
| 1997 | 31,917 | 5659 | 17.7 | | | | | | | 213 | 0.7 | 2453 | 8.1 | 1752 | 5.1 | 25.5 |
| 1999 | 32,497 | 6323 | 19.5 | | | 3658 | 11.3 | | | 286 | 0.9 | 2842 | 9.2 | 1786 | 5.6 | 27.7 |
| 2000 | 32,638 | 6478 | 19.8 | | | 4052 | 12.4 | | | 339 | 1.0 | 2744 | 8.8 | 1842 | 5.5 | 29.0 |
| 2001 | 32,743 | 6798 | 20.8 | | | 4132 | 12.6 | | | 357 | 1.1 | 2740 | 8.8 | 1821 | 5.6 | 30.8 |
| 2002 | 32,469 | 6934 | 21.4 | | | 4169 | 12.8 | | | 336 | 1.0 | 2543 | 8.2 | 1858 | 5.6 | 31.7 |
| 2003 | 32,043 | 7168 | 22.4 | 5533 | 17.3 | 4375 | 13.7 | 607 | 1.9 | 327 | 1.0 | 2603 | 8.5 | 1960 | 5.7 | 33.4 |
| 2004 | 31,405 | 7168 | 22.8 | 6466 | 20.6 | 4803 | 15.3 | 734 | 2.3 | 400 | 1.3 | 2478 | 8.3 | 2076 | 6.1 | 34.3 |
| 2005 | 32,066 | 7851 | 24.5 | 6492 | 20.2 | 4747 | 14.8 | 946 | 3.0 | 453 | 1.4 | 3075 | 10.1 | 2291 | 6.6 | 34.5 |

| 2006 | 32,830 | 8594 | 26.2 | 6751 | 20.6 | 4854 | 14.8 | 1088 | 3.3 | 598 | 1.8 | 3389 | 10.8 | 2317 | 7.1 | 36.3 |
|------|--------|------|------|------|------|------|------|------|-----|-----|-----|------|------|------|-----|------|
| 2007 | 33,606 | 8841 | 26.3 | 6918 | 20.6 | 4882 | 14.5 | 1195 | 3.6 | 731 | 2.2 | 3291 | 10.3 | 2323 | 7.1 | 37.0 |
| 2008 | 34,241 | 9008 | 26.3 | 6792 | 19.8 | 4882 | 14.3 | 1241 | 3.6 | 794 | 2.3 | 3106 | 9.6 | 2306 | 6.9 | 36.0 |
| 2009 | 34,203 | 9076 | 26.5 | 6993 | 20.4 | 4932 | 14.4 | 1280 | 3.7 | 610 | 1.8 | 3026 | 9.3 | 2356 | 6.7 | 36.6 |
| 2010 | 34,459 | 9196 | 26.7 | 7018 | 20.4 | 4916 | 14.3 | 1320 | 3.8 | 806 | 2.3 | 3157 | 9.6 | 2383 | 6.9 | 37.6 |
| 2011 | 35,228 | 9512 | 27.0 | 7393 | 21.0 | 4894 | 13.9 | 1365 | 3.9 | 910 | 2.6 | 3268 | 9.3 | 2513 | 6.9 | 38.2 |
| 2012 | 35,522 | 9607 | 27.0 | 7434 | 20.9 | 4834 | 13.6 | 1365 | 3.8 | 908 | 2.6 | 3116 | 8.8 | 2523 | 7.1 | 38.6 |

*Notes:*
(a) By end of April.
(b) By end of June.
(c) Up to €450 monthly.
(d) Between €450 and €850 monthly.
(e) Results of the Mikrozensus.
(f) Without solo self-employment.
(g) Percentage of overall employment = Overall employment + Solo self-employment.

*Sources*: Federal Statistical Office; Federal Employment Office.

employment pacts at the enterprise level (*betriebliche Bündnisse für Arbeit*) have spread (Massa-Wirth 2007). They constitute a form of 'concession bargaining' whereby pay cuts and changes to working time and work organisation are made in exchange for the avoidance of mass redundancies and the promise of investments.

A consequence of these decentralisation processes is that works agreements are of growing importance (Nienhüser & Hoßfeld 2004). Their number and the issues they regulate have increased since the mid-1980s. Many collective agreements now contain a number of options for regulating issues such as the distribution of working time, work organisation, and pay systems and levels at the enterprise level. As a result, the power of actors at the enterprise level has gradually increased, while that of actors at the sector level has been constrained. The formal structures of industry-wide collective bargaining have remained intact, but its outcomes and functions have changed significantly as final decisions about substantive issues have gradually been shifted to the enterprise level.

The use of opening clauses requires the existence of works councils. However, as explained earlier, many enterprises do not have works councils. Furthermore, the introduction of working-time accounts and the plant-level implementation of agreements add to works councils' workload. The devolution of bargaining authority regarding substantive, distributive issues to the enterprise level also calls into question the strict peace obligation that prevents works councils from taking industrial action.

The established collective bargaining regime has lost its original power to determine pay and working conditions. The balance of power and the division of labour between unions and employers' associations on the one hand, and employers' and works councils on the other, have shifted as the scope of negotiations at the enterprise level has broadened. The distinction between collective bargaining at the industry level and co-determination at the enterprise level has become blurred.

## CONCLUSIONS

The traditional German employment relations system, which has been called the 'paradigm of the highly regulated industrial relations system' (Ferner & Hyman 1998: xiv) and the 'German model of negotiated adjustment' (Thelen 1991) is in decline. Employment relations are no longer as highly regulated and consensus driven.

Since the early 1990s, there has been a gradual disintegration of the German model, particularly in some sectors. There is a slow but general transformation of actors, key institutions and procedural rules. Changes have been incremental and have not been accompanied by fundamental deregulation of the legal framework (Weiss 2013). However, these incremental changes have been far-reaching in their consequences, even though the traditional institutions remain intact.

Meanwhile, there are reasons to doubt that Germany still constitutes the classic example of a CME. This is especially so in the private service sector, reflecting liberalisation and corporate restructuring (Doellgast 2009); institutional complementarities that are mutually reinforcing and contribute to comparative advantages in quality-oriented markets (Hall & Soskice 2001) have lost importance. Further, the traditional approach to corporate governance, with its emphasis on the long-term interests of multiple stakeholders, is gradually being replaced by a rather more neo-liberal, market-driven orientation towards the shorter-term maximisation of shareholder interests (Jackson & Sorge 2012).

There is not a general convergence towards the Anglo-American model described by Colvin and Darbishire (2013), but some similarities are developing, particularly in the trend towards more diversity in employment relations across the economy—between sectors (e.g. traditional manufacturing compared with new private services), enterprises of different sizes (SMEs compared with multinational enterprises, or MNEs) and segments of the labour market. A durable and deeper segmentation into core and peripheral segments of the labour market and of employment relations is a likely outcome.

This trend towards more diversity in employment relations has been caused by internal factors, especially unification and the huge transfer of financial resources to the eastern states, changing modes of work and production, new management strategies to maximise shareholder value and new forms of employment with increased flexibility, as well as external factors, particularly Europeanisation and globalisation.

An outcome of this increasing diversity in employment relations has been increasing inequality, both in terms of earnings dispersion and the incidence of low pay. On both measures, Germany exceeds the CME average and is reaching levels comparable with several LMEs (Jackson & Kirsch 2014: 267). It remains to be seen how the new statutory minimum wage will affect inequality in the years to come.

## FURTHER READING

Hoffmann, R., Jacobi, O., Keller, B. & Weiss, M. (eds) (1998) *The German Model of Industrial Relations between Adaptation and Erosion*. Düsseldorf: Hans-Böckler-Stiftung.

Jacobi, O., Keller, B. & Müller-Jentsch, W. (1998) 'Germany: Facing new challenges', in A. Ferner & R. Hyman (eds), *Changing Industrial Relations in Europe*, 2nd ed. Oxford: Blackwell, pp. 190–238.

Müller-Jentsch, W. & Weitbrecht, H. (eds) (2003) *The Changing Contours of German Industrial Relations.* Munich/Mering: Hampp.

Silvia, S.J. (2013) *Holding the Shop Together: German Industrial Relations in the Postwar Era.* Ithaca: ILR Press.

Weiss, M. & Schmidt, M. (2008) *Labour Law and Industrial Relations in Germany*, 4th ed. Deventer: Wolters Kluwer.

## USEFUL WEBSITES

BDA: <www.arbeitgeber.de/www/arbeitgeber.nsf/id/EN_Home>.

DGB: <www.dgb.de>.

European Observatory of Working Life: <www.eurofound.europa.eu/observatories/eurwork>.

Federal Institute for Vocational Education and Training: <www.bibb.de/en/index.php>.

Federal Ministry of Labour and Social Affairs: <www.bmas.de/EN/Our-Topics/content.html>.

Hans Böckler Foundation: co-determination in Germany and Europe: <www.boeckler.de/37080.htm>.

# A CHRONOLOGY OF GERMAN EMPLOYMENT RELATIONS

| | |
|---|---|
| 1850s–60s | Formation of the first trade unions. |
| 1869 | Foundation of Social Democratic Workers' Party. |
| 1878–90 | Anti-socialist legislation. |
| 1891 | First industrial union—German Metalworkers' Association. |
| 1913 | Association of German Employers' Federations is established. |
| 1914–18 | World War I. |
| 1920 | General strike against right-wing riot (Kapp-Putsch). |
| 1920 | *Works Councils Act.* |
| 1933 | Unions abolished by National Socialist government. |
| 1939–45 | World War II. |
| 1949 | Founding congress of DGB. |
| 1951 | *Co-determination Act* for coal and steel industries. |
| 1952 | *Works Constitution Act.* |
| 1955 | *Staff Representation Act.* |
| 1963 | Lockout of metalworkers. |
| 1967–77 | 'Concerted action'. |
| 1972 | Revision of the *Works Constitution Act.* |
| 1974 | Strike in the public sector. |
| 1974 | Revision of the *Staff Representation Act.* |
| 1976 | *Co-determination Act.* |
| 1984 | Metalworkers' strike and lockout about shorter working week. |
| 1990 | Unification of West and East Germany. Dissolution of the FDGB (Freier Deutscher Gewerkschaftsbund). |
| 1993 | Completion of the European internal market (Maastricht Treaty). |
| 1998–2003 | Alliance for Jobs, Training and Competitiveness. |
| 1999 | Start of the Economic and Monetary Union; Germany is one of the founding members. |
| 2001 | Revision of the *Works Constitution Act.* |
| 2001 | Merger of five service sector unions; foundation of ver.di. |
| 2002 | Unitary framework agreement for pay in the engineering and related industries. |
| 2003 | Failure of the Alliance for Jobs, Training and Competitiveness. |
| 2003 | Strike in the metalworking industry in eastern Germany to reduce working time. |
| 2003–04 | Major reform of labour market, employment policies and parts of the social security systems (Hartz Laws). |
| 2004 | Pforzheim Agreement in the engineering industries; introduction of opening clauses to secure competitiveness and employment. |
| 2008–09 | Most severe economic downturn since the late 1920s but quick recovery. |
| 2015 | Introduction of a statutory NMW. |

# CHAPTER 9

# Employment relations in Denmark

Jørgen Steen Madsen, Jesper Due
and Søren Kaj Andersen

The financial crisis and the economic crisis that struck the Danish economy at the end of 2008 presented a serious challenge to the system of employment relations in Denmark. Nevertheless, there was a gradual upswing from 2013 to 2014. Furthermore, the trade unions and the employers' associations in the private sector managed to renew collective agreements in ways that will improve the competitiveness of the private sector.

Several key developments have nevertheless caused problems between employers and trade unions, and the actors in the political arena. The balance has shifted between the two sides of the scale in the Danish 'flexicurity' model—that is, on the one side income security for wage-earners in case of unemployment, and on the other side the right of employers to flexibly downsize their workforce when necessary. An ambitious attempt in 2011–12 to help solve the crisis by tripartite negotiations failed. Furthermore, a significant number of migrant workers entering Denmark from Central and Eastern European countries led to an intense debate on 'wage dumping' and the undermining of the collective bargaining system. Last but not least, the government's decision to lock out teachers and the subsequent politically imposed outcome of parts of the public sector collective bargaining round in 2013 brought into question the political actors' will to continue to involve employees' organisations, which has traditionally been the norm when regulating wages and working conditions in Denmark.

The difficult relationship between the parties in the labour market and the political actors may become a long-term problem for the Danish system of collective bargaining. The most important factor in this respect is the positive socio-economic effects of the collective bargaining rounds in the private sector, where the parties in three successive rounds of negotiation—in 2010, 2012 and 2014—managed to reach agreements that will improve the competitiveness of Danish companies. This demonstrates the flexibility of the Danish system of regulation, in which regulation of pay takes place via company-level bargaining within framework agreements, which means that adjustments can be made quickly if needed due to slowdowns in growth.

The explanation for this flexibility is to be found in characteristics of Danish labour market regulation, which has deep historical roots. The unification of the labour market actors into confederations at a national level, and the establishment of both the system of collective bargaining and labour law, were all elements that came into being around 1900. Collective bargaining subsequently became the preferred method of regulation for pay and working conditions.

The state has played the role of the third actor in the industrial relations (IR) system (Dunlop 1958). This has occurred in relation to labour market policy, which to a large extent has been formulated within the framework of tripartite agreements. Welfare issues, such as questions of pensions and further training, have also been the subject of tripartite negotiations and agreements, particularly over the last couple of decades. From this perspective, the Danish political economy is a typical coordinated market economy (CME) (Hall & Soskice 2001), with policy development and coordination taking place within a network of key actors, namely trade unions, employers' associations and the political-administrative system.

However, Danish labour market regulation also encompasses clear liberal elements, based on the fundamental political acceptance of self-regulation by the labour market actors. Apart from legislation on freedom of association, there are no specific laws governing the trade unions and employers' associations. Only the Labour Court and the State Conciliation Board on Labour Disputes have a legislative basis. Hence, in relation to the actual regulation, there is only limited legislation.

Denmark has been described as a 'negotiated economy' (Pedersen 2006), which is also known as the 'Danish model' (Due et al. 1993; Due et al. 1994; Due & Madsen 2013; Andersen 2001). The special characteristics and social significance of the employment relations system must be seen in the light of the fact that Denmark is a small country with a population of just under 5.5 million, which in economic terms is greatly dependent on other countries. It is often characteristic of small countries like Denmark that, lacking the ability to protect themselves through protectionist strategies, they develop internal coordination between the state, trade unions and employers in order to be able to adapt to external challenges (Katzenstein 1985).

The industrialisation of Denmark at the end of the nineteenth century was based mainly on agricultural exports. The situation is different today, in that the manufacturing industry accounts for more than half of Danish export revenues. These principally involve the export of machinery and instruments, but also encompass a large number of other products. Denmark's sizeable exports of oil and natural gas from deposits in the North Sea have also contributed significantly over the last three decades. The North Sea oil revenue is now running out, and it is therefore important that Denmark has established itself as a leading-edge country in the field of sustainable energy, especially wind-powered energy. Globalisation over the last three decades has further underlined how dependent the Danish economy is on foreign trade. Imports represented 28 per cent of gross domestic product (GDP) in 1972, but had risen to 50 per cent by 2012, according to Statistics Denmark (2010, 2014). Growth in exports has been even higher, rising from 27 per cent of GDP in 1972 to 55 per cent in 2012. The level fell from 2008 in the wake of the financial crisis, but had already recovered by 2010–11.

The three largest areas of employment in the Danish private sector are the manufacturing industry, financing and business services, and retail trade, hotels and restaurants. Each of these three areas represents around one-quarter of total private sector employment. The other significant areas of employment are construction, transport, and postal and telecommunications services, each of which represents around 10 per cent of private sector employment. The public sector comprises the largest overall area of employment, accounting for more than one-third of total employment (DA 2014).

Unemployment has risen significantly since the start of the global financial crisis in 2008, increasing from a historically low level in the autumn of 2008, when only 3.4 per cent of the total labour force was unemployed. Unemployment reached 7.6 per cent in 2011, and has subsequently fallen slightly to 7 per cent at the beginning of 2014— possibly a sign of an incipient economic turnaround (Eurostat 2014). The total number of people in employment fell by 180,000 persons between 2008 and 2014, indicating that the crisis is not yet over. But unemployment during the current financial crisis has nevertheless remained far below the highest level recorded in the first half of the 1990s, when unemployment peaked at more than 12 per cent. The explanations for the positive employment trend in the decades prior to the global financial crisis include labour market reforms, which emphasised active labour market training, rather than the provision of passive support. Similarly, the development of the collective bargaining system helped to create a more flexible labour market. During the rapid growth era of the 2000s, in-service training and skills development were given a low priority, which made it difficult to react effectively when unemployment again began to rise from 2008. The most recent reforms will therefore once again strengthen training and skills development—for example, by upgrading unskilled workers to the status of skilled workers.

The labour force participation rate in Denmark is high, and at more than 80 per cent of 15- to 64-year-olds, it is among the highest in the Organisation for Economic Cooperation and Development (OECD) countries. The high level of labour force participation among women in particular tends to boost the figures, with more than 76 per cent of Danish women active in the labour market (OECD 2008). Various forms of atypical employment do not generally apply to the Danish labour market. However, the economic boom did create new markets for temporary agency workers, but the number of agency workers was halved during the financial crisis (Stuvøy & Andersen 2013). Agency workers comprise only around 1 per cent of the total labour force.

## LEGAL, ECONOMIC AND POLITICAL BACKGROUND

The fundamental characteristics of Danish employment relations have been prevalent since the establishment of the collective bargaining system. It began with the signing in 1899 of the September Compromise between the two newly founded confederations for wage-earners and employers, the Danish Confederation of Trade Unions (Landsorganisationen i Danmark, or LO) and the Danish Employers' Confederation (Dansk arbejdsgiverforening, or DA).

The nature of the Danish economy at the time, composed of many relatively small handcraft-dominated companies and few large enterprises, meant that employers had difficulty in countering the decentralised wages strategy of the blossoming trade unions—the so-called leap-frogging strategy. As the unions could not be eliminated directly, the employers sought instead to establish a centralised collective bargaining system. The employers also counter-attacked through lockouts, which in 1899 resulted in a nationwide dispute that lasted from spring until September. At the time, this was considered to be the most extensive labour conflict yet encountered, both in Denmark and by international comparisons (Crouch 1993).

Although the new 'basic agreement'—from the September Compromise—created the foundation for an institutionalised collective bargaining system, conflicts between the labour market actors continued in the years after the turn of the century. There was no formal system to handle conflicts. This led to the establishment of the August Committee of 1908 with representatives from the two confederations, LO and DA.

The August Committee of 1908 established a comprehensive labour law system in 1910. Thereafter, rights disputes concerning the interpretation of current collective agreements were to be settled by industrial arbitration, while rights disputes on breaches of the agreements would be handled by a new Labour Court with advocates for the parties, and presided over by professional judges. The rules for industrial arbitration were left to the parties themselves to determine. The guidelines for the Labour Court, on the other hand, were laid down by a special *Labour Court Act*. The same principle applied to another achievement of the August Committee, the establishment of a State Conciliation Board. The new labour court system kept the industrial peace during the agreement periods, and ensured that conflicts could be initiated only in connection with the renewal of the collective agreements, after an appropriate period of notice. The task of the conciliation board was to mediate between the parties during collective agreement negotiations, and thereby further reduce the threat of conflict.

Even prior to the introduction of state support for the labour law system in 1910, legislation had been enacted that was of vital importance for the parties in the labour market. The Act on state-recognised unemployment insurance funds set out the rules for unemployment benefits in accordance with the so-called Ghent system, under which unemployment benefits from 1907 were administered via the unemployment insurance funds of the trade unions. A welfare service—which in many countries is administered by the public authorities—thus came to be placed under the control of the trade unions. In practice, this made membership of an unemployment insurance fund synonymous with membership of a trade union, thereby contributing to strengthening the unions and securing high levels of union density, and consequent high levels of collective agreement coverage. These were necessary ingredients in the development and retention of a form of labour market regulation that was based primarily on collective bargaining.[1]

From the time of the enactment of the supportive labour law legislation, the decisive characteristics of the relations between the parties and the political system were clear. The essential condition for self-regulation—and for the parties to be able to continue to wield decisive influence over subsequent alterations in the supportive procedural legislation—was that the employees' and employers' organisations would be able to arrive at compromises between their different interests, and present joint solutions to the political system. This principle, which has been designated the 'consensus principle', has almost always been adhered to in the history of the collective bargaining system in relation to the legislation that underpins the tripartite system (Due & Madsen 2006).

However, the principle of consensus has been less apparent in legislation that, despite self-regulation, has been enacted to govern the contents of the regulation, such as the *Holiday Act* and the *White-Collar Workers Act*, and with regard to the consultation of the parties in political regulation—not only in relation to labour market policy, but also on broader social issues.[2] There has occasionally been competition between the labour market actors to secure the greatest possible influence, but experience seems to show that the parties are able to secure the most effective and lasting level of influence when they adhere to the consensus principle in this area as well.

The new labour law system did not lead to the immediate realisation of the employers' wish to see a system of coordinated collective bargaining under the control of the confederations, because the individual unions still held on to their right to directly negotiate agreements. The power struggle continued over the degree of centralisation of the collective bargaining system. The differing strategies of the parties were reflected in their internal power structures, with DA becoming characterised by a strong centralisation of power, while the leadership of LO never managed to establish central control over the collective bargaining rights of its member unions.

DA had to continue efforts to develop the centralisation project, and this centralisation phase spanned the first half-century of the history of the Danish collective bargaining system. DA used the threat of sympathy lockouts by employers as a means of securing a unified process. An important change occurred, however, with the amendments to the negotiation rules and the *Conciliation Act* in 1934 and 1936. This established de facto centralisation by extending the powers of the conciliator to put forward settlement proposals and introduce linked coordination through a common ballot for all the involved unions and employers' associations. The principle was that either all of the parties entered into an agreement, or else all participated in a conflict. The conciliator's proposals in mediation attempts thereby became 'the crucial stage in collective bargaining' in Denmark (Galenson 1952: 112).

The 1930s—the first decade of Social Democrat–led governments—also saw the development of the practice of political intervention in industrial conflicts. When the State Conciliation Board was unable to achieve an agreed solution, several times the government chose to intervene to stop industrial conflicts that, in the light of the economic depression of that decade, were regarded as a socio-economic threat.

Since then, interventions by the political system in labour market conflicts have proved to be more the norm than an exception. Industrial conflicts are certainly recognised as being an important element in the Danish model, as a means of forcing the labour market actors to compromise, but if a conflict breaks out with no prospect of an early solution, and there is considered to be a risk of negative economic and/or political consequences, the political parties in the Danish parliament are generally inclined to intervene.

It should be added that the development of the Danish model in the decades prior to World War II was not characterised solely by a tendency towards centralisation. The collective bargaining model also developed from the beginning into a coherent regulatory system with several levels. There were strong relations between unions and employers, not just at the central level but also at the enterprise level, where there was a dense network of shop stewards, union branches and—after World War II—cooperation committees; this helped to secure the effective implementation of the agreements.

The possibility of holding local negotiations on pay was also introduced. The Danish model became a system of considerable depth. From the establishment of the system at the beginning of the twentieth century, a ground-breaking agreement in the iron and steel industry created a system where the actual pay rise was negotiated by the involved parties in the individual companies. The clear risk that centralised collective bargaining might lead to a lack of flexibility was thereby countered in the most export-oriented sector.

A new phase in the history of the collective bargaining system became a reality at the beginning of the 1950s, when the regular collective bargaining rounds began to take place under the control of LO and DA. The phase of central negotiations lasted from the start of the 1950s to the end of the 1970s. From a formal perspective, the individual trade unions and their respective employer counterparts retained their negotiating powers, but due to a division between special and general issues, the result in practice was that the crucial issues were directly negotiated between the confederations—usually with the participation of the State Conciliation Board.

The decades after World War II can justifiably be termed the 'golden age' of the collective bargaining model. It was during this period that the principles introduced at the time of the foundation of the bargaining system came to full fruition. At the same time, however, the high level of centralisation also began to produce problems. The regulation had become too inflexible, and it was difficult for companies to adjust to the increasing level of international competition.

It was also during this period that the public sector labour market began to expand greatly, particularly with the development of the welfare state from the 1960s. The civil service reform of 1969 initiated a development that gradually led to a shift from civil servant status to contractual employment as the dominant form of employment in the public sector. At the same time, a new collective bargaining system was developed on the basis of the old civil service system, under which collective agreements became the new, norm-setting form of regulation. Negotiations on the renewal of these collective agreements were handled via a strongly centralised collective bargaining system, in which the trade unions negotiated collectively from top to bottom via large cartels in the two main areas: the state, and the municipal and county area.

From the mid-1970s, Denmark saw the establishment of its most coordinated rounds of collective bargaining. The two-year agreements were renewed in a coherent process every second year on the basis of the negotiations in the LO-DA area in the private sector. Once negotiations were concluded, the result could be transferred to the public sector. This created a clear hierarchy in the coordinated agreement model, with the competitive industries setting the pattern and the government ensuring that all parts of the public sector adhered to the central principle that, while public employees should not lead the way in pay rises, they should be secured pay rises that more or less corresponded to those of private employees. The other main employer areas in the private sector—agriculture and finance—also renewed their collective agreements at the same rate as the LO-DA area.

## THE EMPLOYMENT RELATIONS PARTIES

### Employers' associations

DA was established in 1896, and quickly gained a strongly centralised power structure. Since the end of the 1980s, many of the formerly numerous small employers' associations have amalgamated to form fewer, larger units under DA. In 2014, of the more than 150 member organisations that existed at the end of the 1980s, just thirteen remain. Of these, three large conglomerates—the Danish Confederation of Industry (Erhvervenes organisation, or DI), the Danish Chamber of Commerce (Dansk erhverv) and the Danish Construction Association (Dansk byggeri) account for almost 90 per cent of the total payroll of enterprises covered by DA. DI alone accounts for 62 per cent of the total (DA 2014). Overall, it thus appeared as if the end result would be a single organisation for each of the three main sectors: manufacturing, service and construction. However, the competition for members has now crossed sectoral boundaries. The amalgamation into a few large member associations has also altered the power structure in DA. From being a confederation in which the daily management held decisive power, DA has developed to become more of a coordinating body for the large organisations—much the same role that has always been played by LO with respect to the member unions.

DA is by far the largest employers' confederation. Since the inclusion of the Danish Confederation of Employers' Associations in Agriculture (Sammenslutningen af landbrugets arbejdsgiverforeninger) in the DA family on 1 July 2012, there have been only two employers' confederations left: the DA and the Danish Employers' Association for the Financial Sector (Finansektorens arbejdsgiverforening, or FA).

As can been seen from Table 9.1, DA and FA together cover 53 per cent of the private sector labour market. To this can be added a few small employers' organisations outside the main confederations. However, companies accounting for approximately 45 per cent of the private sector labour market are not members of any employers' association. This non-member segment has increased steadily from about 40 per cent in 2008. The membership density among employers otherwise showed steady growth up to 2010, when the member associations of DA in particular managed to attract an increasing number of enterprises. This was due less to their function as employers' organisations than to the development of their simultaneous role as special-interest business organisations. DA's organisations by 2010 reached a total membership of about 27,000 companies, but this figure fell to slightly over 24,000 by August 2012.

With the expansion of the welfare state since the 1960s, the number of public sector employees has grown enormously, while at the same time there has been a shift from civil servant status to contractual employment as the dominant form of employment in the public sector. The public sector has thereby acquired increasing importance as an element in the overall system. From the beginning of the 1970s, two main areas underwent development. Local authorities became dominant, as the welfare services are administered by local political units, while the state diminished in size. However, it has always been the minister in charge of public sector pay (usually the minister of finance) who, together with the agency acting as the employer, plays the most decisive role in public sector collective bargaining. The fourteen counties and 373 municipalities negotiated via their two associations, the Association of County Councils in Denmark (Amtrådsforeningen i Danmark) and Local Government Denmark

**Table 9.1 Collective agreement areas in the labour market**

| | Number of wage-earners (000s) converted to full-time equivalents | | |
| | Share of main sector | | Share of overall labour market |
| | No. | (%) | (%) |
|---|---|---|---|
| Private sector | 1356 | 100 | 63 |
| DA | 653 | 48 | 30 |
| FA | 65 | 5 | 3 |
| Other/not organised | 638 | 47 | 30 |
| Public sector | 788 | – | 37 |
| Total | 2144 | – | 100 |

*Sources:* DA, on the basis of special analyses by Statistics Denmark and information from FA (DA 1998, 2007, 2009, 2014: 262)

(Kommunernes Landsforening, or KL), with the larger, KL, taking the leading role. The local government reform of 1 January 2007 reduced the fourteen counties to five regions, and the number of municipalities to 98. Thereafter, the municipalities and regions covered three-quarters and the state sector one-quarter of public employees.

The municipalities have, by and large, retained their position, and still negotiate their collective agreements via KL. The regions—almost the only remaining function of which is the administration of the public hospitals—have a less independent role than the former counties. The regions cannot, for example, levy their own taxes. With respect to collective bargaining, the state has also been given a direct right of veto over the regional area, and consequently the municipalities have not wished to maintain the joint regional–municipal negotiations that formerly characterised negotiations by the counties and municipalities. The regions thus now hold separate negotiations.

## Unions

LO was founded in 1898. It was, and remains, by far the largest confederation of unions in Denmark. Its member organisations mainly represent skilled and unskilled manual workers, but also include groups of salaried employees. LO is the dominant confederation on the employees' side in the private sector, and is also the largest confederation in the public sector labour market.

Most of LO's member unions began at the local level as craft unions, and developed over time into nationwide associations. But from the start there have also been a limited number of industrial unions and general workers' unions. Recent decades have seen a tendency towards concentration in fewer and larger units. In 2014, LO was made up of seventeen member unions, of which the four largest represented 80 per cent of the total membership (Due & Madsen 2005).

LO's power structure has especially been determined by the desire of the major member unions to retain their right to independently negotiate agreements. LO has therefore always functioned more as a coordinating organ for the major unions than as an independent power in itself. However, as the unions have often had divergent interests, LO has been able to acquire independent influence by acting as a mediator between the large member organisations. The LO unions quickly achieved a high level of union density in the urban industries, and thereby the strength to establish collective agreements as the dominating form of regulation in the private sector labour market.

The Confederation of Professionals in Denmark (Funktionærernes of Tjenestemændenes Fællesråd, or FTF) mainly represents professional groups such as nurses, teachers and kindergarten teachers in the public sector, but it also plays a decisive role in the financial sector. These organisations are based around the common educational background of their members, and are thereby characterised by profession-based strategies. In collective bargaining, FTF has had only limited influence, as the right to negotiate lies with the individual member unions. FTF plays a larger political role as the representative of the common interests of its member organisations in tripartite negotiations.

The Danish Confederation of Professional Associations (Akademikerne, or AC) is a confederation of unions representing employees with an academic education. AC covers both the public and private sectors, but its principal weight is in the public sector. In contrast to LO, AC also directly negotiates collective agreements in the public sector labour market, and enjoys the same political role as the other confederations in relation to tripartite negotiations and so on.

The organisational structure in Denmark is influenced by the existence of independent associations in the private sector labour market for the various managerial groups. This trend can be traced back to the September Compromise of 1899, in which the employers had a provision inserted stating that employees who acted as representatives of the employers in the workplaces should not be obliged to join the same unions as the other wage-earners.

The majority of managers are represented by the Organisation of Managerial and Executive Staff (Ledernes hovedorganisation, or LH). LH has only a limited collective bargaining role. Most managers in the private sector are employed on the basis of individual employment contracts. LH and DA have negotiated an overall framework agreement, which lays down guidelines for regulation, but this does not include provisions regarding pay.

The four confederations represent the established union movement in Denmark. One major difference has been that LO and its member unions have always enjoyed a close relationship with the Social Democrats, while the other confederations have been politically neutral—albeit increasingly active on the political front. Over the past decade, LO has severed its formal political and economic ties with the Social Democrats and, although informal ties remain, this has helped to reduce the gap between the confederations. Another sign of closer cooperation between the confederations has been the joint participation by LO, FTF and AC in the European Trade Union Confederation (ETUC).

In recent decades, LO has seen a relative decrease in membership. Although it represented 65 per cent of all organised wage-earners in 1996, LO's proportion had fallen to 49 per cent by 2013. As current alterations in the structure of education and industry encourage a continuation of this trend, the time will come when LO represents only every second trade union member. For the time being, however, LO remains the largest confederation, and possesses decisive influence, as it is the LO unions that play the leading role in collective bargaining with the DA organisations in the private sector. LO enjoys special status in the tripartite negotiations.

While the large confederations have more or less declared peace among themselves, they are still in sharp competition with the alternative—or 'yellow'—organisations. This competition can be traced back to the breakthrough years of the unions, when alternative organisations, often established by the employers, acted as strike-breakers.[3] In Denmark, the Christian Trade Union Movement (CTUM) was established in 1898, at the same time as LO. The CTUM rejected from the start the principle of the right to strike, and was also an integrated part of the Christian employers' association.

The CTUM remained a marginal phenomenon right up to the 1990s; it never succeeded in breaking the collective bargaining monopoly of the established unions, and its membership remained at a low level. In an attempt to alter the situation, the CTUM cut its ties with the Christian employers. At the same time, several other alternative trade unions began to arise. It was not until the mid-1990s, however, that major growth began to occur in the membership numbers of the alternative organisations, and this trend has continued in recent years. As can be seen from Table 9.2, membership of the alternative organisations almost tripled between 1996 and 2008. These unions had a total membership in 1995 of 53,000. By 2008, this figure had grown to 145,000, representing a growth rate of 174 per cent in a period when the total membership of trade unions had otherwise been stagnating. Whereas the alternative organisations were a marginal phenomenon in

**Table 9.2   Confederations of unions' membership**

|  | Member numbers by year (000s) | | | | |
|---|---|---|---|---|---|
|  | *1995* | *2000* | *2005* | *2008* | *2012* |
| LO | 1208 | 1176 | 1142 | 1017 | 872 |
| FTF | 332 | 350 | 361 | 359 | 353 |
| AC[a] | 132 | 150 | 163 | 174 | 192 |
| LH | 75 | 80 | 76 | 76 | 91 |
| Alternative unions[b] | 53 | 68 | 94 | 145 | 218 |
| Other unions outside the confederations[a] | 62 | 55 | 57 | 57 | 58 |
| Total | 1862 | 1879 | 1893 | 1828 | 1784 |
| Wage-earners and unemployed[c] | 2547 | 2614 | 2640 | 2657 | 2648 |
| Union membership (%) | 73 | 72 | 72 | 69 | 67 |
| Excluding alternatives (%) | 71 | 69 | 68 | 64 | 59 |

*Notes:*
(a) To demonstrate the long-term development in AC's total membership, this table includes for 2012 members of the Danish Engineers Association (Ingeniørforeningen i Danmark) and the Surveyors Association (Landinspektorforeningen), although for a short period, from 1 January 2009 to 1 September 2013, these two organisations were actually independent organisations outside AC.
(b) Unions outside the confederations, which also regard themselves as alternatives to the established unions—the 'yellow' unions.
(c) Labour force minus self-employed.

*Sources: Statistical Yearbook*, AKU (Labour Force Survey) and LO statistics.

1995, with a 3 per cent share of total union membership, their 12 per cent share in 2012 has made them more of a real alternative, and therefore a potential threat to the established trade union movement.

## Government

The Danish model, with extensive self-regulation by the parties in the labour market, does not mean that the role of the state as an actor in the employment relations system is insignificant. The role of the state is merely more limited than is the case in some other countries.

Apart from the supportive procedural legislation mentioned above, the collective bargaining system is self-regulating. The relations between the organisations, and the rules for industrial conflicts, are thereby fixed in the basic agreements between the parties in the various bargaining areas. There are, for example, no legislative rules governing the conditions for the formal registration of trade unions. It is, in principle, a free market. However, by entering into sector agreements—which apply both to their own members and to non-union members within the specific bargaining area—the established unions have in practice established a monopoly on the right to collective bargaining. In substance, the legislation is extremely limited. For example, there is no statutory minimum wage. Over the past decade, there appears to have been a renewed tendency towards increased political intervention, reflecting the fact that more welfare issues are now being encompassed by the collective agreements. It can also be seen as an effect of Denmark's membership of the European Union (EU), as various EU directives have been introduced via legislation.

With regard to labour market policy, there has always been formal consultation of the labour market actors in the form of participation in the councils and boards that administer the policy, as well as in the work of the committees and commissions where reforms are prepared and implemented. Apart from this area, though, it should be noted that tripartite cooperation has always been of an ad hoc nature (Mailand 2008, 2011a).

The significant role of the state in the labour market has been concentrated particularly on the growing and stabilising public sector, which has resulted from the development of the welfare state in the second half of the twentieth century.

## PROCESSES OF EMPLOYMENT RELATIONS

Table 9.3 shows coverage of the Danish labour market by collective bargaining. The level of coverage of the collective agreements is very high, with almost 90 per cent of employees covered in the DA and FA areas. The remaining employees belong to some white-collar groups, including university-educated staff and managers employed on individual contracts.

In addition to the two confederations, there are also some smaller employers' associations. However, a very large group of enterprises, encompassing approximately 45 per cent of employees in the private sector labour market, are entirely outside the employers' associations. As a result, it is primarily the ability of the trade unions to enter into adoption agreements with the non-organised companies that has secured them such a high level of collective agreement coverage, which comprises 74 per cent of the private sector. Despite this high level, a quarter of wage-earners in the private sector are not covered by a collective agreement. Their pay and conditions are regulated solely through individual contracts. However, as these contracts are entered into in collective bargaining environments, there is a considerable knock-on effect on the group of non-covered employees.

In the decades following World War II, collective bargaining negotiations in Denmark constituted a coherent system with simultaneous and coordinated negotiations in all major areas. However, the process of decentralisation that began in the 1980s brought about a breakdown in this system. A new pattern has since developed, in which the large LO-DA area negotiates in one year, followed by the remaining areas of the private sector, together with the public sector, in the following year. This has increased the scope for leverage effects. The public sector and

**Table 9.3   Collective bargaining agreement coverage in the labour market**

|  | Number of wage-earners (000s) converted to full-time equivalents | | |
| --- | --- | --- | --- |
| 2012 | Covered by agreement | Total | % covered |
| Private sector | 1006 | 1356 | 74 |
| DA | 573 | 653 | 88 |
| FA | 58 | 65 | 89 |
| Other/not organised | 375 | 638 | 59 |
| Public sector | 788 | 788 | 100 |
| Total | 1794 | 2144 | 84 |

*Sources:* Statistics Denmark (DA 2014: 262).

the financial sector typically set the standard with regard to the development of social welfare elements in collective agreements. However, since the beginning of the financial crisis, any improvements negotiated, for example, in the field of training and skills development have been initiated more by the private sector than by the public sector.

## The determination of pay

The collective bargaining model that has emerged during the past decades has its roots in the economic crisis of the 1970s, when it was becoming more difficult for the two main confederations, DA and LO, to continue the culture of consensus and create joint solutions while satisfying their divergent interests. The collective bargaining of the 1970s began with a major strike in the private sector in 1973, followed by three consecutive political interventions in 1975, 1977 and 1979. By the end of the 1970s, the collective bargaining system was in crisis.

### *Centralised decentralisation*

The answer to the crisis of the 1970s was not further centralisation in the form of an institutionalised tripartite system, as was desired by parts of LO, but rather a movement in the opposite direction, with the focus on the collective bargaining process being returned from the confederations to the sector organisations. However, overall coordination was retained, with a common ballot for the entire LO-DA area via the State Conciliation Board on Labour Disputes.

In addition—especially from the beginning of the 1990s—an organisational centralisation took place, with new, large, sector-wide organisations being formed. Within the bounds of framework-governed collective agreements, these organisations retained overall coordination despite the transferral of negotiations to the parties at enterprise level. This new phase in the development of the Danish model, which took place from the 1980s to the 1990s, may be characterised as 'centralised decentralisation'.

From the time of the establishment of the collective bargaining system, the parties in the iron and steel industry—which the sector must subject to competition—came to constitute the key bargaining area. After the start of the 1990s, this was expanded to include all of the manufacturing industry, with the establishment of a new large confederation, DI, on the employers' side, followed on the wage-earners' side by the Central Organisation of Industrial Employees in Denmark (CO-industri), a coalition of unions, that could match DI.

As well as the displacement in the collective agreement nego-tiations, this period also saw decentralisation taking place in two concurrent processes. First, more collective agreements changed from being standardised pay agreements, with wages centrally determined at the negotiating table, to various kinds of flexible pay systems, with wages determined by negotiations at the enterprise level. Since the mid-1990s, approximately 85 per cent of the overall LO-DA area has encompassed flexible pay systems. At the same time, a development has occurred in recent years in the direction of more individual pay negotiations. While only around 4 per cent of the LO-DA area was covered by collective agreements without specified pay rates in 1993, this had risen to 23 per cent by 2007 (DA 1998, 2007, 2009).

Second, in addition to the negotiation of pay, a transfer of nego-tiating responsibility to the parties at enterprise level also occurred in connection with other areas, particularly over working hours. This has given enterprises greatly enhanced possibilities for introducing flexibility, such as wide-ranging powers to organise flexible working hours. This was achieved through a loosening of the collective agree-ment provisions during the 1990s, with the collective bargaining parties in the manufacturing industry leading the way. This develop-ment provided an opportunity for local trade-offs between the parties, which can be viewed as a form of flexicurity agreement at the enter-prise level.

By international comparisons, Danish companies continue to have very strong local union representation, with approximately 80 per cent of employees represented by shop stewards (Ilsøe et al. 2007; Ilsøe 2008; Navrbjerg et al. 2010).

### Greater scope of the collective agreements

In recent times, there has been an expansion in the scope of collec-tive agreements. While these previously had dealt almost exclusively with wages and working hours, from the start of the 1990s they also began to encompass a number of welfare-related issues. Following a breakthrough in the public sector in 1989 (the LO-DA area), the manu-facturing industry began to develop occupational pensions schemes (arbejdsmarkedspensionsordninger).

Besides occupational pensions, the scope of the collective agree-ments has also been expanded with new provisions dealing with the right to further training, social chapters, sick pay and paid parental leave. A kind of double regulation has developed, under which welfare-related issues such as the right to pay during parental leave are regulated via both collective agreements and legislation. This creates a large area of interplay between the labour market actors and the political players, and legitimises the direct influence of the politicians over the agenda of the various collective bargaining rounds. This in turn places the self-regulation of the parties under pressure.

## European regulation

Denmark became a member of the European Community (EC) in 1973. Since the establishment of the Single European Market in 1993, the EU has in various ways questioned and placed pressure on the existing Danish labour market regulation. This became especially clear in the early 1990s, when a number of labour law directives, and thereby common European legislation, became adopted at European level. These directives were aimed at regulating matters such as working hours, part-time employment, fixed-term work and European works councils.

This regulation is based on legislation (directives) and individual rights. Especially in Denmark, where the employers and trade unions prefer regulating most matters via collective agreements, this triggered worries about whether regulation via collective agreements would be compatible with the EU labour law regulation. Would it lead to a creeping 'legalisation' of the Danish bargaining model, which over time could undermine trade union organisation and displace the bargaining system? In order to assess how the directives should be implemented, a tripartite Implementation Committee was established with representatives from the labour market confederations and the state. In general, the labour market actors first implement the directive provisions via the collective agreements; this is then followed by secondary legislation in the Danish parliament, which ensures that the remaining groups of wage-earners are also covered by the directives. Technically, this added a kind of extension mechanism to the provisions of the collective agreements dealing with the implementation of European labour law directives. Developments over recent years have shown that this did not undermine the collective bargaining system. Furthermore, only a few new EU directives have been adopted since the beginning of the 2000s (Andersen 2003; Kristiansen 2013).

By contrast, the effects of EU law regarding the relations between the EU principle of free movement and the Danish collective bargaining system have proven to be a greater source of conflict in recent years. The tensions have primarily concerned the free movement of services, where the Posting of Workers Directive regulates worker rights. In brief, this directive, adopted in 1996, states that the employment conditions of the home country are to form the basis of the regulation (including taxes and social charges). The exception from this is a core of working conditions (Article 3.1 in the directive), where the host country's rules apply (e.g. working hours, working environment and minimum wages set out in law or generally applicable collective agreements).

The expansion of the EU in 2004 and 2007 to include Central and Eastern European states led to Danish companies—especially in construction—to hire foreign subcontractors who compete with lower labour costs. Without a statutory minimum wage, and without rules capable of rendering collective agreements generally applicable, this meant that it was entirely legal to hire posted Central and Eastern Europeans at wage levels, social contributions and taxes in accordance with home country rules (Dølvik & Eldring 2008; Andersen & Hansen 2008).

Controversies regarding posting of workers led to court cases—the most well known being the Laval case, brought before the European Court of Justice in 2007. This dealt with the degree to which a trade union can place demands on a foreign company with regard to the pay and conditions of workers sent from the home country. The company in question was a Latvian construction company renovating a school in a Stockholm suburb. The Swedish trade union demanded that the company should pay wages according to stipulations in the collective agreement based on supplementary local pay negotiations. The European Court of Justice found this demand to be discriminatory, since it was not made sufficiently clear to the foreign company that it could face such pay demands. With no statutory minimum wages and no legislation rendering collective agreements generally applicable in both Sweden and Denmark, trade unions faced changes in the national implementation of the posted workers directives that limited their possibilities of initiating industrial action against foreign companies. In spite of difficulties in obtaining solid data on pay conditions of posted workers, this seems to have cemented the pay differences between posted workers and locally based workers (Andersen & Hansen 2008). As a consequence, discussion continues as to whether Denmark should introduce some form of legislation that will lead to generally applicable collective agreements. Currently, the dominant employers' associations and trade unions consider this an unacceptable breach with the existing system of voluntary regulation.

## Dispute settlement

The right to initiate conflict is in practice reserved solely for *conflicts of interest*—in connection with the renewal of existing collective agreements, or when entering into collective bargaining in new areas. The parties are in agreement that their potentially conflicting interests during the process of bargaining make it essential that both sides are able to use the weapon of conflict as a necessary threat to force the other side to make concessions. But if the threat of conflict is to be taken seriously, it must be used from time to time, and in recent history there have been four major conflicts. Since the industrial conflict of 1961, a number of strikes have taken place in the labour market, with their basis in the LO-DA area, at twelve- to thirteen-year intervals: in 1973, 1985 and 1998.

In general, the mediation efforts of the State Conciliation Board have proved an efficient means of getting the parties to compromise. This institution functions to a great extent as the parties' own tool, with the conciliator putting forward proposals only if the parties accept this in advance—or at least do not actively oppose it. The conciliation board thus provides a buffer for the negotiators in situations where, due to pressure from their rank and file, it can be difficult for the parties to openly make the necessary concessions. In those instances where the parties have been unable to reach agreement, despite the assistance of the conciliation board, conflict is the only possibility. But only rarely are widespread conflicts in the labour market allowed to go on for very long, due to the established tradition of political intervention.

Although, according to the rules, it is permitted to give notice of strikes and lockouts only in connection with conflicts of interest, this does not mean that the Danish labour market is entirely peaceful. Local disputes often lead to unofficial strikes. In recent years, however, the number of such conflicts has been diminishing. Strikes are thus a rarely utilised means of solving local disputes over the collective agreements. Most conflicts of rights are resolved through the labour law system. The vast majority of disputes are solved locally, solely with advice from the organisations, or at meetings with the participation of the parties to the collective agreement. Disputes rarely progress beyond this level. However, if agreement cannot be achieved, disputes on the interpretation of the collective agreements are handled by industrial arbitration, while the Labour Court handles breaches of collective agreements.

The increasing degree of international regulation has also influenced the Danish system, inasmuch as it can be difficult to accept this form of collective regulation in other, more individually oriented employment relations systems—particularly in relation to the private arbitration system. This resulted in amendments to the Danish IR legislation in 2008, so that the *Labour Court Act* now also lays down guidelines for the treatment of cases through industrial arbitration.

These amendments were undertaken with the agreement of the labour market actors, who thereby hoped to secure the future of the Danish labour law system.

## ISSUES AND TRENDS

The liberal–conservative coalition government in power from 2001 to 2011 initially created problems for the union movement, in that it abolished the monopoly right held by the traditional unions to operate unemployment benefit funds. This monopoly had protected the traditional unions from competition and helped to maintain their membership numbers. But after some time in power during conditions of economic growth, the government attempted to consolidate its position by following a social democratic–style welfare policy and holding tripartite negotiations. Prior to the collective agreement negotiations in 2007, extra public funding was allocated to training and skills development, particularly in the private sector. Furthermore, before the negotiation round in the public sector in 2008, a new tripartite agreement made additional funding available to the public sector.

A positive interaction thus developed between the parties—especially the employees' organisations—and the political system. This had the potential to herald the introduction of a new form of regulation, in which the tripartite arena took over some areas of negotiation from the bipartite collective bargaining arena (Mailand 2008, 2011a); however, it actually proved to be a short-lived anomaly. This became apparent towards the end of the liberal–conservative government's term in office, after Prime Minister Anders Fogh Rasmussen was appointed secretary general of the North Atlantic Treaty Organization in April 2009 and had been succeeded as prime minister by Lars Løkke Rasmussen, also a member of the same Liberal (Venstre) Party.

The first change carried out by the new Lars Løkke Rasmussen government was in labour market policy, when responsibility for job and employment centres was transferred from the state to the individual municipalities (*kommuner*), effectively minimising the real influence of the labour market actors. The second came in the spring of 2011, in the form of a tightening up of the rules for unemployment benefits, reducing the maximum period of benefits from four to two years and increasing the minimum period of new employment needed to subsequently re-enter the system from six to twelve months.

These changes represented a shift in the balance between security and flexibility in the internationally recognised Danish flexicurity system (Andersen & Mailand 2005). Wage-earners now have considerably less financial security in case of unemployment—although security is still at a high level against international comparisons—while the employers' right to 'hire and fire' is no less flexible than before. The unions were weakened by the crisis and could neither slow down the political reform nor obtain better security in employment during the collective bargaining rounds.

The third change was a reform of the retirement rules, which greatly restricted access to the Early Retirement Scheme (Efterløn) and increased the age for eligibility for the state retirement pension from 65 to 67 years. The age for retirement pension eligibility will further increase over time, in pace with the increasing average life expectancy of the population. The Social Democratic Party, which traditionally has had a close alliance with the trade union movement, and the Socialist People's Party went to the election in 2011 with a promise to repeal these changes to the Early Retirement Scheme and to the right to unemployment benefits. However, the new Social Democrat–led coalition government, which took power in October 2011, did not have a sufficient majority in parliament to carry through these intended repeals. The status quo, seen by the unions as real cutbacks, continued to be maintained.

The reason that the new government could not deliver on their campaign promises was that the coalition also includes the Radical Liberal (Radikale Venstre) centre party, which actually holds the balance of power necessary to achieve a majority in parliament. The Radical Liberals had supported the previous government's cutbacks, and were not prepared to change their stance on this, thus giving a de facto majority in parliament and preventing any repeal of the measures already taken. This situation caused great frustration in the union movement. The expectation had been that the new government and the union movement could achieve reinstatement of the previous Early Retirement Scheme through wide-ranging tripartite negotiations. LO had already demonstrated a willingness to negotiate in order to free the very large sums needed to finance the changes. These negotiations did not materialise, and a less ambitious tripartite round, which should have increased the available pool of public financing by 5 billion DKK, was abandoned in the spring of 2012. This was perceived as a major setback for the union movement in general, and for the LO in particular.

The centre-left coalition proved to be more centre than left-wing. In practice, the outgoing centre-right government's economic policy was allowed to continue. A recent consequence of this was that the left-wing Socialist People's Party made its exit from the government coalition in early 2014. The government has also run into a crisis in its relationship with the labour movement, due to problematic collective bargaining rounds in the public sector. This became evident during the 2013 collective bargaining rounds, which culminated in a pro-active government-driven lockout of a specific group of employees for the first time in Denmark—in this case, primary school teachers. As there was no immediate prospect of a negotiated settlement, the conflict was ended by a political intervention, by which the majority in parliament dictated a change in teachers' scheduling of working hours in order to release funds for use in a planned reform of the public schooling system.

This emphasised the significant difference between bargaining systems in the private and public sectors. In the public sector, the employer has a double role as both representative of the employer and representative of the political system—which, with democratic legitimacy, decides the overall economic framework. The terminology 'Danish bargaining model' is normally also valid in the context of the public sector because of this tradition, which has evolved in such a way that wage levels and employment conditions are determined by genuine negotiation rather than by political decree, as was the case in 2013 (Mailand 2013).

The trend towards very direct political intervention in a collective bargaining round was already clear in 2008, when economic growth was still at its peak, and when many political parties were ready to give special concessions to selected groups. This led to an outcome with very high wage increases, but expectations had been so inflated (by the political signals) that a broad conflict still broke out. It seemed like the beginning of more political regulation at the expense of the collective bargaining system—that is, the self-regulation of the nego-tiating parties. However, the conclusion of the negotiation round removed the threat to the self-regulation principle (Due & Madsen 2008, 2009)—until it was reintroduced in 2013.

By 2011, the crisis was so deeply felt that public sector employ-ees in the bargaining process were ready to accept outcomes leading to a decline in real wage levels. Expectations had been tempered by the depth of the crisis (Mailand 2011b). The same situation prevailed in the private sector, although without conflicts between the parties. Both LO and DA have in fact succeeded in three successive rounds of bargaining, in 2010, 2012 and 2014, to achieve outcomes that slowed down cost inflation and thus contributed to strengthen the competitive position of Danish companies. The gradual economic upswing gave a slightly improved economic framework for the 2014 round—which, for example, was used to ensure improvements in training and skills upgrading. During the economic boom leading up to 2008, both sector-level and company-level bargaining challenged the pay policy of improving competitiveness, which has applied since the Common Declaration of 1987. The crisis obliged the parties to return to their old established tracks (Ibsen 2013; Andersen & Ibsen 2013).

The Danish model has therefore worked as intended in the private sector, although it has been in crisis in the public sector. The future prospects for the collective bargaining model seem to be dependent on the extent to which the organisations under LO and DA will adhere to the principles built up around its key guiding principles over most of the 100-year history of the system.

Both the trade unions and the employers' associations continue to observe their consensus-based relationship patterns. The commitment shown by the biggest and most powerful player on the employers' side, the DI, is therefore remarkable. Their annual summit meeting on 24 September 2013 was held under the banner of 'the new Nordic approach', and demonstrated very clear backing by the DI for the values central to the Danish model, such as trust-based relations between management and employees (DI 2013). This does not mean that the Danish model will continue without further challenges, however. There are, as previously mentioned, still problems in re-establishing a balance between the labour market actors and the political parties. These problems are exacerbated by the continuing fall in membership numbers and by the impact of external factors, such as the EU in particular.

## Declining organisation membership

High levels of membership density and collective agreement coverage serve to legitimise the special position of the labour market actors in the Danish model. How far can membership continue to fall before this becomes a problem? Union density rose steadily from the mid-1920s until the mid-1990s, when approximately 73 per cent of employees belonged to unions. Since then, however, union membership has continued to fall, dropping to 67 per cent in 2012. The fall has not been dramatic, but the trend looks likely to continue, and seems especially serious when we consider the sizeable growth in membership enjoyed by alternative unions during the same period.

Part of the explanation for the decline in levels of unionisation lies in the alterations in the former close ties between the unions and the unemployment insurance funds by an Act of parliament which, from 2002, permitted non-trade-specific unemployment insurance funds to be established. Joining the unemployment insurance funds of the alternative unions thereby became a genuine possibility—a factor that has contributed to the growth of these associations.

In general, the trend raises the question of whether the union movement can manage to maintain its legitimacy among wage-earners and employers, as well as within a political system that can be expected to try to exert pressure on the overall bargaining system.

## International pressure

The Danish economy is small and open, which means growth and job creation are inextricably linked with international markets. Accordingly, Danish wealth and welfare to a large extent build on successful economic interaction across borders. It can nevertheless be argued that a twofold international pressure on the Danish collective bargaining system has become even more evident in recent years. First, Denmark seems to be losing investments and jobs as companies outsource or choose to place new activities in low-cost countries. Second, increasing numbers of labour migrants—especially from Central and Eastern Europe—are working for wages and conditions that undercut the wages and conditions of Danes.

During the early phase of the post-2007 global financial crisis, almost 200,000 people lost their jobs in the private sector. Probably most painful was the fact that around 66,000 people became redundant in the manufacturing sector during that period, which represents slightly less than 18 per cent of the total employment in the sector. The slow and somewhat uncertain improvement of the Danish economy since then has led to a stabilisation of the labour market, but prospects of job growth remain weak. Some of the largest Danish companies have increased their profits significantly since 2008, and they have established tens of thousands of new jobs—but not in Denmark. These jobs have been created in subsidiaries abroad. Further, corporate investments have stayed at a low level for the last two decades.

The number of labour migrants from Central and Eastern Europe coming to Denmark rose significantly after the enlargement of the EU with Central and Eastern European states in 2004. This was probably driven first and foremost by the economic boom and labour shortage. However, as the crisis hit the real economy and employment dropped, the inflow of migrants decreased only momentarily, and quickly gained pace once again. This has fuelled debates on social dumping, and different surveys confirm that migrant labour generally is paid less than native employees (Andersen & Felbo-Kolding 2013). Further, it is clear that migrant workers are working primarily in specific sectors such as cleaning, agriculture, accommodation and restaurants, road transport, construction and some parts of manufacturing—mainly low-skilled occupations, typically in domestic market sectors.

The presence of migrant workers means that less skilled Danish workers are facing a new kind of competition for jobs in these sectors. Many of the unemployed are unskilled, which suggests that migrant workers have replaced Danish workers to some degree. Unions see this as the effect of social dumping while the employers' associations stress that employers in these sectors are unable to recruit Danes, who they say do not apply for such jobs. The inflow of migrant workers in some sense can be seen as a functional equivalent to the outsourcing of jobs. The sector in which migrant workers are predominant is the domestic market sector, where functions cannot be outsourced. One possible strategy for employers to reduce costs in this sector is to employ migrant workers.

## CONCLUSIONS

In the twenty-first century, there has been a tendency towards the development of three key pressures that threaten the self-regulation of the labour market actors, and thereby one of the central characteristics of the Danish model. The pressure comes first from the players in the political system, second from the labour market actors at the local level and third from the players at the EU level. Instead of 'centralised decentralisation' with controlled coordination, labour market regulation currently appears to be heading in the direction of a form of multilevel regulation, which is challenging the national collective bargaining actors and the position of the confederations.

In parallel with these broader pressures on the collective bargaining system, three particular factors can be identified that will present a challenge to the agreement system in the coming years. One is the falling union membership numbers. Reversing this trend will be critical for the legitimacy of the unions and for their negotiating power as counterpart to the employers' associations. The second is the increase in migrant workers. The debate on social dumping may well continue. Demographic projections show a continuing decrease in the number of Danes of working age. Should a period of economic growth return, a further significant rise in the number of migrant workers can therefore be expected. Third, conflicts accompanying public sector collective bargaining rounds in recent years have demonstrated that serious rifts exist in the structure underlying this important sector of the labour market. Despite current problems, the Danish model for the regulation of pay and conditions appears to be in a remarkably robust condition. The unions and the employers' associations remain strong, and there continues to be a high level of collective agreement coverage.

## FURTHER READING

Andersen, S.K., Dølvik, J.E. & Ibsen, C.L. (2014) *Nordic Labour Market Models in Open Markets*. Report No. 132. Brussels: European Trade Union Institute.

Due, J., Madsen, J.S., Strøby Jensen, C. & Petersen, L.K. (1994) *The Survival of the Danish Model: A Historical Sociological Analysis of the Danish System of Collective Bargaining*. Copenhagen: DJØF.

Due, J. & Madsen, J.S. (2008) 'The Danish model of industrial relations: Erosion or renewal'. *Journal of Industrial Relations*, 50: 513–29.

Ibsen, C.L. (2014) 'Three approaches to coordinated bargaining: A case for power-based explanations'. *European Journal of Industrial Relations*, March. doi: 10.1177/0959680114527032.

Ilsøe, A. (2012) 'The flip side of organized decentralization'. *British Journal of Industrial Relations*, 50(4): 760–81.

## USEFUL WEBSITES

DA: <http://da.dk>.

FAOS, Employment Relations Research Centre, University of Copenhagen: <http://faos.ku.dk/english>.

LO: <http://www.lo.dk/English%20version.aspx>.

Ministry of Employment: <http://uk.bm.dk>.

National Labour Market Authority: <http://ams.dk/da/Ams/English.aspx>.

## A CHRONOLOGY OF DANISH EMPLOYMENT RELATIONS

| | |
|---|---|
| 1898 | Establishment of two major confederations, LO and DA. The September Compromise—the first basic agreement between the major confederations. |
| 1900 | Pay bargaining at enterprise level became a part of the collective agreement in the iron and steel industry. At the same time, the parties reached an agreement regarding shop stewards. |
| 1907 | The Act on state-recognised unemployment insurance funds set out the rules for unemployment benefits in accordance with the Ghent system, thereby contributing to strengthen the unions. |
| 1908–10 | Representatives from the two major confederations agree in the August Committee of 1908 on a new system of labour law established by an agreement between the parties on arbitration and Acts on a new Labour Court and State Conciliation Board in 1910. The main pillars of the Danish model are in place: self-government of the parties of the labour market with limited legislation on wage and labour conditions and involvement of the confederations in the political processes concerning the labour market in the broadest sense. |
| 1933 | Starting point of a praxis of political intervention in industrial conflicts. |
| 1934–36 | De facto centralisation of collective bargaining between the member organisations of LO and DA by extending the powers of the conciliator to put forward settlement proposals and order a common ballot for all the involved unions and employers' associations. |
| 1947 | The first agreement between LO and DA on works councils in private sector companies. |
| 1969 | The starting point of a renewed public sector IR system based on collective bargaining and the right to take industrial action. Employees covered by collective agreements replace public servants as the major group of public employees. |
| 1950–80 | Centralised collective bargaining under the control of the confederations usual through the board of conciliation. |
| 1970s | The centralised bargaining system is marked by a period of crises, leading to three subsequent political interventions. |
| 1981 | The parties began a renewal of the collective bargaining system. |
| 1987 | In a joint declaration between the confederations of the labour market and the government, the trade unions commit themselves to wage restraint in order to secure the competitiveness of Danish enterprises as well as to safeguard jobs and job creation. |
| 1989 | Structural reform of the DA from a confederation with many small member associations to a confederation dominated by a few large associations. |

| 1989–91 | Establishment of occupational pension funds through the system of collective bargaining. Other welfare issues become part of the collective agreements in the following rounds, expanding the scope of the collective agreements and creating a kind of double regulation of welfare issues through both legislation and collective agreements. An unintended consequence is a growing political pressure on the principle of self-regulation in the Danish model. |
|---|---|
| 1991–92 | The breakthrough of a new sector-based collective bargaining system transferring the bargaining responsibility from the confederations' member organisations at sector level. The role of the key bargaining area is expanded to include all of the manufacturing industry, with the establishment of a new, large employers' confederation, DI, followed on the wage-earners' side by CO-industri. At the same time, the sector organisations agree on a transferral of negotiating responsibility to the parties at enterprise level on wages and working time. These structural changes to the Danish model contain elements of both centralisation and decentralisation, so this new phase in the collective bargaining system can be designated 'centralised decentralisation'. |
| 1998 | A major conflict in the LO-DA area of the private sector is halted by political intervention after two weeks. |
| 2000 | Implementation of EU directives challenges the collective bargaining model, which cannot guarantee that all wage-earners are covered. The problem is solved by a two-phase model: first, the directive is implemented via collective agreements; second, supplementary legislation is introduced which ensures that wage-earners not covered by collective agreements will be embraced by the requirements of the directive. This supplementary legislation is implemented via a new tripartite Implementation Committee. |
| 2008 | The hitherto largest and longest conflict takes place solely on the public labour market covering health care, aged care and child care—that is, more than one-third of all public employees. The conflict is not halted by political intervention, but through a new compromise after more than eight weeks of strike action. |
| 2010, 2012, 2014 | The parties in the private sector manage to reach outcomes in three consecutive bargaining rounds, which will improve the competitiveness of private sector companies. |
| 2013 | The government locks out schoolteachers and then dictates changes in their conditions of work. This is done in a manner that brings into question the will of the political actors to give any real influence to the employees' organisations, as traditionally would be the norm in the Danish model. |

# CHAPTER 10

# Employment relations in Japan

## Hiromasa Suzuki, Katsuyuki Kubo and Kazuya Ogura[1]

Japan's economic context has changed a great deal since the 1980s. In its neighbourhood, there are dynamic East Asian economies that have grown very quickly. There has generally been continuity in Japanese employment relations institutions, as well as the practices of governments, employers and unions. However, many large Japanese enterprises have become multinational enterprises (MNEs), competing in global markets with networks of overseas subsidiaries. Two decades of recession, after the burst of the bubble economy of 1990–91, have prompted Japanese enterprises to dramatically increase their overseas investments. Strategic decisions of MNEs are beyond the scope of national institutions.

Is Japan similar to a coordinated market economy (CME), or is it becoming more like a liberal market economy (LME)? This chapter starts by putting Japanese employment relations into context. It provides some historical background, then discusses the changing roles of unions and employers, and collective bargaining, as well as labour–management consultation and the Japanese employment system. Such current issues as changes of labour market institutions facing global competition with regard to corporate governance, atypical employment and working time are discussed.

With a population of 127 million people and a gross domestic product (GDP) of US$4662 billion in 2013, Japan is the third-largest economy in the world (IMF 2015). Since the early 1980s, the Japanese economy has experienced several distinct eras. First, there was a period of relatively strong growth, stimulated by buoyant domestic consumption; this led to the burst of its bubble economy around 1991. Then followed a decade of economic recessions and difficulties for financial institutions, followed by a period of slow growth up to 2008. Two major events then derailed Japanese economic performance: the post-2007 global financial crisis triggered by the bankruptcy of Lehman Brothers and the 2011 tsunami and associated Fukushima catastrophe. The post-2007 global financial crisis hit the then-booming export industries, such as automobiles and machinery, very hard, while the tsunami impacted strongly on the northern region of Japan, which suffered many casualties. This disrupted supply chains and made it necessary, for safety reasons, to stop most nuclear electricity generation, which had provided 30 per cent of total electricity to Japan.

The financial crisis of 1991 and the burst of the financial bubble were damaging. Previously, the main banks had played a pivotal role in many industrial-financial groups, exemplified by the old Mitsui, Mitsubishi and Sumitomo banks. After the bubble period, these banks and other financial institutions accumulated huge bad loans due to a large drop in asset values (real estate and stocks), and they survived only because of governmental protection and mergers of vulnerable banks. That financial crisis, together with a contraction of domestic demand, plagued the real economy through the 1990s.

In this period, prices were stable and slightly decreased in some years, reflecting technological progress, such as the increasing use of information technology (IT), a decline in consumption and appreciation of the yen. Annual growth rates (GDP) were –0.2 per cent for the period 2001–05 and –0.8 per cent for 2006–10, but in real terms 1.2 per cent for 2001–05 and 0.4 per cent for 2006–10. In 2011, GDP declined by 1 per cent in nominal terms and 0.6 per cent in real terms, mainly due to the tsunami and its aftermath.

Confronted by slow growth and sluggish domestic demand, many Japanese enterprises tried to direct more investment overseas, particularly to the United States, elsewhere in Asia and, to a lesser degree, to European Union (EU) countries. An investment drive to emergent countries—particularly to mainland China and South Asia—accelerated after the mid-1990s when these economies improved their industrial infrastructures and technological standards. Consequently, many Japanese manufacturing enterprises now operate on a global basis. Their overseas turnover may equal or surpass their domestic turnover.

## LABOUR FORCE ISSUES

Japan has a labour force of 66 million and a labour force participation rate of 74 per cent, according to 2012 statistics. About 88 per cent of the labour force is employed; self-employment accounts for only 9 per cent. Japan's labour force peaked in 2000 and, if the present participation rate remains constant, an official estimate predicts a decline of 8.7 per cent (or 6 million persons) by 2030, depending on the rate of economic growth (JILPT 2013). The fertility rate remains low (between 1.3 and 1.4 per cent). About 4 per cent of the labour force works in primary industries, including agriculture and fisheries. Manufacturing, mining and construction (secondary) industries employ 25 per cent, while 71 per cent work in tertiary industries, including services, wholesale and retail, finance, utilities and government. The secondary sector decreased from 33 per cent to 25 per cent of employment between 1990 and 2012. This precipitated a loss of 5.6 million jobs, which indicates the extent to which Japanese manufacturing enterprises have moved activities overseas.

Population ageing is a serious issue on both the supply and the demand sides of the Japanese economy. On average, the Japanese enjoy among the longest lifespans in the world: 86 years for women and 80 years for men. It is estimated that the Japanese ageing ratio (the total number of people more than 64 years old divided by the total population) will be the highest among the major developed countries by the year 2025. Therefore, the government raised the public pension age to 65. Labour force participation is relatively high among elderly people: 76 per cent of men and 46 per cent of women aged 60–64 years were in employment, while 29 per cent of men and 13 per cent of women remained in the labour market after the age of 65 years. The structure of Japan's population will change substantially from a pyramid shape in the 1950s to a top-heavy shape by 2025.

Unemployment was about 1.1 per cent at the end of the 1960s, when the economy enjoyed high growth. The unemployment rate, one of the lowest among developed countries until the mid-1990s, rose to 3.4 per cent in 1997 and 5.4 per cent in 2002 before declining to 4 per cent in 2008. After the post-2007 global financial crisis, unemployment increased to 5.1 per cent in 2009 then fell to 4 per cent in 2013.

The employment situation includes contrasting features. Many elderly workers have difficulties finding jobs, and an increasing number of young workers are unable to find career positions that match their expectations. (They have precarious jobs or they are in atypical employment in the secondary labour market.) On the other hand, some enterprises in IT industries and low-pay enterprises in manufacturing and services find it difficult to hire workers.

The ratio of job openings to job seekers declined from 1.51 in 1990 to 0.64 in 2000, aggravating the disparity between jobs and job-seeker profiles. After 2000, this ratio recovered slowly to 1 in 2007, then declined in 2008 and 2009 before increasing to 0.97 in 2013. The ratio of 1 is an approximate labour market equilibrium. Regional differences are considerable: Tokyo and some industrial centres (Nagoya, Sendai) have a ratio above 1, whereas in rural areas it is below 1, as the employment situation in those areas is worse.

A significant feature of the post-1945 period has been a reduction in the number of average working hours. In the pre-war period, twelve-hour workdays were common. Since then, the number of hours per day has been reduced substantially. However, when the period of slow growth began, the number of working hours declined further, to around 2100 hours per year. In 1987, the legal limit of weekly hours was set at 40 hours. Since the 1990s, the average annual working hours has remained between 1950 and 2000. The increase of part-time workers has tended to lower the average working hours; if we consider only full-time workers, working hours have not declined. One-quarter of full-time male workers aged 30–49 years work more than 60 hours a week. Long working hours are still a major public concern.

## THE POLITICAL CONTEXT

The post-1945 period has seen Japanese politics dominated by the conservative Liberal Democratic Party (LDP). Opposition parties have exerted influence from time to time but, apart from a brief period after the war, none obtained sufficient votes to hold office in national politics. Opposition parties are divided by ideologies. The Japan Socialist Party (JSP) was formed mainly by the radical left and some moderates who had a close relationship with the main union federation, Sohyo. The moderate and small Social Democratic Party had a link with the moderate union movement of Domei, primarily recruited in the private sector. A major political change came after the dissolution of the Soviet bloc, when socialist ideals lost political credibility in Japan, as in many other developed countries.

In the 1990s, the Japanese political scene was characterised by frequent changes of government, as successive elections resulted in fluctuating loss and gain of LDP seats in the lower house (Shugiin) and the upper house (Sangiin). In 1993, for the first time since 1955, a coalition of parties formed a non-LDP government for a short period (less than a year). Then a coalition government, including the LDP, was headed by a leader of the JSP (Tomiichi Murayama). Between 1996 and 2001, the LDP retained its power in alliance with the small but well-organised Buddhist party (Komeito). In 1998, a new Democratic Party of Japan (DPJ) was created, regrouping factions from the LDP, JSP and Social Democratic Party. Between 1993 and 2001, seven governments were formed then collapsed. The electoral basis of the LDP (rural, business and commerce) was gradually eroded during this period without giving birth to a major united opposition party. Unable to get a stable political base, successive governments could not implement the decisive political and economic reforms required to solve the financial and economic problems of the 1990s.

With the election of Junichiro Koizumi as prime minister (2001–06), there was relative political stability. The Koizumi government emphasised a market-oriented approach. Koizumi won several elections with policies such as privatisation of the postal office and deregulation. Due to Koizumi's personal popularity, his government was able to centralise decision-making processes, circumscribing LDP factions and ministerial bureaucracy. The Koizumi government constrained public expenditure by privatising public corporations and by reducing welfare costs. Koizumi resolved the financial crisis of the 1990s, but the period of strong premiership ended with his resignation in 2006.

Following two successive LDP governments, the popularity of the LDP waned so that in 2009, the opposition party, the DPJ, headed by Yukio Hatoyama, won a comfortable majority at the election of the lower house. But he was subsequently criticised for mishandling the delicate American military base issue in the Okinawa islands, and he lost a majority in the election of the upper house. The two DPJ prime ministers who succeeded Hatoyama were unfortunately engulfed in the consequences of the Fukushima disaster, which led to a large number of refugees from radiation. The issue of restarting 50 nuclear electricity plants has divided public opinion and the DPJ. Thus, four years of the DPJ government finished in disillusionment, without achieving any major reforms.

At the end of 2012, the LDP won a landslide election, first in the lower house and subsequently in the upper house, and the conservative Shinzo Abe became prime minister. His government is pursuing an unorthodox economic policy, sometimes termed 'Abenomics', which aims to stabilise the inflation rate at 2 per cent to arrest a lingering deflationary trend by radically increasing the monetary supply through the Bank of Japan. An immediate result of this monetary policy was a rapid depreciation of the yen against the US dollar and the euro (the yen fell by 22 per cent against the dollar and 26 per cent against the euro in a year). Due to rising exports and overseas revenue, many Japanese enterprises posted a very high level of profits for the fiscal year ending in 2014. However, it is too early to assess the effectiveness of the Abe government's economic and monetary policy.

Historically, unions were associated with various parties, including the JSP, the Social Democratic Party and the Japan Communist Party, depending on their dominant ideology. Since its creation in 1998, the main union confederation, Rengo, has maintained a close relation with the DPJ. The relationship between the LDP and Rengo is more distant, but without open hostility. Successful candidates of the DPJ or other small parties are often recommended or supported by unions. Irrespective of the relationships between parties and unions, rank-and-file members of unions tend to vote for candidates of their choice. There has been an increase in voters who do not adhere to particular parties. Consequently, the influence of unions on voters has declined.

## THE JAPANESE EMPLOYMENT RELATIONS MODEL

Given the continued stagnation and the slow recovery of Japan's economy, is the 'Japanese model' of employment relations still viable? From the 1970s, Japan attracted much attention for its favourable economic performance and its 'cooperative' approaches to employment relations, which some claim have supported this economic performance (e.g. Dore 1979).

The international interest in Japanese management and employment relations was perplexing to many Japanese people, as for most of the twentieth century Japan had tried to follow models derived from the West (e.g. the United Kingdom, the United States and Germany). Before the 1973 oil crisis, the Japanese tended to see such countries as much more advanced, and various management techniques and technologies were imported from the West.

Although interest in Japan waned after the decline of its economy in the post-bubble period of the early 1990s, some countries in Asia were still eager to 'import' the Japanese model. In the poor economic climate of the 1990s, some Japanese enterprises (e.g. Toyota, Honda and Sony) modified their management systems in an attempt to survive in competitive world markets. Some large Japanese enterprises, as well as many smaller enterprises, are now shifting their production bases to other Asian countries, including China. To what extent are Japanese production and employment relations systems transferable to other countries?

To begin to answer such a question, some historical background is necessary. Japan's feudal era ended with the Meiji Restoration of 1868. Hitherto, Japan had little contact with Western countries. Industrialisation began in the following decade, a century later than in Britain. Japan's early factories in major industries were begun by the state, but in the 1880s most of them were sold to a few selected families. This was the origin of what was later to become the powerful *zaibatsu* groups of holding enterprises, which were based on these groups' commercial banks.

Although some unions, such as those covering printers and iron-workers, began during this period, the familial basis of industrialisation continued well into the twentieth century. Many factories, especially in the textile industry, had their own dormitories for workers. In some industries, there were master workers (*oyakata*), who were subcontractors—like the early supervisors in Western enterprises. After World War I, there was an acute shortage of skilled workers, and enterprises wanted to recruit workers directly. Hence, large enterprises intervened in the master workers' prerogative to recruit labour. With the rapid development of industries, the system of learning skills through apprenticeships was absorbed into internal on-the-job training systems in Japanese enterprises.

In the paternalistic tradition developed in the 1920s and 1930s, unions did not exert much sustained influence. Faced with pressure from the militaristic regime, unions were dissolved between 1938 and 1943, and the employers' associations were absorbed into the mobilisation for war production.

After Japan's surrender in 1945, the Allied powers' General Headquarters (GHQ) sought to rebuild the organisation of work and employment relations as part of the post-war reconstruction. Many elements of the present model were shaped by American influence after the war.

## Unions

The labour movement developed rapidly under the GHQ's democratisation program. Although much of Japan's industrial base was destroyed during the war, union membership reached pre-war levels four months after the war's end. By 1949, there were 6.6 million union members, a peak density level of 56 per cent. There were, however, some setbacks for the unions. For instance, plans to hold a general strike by the unions in 1947 were suspended by order of the GHQ. Yet the unions recovered and reached a membership of 12.6 million in 1975, with a density of 34 per cent.

After such peaks, union membership and density stagnated before gradually declining year after year. Density was less than 18 per cent with 9.9 million union members in 2013. Unions lost more than 2 million members in two decades. One of the main causes of this decline was a change in the industrial structure, especially the shift towards the service sector. Union density in 2013 varied by industry. Manufacturing industries had 2.7 million members with a density of about 25 per cent. Density rate was higher in the civil service (38 per cent) and in public utilities such as electricity, gas and water (57 per cent). By contrast, union density in wholesale and retail was only 13 per cent. Union membership and coverage also varied greatly according to the size of enterprise in the private sector. While the density was less than 45 per cent in enterprises with more than 1000 employees, it was negligible in enterprises with fewer than 99 employees (only 1 per cent).[2]

The reason why unionisation is relatively high in large enterprises is that most unionised enterprises adopt union-shop clauses whereby newly recruited regular employees have to join the enterprise union. Accordingly, union membership varies with the rise and fall of unionised enterprises or industries. When the firm is expanding, union membership generally rises and vice versa. These union-shop arrangements are common in manufacturing enterprises but hardly applicable to most of the service sector, where enterprises tend to be small and geographically dispersed.

Another cause of union decline has been the general improvement in living standards, which has tended to make employees less enthusiastic about union membership. Pay rises fluctuate according to prevailing macro-economic conditions. Since the peak in 1990, when the pay rise in centralised annual pay negotiations was 5.9 per cent, such pay rises have been minimal, only just keeping pace with prices. These unfavourable outcomes may have discouraged workers' interest in unions. Thus, some argue that unions have outlived their usefulness, and that the centralised mode of pay negotiations is out-dated.

Further, in recent years, there has been an increase in atypical employment, such as part-time workers, seasonal workers, temporary agency workers and fixed-term contract workers. One in three workers is currently considered to be non-regular. As most Japanese unions organise regular employees of the enterprise and exclude non-regular workers, the increase of atypical employment implies a decline in union members. Some industrial unions, such as the large industrial union UA Zensen (e.g. textiles, retails, hotels, food), have tried to organise part-time workers; currently, half of UA Zensen's members are part-time workers. But this is an exception, since the union density among part-time workers remains low—less than 7 per cent.

Why do enterprise unions not organise non-regular employees in the same workplace where they already organise regular employees? The answer relates to the special status enjoyed by regular employees. The word *sei-sha-in* is often used (meaning 'regular member of the enterprise'). The word contains nuances that do not have an equivalent in Western terminology. It means more than being a mere hired worker, and implies belonging to a community formed by people with the same interests. Hence, entry to an enterprise union is generally restricted to the members of that community.

Most unions in Japan are organised not by occupation or by job but by enterprise or establishment. An enterprise union usually consists solely of regular employees of a single enterprise, and includes manual workers and non-manual staff. Excluded are managerial positions (as the law does not permit managerial staff to join unions, to prevent employer interference). Union membership also excludes most of the workers in non-regular status positions (part-time workers, temporary agency workers or fixed-term contract workers).

Many enterprise unions grew sporadically in the period of turmoil after 1945. Some of them developed from the factory- and enterprise-based wartime production committees. As most unions are organised for enterprises or individual plants, there are many unions—more than 25,000, according to the official statistics (2013). Although there are other types of unions, such as industrial, craft and general unions, they are exceptions and play only a marginal role.

Compared with industrial unions, enterprise unions have greater resources and are more powerful. Enterprise unions are autonomous in running their organisations and in promoting their members' interests. They are financially independent and self-supporting. Most union activities occur at the enterprise level, rather than at the federation level. In general, key official union positions are held by regular employees on a temporary secondment from the enterprise—typically of one to three years.

As the enterprise's success greatly influences members' working conditions and employment opportunities, enterprise unions generally have a cooperative attitude towards management. Most employees usually identify with their employer in making decisions that would enhance the competitiveness of the enterprise. A key aspect of the work environment in Japanese enterprises is interdependence, and the belief that the enterprise is a 'community of shared fate', where 'everyone is in the same boat'. The relatively modest pay differentials between managers, non-manual workers and manual workers tend to reinforce the workers' sense of identification with the enterprise. In addition, senior managers, directors and executives, including the chief executive, are likely to have been promoted internally after many years of service. This contrasts with Western countries, where there may be more class differentiation and much larger pay differentials.

Are enterprise unions really independent of the control of theemployer? If an enterprise is unionised, the enterprise union is usually the only organisation that is recognised as representing the employees at the enterprise. Financially, unions are independent from the employer, since full-time union officials are paid from union fees. Employers usually offer various facilities to the union, including an office, but such facilities are offered on a voluntary basis after negotiations between the parties. The availability of these facilities helps establish a basis for cooperative labour–management relations in enterprises.

An advantage of enterprise unions is that their policies are adapted to each enterprise, rather than reflecting sectional craft or political inclination. Employment relations based on enterprise unionism tend to be more flexible than those based, for example, on craft unionism. On the other hand, there are disadvantages from a union's point of view. Newly employed workers automatically acquire union membership and their union dues are 'checked off' from their pay. Thus, employees' union consciousness is generally less than their enterprise consciousness. Union membership usually ceases on retirement, which also reduces the workers' commitment to the union.

Most enterprise unions within the same sector join a sector-specific federation of unions. There are more than 100 such federations. The major functions of these federations include coordinating the activities of the member enterprise unions with the aim of improving pay and working conditions; dealing with problems common to a whole sector; guiding and assisting member unions in specific disputes; and political lobbying in the interest of workers.

These federations belong to national centres, of which Rengo (Japan Trade Union Confederation) is the largest (6.8 million members). There is a small second national centre called Zenroren, which includes some more radical union federations (0.8 million members).

At the national level, unions were long divided into two rival national centres: the left wing Sohyo and the moderate Domei. The first significant step to unite these centres began in 1982, when major union federations of the private sector pertaining to both national centres formed a loose gathering under the name of Zenminrokyo (Japanese Private Sector Union Council). Public sector unions were not included because they were seen as too radical. However, this organisation developed into a larger union centre, Rengo, which did include public sector unions. The new Rengo was established in 1989, when it comprised 78 sector federations with nearly 8 million members. Public sector unions used to be more political and have more power than those in the private sector, but their membership and power diminished after 1978 due to the privatisation of public corporations and the trimming of public services. In the twenty-first century, the most powerful unions are in the private sector.

Rengo has pursued cooperative labour–management relations with employers. Initially, Rengo tried unsuccessfully to play a political role to form an expanded liberal democratic league. During the long recession, its role was restricted to participation in different policy-making and consultation processes at the national level. During four years of the DPJ government, Rengo had regular consultation on political agendas with the government, but after the severe defeat of the DPJ in 2012, Rengo has kept its distance from the Abe government.

## The end of lifetime employment?

The employment system in large enterprises is a complex mix of practices, of which 'lifetime employment' (long-term employment) and seniority-based pay are the best known. Other practices include a policy of recruitment whereby entry to the firm is limited to new graduates without occupational experience. The system also includes on-the-job training, internal promotion and mandatory retirement—generally at 60 years of age. A key role is played by a centralised human resource management (HRM) department, which has strong control functions and reports directly to the chief executive.

Such internal labour market employment systems were consolidated after World War II, particularly during the high-growth period (1955–73). In tight labour market conditions, enterprises had a clear interest in promising regular employees a career in which they expected to be promoted to higher ranks with higher pay related to their length of service. Employment protection was further enhanced by case law concerning limitations on dismissal.

Although the law was silent on collective dismissals (an employment contract could be terminated with advance notice by either party to the contract), the courts ruled that employers should not abuse their right to terminate the employment contract. Dismissals could be justified under specified conditions: reasons for dismissals should be valid; all efforts should be made to avoid dismissals; criteria for choosing workers for dismissal should be fair; and there should be advance consultation with unions. Thus, the court reversed the logic of free employment contracts. Accordingly, large enterprises tend to regard regular employees as fixed costs.

Regular manual and non-manual employees are employed not for specific jobs or occupations, but as general employees. Enterprises prefer to employ new school leavers or university graduates rather than experienced workers who have been trained in other enterprises. Their induction program is designed to encourage them to conform to the enterprise's norms and expectations.

Young recruits start at a comparatively low level of pay, which is based on their educational qualifications. Their pay rises in proportion to their length of service up to a certain age limit. Promotion is based largely on length of service, which is assumed to correlate with the employee's level of skill developed within the enterprise. Therefore, it is disadvantageous for workers to change employers and for employers to lay off employees who have accumulated specific skills required in that particular enterprise. Typically, in the primary labour market, comprising permanent or regular employees working for large enterprises, there is a tacit understanding about the long-term, two-way commitment between employers and employees.

How many employees are really in this lifetime employment system? Official statistics do not give an exact answer. Labour force surveys collect data by types of employment—that is, regular or permanent employment and other types of employment (e.g. fixed-term and part-time employment). Approximately 65 per cent are in regular employment and about 35 per cent in non-regular employment.[3] Regular employment amounted to approximately 80 per cent of total employment in 1990, so it declined significantly after that time, reflecting a change in industrial structures and HRM practices.

Not all regular employees are working in large enterprises that have superior remuneration and career opportunities. Around 35 per cent of employees work in establishments employing more than 500 workers or in the public sector. Employees in large enterprises do not all enjoy good conditions of employment. Supermarkets and package services, for example, tend to employ atypical workers. Given that many large manufacturing enterprises have production sites and replace regular workers with atypical employment, the extent of high-quality career employment has been reduced. Some studies of job tenure suggest that long-term employment patterns continue, despite the long recession and much restructuring. This is probably because long-term employment is a core feature of HRM in Japanese enterprises (Kambayashi & Kato 2011).

The employment system has developed on the basis of a model of male breadwinners. The prototype of the current seniority-based pay system, known as the Densan pay method (1946–47), was designed to cover living expenses of a male employee. Female workers were excluded. In the twenty-first century, female employees are not formally excluded from career employment, but in practice they are still handi-capped by the possibility of career interruptions. Only a small minority of female employees reach higher managerial positions.

## Employers and their organisations

During the period immediately after 1945, there were many violent industrial disputes. These reflected the economic disorder, particu-larly the shortage of food and daily necessities. Neither employers nor workers had much employment relations experience. To counter the union offensive and to establish industrial peace and order, employers organised regional and industrial associations. However, partly due to the 'democratisation' policy of GHQ, employers were often obliged to yield to union pressure, and thus also to an erosion of their managerial prerogatives.

To restore managerial authority, Nikkeiren (Japan Federation of Employers' Associations), was founded in 1948. It was the most important employers' organisation in terms of employment relations, and had multiple functions. It played a major role up to the 1970s, when annual pay negotiations had a significant impact on the national economy. However, the importance of these negotiations waned in the 1980s and 1990s. Business groups felt that a specialised employers' federation in labour matters was no longer necessary. Hence, in 2002, Nikkeiren was merged with the powerful Keidanren (Japan Federa-tion of Economic Organisations) to form Nihon Keidanren (Japan Business Organisation). Most of the functions formerly conducted by Nikkeiren are now the province of Nihon Keidanren, which mainly covers large enterprises.

Nihon Keidanren coordinates and publicises employers' views on employment relations, selects employer representatives to various government commissions, councils and the International Labour Organization (ILO), and provides its member organisations with advice and service on employment relations practices. Nihon Keidanren's members include employers' associations organised at the regional and industry levels. Each year, at the time of Shunto (the Spring Labour Offensive), Nihon Keidanren releases guidelines for employers to follow when dealing with demands from unions during collective bargaining. In this way, although many of them do not have a direct role in bargain-ing, employers' associations play an important role behind the scenes (Levine 1984).

In the past, three factors strongly influenced the magnitude of Shunto: demand and supply conditions in labour markets, consumer price levels, and business conditions or the enterprise's performance (Ministry of Labour 1975). In recent years, however, the main determinant of the outcome of collective bargaining has been the individual enterprise's business performance. Enterprises that are performing well tend to reward good results in the form of six-monthly bonuses instead of a general pay increase. In contrast to the declining power of unions, employers have increased their influence over employees. Many large enterprises in the automobile, electrical machinery, construction and banking sectors have resorted to downsizing, but most enterprise unions have remained quiescent.

## Collective bargaining

What is the form of collective bargaining used in Japan? First, it takes place at the level of enterprise. This means that there is no collective bargaining (collective agreement) at the sector or national level. Federations may coordinate the process of negotiations, but individual enterprises and enterprise unions have autonomy to make their own decisions.

Second, in most unionised enterprises, there are elaborate joint consultation mechanisms, in which union representatives participate. Joint consultation machinery was developed in the 1950s at the initiative of the Japan Productivity Center, which advocated industrial peace in enterprises through dialogue.[4] Joint consultation is seen as a means of information sharing, but many employment relations and related issues are discussed at consultation meetings. The distinction between collective bargaining and joint consultation is blurred, since the same people (top managers and union officials) attend consultation and negotiation meetings.

Third, collective bargaining focuses on pay levels, particularly during the annual pay round. Pay agreements may be concluded separately from agreements on other matters. Most unions conduct pay negotiations during the Shunto annual pay negotiations in March, April and May, while negotiations on other subjects may be conducted at other times. Shunto began in the 1950s at the initiative of major unions. By concentrating annual pay negotiations in spring, the unions wanted to overcome the weakness of dispersed enterprise negotiations. In general, leading sectors negotiate at an early stage to set a pattern for that pay round. Weaker sectors negotiate later to benefit from a spill-over effect. Until the end of the 1970s, Shunto was a national event, as its results influenced the economy in terms of demand and prices. A decline in union density and a sluggish economic climate have helped to change the characteristics of Shunto. Its relative importance in national pay bargaining has declined, with the focus of pay bargaining shifting towards the enterprise level. Increasing differences in the profitability of enterprises, reflecting increased global competition, have been a major reason for this change. However, Shunto is still a significant collective bargaining institution. It includes information sharing and coordination within and between employers and union federations, as well as within enterprises.

The structure of enterprise unions usually corresponds to the organisation of the enterprise and its establishment, department or divisional grouping. If collective bargaining takes place at the central level of a particular enterprise, consultation on safety or conditions of work may be held at the establishment level. In the case of a large group of enterprises, collective bargaining is generally carried out at the group level.

Grievances are often settled informally without recourse to formal procedures. Managers attempt to subdue tensions and conflict, and reinforce a feeling of community. Management and unions established these informal procedures, which seek to avoid formal conflicts, after the late 1940s and early 1950s, when there were many large-scale and lengthy disputes in the mining and manufacturing industries. Radical left-wing leaders led some strikes. Many of these disputes left wounds in employment relationships that were not easily healed.

Although there were many stoppages up to 1975, industrial conflict decreased substantially thereafter. Disputes are usually settled directly between the parties concerned, sometimes with the assistance of a mediator. The central and local labour relations commissions provide conciliation machinery for the private and public sectors. Special commissions act for public sector employees and for seafarers. Nearly all the disputes brought before these commissions are settled by either conciliation or mediation, and relatively few disputes require arbitration. Most disputes presented to the labour relations commissions are those that extend beyond the limits of labour–management relations at the enterprise level. The relative importance of the commissions has declined, as there has been an improvement in cooperation between labour and management at the enterprise level.

Contemporary employment relations are relatively stable, and relations between the parties are generally cooperative. Some see this in a positive light. Others have a more critical perspective, arguing that enterprise unions are too dependent on employers, and that the relationship is one of collaboration and incorporation of unions and employers by the employers. Some enterprise unions are well organised and influence most important managerial decisions, while in other enterprises unions are ineffective.

As many employees expect to work for many years for the same enterprise, they tend to place an emphasis on the improvement of their own working conditions. This may be an unfortunate characteristic of traditional Japanese enterprises, where regular employees want to maintain their positions even at the expense of non-regular employees, such as part-time workers and temporary workers, who are disproportionately female.

Why has the relationship between unions and employers changed so fundamentally since the 1950s? There has been increased global competition, improved standards of living and a shift towards a service-oriented economy. Public opinion is also more conservative than it was in the 1950s. The 1970s oil crises further accelerated the trend in this direction. Despite the long recession since the early 1990s, the number of industrial disputes has not increased. In 1975, the total number of industrial disputes reached a peak of 8435. However, there were only 596 disputes, involving 12,000 workers, in 2012. One of the changes is that most disputes are individual rather than collective. There have also been increased levels of labour turnover. These developments represent challenges to unions as well as to the employment relations system.

## CURRENT ISSUES

### Changes in labour market institutions facing global competition

The geographical context around Japan has changed greatly. Two generations ago, China was still a developing country with a strong socialist legacy. In the twenty-first century, China has become an economic power with a huge appetite for energy, raw materials and new technologies. Korea and Taiwan are strong competitors in many hi-tech industries. Thailand has become a regional centre for certain types of vehicle production (e.g. pick-up trucks) for Japanese car MNEs. Japan used to have a considerable technological and economic advance, but these neighbouring countries have become both competitors and partners. However, Japanese enterprises can also benefit from the proximity of these dynamic markets.

Inside Japan, the social and economic situations are also changing, revealing some long-term problems. There is an ageing population and a decline in the fertility rate, which will result in a decline in the labour force and the total population. There is a sporadic debate about immigration policies, but the issue of foreign workers is currently dormant. Female participation in the labour market has been growing, but many women take up part-time jobs without good career prospects. However, the distinction between regular and non-regular workers, as well as between typical and atypical employment, generates much debate.

In the field of labour law, several important legislative reforms have been adopted since the 1980s: equal opportunity (1985), reduction of statutory hours of work (1987), temporary agencies (dispatching agencies) (1985, 1999), child-care leave (1995) and an amendment to the law of stabilisation of employment (2004), which requires enterprises to offer employment up to the age of 65 years. Two reforms have had considerable impact on the labour market. The amendment to the law of the stabilisation of employment was made in response to the ageing population and the change of the full pensionable age, which was raised from 60 to 65 years. The amended law requires that enterprises should offer employment up to 65 years for all workers who wish to stay in employment. This legal reform was introduced in stages between 2006 and 2013.

Previously, 60 years was the mandatory retirement age in both the private and public sectors. As the law does not specify that the mandatory retirement age should be raised to 65 years, most enterprises have maintained the retirement age of 60, after which they offer a fixed-term contract. This is preferred by enterprises, because upon retirement the open-ended employment contract is terminated and the workers concerned are removed from general pay scales. Hence, enterprises can offer a new fixed-term contract with substantially lower pay, though employees' incomes may be maintained through private pensions and other allowances.

The temporary agency work law is typical of Japan's approach to relaxing regulation. The initial law on temporary agency workers in 1985 (law on dispatching agencies) was aimed at restricting agency workers to be dispatched only to certain technical jobs or specified occupations. After several successive amendments, which enlarged the list of occupations allowed for agency workers, an amendment in 1999 provided that all occupations were open to agency workers, unless forbidden by law (initially this was the case in manufacturing and construction). Since 2004, the use of temporary workers has been legal even in the manufacturing sector, in line with the deregulation policy of the Koizumi government.

The regulation of temporary agency work is very loose; there is no limitation on the renewal of a contract except for a maximum duration of three years. Accordingly, the number of agency workers increased from 0.5 million to 1.3 million between 2004 and 2008. This development was curtailed by the post-2007 global financial crisis, when large manufacturing enterprises reduced production by terminating many temporary work positions. These massive layoffs triggered a public debate for re-regulating temporary agency workers. However, no progress was made during the four years of the DPJ government, because opposition parties had a majority in the upper house. It is estimated that there were nearly a million agency workers in 2012, some 60 per cent of whom were females. Agency workers are paid much less on average than regular workers.

While changes in the legal framework have been only gradual, large enterprises have experienced a transformation in their structures and governance. In the 1980s, most large enterprises in Japan exported their products, but in the twenty-first century many of them are MNEs with production sites in China and elsewhere in East and South-East Asia, the United States and Europe.

Toyota illustrates this transformation. This auto maker, which perfected the famous 'just-in-time' system, had a conservative approach to internationalisation until the 1980s. Toyota opened its first large factory in the United States in 1987 following much US–Japan trade friction. Two decades later, Toyota had a global network of production. In most cases, Toyota's parts makers (e.g. Denso, Aishin) are as globalised as Toyota. By 2012, the total production of Toyota cars was 8.7 million. Overseas production comprised 5.2 million, compared with 3.5 million in Japan. Asia accounted for 2.6 million, followed by North America with 1.7 million and Europe with 0.5 million.

In the same year, 44 per cent of Toyota's profits were from Japan and 56 per cent from overseas subsidiaries. There is a tendency to develop overseas production in other sectors, albeit to a lesser extent. According to an official survey of Japanese enterprises with overseas activities by the Ministry of Economy, Trade and Industry, among manufacturing enterprises a third of their turnover was in overseas subsidiaries in 2012.[5] It had been only 20 per cent in 1995. The number of people employed in Japanese overseas subsidiaries also increased in this period, from 2.3 million to 5.6 million. In manufacturing, two segments alone accounted for 40 per cent of job creation in overseas subsidiaries: transport machines, with 1.4 million, and telecommunication equipment, with 0.8 million. Geographically, most such employment was in Asia, of which China accounted for around a half, followed by Association of Southeast Asian Nations (ASEAN) member countries.

This impressive employment creation outside Japan contrasts with a large reduction in employment in manufacturing in Japan, where total employment was 14 million in 1995 but declined to just over 10 million by 2013. However, job creation abroad should not necessarily be equated with job losses in Japan. Various econometric studies of the employment effects of overseas expansion are inconclusive about those effects in Japan. For example, one study of Japanese MNEs and their overseas subsidiaries for the period 1991–2002 found no correlation between overseas job creation and the employment situation in Japan (Yamashita & Fukao 2010). It may be that those enterprises developing overseas activities are also creating employment in Japan. Nevertheless, in view of the rapid erosion of employment in the manufacturing sector in recent years, there are continuing debates about the implications of overseas expansion for employment in Japan.

Another change is the structure of enterprises. During the late 1990s, many enterprises reorganised themselves through mergers and acquisitions. In addition, sweeping changes in Japan's legal system contributed to the increase in corporate reorganisations.[6] These changes make it easier for enterprises to restructure themselves. Traditionally, large Japanese enterprises did not have an overriding objective only to maximise shareholder value, but they also aimed to further the interests of other stakeholders, including employees. Top managers would put much emphasis on employees' interests.

Yoshimori (1995) surveyed middle managers in five countries (France, Germany, Japan, the United Kingdom and the United States). Respondents were asked to assess the objectives of their firm in relation to the maximisation of shareholder value. More than 70 per cent of managers in the United Kingdom and the United States answered that their enterprise's objective was to maximise shareholder value while only 2.9 per cent gave the same answer in Japan. This result is consistent with other observations which claim that Japanese managers place a higher value on the welfare of their employees. Mergers proposed by top executives have subsequently been cancelled following protests by employees. Some enterprises have introduced anti-takeover measures, or a 'poison pill', to protect the interests of the various stakeholders.

Although employees have limited legal power over top managers, there are several types of employee participation, such as joint labour–management committees (JLMCs), and employee stock ownership plans. JLMCs serve mainly as channels for management to communicate with employees about the business of the firm, any problems and their possible solutions, and management programs or plans for future investment (Shirai 1983). Though not compulsory, most large enterprises have a JLMC to discuss various issues in addition to employment relations, such as investment plans, plant relocation and the introduction of new technologies. According to a survey on labour–management communication, approximately 75 per cent of enterprises with more than 5000 employees had a JLMC. It is assumed that enterprises achieve better performance by having a JLMC (Morishima 1991; Kato & Morishima 2002).

Several changes have occurred that have altered the balance of power between shareholders and employees. First, legal changes have made it easier for enterprises to restructure, such as through mergers and acquisitions. The *Financial Instruments and Exchange Act*, revised in 2007, regulates those who plan to acquire a large proportion of listed enterprises. The *Company Act 2005* established procedures for enterprises to reorganise themselves by various measures, such as mergers and divesture. These changes have made it easier for enterprises and investment funds to acquire shares in other enterprises, through tender offers. Neither of these laws requires enterprises that are restructuring to consult with employees, except in limited cases.

A further important aspect of corporate governance is the change in the ownership structure of enterprises. Japanese enterprises and banks used to have large, stable shareholders. Cross-shareholdings, in which enterprises own each other's shares, declined from more than 15 per cent in 1995 to only 9 per cent in 2008 (Miyajima & Nitta 2011). In addition, ownership by foreigners increased from less than 5 per cent in 1970 to 28 per cent in 2012.

More enterprises are appointing outside directors. Traditionally, a board of directors had several characteristics: there was a strict hierarchy within enterprise boards; the directors were classified as chairperson, president, vice-president, senior executives, executives and non-titled directors; all of these directors were full-time members of the board; and former employees might be promoted to become a director of the firm. Because of these features, boards of directors may have failed to monitor the performance of their firm's president, since presidents faced little pressure from outside directors. Although the proportion of outside directors is still only small, it is increasing. The number of listed enterprises that did not have an outside director declined from 2577 in 2004 to 1623 in 2013. Thus, top managers, aware of the fact that mergers and acquisitions are increasing, face more pressure from financial markets to focus on shareholders' interests.

Another controversial change in HRM relates to the introduction of performance-related pay. Although the definition of performance-related pay varies across enterprises, evidence suggests that increasing numbers of enterprises have been trying to introduce new kinds of pay systems to strengthen the link between pay and performance.[7] A survey of pay determination found that enterprises increasingly place emphasis on performance, with 219 (or 86 per cent) of 254 enterprises having introduced performance-related pay (JILPT 2006). About 62 per cent of enterprises in the survey claimed that performance had become more important in determining pay than before, and 60 per cent said that an employee's ability has more importance than previously. By contrast, for more than 30 per cent of enterprises, the importance of age, education and length of service criteria was decreasing. Less than 10 per cent of enterprises said they put more emphasis on such criteria than before.

Survey-based studies have examined employer responses to performance pay. The 2010 General Survey on Working Conditions asked how enterprises evaluated the introduction of performance-related pay: 23 per cent said 'good', 42 per cent said 'good but needs to be modified', and 24 per cent said 'needs major revision'. The survey also showed that the main problem with performance pay was the performance appraisal: 38 per cent of the enterprises' respondents reported that managers did not have enough skills to evaluate their subordinates. In addition, 53 per cent claimed that it was difficult to compare the appraisals of employees who worked in different divisions of the firm.

One survey asked employees whether they agreed with the general principle that pay should be determined by individual performance (JILPT 2003). More than a quarter (28 per cent) of employees agreed, 60 per cent said that they agreed but were anxious about such a policy, and only 7 per cent of employees said that they did not agree. Among those who felt anxious or who were opposed to this policy, 79 per cent said that they were not confident that their performance or skills were evaluated fairly. In addition, 51 per cent said that performance might depend on the job assigned, rather than on their effort. Nearly two-fifths (38 per cent) were anxious that their income might fluctuate.

## Growth of atypical employment

Atypical employment has tended to increase as regular employment has decreased. About one-third of employees are non-regular workers. Atypical employment covers a wide range of jobs and workers: it includes part-time workers, fixed-term contract workers and temporary agency workers.[8] One of the most important differences between regular and non-regular employees is job security. While most regular workers have an open-ended contract, which is difficult to terminate, similar guarantees are not given to people in atypical employment.

According to the Employment Status Survey (Ministry of Internal Affairs and Communications 2012), regular employees' share of total employment decreased from 78 per cent in 1992 to 62 per cent in

2012, while non-regular employees' share increased from 22 per cent to 38 per cent in that period (see Figure 10.1). The great majority of non-regular employees were part-time workers and in *arubaito* (temporary jobs, such as student jobs). An increasing share of non-regular employees were 'dispatched workers from temporary labour agency (agency workers)'. In the same period, the share of contracted workers increased from 18 to 26 per cent.

Why has atypical employment grown so rapidly in recent years? The reasons are complex and varied. The growth of the service sector is one of the major reasons. For instance, employment by large retail and wholesale enterprises accounts for 11.7 million people, manufacturing for 9.2 million, and medical and welfare services for 6.1 million. In retail and wholesale, chains of convenience stores are major employers of part-time workers and students. Similarly, supermarkets and department stores employ a large number of part-time workers. In these sectors, enterprises like to employ low-paid part-time workers, who may also have more flexibility in terms of their availability.

On average, part-time workers are paid only around 44 per cent per hour of regular workers' pay. With an ageing population, the care industry is also rapidly growing, relying on female part-time workers. Many enterprises may seek to cut their labour costs by replacing regular employees with agency workers or fixed-term contract workers or by subcontracting. There are instances where new factories in the electronics field are operated by a majority of non-regular employees, as automated processes require less qualified personnel than previously.

According to the Survey on the Diversification of the Forms of Employment (Ministry of Health, Labour and Welfare 2010), the most frequent reason why enterprises employed non-regular workers was to save pay costs (44 per cent). This was followed by the need 'to adjust employment volume according to business fluctuations for a day or a week' (34 per cent), 'to save the labour costs' other than pay (27 per cent) and 'to secure qualified or easily disposable workers (24 per cent). (The survey allowed multiple answers.) By replacing regular workers with different types of non-regular workers, enterprises realise cost savings as well as flexibility of employment.

The growth of atypical employment provides an employment opportunity for those who might not otherwise be able to participate in the labour market. Such workers may be older workers, mobile young people (*freeters*), those who experience difficulty finding a first job after school or women who interrupt their career for family reasons, even if they have high educational qualifications. The growth also means that the secondary labour market is getting larger. Entry to regular employment

**Figure 10.1  Changes in the ratio of regular and non-regular employment**

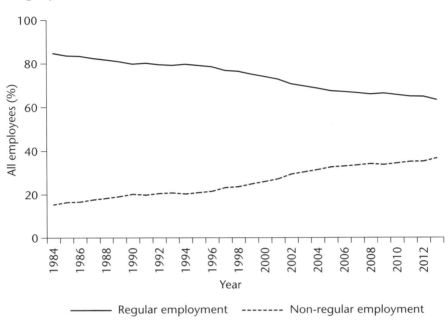

*Source:* Ministry of Internal Affairs and Communications 2012, *Labour Force Survey.*[9]

is limited to new graduates. Hence, there tends to be a strong demarcation between regular and non-regular workers.

## Long working hours

Working time is a serious concern for Japanese workers. According to the Ministry of Health, Labour and Welfare, annual working time per full-time employee (at establishments with five or more employees) was 2038 hours in 1995. It has not changed much, as it was 2026 hours in 2000, 2009 hours in 2010 and 2030 hours in 2012.

Long working time can be divided into two main types. One is overtime work; the other is the relatively short paid annual holidays. As in many other countries, the statutory working time in Japan is 40 hours per week. Overtime is allowed only if the union and management have agreed on such arrangements (Labour Standards Law). The law sets the 'standard' hours for overtime at 360 hours per year. However, there are no legal penalties for enterprises that violate the standard hours.

This is one reason why many enterprises allow their employees to do overtime.

In some cases, employers neither pay additional money for overtime exceeding 360 hours per year, nor keep records of working time. This explains the extent of unpaid overtime. According to the results of a 2005 survey, more than half (52 per cent) of the workers surveyed had received no pay for overtime of at least one hour (JILPT 2005). The most frequently cited reason for overtime work (among regular employees) was 'too much workload', followed by 'want to complete neatly my own job'. These responses illustrate Japanese workers' attitudes towards work and their heavy workloads.

Paid annual leave in Japan is different from that in other developed countries. By regulation, the minimum length of annual leave is ten days for employees with more than six months' service who actually worked for at least 80 per cent of their official working days. They are entitled to one more day for each year of service up to a maximum of 20 days. Most employers apply these minimum requirements. In some cases, workers may take a planned consecutive holiday, but there is no institutional guarantee that the enterprise will grant, for example, a two-week vacation in summer. This partly reflects the weakness of unions, but also to the reluctance of Japanese workers to take such consecutive leave.

Paid annual leave is seen as a kind of buffer against emergencies. For most workers, an emergency is when they are sick. Although many enterprises guarantee their employees sick leave other than paid annual leave, in practice the procedure to take sick leave is complicated (submission of a medical certificate is necessary, and the minimum length of the leave is four days or more), so many workers prefer to take paid annual leave rather than sick leave when they need to be absent for a few days due to a minor illness. Thus, workers tend to accumulate annual leave for emergencies and often lose their annual leave entitlement at the end of the year.

Many enterprises guarantee some special leave for their employees other than paid annual leave. These include summer holidays, year-end or new-year holidays, condolence leave, birthday holidays and marriage leave. In many cases, such special leave or holidays are just for a few days. Reflecting a custom of not having long vacations, Japanese workers tend to take only around half of the paid annual holidays to which they are entitled. Thus, actual working time is generally longer than might be inferred from a list of leave entitlements.

The Ministry of Health, Labour and Welfare does not allow employers to give employees extra pay in lieu of holidays. Its rationale is that, if employers could buy employees' leave entitlements, then employees would be tempted to take less leave, which would be detrimental to their health. Regulations set a ceiling of two years for carry-over of leave. This is to encourage workers to take their full leave entitlements. In practice, however, many workers lose part of their annual leave entitlement. Unions have never given a high priority to annual leave issues.

## CONCLUSIONS

Since the 1980s, there have been significant changes in Japan. These include changes in the Japanese economy as well as employment relations. In terms of macro-economic changes, we note in particular a decline in the relative strength of the Japanese economy in Asia and also in the world, rapid globalisation of Japanese enterprises, a continuing shift towards a more service-oriented economy, and an ageing population.

The Japanese economy has been grappling with economic difficulties since the early 1990s. In contrast with Japan, China has had a high rate of economic growth since it opened to world trade (see Chapter 12). The position of Japan in relation to China and other neighbouring nations has changed. This is different from during the 1980s, when Japanese enterprises had a dominant technological and financial position in Asia.

For a long time, Japanese enterprises were very cautious about overseas development, and preferred to export from Japanese factories. However, the economic context changed in the 1990s, when domestic demand was dampened by recessions and the global competition intensified with American and Korean competitors in terms of new products and technology. Many Japanese enterprises, including medium-sized ones, developed overseas operations in an attempt to make more profits or simply to survive. Many enterprises have transformed themselves into MNEs, with a global network of production, in a relatively short time. In terms of employment relations, this represents a huge change.

In the past, Japanese enterprises boasted about offering 'lifetime' employment, but especially since the 1980s, the job creation may have been outside Japan. When facing competitive pressures, such MNEs change their investment strategies and their corporate governance. Many enterprises are struggling to maintain lifetime employment, consultation with unions and seniority-based pay. To an extent, seniority-based pay is being replaced by performance-related pay, but this has not achieved the promised beneficial results. Globalisation means that MNEs' strategic decisions are being taken at a higher level, so that HRM departments and unions may have little scope to influence them.

Enterprises may consult unions only after the consequences of, say, workplace relocation or enterprise mergers have been realised.

The moves towards a service economy are not new; currently, the service sector accounts for two-thirds of all employment. The segment of wholesale and retail alone employs as many workers as manufacturing. Other segments of services like health and welfare, transport and educational activities are also important. The growth of atypical employment reflects this trend towards a service economy. The service sector employs many part-timers, who include a high proportion of women and students. Most part-time female workers are paid annually less than the 1.3 million yen threshold (around US$13,000) in order to be classified as a dependent family member in terms of tax and social security contributions.

Japan has one of the fastest rates of ageing among developed countries. In 2005, one out of every five people was over 65 years of age, and this proportion is projected to increase to around 40 per cent by 2050. The retirement age will probably be raised, in view of the demographic structure and difficulty of maintaining the public pension scheme. Older workers generally tend to show a strong desire to stay in employment after the mandatory retirement age. Nonetheless, it appears that enterprises are reluctant to employ older workers in high-quality jobs.

There have been several key changes in the Japanese employment system since the 1990s. First, having engaged in labour hoarding during the long recession, enterprises minimised the recruitment of career employees for many years. Consequently, young regular employees (25–35 years) are often overworked, with excessive working hours and little paid leave.

However, there has been a growth of atypical employment. In many enterprises in the service sector, the majority of employees may be part-time or fixed-term workers. There has been a decline in long-term career employment. This echoes the reduction of employment in former public corporations (e.g. telecommunications, national railways) and in large manufacturing enterprises (e.g. steel, electric appliances), which were strongholds of long-term employment. In the past, although lifetime employment used to be offered to only a minority of workers, it was accepted as the norm by management as well as employees. That norm of lifetime employment has been diluted and become fragile.

The issue of atypical employment in Japan poses the question not only of quality of work, but also of the gap between the pool of regular employees and that of non-regular workers. There is almost no possibility for a non-regular worker to become a regular employee.

Non-regular workers are trapped in the atypical pool, whatever the reason for them being in that pool. This is a huge loss of human capital at the individual, enterprise and national levels.

Another disquieting aspect of Japanese employment relations is the absence of a collective dimension. The continuing decline of the unionisation rate and the lack of solidarity among enterprise unions mean that employee voices are barely audible. We can infer from the increasing number of individual disputes that many employees are dissatisfied with their jobs.

The Japanese employment system has been shaped to this point on the basis of the employment practices of large established enterprises. However, the development of the service sector seems to point to the merits of designing a new employment system. This should combine employment security for more workers, including atypical workers, with necessary flexibilities, which enterprises need in the face of economic change and increasing international competition. In sum, aspects of Japanese employment relations seem to be moving to adopt LME-style approaches. However, Japanese employment relations retain similarities with CME-style approaches—albeit with Asian characteristics.

## FURTHER READING

Aoki, M. & Dore, R. (1996) *The Japanese Firm: Sources of Competitive Strength*. Oxford: Oxford University Press.

Jacoby, S.M. (2007) *The Embedded Corporation: Corporate Governance and Employment Relations in Japan and the United States*. Princeton, NJ: Princeton University Press.

Nonaka, I. & Takeuchi, H. (1995) *The Knowledge-Creating Company*. Oxford: Oxford University Press.

Rebick, M. (2005) *The Japanese Employment System: Adapting to a New Environment*. Oxford: Oxford University Press.

Shirai, T. (ed.) (1983) *Contemporary Industrial Relations in Japan*. Madison, WI: University of Wisconsin.

## USEFUL WEBSITES

Japan Institute for Labour Policy and Training: <www.jil.go.jp/english/index.html>.
Japan Productivity Center: <www.jpc-net.jp/eng/index.html>.
Ministry of Health, Labour and Welfare: <www.mhlw.go.jp/English>.
Rengo: <www.jtuc-rengo.org/index.html>.
Statistics Bureau: <www.stat.go.jp/english/index.htm>

## A CHRONOLOGY OF JAPANESE EMPLOYMENT RELATIONS

| | |
|---|---|
| 1868 | Meiji Restoration ends the feudal era. |
| 1880 | Early government factories are sold to family groups, the genesis of *zaibatsu* (holding companies). |
| 1894–95 | Sino-Japanese War. |
| 1904–05 | Russo-Japanese War. |
| 1911 | Factory Law promulgated. |
| 1912 | Founding of Yuaikai (Friendly Society). |
| 1921 | Founding of Nippon Rodo Sodoumei (Japan Labour Foundation). |
| 1931 | Pre-war record for the large number of industrial disputes. The Manchurian Incident starts. |
| 1937 | Sino-Japanese War starts. |
| 1938 | National General Mobilization Law enacted, which gives the government powers to control vast areas of life and business. |
| 1940 | Organisations of workers and farmers dismissed. Dainihon Sangyo Hokokukai (Great Japan Federation of Patriotic Industries) inaugurated. |
| 1945 | The end of World War II. Trade Union Law promulgated (implemented 1946). |
| 1946 | Sodomei (Japanese Confederation of Labour) organised. Labour Relations Adjustment Law promulgated. Constitution of Japan promulgated (implemented May 1947). Nichirokaigi (Congress of Labour Unions of Japan) organised. |
| 1947 | GHQ orders suspension of February general strike. The Labour Standard Law promulgated. |
| 1948 | Nikkeiren (Japan Federation of Employers' Association) formed. Trade Union Law and Labour Relations Adjustment Law revised. |
| 1950 | Korean War starts. Conference for organising Sohyo (General Council of Trade Unions of Japan). |
| 1954 | Zenro (All Japan Federation of Labour Unions) formed. Sohyo consolidates five industry-level offensives into a united wage rise in spring. |
| 1959 | Minimum Wages Law passed by the Diet. Labour disputes at Miike Coal Mines. |
| 1965 | Japan ratifies the ILO's Convention 87. |
| 1974 | The biggest strike in the history of the Spring Offensive— about 6 million participants. |
| 1982 | Zenminrokyo (Japanese Private Sector Trade Union Council) formed. |
| 1986 | Equal Employment Opportunity Law (amended) introduced. |

| | |
|---|---|
| 1987 | Rengo (Japanese Private Sector Trade Union Confederation) formed. Revision of Labour Standard Law (promotion of shorter working hours). Privatisation of the national railways. |
| 1988 | Start of new Rengo (Japan Trade Union Confederation), which merges the public sector unions. |
| 1990 | Revised *Immigration and Refugee Recognition Act*. Fall of the Nikkei index heralds the end of the bubble period. |
| 1997 | Financial crisis peaks with the bankruptcy of some large financial institutions (Yamaichi Securities, Hokkaido Takushoku Bank). |
| 1999 | Amendment of the Temporary (Dispatching) Agency Law relaxes restrictive provisions. |
| 2001 | Junichiro Koizumi becomes prime minister. Law on settlement of individual industrial disputes. Unemployment ratio at a high level of 5.5 per cent. Ministry of Health merges with Ministry of Labour (Ministry of Health, Labour and Welfare). |
| 2002 | Merger of two employers' federations, Keidanren and Nikkeiren, into Nippon Keidanren (Japan Business Federation). |
| 2005 | LDP wins the lower house general election. Privatisation of postal services. |
| 2006 | Resignation of Koizumi. Shinzo Abe becomes prime minister. |
| 2007 | DPJ and other opposition parties win a majority in the upper house. |
| 2008 | Resignation of Takeo Fukuda (LDP). Taro Aso (LDP) becomes prime minister. Manufacturing enterprises suffer from a huge drop in export markets following the global financial crisis. Protests about dismissed temporary workers, with large media coverage. |
| 2011 | (March) Huge earthquakes followed by a tsunami devastate parts of northern Japan and caused a major accident at Fukushima nuclear electricity generator. Many people displaced. Most nuclear plants in Japan cease operation. |
| 2012–13 | LDP wins the general election of both houses of parliament. Shinzo Abe becomes prime minister and launches a new monetary policy, 'Abenomics'. |
| 2014 | Shinzo Abe re-elected as prime minister. |

# CHAPTER 11

# Employment relations in South Korea

## Byoung-Hoon Lee[1]

Some analysts see South Korea (the Republic of Korea, hereafter Korea), along with Japan, as having certain similarities with the coordinated market economies (CMEs) variety of capitalism category identified by Hall and Soskice (2001). The similarities are only approximate; nevertheless, Korea is an exemplary case of relatively late industrialisation. Its late development can be attributed to Japanese colonial occupation (1910–45), division of the nation (1945–48) and the Korean War (1950–53). Despite its late industrialisation, the country has achieved remarkable 'compressed development' since the early 1960s, due to successful export growth at an annual rate of 30 per cent, as well as average economic gross domestic national product (GDNP) growth at an annual rate of more than 8 per cent for 30 years. Until 1987, the 'compressed economic growth' was led by the authoritarian state, pursuing a policy of export-oriented industrialisation. Korea has a population of more than 50 million, and is ranked fifteenth in the world in terms of GDNP (US$1198 billion). Korea's per capita gross domestic product (GDP) has risen from $87 in 1962 to $25,973 in 2013, and it has been a member of the Organisation for Economic Cooperation and Development (OECD) since 1996.

Korea has had a tumultuous trajectory towards democratisation, especially since 1987. After national liberation in 1945, the country was governed by a US military government until 1948. The republic system was founded by the first president, Syngman Rhee, who was ousted by student demonstrations in 1960. President Chung-hee Park, who took power through a military coup in 1962, built an authoritarian regime to lead the export-oriented industrialisation over his eighteen-year presidency (1962–79), which ended with his assassination. President Doo-hwan Chun, who gained power by military coup in 1980, continued the authoritarian leadership. In June 1987, the growing power of the civil society pressured the ex-military ruling group to proclaim the Declaration of Democratisation, which provided critical momentum for political democratisation. After the two terms of Presidents Tae-woo Roh and Young-sam Kim, Dae-jung Kim won the presidential election against the backdrop of the economic crisis at the end of 1997, the first peaceful power shift to an opposition party in the history of Korea. After a decade (1998–2007) of liberal governments led by Presidents Dae-jung Kim and Moo-hyun Roh, Presidents Myung-bak Lee and Geun-hye Park (the daughter of Chung-hee Park) won the elections of 2007 and 2012 respectively. Their conservative governments have pursued 'business-friendly' economic and employment relations reforms.

This chapter delineates the development of employment relations in Korea, mainly focusing on the post-1960s period of industrialisation, and discusses the principal characteristics of key parties and the processes and issues in the employment relations system.

## DEVELOPMENT OF EMPLOYMENT RELATIONS

Until the early 1960s, Korea was an agricultural economy: 63 per cent of the national labour force worked in the primary sector in 1963. As the government, led by President Park, launched successive economic development plans after 1962, the country's economy was transformed by export-oriented industrialisation over the next three decades. The 'Korean model' of industrialisation was shaped by the government-led economic development (Lee 2003). During this period, it was the government that set the goals and policy of economic development, determining the allocation of financial capital and the application of industrial technologies. It promoted the growth of business conglomerates, called *chaebol*, as partners in its export-driven policy, resulting in their dominance in Korea's current economic structure.

From 1962 to 1987, employment relations in Korea were controlled by the government's interventionist employment relations policy, geared to guarantee the supply of cheap, strike-free labour deemed necessary for economic growth. The so-called developmental state made it illegal for workers to take collective industrial action and to organise independent unions. Nevertheless, employers were able to deploy managerial prerogatives in setting pay and working rules. Since unions were too weak to voice their members' discontent, the state and the employers were generally the most powerful parties in employment relations until 1987. The Federation of Korean Trade Unions (FKTU)[2] and its affiliates were under strict state control, and colluded with management instead of actively representing rank-and-file interest. As a result, employment relations were largely quiescent under state-led industrialisation. Industrialisation caused unemployment to fall from more than 8 per cent in 1963 to less than 4 per cent in 1986 (Kim & Sung 2005).

Union membership gradually increased as Korea industrialised in the 1960s and 1970s. However, as illustrated in Table 11.1, it plunged in the early 1980s and continued to decline into the mid-1980s as President Chun pursued a hard-line policy towards unions. Nonetheless, independent union activism associated with the student movement challenged the government and the impotent FKTU leadership from the late 1970s.

In late 1987, the Great Labour Struggle following political democratisation led to the dismantling of the state-controlled employment relations system. Faced with a union movement that had taken the offensive, the government abandoned its interventionist employment relations policy and officially recognised the autonomy of unions and managers in dealing with workplace issues. As a consequence, the number of unions nearly tripled (from 2742 to 7883) between 1986 and 1989. Union membership nearly doubled from about 1 million to almost 2 million, and union density also grew from less than 12 per cent to almost 19 per cent. The growth of the labour movement created a change in the balance of power between workers and management. Management's power over workers was reduced, and unions in many large enterprises took control of the shop floor. Employers had to accept pay increases, improve working conditions and establish corporate welfare programs. Between 1987 and 1989, average nominal annual pay increases exceeded 12 per cent in all sectors. In manufacturing, average nominal pay increased by 18 per cent annually during the same period.

However, union membership and density both began to fall in the early 1990s because of the economic slump, the government's return to interventionist-style employment relations policies, significant improvements in working conditions including pay, and waning public sympathy towards militant unionism after the collapse of the Soviet bloc in the early 1990s (Lee & Lee 2003). The downward trend in union membership continued until 1998.

By the early 1990s, globalisation had increased Korea's concern with the international competitiveness of its economy. To lessen labour–management confrontation, the government adopted a social dialogue model, involving tripartite consultation among unions, employers and

**Table 11.1  Indexes of employment relations**

| | Unions | | | Labour disputes | | |
|---|---|---|---|---|---|---|
| Year | Union members (000s) | Union density (%) | Number of unions | Number of strikes | WDL (000s) | Unemployment (%) |
| 1970 | 473 | 13 | 3500 | 4 | 9 | 4.4 |
| 1975 | 750 | 16 | 4091 | 52 | 14 | 4.1 |
| 1980 | 948 | 15 | 2635 | 206 | 61 | 5.2 |
| 1985 | 1004 | 12 | 2551 | 265 | 64 | 4.0 |
| 1986 | 1036 | 12 | 2675 | 276 | 72 | 3.8 |
| 1987 | 1267 | 14 | 4103 | 3749 | 6947 | 3.1 |
| 1988 | 1707 | 18 | 6164 | 1873 | 5401 | 2.5 |
| 1989 | 1932 | 19 | 7883 | 1616 | 6351 | 2.6 |
| 1990 | 1887 | 17 | 7698 | 322 | 4487 | 2.4 |
| 1991 | 1803 | 15 | 7656 | 234 | 3271 | 2.4 |
| 1992 | 1735 | 15 | 7527 | 235 | 1528 | 2.5 |
| 1993 | 1667 | 14 | 7147 | 144 | 1308 | 2.9 |
| 1994 | 1659 | 13 | 7025 | 121 | 1484 | 2.5 |
| 1995 | 1615 | 12 | 6606 | 88 | 393 | 2.1 |
| 1996 | 1599 | 12 | 6424 | 85 | 893 | 2.0 |
| 1997 | 1484 | 11 | 5733 | 78 | 445 | 2.6 |
| 1998 | 1402 | 11 | 5560 | 129 | 1452 | 7.0 |
| 1999 | 1481 | 12 | 5637 | 198 | 1366 | 6.3 |
| 2000 | 1527 | 11 | 5698 | 250 | 1894 | 4.1 |
| 2001 | 1569 | 12 | 6148 | 235 | 1083 | 3.8 |
| 2002 | 1538 | 11 | 6506 | 322 | 1580 | 3.1 |
| 2003 | 1550 | 11 | 6257 | 320 | 1299 | 3.4 |
| 2004 | 1537 | 10 | 6107 | 462 | 1199 | 3.5 |
| 2005 | 1506 | 10 | 5971 | 287 | 848 | 3.5 |
| 2006 | 1559 | 10 | 5889 | 138 | 1201 | 3.3 |
| 2007 | 1688 | 11 | 5099 | 115 | 536 | 3.0 |
| 2008 | 1666 | 10 | 4886 | 108 | 809 | 3.0 |
| 2009 | 1640 | 10 | 4689 | 121 | 627 | 3.4 |
| 2010 | 1643 | 10 | 4420 | 86 | 511 | 3.4 |
| 2011 | 1720 | 10 | 5120 | 65 | 429 | 3.0 |
| 2012 | 1781 | 10 | 5177 | 105 | 933 | 2.8 |
| 2013 | 1848 | 10 | 5305 | 72 | 638 | 3.1 |

*Notes:*
Union density = Union members ÷ Total number in the labour force × 100.
Numbers rounded. Unemployment rate = The unemployed (in one week job search) ÷ Total number in the economically active population × 100.

*Sources:* MoEL (2014); KLI (2014).

government. With the assistance of the government, the FKTU and the Korea Employers Federation (KEF) reached nationwide agreements on pay increases and employment policy in 1993 and 1994. The FKTU–KEF agreements were used as a guideline for pay negotiations at the enterprise level. But in 1995, these nationwide consultations were halted as the FKTU was discredited for supporting the government's wage restraint policies.

The government led another tripartite initiative, the Presidential Commission on Industrial Relations Reform (PCIRR), in May 1996. The commission was formed as an advisory body to the president, and consisted of representatives from unions, employers' associations, public-interest and academic groups. The PCIRR provided an open forum for social dialogue among those various stakeholders with regard to labour law reform. The PCIRR included representatives of the Korean Confederation of Trade Unions (KCTU), the national centre of democratic unions that was founded in November 1995, but had not been legally recognised.

Following a series of public hearings, sub-committee workshops and plenary sessions, the PCIRR submitted to President Young-Sam Kim a set of proposed changes to labour legislation. However, on 26 December 1996, the government and the ruling party passed their own bill revising the existing labour laws, while opposition law-makers were absent from the parliament. The government's unilateral revision of labour legislation, which placed more emphasis on labour market flexibility than on labour rights and unionisation, triggered nation-wide strikes and anti-government protests in late 1996 and early 1997. Under greater pressure from unions and the international community, the government abandoned its unilateral 1996 revision of the labour laws and eventually revised them after consultation with opposition parties in March 1997.

The foreign exchange crisis of November 1997 that precipitated an economic recession severely affected Korea's employment relations. It triggered extensive restructuring and massive downsizing by the government and businesses. The focus of employment relations shifted from economic issues, such as pay and fringe benefits, to jobs and employment; this was accompanied by a sharp increase in the intensity of industrial conflict. Unions made unprecedented concessions in 1998 and 1999, by agreeing to pay freezes and reduced bonuses and welfare programs. For example, the total pay decrease in 1998 was only 2.7 per cent. Widespread downsizing at unionised enterprises caused union membership to decline sharply—by 197,000 between 1997 and 1998. However, union membership and density rose slightly in 1999 when a new law allowed teachers to form unions for the first time. Since then, union membership has rebounded to more than 1.8 million, but union density had dropped to around 10 per cent by 2013 (see Table 11.1).

Confronted by the economic crisis, the government resumed its policy of social dialogue. President-elect Dae-jung Kim established the Tripartite Commission in January 1998 to promote cooperation among government, unions and employers in overcoming the economic crisis. In February 1998, the commission concluded a historic social pact covering an extensive agenda, including the extension of employment insurance coverage, procedures for redundancies (layoffs) and dispatched labour, and guaranteed employment relations rights for teachers and public servants (Lee 2003). The social pact helped to end the economic crisis by improving the country's credibility among foreign financial institutions. Immediately after signing the social pact, however, the KCTU leadership faced strong criticism from its members for agreeing to the dismissal of redundant workers. As a result, the KCTU withdrew its participation from the commission, bringing to a halt the commission's first round of policy consultations.

The second round of Tripartite Commission consultations began in June 1998. The main objectives in this round were to monitor the implementation of agreements made in the first round and to promote tripartite consultations on economic restructuring, particularly with regard to the banking, finance and public sectors. The second round reached tripartite agreements on detailed policy proposals, including the legalisation of teachers' unions and integration of the two-tier health insurance system. The second round ended in early 1999 when the KCTU again withdrew from the commission.

Although a third round of consultations began in September 1999, the commission's role in promoting tripartite dialogue had been seriously weakened by the confrontations between the KCTU and the government. As a result, since 2000, the Tripartite Commission has been unable to contend with many pressing employment relations issues, such as intensified labour market segmentation, the proliferation of non-regular employees and jobless economic growth. Such issues were precipitated by the neo-liberal reforms following the 1997 economic crisis (Lee 2005).

Since 1997, the quality of working life has deteriorated for many people. There has been a rapid increase in the size of the non-regular labour force, discrimination against non-regular workers and a decrease in decent jobs. Issues of employment status, enterprise size and gender have become more serious, increasing the segmentation of labour markets and resulting in a worsening quality of employment relations.

Since the early 1990s, particularly in the aftermath of the economic crisis, there have been increasing disparities between regular employees of large enterprises and the remainder of the workforce, in pay, welfare benefits, job training, employment conditions, and legal and union protection. Meanwhile, the employment relations system has undergone structural change—for example, the spread of industrial unionism and the revision of labour laws to meet global standards. In particular, the institutional reforms—including allowing multiple unionisation at the establishment level—have had a profound impact on the reshaping of employment relations, mainly weakening the leverage of unions.

In summary, since the 1960s, employment relations in Korea have been transformed by industrialisation, democratisation, globalisation and the post-2007 global financial crisis. After 1987, Korea's employment relations, controlled by the state until 1987, changed to embrace more social dialogue and regulation—albeit in the face of a steady decline in union density. However, since 1997, employment relations have included aspects of confrontation and labour market polarisation.

## THE EMPLOYMENT RELATIONS PARTIES

### Unions

The late 1980s witnessed remarkable changes in the composition of unions, as well as an explosive growth in the labour movement. First, the most unionised sector changed from textiles, where the workforce was predominantly female, to metal and chemical industries, mostly employing men.[3] This reflects the change in Korea's economic structure in the 1980s. Since 1987, male-dominated unions organised in heavy industries have led the union movement. The membership of non-manual unions in such industries as banking, mass media and health care also rose sharply in this period. Second, many of the newly organised unions were critical of the FKTU's submission to the government's employment relations control policies before 1987, and rejected affiliation with the FKTU. Those independent unions espoused 'democratic unionism' and formed their own federations in the late 1980s that merged with the KCTU in 1995.

The union movement is divided into four groups, as illustrated in Table 11.2. The FKTU, the largest national centre, with 28 affiliates, takes a moderate stance towards the government and employers. By contrast, the KCTU, which gained legal recognition in 1999 and has fifteen affiliates, tends towards militant activism. The Korean Labor Union Confederation (KLUC), which was established as the third national centre in 2011, after the legislation allowing multiple unionisation, has a more conciliatory attitude towards the government and employers. The FKTU, which lost its exclusive official recognition in 1987, continued to lose members. Its membership fell to 755,000 by the mid-2000s, but rebounded to 820,000 in 2013. The KCTU grew from 420,000 in 1995 (at the time of its establishment) to 626,000 in 2013. The membership of independent unions that withdrew their affiliation from the FKTU and the KCTU almost doubled, from 176,700 in 2006 to 381,575 in 2013, as shown in Table 11.2. The growing membership of independent unions might reflect their concern with the national centres' confrontation with conservative governments. It might also reflect the prohibition of employers paying wages to union officials, which is having a damaging impact on unions' finances.

The majority of unions in Korea are enterprise based. Enterprise unions have considerable autonomy in union administration and collective bargaining at the enterprise level. In the early 1960s, President Park forced unions to restructure along industrial lines, but in the early 1980s, President Chun legislated for enterprise unions. Since the late 1990s, unions have aimed to revert to industrial unionism and centralised bargaining to strengthen their socio-political power.

**Table 11.2    Number (%) of unions and union members by national centre affiliation**

| | 2006 | | 2013 | |
| --- | --- | --- | --- | --- |
| Union affiliation | No. of unions | No. of union members (000s) | No. of unions | No. of union members (000s) |
| FKTU | 3429 (58.2) | 755.2 (48.4) | 2313 (43.6) | 820.0 (44.4) |
| KCTU | 1143 (19.4) | 627.3 (40.2) | 356 (6.7) | 626.0. (33.9) |
| KLUC | – | – | 100 (1.9) | 20.2 (1.1) |
| Independent unions | 1317 (22.4) | 176.7 (11.4) | 2536 (47.8) | 381.6 (20.7) |
| Total | 5889 (100) | 1559.2 (100) | 5305 (100) | 1847.6 (100) |

*Source:* MoEL (2014).

In 1998, the Korea Health and Medical Workers Union (KHMWU) was the first to revert to industrial unionism. Subsequently others followed suit, including the Korea Finance Industry Union (KFIU) and the Korea Metal Workers Union (KMWU). As a consequence, membership in industrial unions grew from 10 per cent of total union membership in 1996 to about 56 per cent in 2011 (Lee & Kim 2013). In particular, the KCTU resolved to complete its return to industrial unionism by the end of 2007, and by 2012 nearly 84 per cent of its members were affiliated with industrial unions. In contrast, the FKTU has been less active at restructuring, and only 20 per cent of its members are organised in industrial unions. Non-regular workers made another attempt to organise community-based general unions to try to cope with the growing flexibility and mobility of labour markets. Almost 63 per cent of large enterprises with more than 300 employees are unionised, even though union density remains very low at only 10 per cent. The unionisation of regular workers is 17 per cent, whereas that of non-regular workers is only 3 per cent.

## Employers

Until 1987, employers, who relied on the government's interventionist employment relations policies to restrain workers' collective activities, imposed authoritarian supervision over workers. Before 1987, employers practised militaristic control, imitating direct supervision of the rank and file by force (Park 1992). However, the explosive growth of unions in 1987 transformed corporate-level employment relations from domination by management towards a more balanced power relationship. As a result, unions were able to exercise a degree of shop-floor control in many enterprises. In addition, unions pressed managements to concede high pay increases and improvements to working conditions and welfare programs. Further, unions persuaded enterprises to abolish job evaluation schemes, which had been used for determining employees' pay in a discriminatory manner and were therefore a cause of discontent.

From the early 1990s, employers took a hard line in employment relations. Against the economic downturn that hit the Korean economy around the end of the 1980s and in the early 1990s, employers launched their 'new management strategies'. The strategies had three pillars: new personnel policies, flexible working systems and union suppression. The new personnel policies included the introduction of flexible pay systems (e.g. pay for performance and job capabilities) and the restoration of job evaluation. At the workplace level, employers extended the use of automation technologies to promote flexible labour processes and increased labour productivity. The growing implementation of advanced production technologies was also intended to reduce management's reliance on a recalcitrant workforce. Considerable management efforts were expended on restricting the militant activities of unions by imposing strict penalties on union officials and activists for organising illegal industrial action. As a core part of the union-suppression strategies, the 'no work, no pay' policy was reinforced to prevent unions from taking strike action. Therefore, new management strategies were pursued primarily to weaken the strong shop-floor power of unions and make labour processes more flexible.

Against the backdrop of the economic crisis of 1997, massive restructuring took place, particularly in the finance and public sectors, and among large private enterprises. Management at those large enterprises commonly took action to downsize regular employees by permanent layoffs and/or early retirement in the context of economic crisis, while extending the use of the non-regular labour force and outsourcing business operations in the later period of business recovery. As a consequence, the employment practices of internal labour markets developed by those large enterprises in the period of economic prosperity, which had followed the Japanese model, were crucially weakened during the economic crisis. In the post-1997 period, it has been common for large enterprises to resort to external labour markets by increasing the use of the non-regular workforce and undertaking organisational re-engineering on a regular basis, following the American business model. It is noteworthy that wide variations of employment relations exist among the business conglomerates, which have exerted dominant influence over the Korean economy and national employment relations. For instance, Samsung, the first business conglomerate, has strictly pursued a human resource management (HRM) model that avoids unionisation; Hyundai Motor Group, the second conglomerate, has taken a confrontational stance towards unions; LG (the third conglomerate) and SK (the fourth) have maintained a relatively cooperative relationship with their unions. By contrast, small and medium-sized enterprises (SMEs) often have poor employment relations practices, sometimes below statutory labour standards. This reflects their inferior financial capabilities and out-dated management styles.

There are three significant contemporary employers' organisations that have substantial influence over national-level employment relations: the KEF, the Korean Chamber of Commerce and Industry (KCCI), and the Federation of Korean Industries. The KEF, which was established in 1970 and represents about 3300 enterprises in the manufacturing and service sectors, has been the official voice of Korean employers at national-level negotiations and consultations regarding employment relations issues. This association was invited as their employer representative to membership of the PCIRR and the Tripartite Commission. The rapid growth in the labour movement in the late 1980s and the government-initiated tripartite efforts since the 1990s have made the KEF a body of growing significance. The KCCI is the oldest employers' association, founded in 1884. It represents about 45,000 enterprises in all business sectors, based upon the *Chambers of Commerce and Industry Act 1952*. The KCCI has been treated as an employer representative for social dialogue concerning labour law reforms during recent years. The Federation of Korean Industries, which was formed in 1961 and is mainly composed of 380 large enterprises (including business conglomerates), has also exercised substantial influence on the government's employment relations policy and on labour legislation by the congress on behalf of business conglomerates interests.

## Government

Before 1987, the government played an active role in promoting economic growth and suppressing workers' collective action. It focused on job creation and paternalistic regulation of employment relations. After 1987, however, the government shifted its employment relations policy from authoritarian control to social dialogue. In the early 1990s, it became concerned with national economic competitiveness and recurrent labour–management confrontation, and adopted a tripartite model for promoting cooperative relations between unions and employers.[4] Tripartism, led by the government, started with the National Economic and Social Council, formed in 1990. It went through the stages of the national-level FKTU–KEF pay negotiations in 1993 and 1994, and the PCIRR's policy consultation for labour law reforms in 1996, to the Tripartite Commission in early 1998. The Tripartite Commission was renamed the Economic and Social Development Commission, and its agenda of policy consultation was expanded with the revision of the law in April 2007. This commission now operates as a presidential advisory board for policy consultations concerning employment relations and social issues. Despite the 25 years of tripartism and some notable achievements—particularly in overcoming the economic crisis in 1997—the social dialogue has gained little credit with unions, which claim that it is a cosmetic for government-initiated policy-making and is hindered by the recalcitrance of employer representatives. In addition, union

276

members have stigmatised the commission as being responsible for the adoption of neo-liberal labour market flexibility, and for doing little to resolve the social problems resulting from labour market polarisation.

The government established a section to administer employment relations policies in 1963. It became the Ministry of Employment and Labour in 2010. The ministry covers all work-related areas, including labour standards, employment relations, employment insurance and equality, vocational training and occupational safety. It consists of two offices (policy planning and employment policy) and three divisions (labour–management cooperation, labour standards and employment health and safety). The ministry has six regional administration offices located in major cities—Seoul, Pusan, Incheon, Daegu, Incheon and Kwangju—and 40 regional offices. In the regional offices, more than 1300 labour inspectors are charged with policing and supervising working conditions in accordance with the *Labour Standards Act*, and taking action to prevent and deal with employment relations disputes at enterprises in their regions. Two commissions, affiliated with the Ministry of Labour, play a crucial role in shaping nationwide employment relations. The Labour Commission, which consists of three parties—unions, employers and public-interest groups—adjudicates such employment relations cases as unfair labour practices, unfair dismissal and work discrimination, and mediates industrial disputes. The Minimum Wage Commission, which consists of 27 members evenly representing unions, employers and the public interest, manages the negotiations among the three parties and the determination of the annual minimum pay.

Unions have been critical of the submissive role and position taken by the Ministry of Labour and its predecessors, giving priority to economic growth from throughout Korea's post-war development. Since President Dae-jung Kim's administration (1997–2002), the government has promoted a new labour–management culture and workplace innovation, as it regards confrontational labour–management relations as a major constraint on national competitiveness. The government is the largest employer in Korea, employing 1.62 million people, including civil servants (slightly more than a million), public school teachers (more than a third of a million), and employees of public enterprises and institutes (more than a quarter of a million). Teachers and civil servants were given legal labour rights to organise and bargain (excluding strike action) in 1999 and 2004 respectively. Given the statutory constraints on union activities, the public sector is highly organised, with union density of just under 27 per cent for civil servants, approximately 25 per cent for teachers and 44 per cent in public enterprises. Therefore, the government has substantial influence over the employment relations of the private sector through the results of its collective bargaining with unions in the relatively large public sector.

## PROCESSES OF EMPLOYMENT RELATIONS

### Collective bargaining and dispute resolution

Collective bargaining is regulated by the *Trade Union and Labour Relations Adjustment Act* (TULRAA). Collective bargaining in most unionised enterprises is conducted primarily at the enterprise level, in accordance with the enterprise-based union structure. The transport sector (e.g. taxi and bus) and the textile sector are exceptions, in that those sectors traditionally have maintained regional or sectoral bargaining practices. As the TULRAA, amended in 1997, stipulates that no collective agreement shall have a valid term exceeding two years, collective bargaining takes place every year in most unionised enterprises. In practice, collective bargaining on pay is conducted every year, while bargaining to determine other working conditions and other contractual terms is conducted every two years.

Even though the collective bargaining structure is basically decentralised, two national centres and the employers' associations have had substantial influence on enterprise-level bargaining through their bargaining proposals. As demonstrated in Table 11.3, the FKTU and the KCTU have proposed bargaining guidelines for pay increases and other contractual changes (e.g. the reduction of working hours, employment security, regular employment of non-regular workers in recent years) at the beginning of every year; these serve as an influential reference to enterprise-level collective bargaining. In response to the national union centres' bargaining proposal, the KEF offers its own bargaining guidelines to member enterprises. Moreover, the national union centres and the KEF are involved in bargaining processes to set the minimum wage through the Minimum Wage Commission every year.[5]

Industrial unions, reorganised by the organisational integration of enterprise unions over the past fifteen years, have demanded centralised bargaining, which is distinct from the decentralising trends of bargaining structure in Western countries. In particular, three major industrial unions, the KMWU, the KHMWU and the KFIU, have made progress in making national agreements with their employers' associations. The KMWU has a three-level bargaining structure, comprising the national, regional and enterprise levels, while the KHMWU and the KFIU have two tiers: national and enterprise levels. Centralised

**Table 11.3   Trends in labour–management pay proposals and contractual pay increases**

| | Average pay increases (%) | Pay increase proposals (%) | | |
|---|---|---|---|---|
| | | KEF | FKTU | KCTU |
| 1988 | 13.5 | 7.5–8.5 | 29.3 | – |
| 1989 | 17.5 | 10.9 (8.9–12.9) | 26.8 | 37.3 |
| 1990 | 9.0 | 7.0 | 17.3–20.5 | 23.3 |
| 1991 | 10.5 | 7.0 | 17.5 | 22.2 |
| 1992 | 6.5 | 5.7 (4.7–6.7) | 15.0 | 25.4 |
| 1993 | 5.2 | 4.7–8.9 | (c) | 18.0 |
| 1994 | 7.2 | 5.0–8.7 | | 16.4 |
| 1995 | 7.7 | 4.4–6.4 | 12.4 | 14.8 |
| 1996 | 7.8 | 4.8 | 12.2 | 14.8 |
| 1997 | 4.2 | (a) | 11.2 | 10.6 ±3 |
| 1998 | 0.0 | (b) | 4.7 | 5.1–9.2 |
| 1999 | 2.1 | (a) | 5.5 | 7.7 ±1.5 |
| 2000 | 7.2 | 5.4 | 13.2 | 15.2 |
| 2001 | 6.0 | 3.5 | 12.0 | 12.7 |
| 2002 | 6.7 | 4.1 | 12.3 | 12.5 |
| 2003 | 6.4 | 4.3 | 11.4 | 11.1 |
| 2004 | 5.2 | 3.8 | 10.7 | 10.5 |
| 2005 | 4.7 | 3.9 | 9.4 | 9.3 |
| 2006 | 4.8 | 2.6 | 9.6 | 8.0–12.6 |
| 2007 | 4.8 | 2.4 | 9.3 | 9.0 |
| 2008 | 4.9 | 2.6 | 9.1 | 8.0 |
| 2009 | 1.7 | – | – | 4.9 |
| 2010 | 4.8 | (a) | 9.5 | 9.2 |
| 2011 | 5.1 | 3.5 | 9.4 | – |
| 2012 | 4.7 | 2.9 | 9.1 | – |
| 2013 | 3.5 | – | 8.1 | (d) |

*Notes:*
(a) Pay freeze.
(b) Labour cost reduction by 20%.
(c) National level agreement by KEF and FKTU.
(d) Increase by 219,170 Korean won per month.

*Source:* KLI (2014).

industrial bargaining has declined, however, due to opposition from employers—particularly business conglomerates—and from conservative governments.

The dispute procedure is stipulated in the TULRAA. According to this law, the parties are obliged to enter into mediation with the Labour Commission. Prior to the revision of the TULRAA in 2007, the government was able to award compulsory arbitration for resolving disputes at public enterprises providing essential services (water, electricity, gas, oil, telecommunications, railroads, hospitals, inner-city bus services and banking services). The revised TULRAA abolishes compulsory arbitration, and instead prohibits unions from engaging in strike action in essential services in public enterprises.

In 2010, when multiple unionism was allowed at the level of the establishment, an additional legal procedure was required to regulate bargaining between multiple unions. Multiple unions can agree to form a joint bargaining team to negotiate with their employer. If multiple unions fail voluntarily to form a joint bargaining team, a union that represents a majority of workers in the establishment can have the exclusive right to bargain with the employer, and minority unions are required to accept the majority union's bargaining.

## LMC

The Labour–Management Council (LMC) is an institutionalised channel for promoting communication and cooperation between employees and management. The government enacted the *Labour–Management Council Act* in 1980, making it mandatory for all establishments with more than 50 workers to establish a council. Despite this statutory obligation, only a limited number of enterprises formed LMCs before 1987. However, confronted with increasing disputes following democratisation in 1987, management tried to promote cooperation with workers by implementing the LMC legislation. As a result, enterprises with LMCs rapidly increased, to over 14,000 in the early 1990s.

In 1997, the *Labour–Management Council Act* was replaced with the *Act Concerning the Promotion of Worker Participation and Cooperation*. The new Act stipulates that all enterprises with more than 30 workers must form a council and hold meetings every quarter. In accordance with the new law, the number of enterprises that formed LMCs almost doubled between 1996 (15,234) and 2001 (29,348). The number of LMCs continued to grow, reaching 45,456 in 2012.

The LMC is composed of equal numbers of representatives from employees and management—usually between three and ten persons from each side. When an enterprise has a union that represents a majority of workers, the union's leaders are entitled to participate in the LMC as employee representatives. According to the *Act Concerning the Promotion of Worker Participation and Cooperation*, workplace issues to be dealt with by the LMC fall into three categories: issues requiring prior consent by employee representatives (i.e. training and development plans, fringe benefit programs, in-house welfare funds, grievance handling and joint labour–management committees, or JLMCs); issues of consultation with employee representatives (i.e. human resource planning, workplace renovation and new technologies, prevention of industrial accidents, redundancy adjustment, working time rescheduling, pay system changes and revision in work rules); and issues to be reported (i.e. corporate strategies and performance, quarterly production plan, personnel issues and the enterprise's financial situation). Many unions use LMC meetings as an extension of their collective bargaining, while top management at many enterprises is indifferent to the feasibility of cooperation and communication promoted by the LMC.

## KEY ISSUES

### Labour market issues: Non-regular labour, widening pay gap and working hours

The 1997 economic crisis was a shock to labour markets. Most enterprises that had achieved sustained growth and maintained the conventional human resource policy of 'lifetime employment' before 1997 then undertook extensive restructuring of their businesses and employment practices. This resulted in a fundamental change to employment relations in Korea. According to a survey conducted in 2000, 66 per cent of enterprises downsized after the economic crisis. This shows the huge extent of corporate restructuring at the time (Park & Roh 2001). The survey showed that 74 per cent of respondents fostered spin-off enterprises and that nearly 58 per cent outsourced part of their business. Those enterprises then recruited non-regular labour to fill what previously had been regular jobs after the economy recovered in 1999. There was a sharp rise in unemployment during the 1997 economic crisis, but there was a notable reduction in unemployment in the recovery phase of the early 2000s. The unemployment rate remained low, at 3 per cent, from 2001 until 2008—the lowest among the OECD countries. Immediately after the post-2007 global financial crisis, unemployment in Korea was only 3.4 per cent, and had declined to 2.8 per cent by 2012.

However, the biggest problem with Korean labour markets is the worsening employment structure, mainly derived from the sustained decline in good jobs and the widening disparity between good and bad jobs. The loss of good jobs at large enterprises has been due mainly to management's determined policy to carry out downsizing and outsourcing. Employee numbers at enterprises with more than 500 employees decreased from 2.1 million in 1993 to 1.3 million in 2005. As a result, the large-enterprise workforce's share of the total wage-labour population declined from more than 17 per cent to less than 9 per cent during the same period (Kim 2005). Moreover, the process of de-industrialisation has accelerated since the mid-1990s, resulting in a reduction in the number of manufacturing jobs. This change in the composition of sectoral employment is associated with a lowering in the quality of jobs. Between 1997 and 2012, the percentage of employment accounted for by the manufacturing sector declined from 21.4 per cent to 16.6 per cent, while that sector's share of GDP increased from 26.3 per cent to 31 per cent.

The number of non-regular workers has grown sharply since the economic crisis. Thus, the excessive use of and discrimination against such temporary employees has become a major issue. The share of non-regular employment increased from approximately 27 per cent of the working population in 2002 to 37 per cent in 2004. Owing to the government's strengthened regulation over the use of contingent workers, reflecting societal concern about inferior employment conditions, the size of the non-regular workforce has since declined to less than 33 per cent.[6] As many as 88 per cent of non-regular workers are employed at small establishments (those with fewer than 100 employees).

The increasing polarisation of labour markets is exemplified by the growing gap in overall employment conditions, including pay and fringe benefits, between the primary sector for regular workers at large enterprises and the secondary sector for workers in small enterprises and non-regular employees. There has been a growing pay discrepancy between large and small enterprises. For example, the average pay in small enterprises with between ten and 29 employees declined from 90 per cent of the average pay in large enterprises with more than 500 employees to about 59 per cent between 1986 and 2007.[7] The pay level of small enterprises employing five to nine workers is less than 52 per cent of the pay in large enterprises that have 300 employees or more. The pay gap between regular and non-regular workers also increased. For instance, the monthly pay of non-regular workers dropped from 67 per cent of regular workers' pay in 2002 to 56 per cent in 2013.

Moreover, labour market polarisation is evident in worker fringe benefits and HR development. The discrepancy in enterprise-level expenditures on fringe benefits and training between large and small enterprises has been constant over the past fifteen years. Large enterprises with more than 1000 employees expend twice as much on fringe benefits, and eight times more on training, than small enterprises with between ten and 29 employees. Most non-regular workers have been excluded from statutory welfare and labour standards. About 40 per cent of these workers benefit from statutory welfare programs, such as national pensions, medical insurance and employment insurance. Only 25–33 per cent of those non-regular workers are protected by legal labour standards, including extra work premiums and paid vacation.

As in Japan, an additional problem with polarised labour markets is the lack of job mobility between the primary and secondary sectors. Many studies have shown that non-regular jobs are trapped in the peripheral sector, rather than functioning as 'stepping stones' to regular jobs (Nam & Kim 2000; Han & Jang 2000). Workers in large enterprises have experienced job insecurity, just as small-enterprise and non-regular workers have. Employees at large enterprises have much shorter tenures than their counterparts in the United States and Japan (Jung 2006). Even workers at unionised large enterprises have been threatened by management-led restructuring initiatives, including outsourcing, spin-offs, business re-engineering, the reallocation of production facilities and the use of non-regular labour.

Labour market polarisation results not only from the external shocks of the economic crisis, but also from the strategic choices of employment relations actors and their political interactions. Growing labour market segmentation in Korea can be attributed to neo-liberal economic reforms, led by the government in the post-1997 period; large enterprises' exploitative profit maximisation, making small suppliers more inferior and resulting in a sharp increase of non-regular labour; and business unionism focusing on the protection of union members' egoistic interest, excluding a majority of unorganised labour. As a consequence, the polarisation of the labour market has tended to worsen. There has been growing concern that labour market polarisation results in social disintegration, as indicated by the sharp rise in the number of crimes and divorces, and that it weakens the sustainability of economic growth.

Although Korea introduced the 40-hour week by law in 2003, it has recorded the most annual working hours (e.g. 2090 hours in 2011) of the OECD member countries. During recent years, the government has made policy efforts to reduce working hours as a

key means to create decent jobs. While the Lee Myung-bak government attempted to constrain extra working hours and holiday work,
the Park Geun-hye government has taken steps to create permanent
part-time jobs with its policy goal to increase the employment level.
In this political context, Hyundai auto company and its labour union
reached a significant agreement to implement a two daily work-shift
system to reduce working hours and get rid of night-shift work in
2012, which has since diffused through the auto industry and other
manufacturing sectors.

## Transforming employment relations and weakening unions

Employment relations have been more adversarial in the post-1997
period than beforehand. As illustrated in Table 11.1, the number of
labour disputes declined to below 100 in the mid-1990s, but grew
sharply after 1997 and peaked at 462 in 2004. The number of labour
disputes continued declining, to 65 in 2011, but increased to 105
in 2012. Despite the general decreasing trend in disputes, employment relations continue to be unstable, reflecting mistrust between
the parties. The instability of employment relations has been seen as
a crucial constraint on national economic competitiveness, with the
IMD's World Competitiveness report indicating that Korea is falling
considerably in relation to, for example, Japan, Taiwan and Singapore.

While the labour disputes during the economic crisis of 1998 and in
the following years took place largely due to government-led and
employer-driven restructuring, many labour disputes in the 2000s have
been associated with non-regular employment and industrial bargaining. Since the start of the twenty-first century, the growing presence
of non-regular labour has been a contentious issue in employment
relations. The national labour centres (the FKTU and the KCTU) and
non-government organisations (NGOs) have launched campaigns
demanding legislation to constrain employers from using non-regular
employment. Moreover, non-regular workers have organised their own
unions in sectors such as auto manufacturing, transport, construction
and public administration, and have engaged in militant collective
action, demanding improvements to their working conditions and
regular status.

Employers resist the unionisation of non-regular workers, and
sometimes there are conflicts with regular workers' unions. After
2006, when the laws to protect non-regular labour were enacted,
many enterprises terminated their contracts with non-regular workers
and replaced them with subcontracted labour, which resulted in

confrontations with the dismissed non-regular workers. Even though the union density of non-regular workers was less than 3 per cent during the 2000s, the excessive use of and discrimination against non-regular labour has created acute tensions in employment relations at the national and enterprise levels. Since the late 2000s, subcontracted workers in manufacturing industries have been at the centre of non-regular labour issues, in that many of them organised themselves to protest against employers breaking labour laws, to engage in law suits and to take industrial action. The massive downsizing at Sangyong Motor and Hanjin Heavy Industries has resulted in passionate union–management confrontations and triggered citizens' voluntary campaigns to protest management's unilateral layoffs.

Industrial unionisation—mainly initiated by KCTU affiliates—was successful until the late 2000s, but industrial unions have little presence in each sector, and limited concentration of organisational resources (e.g. financial funds and union staff). They face employer opposition to industry-level bargaining, and there has been little extension of industrial contracts to the unorganised or non-regular workforce (Lee 2002). With conservative anti-union governments, the opposition of employers to the industrial unions' demand for centralised collective bargaining has become even stronger, and there have been few moves towards centralised bargaining.

The prohibition of wage payments to union officials and the permission of multiple unionisation at the establishment level[8] were implemented in 2010, after the ten-year suspension of those TULRAA clauses. This change in the institutional framework of employment relations has had a damaging impact on labour unions, particularly KCTU affiliates. Employers encouraged the organisation of a cooperative second union to weaken the existing militant union by taking advantage of the multi-unionisation clause. Given the prohibition of employers paying wages to union officials, a new clause was adopted to provide paid time off for union officials. However, the paid time off system has reduced the number of full-time union officials working on union activities by 24 per cent. Moreover, some employers resorted to union-busting consultancies to destroy recalcitrant unions, which became a scandal at the end of the Lee Myung-bak government.

The Park Geun-hye government imposed a large sum of compensation as damages on the striking Korean Railway Workers Union, which launched collective action against the government's plan to privatise the national railways in 2013. The claims for compensation against unions' collective action have become a focus of labour law reforms, demanded by unions and NGOs. Public sector unions have raised other issues: civil servants and teachers have complained about the restriction on collective bargaining and industrial action by the current laws. They are also critical of the statutory extension of the 'strike-free' essential services, a policy introduced in 2007. Therefore, public sector employment relations remain contentious in Korea. Confronted by the unfavourable change in employment relations laws and employer anti-unionism, unions have been losing their bargaining power and organising capacity.

## CONCLUSIONS

Under the developmental regime (1961–87), employment relations in Korea were largely shaped by the government-led economic growth policy. Since 1987, there have been remarkable changes in employment relations at the macro level as well as at the workplace level, along with the compressed development of the political economy, such as industrial restructuring, democratisation and economic crisis. The post-democratisation period included the growing segmentation of labour markets and the institutionalisation of employment relations. After the 1997 economic crisis, employment relations in Korea began another round of structural transformation, with some similarities to a market-driven model. Employment relations in the post-1997 period are characterised by precariousness and polarisation, exemplified by the proliferation of the non-regular workforce and the widening pay gap, as well as employer dominance, supported by the government's neo-liberal policies. At present, social dialogue, led by the Tripartite Commission, is marginalised, and organised labour has been weakened. Hence, aspects of Korean employment relations seem to be moving towards a form of liberal market economy (LME)–style framework—albeit with Asian characteristics.

## FURTHER READING

Choi, J. (1989) *Labor and the Authoritarian State: Labor unions in South Korean manufacturing industries, 1961–1980*. Seoul: Korea University Press.

Kim, D. & Bae, J. (2004) *Employment Relations and HRM in South Korea*. Aldershot: Ashgate.

Koo, H. (2001) *Korean Workers: The Culture and Politics of Class Formation*. Ithaca, NY: Cornell University Press.

Lee, B. (2007) 'Militant unionism in Korea', in S. van der Velden, H. Dribbusch, D. Lyddon & K. Vandaele (eds), *Strikes around the World, 1968–2005*. Amsterdam: Aksant, pp. 155–72.

Lee, W. (ed.) (2004) *Labor in Korea, 1987–2002*. Seoul: Korea Labour Institute.

## USEFUL WEBSITES

Human Resources Development Service of Korea: <www.hrdkorea.or.kr/ENG>.
KEF: <www.kefplaza.com/kef/kef_eng_intro_1.jsp>.
Korea Employment Information Service: <http://eng.keis.or.kr/main/eng.do>.
Korea Labor Foundation: <http://inosa.or.kr/eng/front/main.act>.
Korea Labor Institute: <www.kli.re.kr/kli_ehome/main/main.jsp>.
Ministry of Employment and Labour: <www.moel.go.kr/english/main.jsp>.

## A CHRONOLOGY OF KOREAN EMPLOYMENT RELATIONS

| | |
|---|---|
| 1876 | Japan forcefully opens up feudal Chosun. |
| 1888 | First unionised strike, by gold miners. |
| 1898 | Korea's first union, the Seongjin Stevedores' Union, formed. Chosun mining strike. |
| 1910 | Japan occupies Korea. |
| 1919 | (1 March) National Independence Movement. |
| 1920 | First national organisation, Chosun nodong-kongjeahoe (Chosun Labour Fraternal Association), is initiated by the liberal intelligentsia. |
| 1922 | Socialist-oriented Chosun nodongyeon-maenghoe (Chosun Labour Confederation) formed. |
| 1924 | Chosun nonong chongyeonmaeng (Chosun Labour and Farmer Confederation) formed. *Law and Order Maintenance Act* represses national unionism. |
| 1929 | First general strike, in Wonsan. |
| 1938 | Unions prohibited with onset of China–Japan War. |
| 1945 | Korea is liberated from Japanese and US AMG established. National and Provincial Mediation boards begin. Chun pyung (General Council of Korean Trade Unions) is formed. |
| 1946 | Child Labour Law and Basic Labour Law are enacted. Labour Department is established. September National Strikes are called. Daehan dogrib chockseong nodong chongyeonmyeng (General Federation of Korean Trade Unions) formed. |
| 1947 | Chun pyung banned by the AMG. |
| 1948 | Syngman Rhee elected president of the First Republic of Korea. Five-Year of Economic Rehabilitation Plan aims at economic independence from consumption aid. |
| 1950–53 | Korean War. |
| 1953 | *Trade Union Act*, *Labour Standards Act*, *Labour Dispute Adjustment Act* and *Labour Relations Commission Act*. |
| 1957 | (December) Chosun Textile Company dispute in Pusan splits FKTU. |
| 1959 | Cheonkuk nodongjohab hyeobuiehyo (National Council of Trade Unions) formed. |
| 1960 | April 19 Student Revolution deposes Syngman Rhee. Chang Myeon government is elected. FKTU and National Council of Trade Unions merge to form a new national centre: Cheon-nohyeob. |
| 1961 | General Park Chung-hee takes power in a military coup in May. FKTU is restructured into twelve industrial union associations. |
| 1963 | Park Chung-hee elected president of Third Republic of Korea. Labour laws revised. |
| 1970 | Restrictions on unionism in foreign-owned enterprises. |

| 1971 | Law Concerning the Special Measures for Safeguarding National Security gives Park Chung-hee a lifetime presidency. Compulsory arbitration is extended to all industries. KEF established. |
| --- | --- |
| 1975 | *Labour Standards Act* extended to enterprises with between five and fifteen employees. |
| 1979 | Park Chung-hee assassinated. |
| 1980 | Military coup by General Chun Doo-hwan. |
| 1981 | *Labour–Management Council Act, Industrial Safety and Health Act* and *Minimum Wage Act*; scope of *Industrial Accident Insurance and Compensation Act* extended. |
| 1987 | (29 June) Democratisation Declaration; subsequent Great Labour Struggles. |
| 1991 | Cheonnohyup (Korea Trade Union Congress) formed. Korea joins the ILO. |
| 1995 | Minjunochong KCTU formed. |
| 1996 | PCIRR formed. Korea joins OECD. December amendments to labour laws provoke public outcry. |
| 1997 | Wave of general strikes organised by KCTU and FKTU, followed by the revision of amended labour legislation. Asian financial crisis. |
| 1998 | Kim Dae-jung government begins. Presidential Tripartite Commission agrees to introduce more labour market flexibility, including layoffs for managerial reasons and use of dispatched labour. KHMWU established as first industrial union. |
| 1999 | Unemployment rate jumps to record high, 8.5 per cent, in February; KCTU withdraws from participation in Tripartite Commission. General strike called by KCTU to protest IMF's restructuring programs, but fails to gain widespread support. |
| 1999 | Teachers granted legal right to form a union. KCTU is officially recognised by government. |
| 2001 | Tripartite Commission postpones enforcement of labour law clauses concerning multiple unions at enterprise level and prohibition of payment of full-time union officials by the end of 2006. Tripartite Commission agrees to reduce standard working hours to 40 hours per week. |
| 2003 | Roh Moo-hyun government begins. Transport workers' (truck drivers') union calls general strike to demand labour rights for self-employed workers. |
| 2004 | Tripartite Commission reaches the Social Pact for Job Creation. |
| 2005 | FKTU and KCTU call a joint general strike to demand the enactment of non-regular labour protection laws. |
| 2006 | Public servants are granted the legal right to organise unions and engage in collective bargaining. Tripartite Commission |

|      | agrees again to postpone the enforcement of the labour law clauses concerning the operation of multiple unions at enterprise level and prohibition of payment of full-time union officials until the end of 2009. Non-regular labour protection laws are passed. |
|------|------|
| 2007 | Tripartite Commission is renamed Economic and Social Development Commission of Korea. |
| 2008 | Lee Myung-bak government begins. President Lee announces 'MBnomics', which includes business-friendly labour market deregulation to promote labour market flexibility. |
| 2009 | Government campaigns for a work-sharing program and adopts active labour market policy to create jobs through youth internships and public works projects. Social pact is agreed between unions, employers, civic groups and the government to overcome the impact of the post-2007 global financial crisis. |
| 2010 | The revised labour law clauses prohibiting multiple unionisation at the enterprise level and of employers paying wages to union officials. Time-off system allowing union officials' paid activities. |
| 2013 | Park Gyun-hye government takes office. Ageing workforce law is enacted, extending the compulsory retirement age to 60. |
| 2014 | A social pact is agreed to promote labour market reform. The court decides key labour issues concerning non-standard workers (i.e. subcontracted worker status) and regular pay, which is applied to the calculation of overtime and holiday pay. This becomes a hot issue between employers and unions, which is handled by the courts. |

# CHAPTER 12

# Employment relations in China

## Fang Lee Cooke

The People's Republic of China (hereafter China) was founded on 1 October 1949 and has since been ruled by the Chinese Communist Party (CCP). Following China's opening up from a state-planned economy in the late 1970s, the contemporary Chinese economy has been described by foreign commentators and scholars as 'Chinese capitalism' (e.g. Guthrie 1999; Gabriel 2006; Redding & Witt 2007; Huang 2008; Kennedy 2011) or 'authoritarian capitalism' (Witt & Redding 2014). The Chinese government prefers to call it the 'marketisation with Chinese socialist characteristics', to signal its departure from the state-planned regime, but without (at least publicly) abandoning the socialist ideology.

Commentators outside China also use the term 'state capitalism' to emphasise continuing state intervention as a defining feature of the country's liberalising economy. This state capitalism is characteristic of a developmental state, and manifests itself in various forms, including the dominance and existence of a significant number of state-owned enterprises (SOEs) that are managed in a capitalist manner, particularly in key industrial sectors or as lead enterprises of the industry; strong state control in the allocation of resources to privately owned businesses; and state intervention to protect the growth of large enterprises, often state invested or state connected, with national strategic interests. The Chinese economy is a 'mixed economy' characterised by 'a blend of market-driven, government-controlled and *guanxi* (relationship)-based culture', with strong management implications (Si et al. 2008: 932). Within this system, foreign capitalists, private entrepreneurs and local authorities interact to (re-)construct market-friendly institutions. Political power and social relations are mobilised and consolidated to achieve their respective goals (Cooke 2013).

With a population of over 1.36 billion, China is the world's most populous country, and in terms of one indicator, it became the largest economy in the world in 2014.[1] The gross domestic product (GDP) per capita of China is more than US$6500 (*The Economist* 2014). The labour market participation rate is high, in part because the social security system is basic, with only limited coverage. More than 56 per cent of the population is in employment (more than 764 million people) and nearly half of those employed are in urban areas (NBSC 2012).

Compared with their counterparts in other countries, Chinese women have a relatively high employment participation rate, making up more than 37 per cent of the total workforce in full-time employment in urban areas (NBSC 2012). Part-time employment is unusual in China, partly as a result of the low-pay, full-employment policy adopted by the government during the state-planned economy period. It is also driven by the Marxist emancipation thesis, in which women were encouraged by the state to participate in employment to gain financial independence and enhance their political and social status. In addition, women's high employment participation rate is underpinned by the work ethic in the Chinese collectivist culture, which treats work as an obligation and advocates that each should contribute to society to be entitled to benefit from it.

The development of the labour market of socialist China can be divided into three periods. The first was a highly regulated—or, more precisely, controlled—labour market through administrative policy during the state-planned economy. Labour mobility was highly restricted, monitored by the *hukou* system—a household registration system where individuals are registered with the local authority where they were born and where they live. The population was divided by two residential statuses: urban and rural. Rural residents were not allowed to enter urban areas for employment. This restriction was gradually removed during the period of deregulation that followed, between the 1980s and early 2000s, when millions of farmers migrated to urban areas for employment and millions of SOE employees were laid off and forced to seek re-employment in the labour market for the first time.

The enactment of three major employment-related laws in 2008 (see below) marked the beginning of the third period, in which the government has sought to re-regulate the labour market, through legislative intervention, to provide greater employment protection to workers—particularly those outside the state sector. Dealing with labour market transformation has been one of the most challenging tasks facing the Chinese government (Fleisher & Yang 2003). And employment relations at the workplace level have been developed within this broader context of labour market transformation.

China's political economy, characterised by the enduring strong state intervention, a weak collective bargaining regime and the large size of its economy and workforce, makes China an interesting country to study. It brings a rather different perspective from those of the developed economies in this book. This chapter includes three main sections, in addition to this introduction and a conclusion. The first section outlines the changing role of the parties, including the state, the unions and the workers. The second examines the processes of employment relations by focusing on the development of collective consultation and collective contract, as well as labour disputes resolution. The third section discusses a few current issues that are confronting the state, employers and workers in China, which may have a broader impact on its economy.

## THE MAJOR PARTIES

### The role of the state

As China is a socialist country with the legacy of a state-planned economy embedded in its political economy, the role of its government— or more broadly the state—is dominant as an employer, a legislator and an economic manager. This is despite state sector employment making up a shrinking proportion of the total employment since the early 1980s. For example, in 1978, the year when China adopted its 'open door' policy, more than 78 per cent of the urban workforce was employed in the state sector. This had been reduced to around 19 per cent by 2012 (see Table 12.1). The sharp decline of employment in the state sector, particularly from the late 1990s, was achieved mainly through downsizing, plant closures and privatisation of SOEs as part of the state-driven reform. Started in the early 1990s with the purpose of revitalising the out-moded and largely loss-making SOEs, the momentum of SOE reform reached its peak in the late 1990s after Premier Zhu Rongji announced his SOE reform plan in 1997. Poor-performing SOEs were given three years to 'sort themselves out'. In the ensuing five-year period between 1998 and 2002, more than 27 million workers were laid off (NBSC 2003).

In the meantime, the private sector was encouraged to grow (Garnaut & Huang 2001; Saich 2001) through the removal of policy restrictions and operational barriers, and the provision of financial incentives. The sector provides employment opportunities for those

**Table 12.1  Employment statistics by ownership in urban and rural areas (000,000s)[a]**

| Ownership type | 1978 | 1980 | 1985 | 1990 | 1995 | 1998 | 2000 | 2005 | 2012 |
|---|---|---|---|---|---|---|---|---|---|
| Total | 402 | 424 | 499 | 648 | 681 | 706 | 721 | 758 | 767 |
| Urban employed persons | 95 | 105 | 128 | 166 | 191 | 207 | 232 | 273 | 371 |
| State-owned units | 75 | 80 | 90 | 104 | 113 | 91 | 81 | 65 | 68 |
| Collectively owned units | 21 | 24 | 33 | 36 | 32 | 20 | 15 | 8 | 6 |
| Cooperative units | – | – | – | – | – | 1 | 2 | 2 | 2 |
| Joint ownership units | – | – | 0.38 | 1 | 0.53 | 0.48 | 0.42 | 0.45 | 0.39 |
| Limited liability corporations | – | – | – | – | – | 5 | 7 | 18 | 38 |
| Shareholding corporations | – | – | – | – | 3 | 4 | 5 | 7 | 12 |
| Private enterprises | – | – | – | 0.57 | 5 | 10 | 13 | 35 | 76 |
| Units with funds from Hong Kong, Macao and Taiwan | – | – | – | 0.04 | 3 | 3 | 3 | 6 | 10 |
| Foreign-funded units | – | – | 0.06 | 0.62 | 2 | 3 | 3 | 7 | 13 |
| Self-employed persons | 0.15 | 0.81 | 5 | 6 | 16 | 23 | 21 | 28 | 56 |
| Rural employed persons | 306 | 318 | 371 | 473 | 489 | 493 | 489 | 485 | 396 |
| Township and village enterprises | 28 | 30 | 70 | 93 | 129 | 125 | 128 | 143 | – |
| Private enterprises | – | – | – | 1 | 5 | 7 | 11 | 24 | 37 |
| Self-employed persons | – | – | – | 15 | 31 | 39 | 29 | 21 | 29 |

*Notes:*
Numbers rounded.
(a) Since 1990, data on economically active population, the total employed persons and the sub-total of employed persons in urban and rural areas have been adjusted in accordance with the data obtained from the Fifth National Population Census. As a result, the sum of the data by region, by ownership or by sector is not equal to the total. [Original note from NBSC 2003: 123.]

*Sources:* Adapted from NBSC (2003: 126–7; 2010: 117; 2013).

displaced by their state employer, new workers from urban areas and rural migrant workers. Once marginal and marginalised in the state-planned economy due to the ideological clash between capitalism and socialism, the private sector then took a major stake in the economy. This is despite the majority of the firms in this sector being relatively small, low technology based and competing mainly on price. Similarly, foreign invested enterprises (FIEs), and those funded from Hong Kong, Taiwan and Macao, have been given more autonomy to operate in China since the mid-1990s, including permission to set up wholly foreign-owned enterprises. FIEs are no longer required to set up joint ventures as their entry mode. They are also given more autonomy in determining their employment policy.

A series of labour laws and regulations have been promulgated by the government since the 1980s, symbolised by the launch of the Labour Law of China (enacted in 1995). In 2007, the government increased its legislative activities and passed three major employment-related laws to take effect from 2008: the much-debated Labour Contract Law (amended in 2013), the Employment Promotion Law and the Labour Disputes Mediation and Arbitration Law. In 2011, the Social Security Law was enacted. The promulgation of these laws signals the government's renewed and stronger determination to increase the level of protection of its workforce. Employees are afforded greater power to seek justice through legal channels when these laws are violated by employers. In addition, the government has issued regulations, including the Special Regulation on Minimum Wage (2004), the Regulations on Employment Services and Management (2008) and the Interim Provisions on Labour Dispatch (2014), that are aimed to support the amendments of the Labour Contract Law (2013) and tighten the use of agency employment.

These labour laws and regulations provide a legal framework within which employment relationships are governed and labour markets regulated, at least in principle. The primary objective of their implementation is to achieve a more efficient and equitable labour market. In parallel, a system for labour dispute resolution was developed. It has been argued that, with 'the major exception of freedom of association', the labour standards established by the series of labour laws and regulations of China 'are not markedly inferior to those of comparable countries and indeed many developed nations' (Cooney 2007: 674). However, the lack of effective enforcement remains problematic (Taylor et al. 2003; Cooke 2012). While implementation failures are a characteristic of all regulatory systems (Cooney 2007), the Chinese system is frustrated by the multiplicity of employment-related laws, directive regulations and administrative policies issued at central, provincial and municipal government levels, the ambiguous status of some of these regulative instruments and the confusing channels through which employees can seek to secure compliance with laws (Potter 1999; Cooney 2007).

In addition, it has been argued that employment-related regulations are targeted primarily at those in the formal employment sector with formal employment relationships (Hu 2004). There is considerable ambiguity about whether certain laws and regulations should apply to the informal sector and to workers in informal employment (discussed further below). Employers also tend to take advantage of these regulatory loopholes and argue for exemptions (Cooke 2011). The amendment of the Labour Contract Law in 2013 and the adoption of the Interim Provisions on Labour Dispatch (2014) are both attempts by the government to stem creative non-compliance. While the labour laws carry more legal power, they provide only limited regulation of the labour market. Although the labour market–related regulations have some effect, these regulations, together with a series of other employment-related regulations, are essentially administrative policy regulations that have limited authority and enforceability (Hu 2004).

A feature in the Chinese laws and regulations is that the central government provides a broad framework. It is up to the local governments to devise their localised regulations based on the national framework to suit local characteristics. This flexibility is needed in a vast country like China, with significant economic disparities across the regions. But the decentralisation of interpretation and enforcement also opens up opportunities for implementation slippage. The power and determination of local government officials and labour authorities may be undermined by the priority of economic development; some of them may even be co-opted by employers.

## Employers

Unlike employers' associations in developed economies, which are developed and provide a range of services to their member employers and form pressure groups to influence government policy and legislation, employers' associations in China are much less well established. The China Enterprise Confederation (CEC)/China Enterprise Directors Association (CEDA) and the All-China Federation of Industry and Commerce (ACFIC) are the two main official employer/business associations that the state recognises at the national level as the representatives of employers' interests. Like other major non-government organisations (NGOs) recognised by the Chinese government, both operate under the leadership of the CCP.

The CEC was established in 1979 and the CEDA in 1983. The two NGOs merged into one institution in 1988. The subordination to state control means that the CEC/CEDA has limited autonomy beyond state-sanctioned activities (see Unger 2008 on the relationships between associations and the state). Nevertheless, the lobbying power of Chinese employers is rising. They are able to form pressure groups rapidly to exert pressure on the government if forthcoming regulations and policies are likely to have a significant negative impact on their business environment. The drafting of the Labour Contract Law (2008) is a good example—the final version was watered down from the draft version as a result of employers lobbying to maintain flexibility in hiring and firing.

Established in 1953, the ACFIC, also called the All-China General Chamber of Industry and Commerce, is a chamber of commerce with enterprises and personnel from the private economic sector as its main component. It is a channel for the CCP and the government to liaise with the private sector, an aid to the government in administering and serving the private economy. In 2008, ACFIC added an employment relations function and was recognised by the state as a representative of employers in national tripartite consultations in 2010. ACFIC's espoused functions and tasks include promoting harmonious labour relations, participating in coordination of labour relations, promoting social harmony and stability, and representing and safeguarding the legitimate rights and interests of the private sector (see ACFIC 2015).

As mentioned, the state is no longer as dominant, though it is still a major employer in the urban sector. Private firms and FIEs are becoming major employers too. Employers of different ownership forms operate in different historical, legislative, economic and labour market contexts. Their business strategies and employment policies are heavily influenced by the context. Outside the state sector, employment relations are shaped mainly at the enterprise level, and display different characteristics across various ownership forms, as we show in this chapter.

## Workers

Not only has the Chinese government's economic policy triggered radical changes to its economic structure; it has also brought about fundamental changes in the ideological identity and demographic profile of its workers. These changes have diverse implications. During the state-planned economy period, Chinese workers were relatively homogeneous, consisting largely of employees in urban areas who were employed primarily by the state. The status of workers under socialist China was political as much as it was economic. Workers were regarded by the state as the 'masters' of the country (see Sheehan 1999). The term 'working class' differentiated urban workers from those in rural areas (peasants). The former enjoyed a high level of social welfare and benefits. By contrast, the latter were relatively deprived. Employment relations in the state sector were portrayed as harmonious, with workers participating in the democratic management of the workplace and production activities through their union organisations and worker representatives.[2]

The reforms in SOEs since the late 1980s have led to profound changes in employment relationships between the workers and their state employers. An important change is the end of employment security and the reduction of workplace welfare provision. These changes have undermined, and in some cases almost ended, paternalistic bonds between the state employer and its workers. A significant proportion of the labour discontent and disputes has come from those who have been affected negatively by these changes. However, a number of SOEs have transformed themselves successfully, and continue to perform very well (e.g. see Nolan 2001). This is particularly the case for the extremely large SOEs that are controlled directly by the central government (*yiangqi*). Well-performing SOEs continue to adopt a paternalistic management style, offering even better welfare benefits to their employees than they once did as a result of the improved performance of the enterprise (Chan & Unger 2008).

Meanwhile, the opening up of the economy has attracted millions of rural migrant workers seeking employment in urban areas. They have played a pivotal role in China's recent economic development. The inflow of rural migrant workers to urban areas started in the late 1980s, and there are now probably more than 262 million rural migrant workers engaging in urban employment (*China Labour Bulletin* 2014). Most of the rural migrant workers have informal employment status, even though they have been working in urban areas or doing the same job for many years on a full-time basis. Inferior employment terms and conditions, in terms of job security, pay level and working conditions, are a distinctive feature of this category of workers. Most of them have no written employment contract, little training, few rest days, no social security and little health and safety protection. They work long hours, live in poor conditions and are largely unorganised and unrepresented (e.g. Chan 2001; Gallagher 2005; Lee 2007; Pun & Smith 2007). Delays in getting paid are common, especially in the construction industry (Cooke 2008).

The inferior employment conditions endured by rural migrant workers are a legacy of the non-egalitarian socialist development strategy adopted by the government, in which urban development has been achieved at the expense of rural populations (e.g. Solinger 1999; Meng 2000). Institutionalised discriminative practices continue when rural migrant workers enter urban employment. Although efforts have been made by the government to eliminate discriminative practices since the 1990s through regulatory and policy intervention, the lack of comprehensive legislative coverage and effective enforcement in the private and informal sectors means that these workers remain largely unprotected (Cooke 2011).

In sharp contrast to the above two groups of workers is the younger generation of university graduates employed in government and public sector organisations, well-performing private firms and prestigious multinational enterprises (MNEs). Following the expansion of higher education in the early 2000s, China has produced millions of university graduates each year, in addition to thousands who have been educated overseas. For example, the number of university graduates grew from 2.12 million in 2003 to almost 7 million in 2013 and a predicted 7.27 million in 2014 (China Education Online 2013). However, the prospect of gainful employment has not been achieved by all of them, so the term 'ant tribe' (*yizu*) has been coined to describe the expanding force of under-employed or unemployed university graduates.

Meanwhile, the well-documented talent shortage in China (e.g. Farrell & Grant 2005; Malila 2007; Cooke et al. 2014) means that some of them hold a high level of bargaining power in determining their terms and conditions. Enterprises are relying on financial rewards (e.g. pay rises, bonus and stock options) and career development opportunities as the main mechanisms to attract and retain talented and experienced employees (Wang et al. 2007; Cooke 2012). This new generation of workers—particularly the post-1980s generation (i.e. those who were born after the implementation of the one-child policy in the 1980s)—tends to have different values and a very different work ethic from those of the older generation of workers, who were more influenced by the traditional Chinese cultural values and socialist work ethics such as loyalty, obedience and diligence. Young graduate employees have little knowledge about the unions (Cooke 2012), and seem to be more materialistic, with stronger career aspirations and a keen desire to progress (Arkless 2007; Malila 2007; Cooke 2012).

## Unions

Only one union—the All-China Federation of Trade Unions (ACFTU)—is recognised by the Chinese government. The ACTFU–CCP tie dates back to the 1920s (the union was founded in May 1925), when grass-roots union organisations served as the party member recruitment bases and provided vital support to the CCP by mobilising workers. Since the founding of socialist China, the ACFTU has become one of the eight 'mass organisations' that have the function of organising and represent-ing specific social groups, such as women, youth and workers. A distinct feature of these political organisations is that they have to be recognised and led by the CCP. This institutionalises superior and subordinate rela-tionships between the party and the mass organisations, depoliticises the relationship and tries to disguise any conflicts and power strug-gles between these organisations and the state. Although the relation-ship between the party and the ACFTU has not always been smooth, attempts by the ACFTU to gain greater power and autonomy have been suppressed by the party (You 1998; Sheehan 1999). Similarly, attempts to form autonomous workers' unions are suppressed, as was the case during the Tiananmen Square incident in 1989.

The governance structure of the ACFTU branches includes vertical and horizontal reporting lines. They are under the dual control of the local government at the lower levels and their organisational branch at higher levels. ACFTU branches are responsible for liaising with union organisations at the enterprise level, where they have to win recogni-tion from employers.

The roles and responsibilities of the unions are set out by laws: the Trade Union Law (1950, 1992, amended 2001), the Labour Law (1995) and the Labour Contract Law (2008). According to the Trade Union Law (2001: Article 6), 'the basic function and duty of the trade unions is to safeguard the legal rights and interests of the employees. While upholding the overall rights and interests of the whole nation, trade unions shall, at the same time, represent and safeguard the rights and interests of employees'. Article 7 further stipulates that the 'trade union shall mobilise and organise the employees to participate in the economic development actively, and to complete the production and work assignments conscientiously, educate the employees to improve their ideological thoughts and ethics, technological and professional, scientific and cultural qualities, and build an employee team with ideals, ethics, education and discipline'.

According to Martin's (1989: 78) typologies, the Chinese trade unions fall within the 'authoritarian' category as the 'state instruments', carrying out a 'decisively subordinate role' that is 'concerned with *both* production and protection'. The unions' primary responsibility is the state (Martin 1989), the interests of which are not necessarily aligned with those of the workers. Under the socialist system, in which the state employer and the workers are perceived to share the same interests, the unions' main functions are to organise social events, take care of workers' welfare, help management implement operational decisions, organise skill training, raise employee morale and coordinate relations between management and workers (Verma & Yan 1995). They carry out these functions effectively by acting as a 'conveyor belt' between the CCP and the workers (Hoffman 1981). The way the ACFTU is operationalised has led to questioning by global union organisations, labour movement activists and scholars about its legitimacy as a genuine union (e.g. Taylor & Li 2007).

Since the mid-1990s, when SOEs shed millions of their workers, skill training and assisting laid-off workers to regain employment have been two major functions of the unions. With the growth of new ownership forms outside the state sector and the concomitant social welfare reforms in the state sector, the welfare role of the state has been diminishing. The formerly relatively harmonious management–labour relations have been replaced by relations that are characterised by conflicting interests, more disputes and increasing inequality in contractual arrangements between capital and labour. However, the role of the unions—or, more specifically, the union officials' perception of their duties—has not changed sufficiently to reflect the new reality. Union officials generally lack the resources, power, skills and legal knowledge to fulfil their collective bargaining role and to defend their members' rights (Warner & Ng 1999; Cooke 2012). They are often ineffective in representing workers' interests against management prerogatives, and sometimes even side with management (e.g. Clarke 2005).

Nevertheless, the ACFTU is the largest national union confederation in the world, measured by its official membership (Warner & Zhu 2010). As shown in Table 12.2, union density has been consistently high, at more 90 per cent, since 1990 in workplaces where union organisations are established. The number of grassroots union organisations has grown substantially since 2009. So has the number of full-time union officials in union branches, after experiencing a brief period of decline between 2001 and 2004 when union organisations underwent a period of restructuring and downsizing as part of the state sector reform. Nevertheless, the high level of membership in unionised workplaces has not brought real power to workers. Once a union is established in an enterprise—particularly in the urban sector—it is almost mandatory for its employees to become members.

The majority of studies on the Chinese unions have taken a union-bashing approach, highlighting their inadequacy in organising and representing workers' interests. Much less attention has been paid to

**Table 12.2   Enterprise union membership**

| Year | Grass-roots unions (000s) | Employees (000s) | Female employees (000s) | Members (000s) | Female members (000s) | Union density (%) | Full-time union officials (000s) |
|------|------|------|------|------|------|------|------|
| 1952 | 207 | 13,932 | – | 10,023 | – | 71.9 | 53 |
| 1962 | 165 | 26,671 | – | 19,220 | – | 72.1 | 86 |
| 1979 | 329 | 68,972 | 21,717 | 51,473 | – | 74.6 | 179 |
| 1980 | 376 | 74,482 | 25,186 | 61,165 | – | 82.1 | 243 |
| 1985 | 465 | 96,430 | 35,967 | 85,258 | 31,492 | 88.4 | 381 |
| 1990 | 606 | 111,569 | 42,910 | 101,356 | 38,977 | 90.8 | 556 |
| 1995 | 593 | 113,214 | 45,153 | 103,996 | 41,165 | 91.9 | 468 |
| 2000 | 859 | 114,721 | 45,345 | 103,615 | 39,173 | 90.3 | 482 |
| 2005 | 1174 | 159,853 | 60,163 | 150,294 | 55,748 | 94.0 | 477 |
| 2006 | 1324 | 181,436 | 67,193 | 169,942 | 61,778 | 93.7 | 543 |
| 2007 | 1508 | 204,524 | 74,945 | 193,290 | 70,422 | 94.5 | 602 |
| 2008 | 1725 | 224,875 | 81,688 | 212,171 | 77,738 | 94.4 | 705 |
| 2009 | 1845 | 245,353 | 86,526 | 226,344 | 82,484 | 93.3 | 746 |
| 2010 | 1976 | 253,454 | 92,881 | 239,965 | 88,715 | 94.7 | 864 |
| 2011 | 2320 | 273,047 | 102,112 | 258,851 | 97,636 | 94.8 | 998 |
| 2012 | 2663 | 293,715 | 110,145 | 280,213 | 106,110 | 95.4 | 1079 |

*Note:* Since 2003, statistical coverage of the number of grassroots unions has been adjusted. [Original note in NBSC 2010.]

*Sources:* Compiled from NBSC (2010: 885; 2013: 927).

the institutional environment in which unions need to gain recognition, and the diversifying organising strategies deployed by the ACFTU at the operational level. Kim et al. (2014) and Liu (2010) are among the few exceptions. Drawing on a large dataset and a dual institutional pressure perspective, Kim et al.'s (2014: 34) study of union recognition by foreign MNEs in China concludes that a foreign firm is more likely to recognise unions if the legitimacy of collective representation is high in its home country and 'if it is located in a Chinese city where union recognition is prevalent among Chinese-owned firms'. Similarly, Liu (2010: 30) argues that the ACFTU is not a monolithic organisation; instead, 'there is considerable variation within ACFTU in terms of local union organising strategies', and different patterns of organising may have 'vastly different consequences for the future of trade unions and collective bargaining in China'.

A small number of studies provide a more balanced assessment of the ACFTU. For example, the senior leadership of the ACFTU has been regarded as instrumental in pressing for collective regulation in labour legislation (Clarke & Pringle 2009; Taylor & Li 2010). Similarly, Chen (2007: 65) acknowledges the ACFTU for 'its effort to promote the pro-labour legislation', particularly in drafting the Labour Contract Law and the Labour Disputes Mediation and Arbitration Law. In addition to their legislative role, unions also have a direct economic impact, particularly in the enforcement of mandatory social insurance, although evidence about union influence on pay is inconclusive (e.g. Yao & Zhong 2013).

## THE PROCESS OF EMPLOYMENT RELATIONS

### Collective consultation and collective contracts

The notion of collective bargaining was first introduced in employment relations in China in the early 1990s, after the Trade Union Law (1992) authorised unions at the enterprise level to conclude collective contracts with employers. The state prefers the term 'collective consultation' rather than 'collective bargaining'. It holds that consultation is a more constructive approach than bargaining, as the former conforms to the Chinese culture of non-confrontation and conflict avoidance. In 1994, the Provisions on Collective Contracts was issued by the Ministry of Labour, which provided detailed regulations to support the collective contracts provision outlined in the Labour Law of 1994 (see Taylor et al. 2003; Brown 2006 for more detailed discussion). Unions have been given the official role of representing workers in consultation with employers. This position of the unions has been reinforced and expanded in the subsequent amended Trade Union Law (2001) and the improved Provisions on Collective Contracts (2004), which superseded the 1994 version. According to the Trade Union Law (2001), a union shall represent employees in the negotiation and signing of a collective contract. Matters that can be concluded in a collective contract may include pay, working time, rest breaks, vacations, occupational safety and health, training, insurance and welfare. In addition, local labour authorities are responsible for facilitating and monitoring the consultation process.

The establishment of this tripartite consultation system is an important mechanism for the government, unions and enterprises to strengthen social dialogue and cooperation in coordinating labour relations. Achievements have been made in the period since this system was implemented. Collective contracts are widening to cover a range of aspects of labour standards, though pay remains the major issue (Zhang 2006). The ACFTU is also pushing for collective contracts that provide large coverage, such as region-based and industry-wide collective contracts.

However, there is still scope to improve the collective contract system that has been developed since the late 1990s (Brown 2006; Clarke et al. 2004). The collective consultation system does not provide an independent framework for regulating employment relations. Most collective contracts are standard agreements made between the employer and the union without the direct involvement of workers or any real negotiation process. Where there is collective bargaining, it takes place mostly at the enterprise level. The government is trying to promote industry-based bargaining, or multi-establishment bargaining for enterprises (often MNEs) that have operations in various parts of China. But region-wide or nationwide collective contracts may be too broad to reflect local needs. This gives managers an excuse to ignore local union representatives (Cooke 2011). Wal-Mart (China) is one example (China Labor News Translations 2008).

## Resolution of labour disputes

A labour dispute reconciliation system was established in the early 1950s. After a period of disruption during the Cultural Revolution (1966–76), the system was resumed in 1987 with the promulgation of the Temporary Regulation for Labour Disputes Reconciliation in State-Owned Enterprises. This was amended in 1993 and implemented as the Labour Disputes Reconciliation Regulation. The regulation was later incorporated into the Labour Law (1995), which forms the legal basis for settling labour disputes. The Labour Law officially brought all labour disputes in all enterprises under the jurisdiction of the formal dispute resolution system (Cooke 2008).

The labour dispute resolution system consists of three stages: mediation, arbitration and litigation (see Taylor et al. 2003 for a more detailed description). Mediation is the initial procedure; it usually takes place in the enterprise where the dispute occurs through a mediation committee consisting of representatives of the employer, the employees and the union or a third party who is acceptable to both parties to the dispute. Resolution of the dispute through consultation and voluntary mediation is the approach encouraged by the state. Any agreements made at this stage and beyond are legally binding. If this approach fails, then one of the two parties in dispute can apply to the Labour Dispute Arbitration Committee for resolution. An arbitration committee will then be formed to arbitrate the dispute. A dispute case can also be submitted directly to the arbitration committee without going through the initial stage of mediation at the enterprise level if it is felt that mediation is unlikely to settle the dispute. However, a dispute case will not be accepted for lawsuit until after it has been through the arbitration procedure. Cases resolved by the arbitration committees are classified as being settled by mediation, arbitration or other means. If either party is not satisfied with the arbitration ruling, then the case can be appealed at the local People's Court. At each stage, emphasis is made on resolving the conflict through negotiation, mutual understanding and voluntary agreement between the parties directly involved. Labour disputes are categorised as individual or collective disputes.

Several characteristics have emerged from the rising trend of labour disputes since the adoption of the Labour Law (1995), which peaked in 2008 and 2009 following the enactment of the Labour Contract Law and the Labour Disputes Mediation and Arbitration Law in 2008 (see Table 12.3). First, the number of labour disputes accepted by the arbitration committees at all levels had been rising in the 2000s before starting to decline from 2010. This is due to the strong promotion of mediation by the state to maintain a harmonious society, sometimes by forcing arbitration applications back down to workplaces for mediation (Cooke 2012). As we can see from Table 12.3, the proportion of cases settled by mediation has been increasing steadily since 2007, from about 35 per cent in 2007 to 47 per cent in 2012. In addition, a substantial number of cases are mediated outside the arbitration system. Nevertheless, we do not know the level of satisfaction with mediation and arbitration of those involved, which could assess their relative efficiency and effectiveness.

Second, pay, social insurance and termination of employment contract have been the major causes of disputes. Third, the proportion of cases won by workers appears to be significantly lower than the proportion of cases submitted by them, and appears to have been in decline, from 46 per cent of the cases being won by the workers in 2007 to only 33 per cent in 2012. In comparison, the decline of cases won by employers has been much less pronounced, from about 14 per cent of the cases being won by employers in 2007 to 12 per cent in 2012.

In addition to the official labour disputes resolution system, workers rely on other channels to voice their grievances and seek

**Table 12.3   Number of labour disputes and settlements (by year)**

|  | *2007* | *2008* | *2009* | *2010* | *2011* | *2012* |
|---|---|---|---|---|---|---|
| Cases from previous year | 25,424 | 33,084 | 83,709 | 77,926 | 42,308 | 36,151 |
| Cases accepted in current year | 350,182 | 693,464 | 684,379 | 600,865 | 589,244 | 641,202 |
| Collective labour disputes | 12,784 | 21,880 | 13,779 | 9314 | 6592 | 7252 |
| Cases filed by workers | 325,590 | 650,077 | 627,530 | 558,853 | 568,768 | 620,849 |
| *Cases by cause of dispute* | | | | | | |
| Remuneration | 108,953 | 225,061 | 247,330 | 209,968 | 200,550 | 225,981 |
| Social insurance | 97,731 | – | – | – | 149,944 | 159,649 |
| Change of labour contract | 4695 | – | – | – | – | – |
| Termination of labour contract | 80,261 | 139,702 | 43,876 | 31,915 | 118,684 | 129,108 |
| Workers involved | 653,472 | 1,214,328 | 1,016,922 | 815,121 | 779,490 | 882,487 |
| Collective labour disputes | 271,777 | 502,713 | 299,601 | 211,755 | 174,785 | 231,894 |
| Cases settled | 340,030 | 622,719 | 689,714 | 634,041 | 592,823 | 643,292 |
| *Cases settled by means of settlement* | | | | | | |
| Mediation | 119,436 | 221,284 | 251,463 | 250,131 | 278,873 | 302,552 |
| Arbitration lawsuit | 149,013 | 274,543 | 290,971 | 266,506 | 244,942 | 268,530 |
| Others | 71,581 | 126,892 | 147,280 | 117,404 | 69,008 | 72,210 |
| *Cases settled by result of settlement* | | | | | | |
| Lawsuit won by employing unit | 49,211 | 80,462 | 95,470 | 85,028 | 74,189 | 79,187 |
| Lawsuit won by workers | 156,955 | 276,793 | 255,119 | 229,448 | 195,680 | 213,453 |
| Lawsuit partly won by both parties | 133,864 | 265,464 | 339,125 | 319,565 | 322,954 | 350,652 |
| Cases mediated | 151,902 | 237,283 | 185,598 | 163,997 | 194,338 | 212,937 |

*Sources:* Compiled from NBSC (2010: 885; 2013: 927).

justice—for example, letters and petitions (Thireau & Hua 2003), workplace industrial actions, and street protests, which are often spontaneous (Chan 2001; Chen 2003; Gallagher 2005; Lee 2007). Official statistics on labour disputes reveal only a partial picture. The precise number of labour disputes, industrial actions and street protests, and the total number of those who are involved, may not be recorded. Another development in is industrial action–driven collective bargaining, especially in MNE-funded manufacturing plants such as Honda (Nanhai) and Foxconn (Cooke 2014; Elfstrom & Kuruvilla 2014). Negotiations take place after strikes (see below).

## Labour market flexibility

The key features in the labour deployment strategy adopted by enterprises in developed economies to combat labour and skill shortages and the pressure of global competition include temporary employment, job sharing, annualised hours, and part-time and seasonal work. Chinese labour market flexibility is achieved through the rapid expansion of the informal employment sector, including agency employment. The primary motives are cost savings (from employers' perspectives) and the creation of employment opportunities (from the government's perspective). China has been experiencing a change from a rigid internal labour market dominated by the state sector to an increasingly informal and unprotected labour market since the mid-1990s. Redundant SOE workers and former rural migrant workers constitute most of those in informal employment. Increasingly, though, university graduates are also joining the informal employment ranks through a variety of job-placement schemes (e.g. internships, trainee schemes, long probation, in-sourcing, agency employment) innovatively introduced by employers to avoid formal employment commitments. The main causes of university graduates' unemployment, under-employment and insecure employment include the rapid expansion of higher education, the absence of skills sought by employers and a lack of work experience.

The opening up of the economy to the private sector and foreign investment since the mid-1990s, and the government's prioritisation of the interests of capital rather than those of labour in the interests of economic development, have led to widening income disparities across different social groupings and regions. The Gini coefficient[3] has been recorded to be above 0.4 (the international warning line) since 1992, and it has subsequently increased. According to *The Economist* (2013), China's Gini coefficient was 0.474 for 2012, having peaked at 0.491 in 2008. Low wages for workers with undifferentiated skills have been a main cause of income disparities. Li et al.'s (2014) analysis of the nationally representative China General Social Survey data suggests that the average level of under-payment was almost 44 per cent in the period 2003–08, which is substantially higher than generally estimated in developed economies.

## Employment agencies

Accompanying the rise of informal employment has been a significant growth since the mid-1990s in the number of employment agencies tailored for the lower end of the labour market. Despite being around since the mid-1990s (Xu 2009), employment agencies represent relatively new institutional actors in employment relations. Most employment agencies and job centres have been set up by, or under the auspices of, local governments to provide services at the lower end of the labour market. In 2001, there were nearly 27,000 employment agencies, 70 per cent of them funded by local governments at various levels as part of the multi-level employment services network. By 2009, the number of employment agencies had grown to more than 37,000. The number of employees working in employment agencies had increased from fewer than 85,000 in 2001 to 126,000 in 2009 (NBSC 2002, 2010). This significant growth was a response to the large-scale downsizing in the state sector, the inflow of rural migrant workers to urban areas to seek employment and the growing number of unemployed school leavers and university graduates (Li et al. 2006). More importantly, it was an opportunistic growth that stemmed from the enactment of the Labour Contract Law in 2008. While the objective of the law was to offer a greater level of employment protection to workers, an unintended consequence has been the dismissal of long-serving employees, stopping recruitment and the use of agency employment (Cooke 2012). This necessitated the amendment of the Labour Contract Law in 2013 and the introduction of the Interim Provisions on Labour Dispatch (2014).

According to the Employment Agency Regulation of 1995, employment agencies established by local labour authorities should be non-profit-making, whereas those set up by private enterprises unrelated to the authorities can be either profit-making or non-profit-making. Most employment agencies charge service fees, often beyond the price set by the local authority. Employment agencies have been criticised for their lack of professionalism, up-to-date market information and ability to coordinate various organisations related to labour market services. Their training function is under-resourced and poorly equipped. Their training content is out-dated, and fails to reflect what is most needed by employers (Li 2000). The legitimacy of employment agencies as labour market brokers is also questioned by job seekers (Li 2003; Mu 2003). Despite all these limitations, employment agencies play an increasing role in the labour market, and agency employment forms a part of employers' staffing strategies. It remains to be seen how effective the amendment of the Labour Contract Law and the Interim Provisions on Labour Dispatch are in offering an enhanced level of protection to workers.

## The rising level of labour disputes and workers' bargaining power

A key feature of employment relations since the mid-2000s has been the increasingly public and high-profile protests and strikes under-taken by workers to seek justice in both the public and private sectors. According to the ACFTU, there were nearly 10,000 collective disputes in a year, including strikes, go-slows, appeals and demonstrations (Lu 2010). Similarly, the *China Labour Bulletin* (2014) recorded nearly 1200 strikes and worker protests between mid-2011 and the end of 2013. These actions included high-profile strikes organised by workers seeking improved terms and conditions in MNE establishments in various major cities; protests from taxi drivers over high costs, cumbersome local government regulations and enterprise charges; protests from teachers in remote regions over pay arrears; and protests about poor terms and conditions of sanitation for workers hired (some via subcontracting) by local governments.

These events are officially referred to as 'mass incidents' to disguise or underplay their disruptive and antagonistic nature. This euphemism partly reflects traditional Chinese culture, characteristic of confrontation avoidance and harmony-seeking. It also reflects a political ideological demand to maintain stability. The right to strike is neither denied nor granted in the Chinese labour laws. The state-controlled ACFTU does not have the right to organise industrial action. Strikes are dealt with by local governments pragmatically as and when they emerge in the absence of legal guidance (Cooke 2013).

In developed economies, industrial action usually takes place as organised events following the failure of negotiations to reach an agreement. By contrast, such attempts at dispute resolution in China in recent years have occurred in the reverse order, with strikes and protests taking place without any forewarning and before negotiation has been attempted to settle the dispute. These spontaneous events often take the enterprise, union and government by surprise, and exert an enormous amount of pressure on unions and the government to deal with the situation rapidly to avoid contagion (Cooke 2013).

Within the domestic private sector, a diverse range of expressions of worker discontent and power wrestling with proprietors—often covertly and subtly, and on a day-to-day basis—has been found. These include, for example, slack attitudes, low efficiency, material waste, go-slows, sabotage, a low level of organisational citizenship behaviour and a high level of negligence (e.g. Liu & Yuan 2005; Cooke 2013).

The above instances of confrontational industrial action and covert expressions of discontent suggest that Chinese workers are increasingly becoming aware of their rights and willing to advance their interests through self-organising and other forms of expression. They are not powerless, although many workers still have poor terms and conditions of employment (Cooke 2013; also see Box 12.1).

Labour NGOs, including international and domestic ones, are emerging industrial relations (IR) actors, and have been playing a growing role, particularly in southern China. They have been developing the rights awareness of workers and facilitating pay negotiations and dispute settlement. In some cases, they have been pivotal in strike-driven collective bargaining (e.g. Cooke 2012; Lee & Shen 2011).

---

### BOX 12.1 HONDA (NANHAI) STRIKES

On 17 May 2010, a high-profile strike took place, involving some 1900 workers and interns in the Honda (Nanhai) car component plant in the Pearl River Delta region of south-eastern China. Striking workers were demanding substantial pay increases, better pay and conditions for student interns who were one-third of the workforce, job security and, most importantly, a union to be elected by and accountable to the workers at the plant. The strike, which lasted for two weeks and paralysed Honda's whole operation in China due to the 'just-in-time' production mode, ended in a total victory by the workers, who were given a 24 per cent pay rise and a promise of democratic union elections. This success inspired other Honda plants in China, whose workers also went on strike and won substantial wage increases. Workers' successful industrial actions in Honda have also inspired their counterparts in other foreign plants in China, including Toyota and Hyundai, to follow suit.

The strike was initially led by two workers; they were later sacked by Honda. Workers then refused to send representatives to negotiate with management for fear of being singled out for reprisals. They wore face masks and uniforms to conceal their identities during the strike action. Young and information technology (IT) savvy, the workers used internet chat rooms and other social networks to organise the strike and maintain communication. As the strike continued, the workers not only developed higher consciousness of the importance of having a formal organising body through the setting up of a democratic union in their factory, but also employed Professor Chang Kai, the influential Beijing-based IR scholar, as their expert adviser to guide them through the negotiations with management. Honda (Nanhai) raised wages three times in 2010 as a result of the collective bargaining between the workers and the company.

When the strike started, ten union officials tried to shut down the workers' picket line, although a thin apology from the local government was made afterwards (Watts 2010). This suggests that peacekeeping rather than defending worker rights was the main priority of the unions. It also showed that the local unions were not well equipped to handle strikes. Under heavy public criticism, the union's attitude changed as the strike went on, and it became more proactive in facilitating the negotiation process.

The Honda (Nanhai) case and other similar cases highlight the growing mobilisation of labour activism in channelling worker demands and the impact of worker-led collective bargaining. However, these achievements have been made possible with the support of other key institutional actors, including lobbying by the government and unions to broker deals, and the involvement of media, scholars and other pressure groups (Xie 2011). Nonetheless, the success of such worker-led collective bargaining, facilitated by worker-elected representatives rather than state- or enterprise-appointed union officials, suggests that effective bargaining can take place only when workers play an active part in it, with the support of state institutions and other actors. In many ways, the government's continuing involvement in dealing with labour disputes reflects the institutional inefficacy in dispute resolutions and the low level of confidence from the workers in this system (Cooke 2013).

*Sources:* China Labor News Translations (2010); Martin (2010); Watts (2010).

## CONCLUSIONS

Employment relations in China have undergone significant changes during the process of economic reform, notably in how the interests of workers are defined, challenged and defended. Characteristics of employment relations are diverging across different ownership forms, sectors and groups of workers. This is a trend that reflects those in developed economies in spite of fundamental contrasts that remain— in particular, union independence and strength. Due to the lack of representational strength of the unions and employers' associations, employment relations are shaped largely between the employer and the workers, with the majority of workers having little bargaining power. Where changes in employment practices are taking place, these often follow employment-related laws and regulations. The role of the state therefore continues to be crucial in shaping employment relations. However, despite the government's desire to create a more humanistic employment environment for workers through tightening legislative governance and a more harmonious society, the intended effect of laws and regulations is not always achieved. Employers continue to find ways to bypass legal constraints. Many workers may tolerate exploitative employment practices for fear of job losses, while others mobilise their bargaining power to advance their interests.

Unions are active mainly in the state sector, and in private enterprises that have strong government ties, although new initiatives of organising—such as special unions for smaller enterprises, community unions for the unemployed and project unions for construction sites—are promoted to organise those outside the state sector. Unions largely play a welfare role, which is inadequate for representing those in the private sector and those working in poorly managed SOEs. It is therefore not surprising that the level of disaffection with unions is high among SOE workers, who have experienced radical changes with worsened employment outcomes. The level of union identification is low among rural migrant workers; this reflects their unmet representation needs. In comparison, public sector employees are more receptive to, and vocal in their demands for, the welfare role of the unions. In this sector, employment relations remain relatively stable, and are less challenged by the market economy. And there is plenty of scope for the unions to improve their (welfare) functions (Cooke 2012).

More broadly, the welfare role of the unions continues, as it reflects both the government's ideology of building harmonious employment relations and the traditional Chinese culture. Benevolent paternalism, collectivism and harmony are some of the key characteristics of Chinese culture, which feature prominently in workplace relations.

The workplace plays an important role in providing social bonding activities to develop and maintain a harmonious relationship among employees, and between employers and their workforce. The provision of employee welfare and employee entertainment is traditionally seen by the Chinese as an important ingredient to improve the morale and commitment of the workforce and enhance the productivity of the firm (Cooke 2012). Unions help with organising social events and providing the welfare role required to improve the working and family life of employees. This role is particularly important when the HR function in the majority of Chinese enterprises is underdeveloped.

To some extent, the ideal form of employment relations promoted by the government—one that is influenced by Chinese culture—can be compared with the neo-pluralistic approach to contemporary employment relations promoted by certain scholars in more developed economies. It is an approach that emphasises social cohesion and stresses the importance of social values over interests, cooperation over conflict and trust over power (Ackers 2002). There has been a diversification of unions' constituencies; this is consequential of the growth of the market economy. The changing context presents opportunities as well as challenges to the unions. It requires them to adopt different roles and organising strategies, especially at local levels, to address diverse needs and interests if they are to maximise their continuing potential.

## FURTHER READING

Chan, C.K.C. (2010) *The Challenge of Labour in China: Strikes and the Changing Regime in Global Factories*. London: Routledge.

Chen, F. & Xu, X. (2012) '"Active judiciary": Judicial dismantling of workers' collective action in China'. *China Journal*, 67: 87–108.

Howell, J. (2008) 'All-China Federation of Trades Unions beyond reform? The slow march of direct elections'. *China Quarterly*, 196: 845–63.

Kim, S., Han, J. & Zhao, L.K. (2014) 'Union recognition by multinational companies in China: A dual institutional pressure perspective'. *Industrial and Labor Relations Review*, 67(1): 33–59.

Taylor, B. & Li, Q. (2010) 'China's creative approach to "union" organizing'. *Labor History*, 51(3): 411–28.

## USEFUL WEBSITES

ACFTU: <www.acftu.org.cn>.

China Labor News Translations: <www.clntranslations.org>.

*China Labour Bulletin*: <www.clb.org.hk/en>.

Ministry of Human Resources and Social Security: <www.mohrss.gov.cn>.

## A CHRONOLOGY OF CHINESE EMPLOYMENT RELATIONS

| | |
|---|---|
| 1949 | Founding of socialist China, ruled by the CCP. |
| 1950 | Enactment of the Trade Union Law. |
| 1966–76 | Chinese Cultural Revolution, during which production activities were slowed down or stopped, with the national economy on the brink of paralysis. |
| 1978 | Beginning of China's open door economic policy, which has led to the growth of FIEs and private firms with different employment policies from SOEs. |
| 1992 | Enactment of the Second Trade Union Law. |
| 1992 | Southern Tour by Deng Xiaoping, the architect of China's market economy; he gave a speech that endorsed the role of private entrepreneurship, leading to the rapid growth of the private sector, which has become a major employer. |
| 1993 | Enactment of the Enterprise Minimum Wage Regulation, which first set the monthly minimum pay for full-time workers. |
| 1994 | Ministry of Labour issues the Provisions on Collective Contracts, which provided details of the collective contract system outlined in the Labour Law. |
| 1995 | Enactment of the Labour Law—the first major piece of employment law in China. |
| 1997 | Beginning of the radical restructuring of SOEs, which led to millions of workers being made redundant. |
| 2000 | Ministry of Labour and Social Security issues the Collective Wage Consultation Trial Implementation Measures, requiring employers and workers (represented by managers and unions) collectively to consult about pay. |
| 2001 | Amendment of the Trade Union Law. China joins the World Trade Organization, which intensifies competition and puts pressure on Chinese enterprises to change their business and employment practices. |
| 2003 | Premier Wen Jiabao and President Hu Jintao take office; this marks the beginning of the pursuit of an economic development policy that emphasises social justice, social harmony and environmental protection instead of the efficiency-driven economic development policy of their predecessors. |
| 2003 | Premier Wen Jiabao initiates a government-led campaign in an attempt to solve the delayed pay problem endemic in industries employing primarily rural migrant workers—especially the construction industry. |
| 2003 | The ACFTU launches a drive to recruit rural migrant union members; it also leads the campaign to put pressure on FIEs to recognise unions. |

| | |
|---|---|
| 2004 | Ministry of Labour and Social Security issues the Provisions on Collective Contracts, which regulate collective negotiations and the signing of collective contracts. |
| 2007 | Many enterprises, including large and well-performing enterprises of all ownership forms, dismiss long-serving workers and rehire them under different contracts to avoid legal responsibility in anticipation of the forthcoming Labour Contract Law. |
| 2008 | Enactment of the Labour Contract Law, the Promotion of Employment Law and the Labour Dispute Mediation and Arbitration Law. |
| 2011 | Enactment of the Social Security Law. |
| 2013 | Amendment of the Labour Contract Law. |
| 2014 | Adoption of the Interim Provisions on Labour Dispatch. |

# CHAPTER 13

# Employment relations in India

## Anil Verma and Shyam Sundar[1]

With a population of more than 1.2 billion people, the Republic of India (hereafter India) is the second most populous country in the world; it is also the world's largest democracy. India has developed its employment relations system from its origins in British India, going back to the growth of industry in the nineteenth century. The legal foundation for unions, collective bargaining and worker rights in general has its roots in British common law, though the key players in India charted their own course for most of the twentieth century. India is a large multi-party democracy with a diverse population in terms of ethnicity, language, religion and caste. These characteristics also influence its employment relations. Most unions are concentrated in large enterprises and in government-related sectors. A majority of India's workforce is rural, and employed in the so-called informal sector. Unions are scarce in both these spheres, resulting in a very low total union density.

In the mid-1990s, India embarked on a new round of economic reforms, largely based on liberalising its economy, which had been highly regulated. The New Economic Policy, introduced in 1991, marked a decisive shift from heavy regulation to liberalisation, privatisation and globalisation (LPG). These reforms were introduced after a long period of sluggish economic growth, which had averaged 3 per cent per year during the years 1971–80. In the ten years between 1996 and 2005, after the introduction of the reforms, growth accelerated to an average of more than 6 per cent per year, and in the period 2006–11 it was even higher, at more than 8 per cent per year. However, growth slowed down to less than 6 per cent in 2012–13.

The hypothesis underlying this debate is that India should reform its labour and employment regulations so that a more flexible and responsive regime can facilitate sustainable economic growth. While there is general agreement that such reforms are urgently needed, no consensus exists about the best way to move forward. Indian labour laws—at least on paper—are considered to be among the most favourable to workers anywhere in the world. Employers face severe restrictions on their ability to discipline or lay off workers, or to close a plant (Ahsan & Pages 2009). While some reform is needed to create a more growth-friendly climate, merely making it easier to fire workers is unlikely to be the most effective reform. By providing a historical and institutional context for the development of India's employment relations, we provide analytical insights into the links between labour regulation, labour flexibility and the aspirations of India's citizens to create prosperity through sustainable long-term growth.

We provide a description of the framework of the employment relations system, followed by a review of the economic reforms of the 1990s. We describe the historical context, then consider the challenges that the employment relations system faces in facilitating economic growth while ensuring fairness and equity for workers. We then show that Indian developments do not fit neatly into categories such as liberal market economies (LMEs) or coordinated market economies (CMEs), as elaborated in the Varieties of Capitalism (VoC) framework (Hall & Soskice 2001). The developments also defy the notion that India is simply transitioning from being a CME to an LME.

Before the current period of economic liberalisation from the early 1990s, India exhibited many characteristics of a CME. Later, many of the economic reforms that led the high economic growth rates in the next dozen years did open up Indian markets to greater flows of capital, both across and within Indian borders. Yet, in terms of labour policy, India is less likely to mimic the extent of liberalisation experienced by the labour markets of LMEs. While there is some liberalisation of workplace regulation in the private sector, achieved through collective bargaining, and also in non-union workplaces, it is unlikely that there will be a change to labour laws in the manner in which many states in the United States have reduced collective bargaining and unionisation rights for public sector workers.

The Indian case is not unique in this regard. Other Asian economies, such as Japan, South Korea and China have also followed their own paths, which allow for a bigger role for the state in employment relations compared with the LMEs of Europe or North America. Perhaps this is an Asian model—one that seeks high economic growth rates by liberalising economic policies while maintaining a strong role for the state in social policy, including employment relations policy.

## HISTORICAL DEVELOPMENT OF EMPLOYMENT RELATIONS

India became independent of the United Kingdom in 1947. In the immediate post-1947 period, India chose the state-led, planned, import-substituting industrialisation model to foster economic progress. After 1947, a consensus emerged among the leaders that a compulsory adjudication–led state intervention model would best serve the national interest. The collective bargaining model was seen as 'desirable' but 'impractical', and was to play a secondary role; it was shelved for the future (see Ramaswamy 1984). The elements of the state intervention model include labour laws and emergency decrees, compulsory conciliation of industrial disputes in the public utilities (industries as notified by the government on public interest, distinct from essential industries), regulation of strikes and lockouts, compulsory adjudication of industrial disputes by labour judiciary and their awards, special intervention by the Supreme Court and the case laws (judgments and awards), quasi-judicial functions of labour administrators, labour inspection and administration and so on. These institutions of the state determine the substantive and procedural rules of the system, which are usually made by the bipartite processes elsewhere.

State intervention does not mean suppression of labour rights. The federal-democratic-pluralistic model of polity adopted assures fundamental rights, which include the right to form associations (unions), the right to education and the freedom of industrial action subject to legal regulation. India has ratified *only four* of the eight core conventions (the unratified conventions relate to freedom of association and collective bargaining and child labour) and three of the four 'governance' conventions of the International Labour Organization (ILO.) But the constitutional guarantees and the liberal-pluralist legal framework uphold the principles contained in the core conventions, and India's record in respecting the principles of freedom of association is better than that of other countries in Asia (Venkata Ratnam 2006).

Under India's Constitution, labour is on the Concurrent List, a list of policy areas in which both the central (federal) and state governments are empowered to legislate. There are more than 40 central labour laws and more than 150 state labour laws that seek to regulate various aspects of the labour market and employment relations, such as working conditions, wages, industrial relations (IR), social security and labour welfare.[2] The scope of each of these labour laws is limited by criteria such as the nature of industrial activity (seasonal or not), pay levels and size of enterprise (as measured by the number of workers).

Most labour laws apply only to the organised sector—that is, those establishments that employ more than nine workers; they do not cover the unorganised (or informal) sector. Even within the organised sector, their coverage is far from complete (see IHD/ISLE 2014). In this sense, a divide between the organised and unorganised sectors is created by the policy itself.

The legal framework for employment relations regulation has remained virtually unchanged, notwithstanding a few attempts at reform. The rising incidence of industrial disputes, violent and undisciplined industrial conflicts, delays in delivery of industrial justice in the past and the dynamics of globalisation in the post-reform period, among other factors, has prompted many reform initiatives since the mid-1960s. Several commissions (the National Commission on Labour in 1966, the Sanat Mehta Committee in 1982, the Second National Commission on Labour in 2002) made recommendations, which have not been fully implemented. The failure to reform can be attributed largely to a lack of consensus among the actors and an absence of political will for reform.

## THE EMPLOYMENT RELATIONS PARTIES

### Unions and workers' organisations

Collective activities of workers in the industrial era can be traced to the early 1880s, with the formation of the Bombay Millhands' Association in 1890 and the Amalgamated Society of Railway Servants of India and Burma in 1897. Some commentators see these initial formations as no more than strike committees, and as lacking trade union and class character (Sharma 1982). India's first continuing union was the Madras Labour Union, a general union formed in 1918. India's first national union federation, the All India Trade Union Congress (AITUC), was formed in 1920.

The *Trade Unions Act* of 1926 provided for voluntary registration of unions (including employers' organisations), subject to compliance with rules and regulations framed in the law, and offers immunities from civil and criminal conspiracies for the conduct of legal union activities. From 1926 to 2001, any seven persons could form a union, a law which was criticised as being too lax and was seen to have contributed to the multiplicity of unions. Following the 2001 amendment to the Act, 10 per cent of the workforce, or 100 workers—whichever is less—has been necessary for the formation of a union, subject to a minimum of seven people. This law provides merely for voluntary registration of unions, and not for their recognition for collective bargaining (Venkata Ratnam & Verma 2011). This shortcoming in the law has been detrimental to the growth of collective bargaining and has contributed to strife in employment relations (see Tulpule 1978; Gopalakrishnan 2009).[3]

The poor quality of union membership data from the Ministry of Labour makes it difficult to estimate union density. On average, only about 10 per cent of registered unions in India submit their annual returns on membership. Estimates suggest that, depending on the source of information (labour force data or the organised sector employment data), union density varies from less than 5 per cent to around 30 per cent (IHD/ISLE 2014).

Since 1920, when the AITUC allied itself with the Indian National Congress (the Congress Party), Indian unions have affiliated with a political party. Initially, when the AITUC was the only union confederation, it comprised various factions from the nationalist Congress Party (including socialists and communists). These tensions led to splits when the Congress Party formed its own union confederation, the Indian National Trade Union Congress (INTUC) in 1947. Further splits in the union movement took place as the socialists and radicals broke from their parent bodies after the formation of their own political parties. The socialists formed the Hind Mazdoor Sabha (HMS) while the radicals formed two splinter unions, United Trade Union Congress (UTUC) and UTUC (Lenin-Sarani) (see Sharma 1982). The group subscribing to Hindu nationalism formed the Bharatiya Mazdoor Sangh (BMS) in 1955.[4] The Communist Party of India (CPI) split over issues relating to the Indo-China War in 1962 and the Communist Party of India (Marxist), or CPI(M), was born in 1964. The Centre of Indian Trade Unions (CITU) was formed in 1970 as the labour wing of the CPI.

The Dravida Munnetra Kazhagham in Tamil Nadu (in 1970) and the Shiv Sena in Maharashtra (in 1966)—both powerful regional political parties—formed their own labour wings. Splits in these political parties over the years have led to corresponding splits in their labour wings as well (Ramaswamy 1984, 1988). The Ministry of Labour carries out membership verification exercises of Central Trade Union Organisations (CTUOs) to assess their membership for representation in tripartite and international meetings. Table 13.1 shows the relative sizes and political affiliation of the CTUOs.

Despite the dominance of 'political unionism' as illustrated in Table 13.1, there are also some large and effective enterprise unions. Labour leaders such as R.J. Mehta and Dr Datta Samant in Mumbai, R. Kuchelar in Chennai and Michael Fernandes in Bengaluru have

**Table 13.1 Membership of CTUOs[a]**

| CTUO | Membership (000s) | Political affiliation |
|---|---|---|
| BMS[5] | 6216 | BJP |
| INTUC | 3954 | Indian National Congress |
| CITU | 2678 | CPI (M) |
| AITUC | 3442 | CPI |
| HMS | 3338 | Non-political |
| UTUC (Lenin-Sarani)[b] | 1373 | Socialist Unity Centre of India (communist) |
| LPF | 612 | Dravida Munnetra Kazhagham (regional party with Dravidian ideology) |
| UTUC | 607 | Revolutionary Socialist Party |
| AICCTU | 640 | CPI (Marxist-Leninist) |
| TUCC | 733 | All India Forward Bloc (left-leaning) |
| SEWA | 688 | Non-political |
| Total | 24,885 | |

*Notes:*
(a) Union federations having verified membership of at least 0.5 million which includes at least four states and four industries including agriculture. Numbers rounded.
(b) Known as All India United Trade Union Centre.

*Source:* Government of India, Ministry of Labour and Employment, Notification No. L–52025/20/2003-IR(Imp-I), (Mimeo).

formed or led independent or enterprise-based unions (Davala 1996; Ramaswamy 1988). The success of enterprise unions has led to a surge in union membership and activity at the enterprise level, and has thus contributed to the vitality of the labour movement. Nevertheless, some argue that enterprise unions lack a class character, and could not make system-level impacts (Sengupta 1993). There are other forms of unionism, namely craft unionism (in Indian railways and civil aviation), industry or sector unionism (in banks, insurance and the steel industry), caste and gender unionism, and so on (see IHD/ISLE 2014). The result is a fragmented and diverse pattern of organisation of workers.

## Trends in unionism in the post-reform period

Four features of union movement in the post-reform period merit attention: weakening of the politics–unions nexus; unity and coordination in the union movement; inclusivity of conventional unions; and strengthening and formation of union organisations in the informal sector. Unions increasingly have realised that all major political parties, irrespective of stated ideology, tend to lean towards liberal economic and labour policies when in power (Ramaswamy 1988; Bhattacherjee 1999; Shyam Sundar 2009b).

## Workers' organisations in the informal sector

The part-arrogant and part-indifferent attitude of mainstream unions towards the informal sector has spurred the rise of several union-like workers' organisations. However, the CTUOs have sought to correct their historical guilt in ignoring the informal sector workers, and their verified membership grew significantly between the 1980 and 2002 membership verification surveys (John 2007). This did not prevent them from adopting an encompassing perspective towards the non-government organisations (NGOs) that have been organising workers in the informal sector. The conflict between the mainstream unions and the new forms of labour organisations, including the well-established Self Employed Women's Association (SEWA), is based on the premise that the latter are non-membership based and externally (often dubiously) funded organisations—unlike the representative and democratic union organisations (Shyam Sundar 2009b).

SEWA, formed in 1971, is the most notable of the new forms of labour organisation. Though it was registered as a union, it has combined the functions of a union, a cooperative and an advocacy group, and has grown to be seen as a CTUO. It has participated at the international level in networks like Women in Informal Employment: Globalising and Organising and played an important role in the adoption by the ILO of Convention 189 for regulation of domestic work. SEWA was also instrumental in the creation of organisations and networks like StreetNet and the National Centre for Labour (NCL).

Although the National Alliance of Street Vendors of India formed in 1998, it was not registered as an independent organisation until 2003. It has 373 organisations representing nearly 300,000 street vendors as paying members from 20 states of India (Bhowmik 2005). In 2014, the central government passed a law to offer the right of street vending, subject to regulations.

The NCL is a confederation of organisations engaged in advocating for informal sector workers. It worked with the National Campaign Committee for Central Legislation on Construction Labour, headed by ex-Supreme Court Justice the late Krishna Iyer, in mobilising support for the *Building and Other Construction Workers Act* in 1996. The NCL has also fought for implementation of the law in various states through litigation in the Supreme Court (Venkatesan 2012). Both these organisations effectively combined advocacy with litigation to advance the interests of informal sector workers (IHD/ISLE 2014).

## Unions and the emerging sectors

Unions have found it difficult to organise workers in growth sectors like information technology (IT) and IT-enabled services, large retail outlets (shopping malls), garment-making, private hospitals and clinics, multinational and private sector banks and in special economic zones (SEZs). These workers are hard to unionise for both demand- and supply-side reasons. Many of these workers regard themselves as being 'different' from industrial and manual workers. At the same time, many of their employers see unions as unnecessary or undesirable in the workplace. Employer opposition to unions can take a soft form of opposition through the 'pro-employee' human resource management (HRM) policies or a hard form of anti-union policy of threats, coercion or intimidation. In many locations, such as the SEZs, workers have the legal right to unionise, but in practice they are unable to exercise their right for a variety of reasons (Shyam Sundar 2010a). These situations have created a gap in representation between what the law permits and actual representation in practice.

## Employers' organisations

For early employers' organisations such as the chambers of commerce (e.g. Federation of Indian Chambers of Commerce, formed 1927), the main focus was on *trade* interests rather than on employment relations. Along with the chambers of commerce, employers' organisations did develop in specific industries and regions such as textiles and plantations in Tamil Nadu, Maharashtra and West Bengal. For them, employment relations issues were important (e.g. Southern India Mills Association in Coimbatore in 1933,[6] and the United Planters' Association of Southern India in Tamil Nadu in 1893).[7] The establishment of an industry association so early in the development of textiles facilitated industry-wide bargaining in the cotton textile industry (Ramaswamy 1977).

At the national level, the All India Organisation of Employers (AIOE) and the Employers' Federation of India (EFI) were formed in 1932–33, with employment relations as their main mandate. Employers' organisations could be formed under any of three laws: the *Trade Unions Act 1926*, the *Societies Registration Act 1860* and the *Companies Act 1956* (revised in 2012). The main employment relations activities of employers' organisations are to act as a pressure group to influence public policies on labour; to advise their members on employment relations issues; to represent employers in the tripartite and bipartite agencies at national and international levels; to represent their members in industrial dispute resolution agencies; and to share information on IR and technical aspects.[8]

The AIOE and EFI worked separately in their early years, but they joined in 1956 to set up the Council of Indian Employers (CIE) to coordinate their activities. Both are also members of the International Organisation of Employers (IOE). The Confederation of Indian Industries started as the Engineering and Iron Trades Association (1895), but adopted its current name in 1992.[9] It deals with such matters as employment relations, human resource (HR) development and gender issues.[10] However, it does not represent employers in the tripartite and bipartite agencies at the national level and at the ILO's International Labour Conference.

In the public sector, the New Horizon society was established in New Delhi in 1970. This was later converted into a confederation for all central public sector enterprises, the Standing Conference of Public Sector Enterprises (SCOPE). SCOPE was formally recognised by the government in 1976,[11] when it also joined the CIE. The guidelines for wage negotiations and the HR development policies for the central public sector enterprises are coordinated by the Department of Public Enterprises.[12]

## INDUSTRIAL RELATIONS PROCESSES: THE INSTITUTIONAL CONTEXT

The state agencies determine the substantive and procedural rules of employment relations, and elaborate machinery has been created to prevent and settle industrial disputes. The *Industrial Employment (Standing Orders) Act 1946* was enacted to regulate terms and conditions of employment and to ensure 'standardisation' of the rules across employers through a model standing order, as well as to provide for adoption of principles of natural justice before employees are dismissed (e.g. for misconduct). The *Industrial Disputes Act 1947* seeks to prevent industrial disputes through works committees (bipartite enterprise-level councils) and grievance procedures at enterprise level; prevent and resolve industrial disputes (apprehended and actual disputes) through conciliation and adjudication, collective bargaining and voluntary arbitration; define unfair labour practices; define and regulate (by prohibition) the legality of strikes and lockouts; and regulate employer industrial actions like redundancies and retrenchments of employees and closure of establishments.

Consistent with its state interventionist traditions, the law provides for compulsory conciliation and adjudication (subject to failure of conciliation) of industrial disputes in the public utilities. Such intervention is optional in other workplaces, except where a notice of a strike and lockout has been issued. Voluntary arbitration is provided as another option after conciliation and before compulsory adjudication. The settlement reached in conciliation and the awards given by voluntary arbitrators or compulsory adjudicatory agencies (a labour court or industrial tribunal) apply to all parties and their successors, be they employers, employees or others who may have been involved in the adjudication. Collectively negotiated agreements apply *only* to the parties to the employment relationship. The threat of compulsory adjudication (the government has discretion to refer any impasse for such compulsory arbitration) and the *wider* applicability of adjudicated awards may have incentivised the parties to prefer adjudication and compulsory conciliation to voluntary negotiation. The effect has been to juridify IR (Saini 1991) and weaken bipartisanship (Tulpule 1978).

The absence of national regulation for determining a bargaining agent and related controversies have been detrimental to the development of collective bargaining. A few states have enacted such legislation (including Maharashtra, Gujarat, Madhya Pradesh, West Bengal and Orissa). Regulations concerning strikes make legal strikes almost impossible (see Ramaswamy 1984). Government employees do not enjoy the right to strike, and strikes are not a fundamental right in India (Shyam Sundar 2009b). The coverage of collective bargaining is extremely limited; it is estimated to be only around 2 per cent (Venkata Ratnam 2003). Ironically, the dynamics of globalisation have strengthened collective bargaining in some sectors and workplaces. Adjudication has become costly as competitive product markets tend to demand quick settlements of industrial disputes. The parties have realised that adjudication is an easy alternative, and hence it was much used during the command economy regime. However, collective bargaining has much to offer, and negotiated outcomes have more legitimacy than decisions of third parties (Ramaswamy 1988).

## Dispute settlement

Consultative institutions at the macro level include the Labour Ministers' Conference and tripartite institutions such as the Indian Labour Conference and the state-level Labour Advisory Boards. Consultative institutions at the micro level include works committees (statutory councils under the *Industrial Dispute Act 1947*) and voluntary joint management councils. These institutions allow for consultation as an alternative to the legalistic compulsory adjudication model. Consultative institutions can facilitate industrial peace and help create voluntary rules for issues such as recognition of unions that are not covered by regulation. But these institutions have not been productively employed, especially in the post-reform period (Venkata Ratnam 2006). The statutory tripartite institutions are not constituted in a timely way in many states. Furthermore, their composition does not include the necessary expertise. The ILCs have degenerated into talking shops, and their unanimous recommendations are invariably not implemented by the government (Shyam Sundar 2011).

## Labour–management conflict

The economic reforms might have been expected to decrease industrial conflict because of the shift in bargaining power to favour capital, the weakening of collective institutions and the establishment of pro-market state policies. The government claimed in 2003 that employment relations were 'harmonious', and pointed to a decline in strikes (see Shyam Sundar 2009b). However, the tensions arising out of the economic reforms and the related conduct of employers have resulted in an increase in the incidence of labour–management conflicts (see Table 13.2).

While the number of work stoppages has decreased, the incidence of worker involvement in work stoppages and the volume of working days lost (WDL) due to work stoppages have risen since the late 1990s. There are at least two features of employees' protests to discuss. The mobilisation of employees in strikes (measured by WI/N and WI/WS—that is, the average size of strikes) has increased substantially during the post-reform period (see Table 13.3). Why has there been an increase in the mobilisation of employees in work stoppages? The reasons include the incidence of all-India strikes (more than a dozen since the mid-1990s), an increasing incidence of work stoppages in the public sector (see Shyam Sundar 2010b), lockouts by larger establishments and disputes about issues that have arisen from the reforms and

**Table 13.2   Indicators of work stoppages**

| Period | WS/N[(a)] | WI/N[(b)] | WDL/N[(c)] | WI/WS[(d)] | WDL/WI[(e)] | WDL/WS[(f)] |
|---|---|---|---|---|---|---|
| 1992–95 | 4.9 | 37 | 814 | 752 | 22 | 16,530 |
| 1996–99 | 4 | 40 | 766 | 1006 | 19 | 19,156 |
| 2000–03 | 2.3 | 46 | 995 | 1942 | 22 | 42,458 |
| 2004–07 | 1.6 | 70 | 943 | 4293 | 13 | 57,661 |
| 2008–10 | 1.4 | 54 | 689 | 3976 | 13 | 51,175 |
| 1990s | 4.9 | 41 | 821 | 885 | 11 | 10,072 |
| 2000s | 1.9 | 59 | 900 | 5127 | 6 | 30,485 |

Notes:

Work stoppages include strikes and lockouts. Some numbers rounded.

(a) Number of work stoppages per 100,000 employees in the organised sector.
(b) Number of workers involved in work stoppages per 1000 employees.
(c) Number of WDL due to work stoppages per 1000 employees.
(d) Average size of the work stoppage.
(e) Average duration of the work stoppage.
(f) Average volume lost of the work stoppage.

Sources: Indian Labour Statistics; Indian Labour Year Book (Shimla: Labour Bureau), Government of India.

restructuring processes. Such disputes illustrate a widening of the agenda of workplace conflict.

As a result of such conflict, the central and state governments have shied away from making any changes in the legal framework for employment security, and from initiating full-scale privatisation, with a few exceptions. Some of the major causes of industrial disputes include union recognition, aggressive state policies to demonstrate a conducive labour climate for attracting and retaining new investments, alleged exploitative and tough work conditions, redundancies and hiring of contract labour employment (Shyam Sundar 2010b). Let us offer some illustrations.

Workers in Honda Motorcycles in Haryana sought recognition of their unions in 2005. When the employer refused, it led to much violence from both workers and the police. These events were covered

**Table 13.3    Lockouts, workers involved in and WDL through lockouts, as proportion (%) of total work stoppage**

| Period | Lockouts | Workers involved in lockouts | WDL in lockouts |
|--------|----------|------------------------------|-----------------|
| 1985–90 | 22 | 15 | 58 |
| 1992–95 | 36 | 32 | 63 |
| 1996–99 | 39 | 30 | 60 |
| 2000–04 | 48 | 24 | 74 |
| 2005–09 | 47 | 6 | 59 |

*Notes:* Numbers rounded.
The year 1991 has been omitted as it was a transition year that does not fit well into either the pre- or post-reform period.

*Source:* Indian Labour Statistics, *Indian Labour Year Book* (Shimla: Labour Bureau), Government of India.

widely in the media, and the images traumatised the whole nation (Saini 2005). In 2008, Hyundai Motor India Limited refused to recognise the free and independent union, the HMI Employees' Union; the company victimised the union leaders and sought to reach a collective agreement with a management-nominated workers' council. This provoked several strikes and worker protests. Similarly, the Madras Rubber Factory preferred a 'company union' to a free and independent union formed by a majority of the workers in its plant in Arokkonam in Tamil Nadu (Gopalakrishnan 2009; Shyam Sundar 2010b).

Instances of violence and death of managers, union leaders and workers have been reported in conflicts in the twenty-first century (see Shyam Sundar 2012).[13] Employers have been more aggressive in initiating lockouts since the 1990s (see Table 13.3).The post-reform period: Indications of a policy shift towards the informal sector

During the post-reform period, the institutional framework for employment relations changed at the local level while remaining relatively unchanged at the national level. At the same time, the informal economy posed serious challenges for the national development model pursued by policy-makers. The government responded by constituting the National Commission on Enterprises in the Unorganised Sector (NCEUS), chaired by Arjun Sengupta. The NCEUS submitted reports on social security, working conditions and the challenge of creating employment.

The government introduced the *Unorganised Workers' Social Security Act* in 2008, in a much-diluted form from the one recommended by the NCEUS. The National Rural Employment Guarantee Scheme was introduced in 2006. This guaranteed unskilled work for rural families for 100 calendar days in a year at the minimum wage as fixed by the government. The government also introduced the Rashtriya Swasthaya Bima Yojana, a free medical insurance coverage of 30,000 INR, including free hospitalisation for families below the poverty line.[14] The *National Food Security Act*, enacted in 2013, obliges the government to provide food grains at subsidised prices to approximately two-thirds of India's population. Under this Act, households have the right to purchase 5 kilograms of cereals per month per eligible person at subsidised prices. These are some of the major state initiatives that address work and social security needs of workers in the unorganised sector.

## Trends in collective bargaining

Some employers—especially the multinational enterprises (MNEs)—have adopted union-avoidance and aggressive union-busting tactics. Many enterprises have achieved de facto workforce flexibility by reducing their regular workforce (the 'bargainable category' of workers) using a variety of tactics, such as constraining recruitment, attrition, coerced or voluntary separations, creation of pseudo-managerial job categories, outsourcing of work both on and off site, closure of selected operations and/or relocating them to non-union sites, and the use of lockouts as 'closures in disguise' (Shrouti & Nandkumar 1995). Such employer strategies have weakened collective institutions.

In general, globalisation has intensified competition. Employers argue that the employment relations actors need to shift from conventional 'distributive bargaining' to 'productivity bargaining' in order to remain competitive in the global context (Shyam Sundar 2014). Unions have conventionally viewed productivity bargaining with suspicion, regarding it more as a management ploy to limit worker gains, and have instead preferred bargaining for pay increases based on the cost of living. Many employers realise that they need worker cooperation to get positive outcomes from work processes (e.g. lower costs, higher quality and high productivity), or they will have to face even higher costs of work disruptions, low morale and loss of productivity. Unions, on the other hand, face the threat of non-recognition and being completely marginalised. Unions have an incentive to earn back their legitimacy and bring employers back to the negotiating table by mixing cost-of-living and productivity objectives to bargain for pay increases and to allow concession bargaining during economic downturns. It could be a win–win game for both if they accept productivity bargaining and use their power to negotiate gains within it.

Unions are increasingly likely to engage in productivity bargaining under certain conditions, such as no reduction in the size of the workforce, no increase in workers' efforts and productivity not being the sole criterion for pay increases. Generally, the formula for improving productivity has involved higher utilisation of resources, an increase in productive hours—for example, by excluding non-productive hours (e.g. tea and lunch time, rest and fatigue time, change of clothing time) from paid hours, and through work reorganisation to adopt multiskilling, multi-machining, waste reduction and quality improvement (Shyam Sundar 2014). In public sector enterprises, the Department of Public Sector guidelines for collective bargaining require enterprises to link pay with the performance of the employees and of the enterprise.

In India, collective bargaining has been conducted at various levels: enterprise, industry and region (in cotton textiles, jute, plantations), and sector and national (in steel, cement, banking and insurance). Employers have pressed for decentralised collective bargaining in response to competitive pressures in the hope that market forces would discipline the rent-seeking behaviour of unions in terms of pay and benefits (SNCL 2002). In the private sector, enterprise-level bargaining has gradually been replacing industry-wide bargaining, even where industry-wide bargaining had previously been the norm (Bhattacherjee 1999; Shyam Sundar 2009a, 2010c).

Unions have been able to mobilise certain marginalised sections of the workforce (e.g. contract workers) and to negotiate significant benefits, such as employment security and regular collective contracts (Shyam Sundar 2011). Most unions realise that, despite being pitted against each other in competition for jobs, the two groups of workers (regular employees and contract workers) face common challenges, such as lack of employment security, low pay and inadequate working conditions. The employers also recognise the need to negotiate terms for contract workers for increasing cooperation between the two categories of workers in bargaining (Shyam Sundar 2010b).

## Labour market reforms

The government has been successful in introducing economic reforms, which are summarised by the initialism LPG (liberalisation, privatisation and globalisation). Indian and foreign MNE employers have cited these economic reforms to demand corresponding liberalisation of the labour market and its institutions.

India's restrictive labour laws make summary dismissal of workers difficult, even on the grounds of serious misconduct. Regulations require that industrial establishments[15] employing more than 99 workers must seek prior permission from the government to lay off workers, to close an establishment or even, under certain conditions, to terminate contract labour. These provisions are criticised as creating 'rigidities' in the employment system, because they constrain employers' ability to make changes in operations in response to changes in product markets or the economy. Problems compound for the employers, given the plethora of labour laws, the complexity of which makes compliance challenging even for the most capable and well-meaning employers. Labour inspectors are often accused of being over-inquisitive and, in some cases, of demanding bribes to cut short required inspections (Pages & Roy 2006).

Some attribute the jobless growth of the 1980s to the rising power of unions, an increase in the number of industrial disputes, restrictive employment laws and rising real wages (Shyam Sundar 2009c). Econometric analyses using data from the organised manufacturing sector have generally shown the *detrimental* effects of restrictive labour regulation on employment growth, output and poverty reduction (Ahsan & Pages 2009; Besley & Burgess 2004; Goldar & Aggarwal 2012). These results suggest that a more flexible labour regime would result in greater job creation and real gains in income, which in turn would lead to a reduction in poverty.

However, the flexibility hypothesis is contested. Other studies—including macro-economic studies (e.g. Roy 2002; Deakin & Sarkar 2011), micro-survey-based studies (Deshpande et al. 1998; Deshpande et al. 2004) and state-level studies of labour regulation (quoted in Papola et al. 2008)—question the flexibility hypothesis. These studies broadly show that the restrictive job security clauses were not responsible for the slowdown in employment growth. Notwithstanding restrictive labour laws, employers enjoyed considerable flexibility in hiring and reducing their workforce, so that labour regulation was not so problematic; this was shown by steep reductions in enforcement such as labour inspections and prosecutions. Moreover, some critical scholars have argued that the pro-flexibility econometric studies relied on faulty measures of key variables (Bhattacharya 2009). Since the economy did not generate many jobs—even during periods of high growth (more than 8 per cent)—it can be argued that factors other than lack of flexibility might lie behind anaemic job creation. Others argue that jobs were created, but mostly in the informal sector, given the rigidities of the formal labour market (e.g. Mehrotra et al. 2012).

## The labour market flexibility strategy of the government

The evidence in the flexibility debate is therefore inconclusive, and the government has taken an ambivalent attitude to labour law reforms. While the government sometimes seems to accept the inflexibility hypothesis (Government of India 2006), it has also acknowledged that the *Industrial Disputes Act* has not proved an obstacle to downsizing, and that the scope of prohibition of contract labour has not been wide. At the same time, it recognises that the *Industrial Disputes Act* does create a psychological block against the creation of new enterprises, which makes it difficult 'to cope with large size orders from retail market chains' in some product lines (Government of India 2008).

The government has been inclined to introduce labour reforms to facilitate attracting and retaining capital. The political-economic argument is that, although there are relatively few workers in the organised sector compared with the unorganised sector, they are well organised and can inflict high costs on the government and society (Varshney 1999). Three issues have brought labour reforms to the centre of national politics: labour policies of the government, public sector reforms and the labour flexibility measures. More than a dozen all-India strikes and agitations have taken place in recent years (discussed below). The central government postponed reforms several times to try to avoid this type of conflict.

However, the Bharatiya Janata Party (BJP)–led National Demo-cratic Alliance government has taken some bold initiatives to introduce reforms at the central level. It has introduced amendments to the *Factories Act 1948*, the *Apprentices Act 1971* and the *Labour Laws (Exemption from Furnishing Returns and Maintaining Registers by Certain Establishments) Act 1988*. The last of these laws was passed by the upper house in November 2014.[16] The central government has also directed the central labour offices and the state labour departments to rationalise 'governance' of employment relations through removing the so-called Inspector-raj and moving to e-governance.[17]

With labour reform measures being stymied by several obstacles at the central government level, attention has shifted to the state level. Labour is on the Concurrent List of the Constitution, which gives state governments power to legislate in the area of labour policy.[18] The state governments are in competition for mobile capital, so to attract capital they may offer incentives, including labour flexibility. Reforms at the state level would 'localise' worker protests and allow for breakthroughs in some regions that have proved elusive at the national level (Shyam Sundar & Venkata Ratnam 2007).

State governments have undertaken two types of reform measures and initiatives: 'hard' reforms that explicitly rewrite the formal rules and 'soft' reforms (reforms by stealth), which effectively change practice by limiting application and enforcement of the formal rules (Bardhan 2002; Shyam Sundar & Venkata Ratnam 2007). The government of Rajasthan has amended three labour laws (the *Factories Act 1948*, the *Industrial Disputes Act 1947* and the *Contract Labour (Regulation and Abolition) Act 1970*), which have been endorsed by the president as required under the Constitution; any amendment to the central law by a state government on a subject on the Concurrent List that is inconsistent with the central law needs the consent of the president. The achievement of securing hard labour law reforms by the Rajasthan government is a game-changer in the politics of labour policy in India, as more state governments are inclined to follow the Rajasthan model.

Soft reforms involve making no changes to the formal institutional framework, but allow employers to introduce changes in terms of labour reforms. The government simply looks the other way when employers resort to them (Bardhan 2002: 128). State governments have adopted a mix of soft and hard policies. (Table 13.4 illustrates these two contrasting types of reforms.)

## CONCLUSIONS

India is characterised by a plethora of labour laws, long-standing employees' and employers' organisations and a variety of dispute settlement processes, including jurisprudence from the courts. Nevertheless, the regulation of employment relations has not kept pace with economic and social changes in India and other countries. There is much potential to reform India's employment relations regulations, especially if the country is to be responsive to the needs of its employment relations actors.

Employment relations policy in India has focused mostly on the 7–8 per cent of the labour force employed in the organised sector. Therefore, the employment relations challenges are different from those in many other countries, especially the developed economies. India has too many laws offering too much protection to the few and too little protection to the many.

Given the pluralism in the Indian labour market, the government is faced with a paradox: how to moderate the 'excessive' (at least on paper) protection of a relatively small category—the organised labour

## Table 13.4  Typology of employment relations reforms

| Hard reform | Soft reform |
| --- | --- |
| The Maharashtra government amended the *Contract Labour Act* (Sections 1 and 10) in 2005 to deem certain ancillary activities (e.g. canteens, gardening, cleaning, security, courier services, transport of raw material and finished products, loading and unloading of goods) performed on the premises of an establishment in SEZs and the work in the establishments declared 100 per cent export units by the government as 'temporary and intermittent work'. The amendment takes these activities out of the purview of the *Contract Labour Act* (Shyam Sundar 2009a). | Several states have introduced reforms that effectively reduce the coverage of inspections by exempting sectors, reduce the frequency of inspections, limit the discretion of junior inspectors by requiring prior authorisation from superiors, and provide for self-regulation in the form of self-certification. |
| The Rajasthan government amended the *Industrial Disputes Act 1947* to weaken the requirement for prior government permission before redundancies and closure of establishments from the threshold of enterprises employing 100 or more workers to those employing 300 or more workers. | Some state labour departments may delay or refuse registration of unions; they may also inform concerned employers of the registration request and apparently seek endorsement from the employer before accepting registration. Such actions are ploys to defeat workers' efforts to unionise in the face of opposition by the employer. |

*Source:* Shyam Sundar (2009a, 2010a); Tripathy (2014).

force—and how to enhance social protection of the majority of the labour force in the unorganised sector. For the next few decades, India will have a demographic 'dividend' in terms of a young work-force. Nevertheless, most of them still need basic education, vocational skills training, health services and social security. Unless such needs are met adequately, the so-called demographic dividend could turn into a demographic liability. Perhaps the most glaring weakness of the employment relations system in India is 'its failure to include all workers' (Hill 2009).

There is a long list of potential reforms. However, there is little consensus over exactly where the reforms should begin. We have identified some specific areas as well as the big issue of labour flexibility. For example, one specific area concerns labour administration. Labour administrators in India have large discretionary powers without commensurate accountability, training or infrastructure to handle them. It is necessary to build a cadre of professionals in labour administration and the labour judiciary. It is also necessary to achieve a greater awareness and understanding of alternative dispute resolution procedures. The employment relations partners should work together to promote arbitration. To this end, training and certification of arbitrators should be encouraged and mechanisms developed on a scale commensurate with the needs in this area. There is also a need to strengthen the *labour lok adalats* (people's labour courts) whereby the labour adjudication process is expedited closer to the place of work of the affected parties without recourse to vexatious time- and money-consuming legal procedures.[19]

The government has not revived the special national tripartite mechanism it initiated when its predecessor launched the economic reforms in 1991 to work for a consensus on 'flexicurity' (a trade-off between flexibility and security). Compensation for affected workers in the form of income protection can be traded in exchange for relaxing labour laws to accommodate employers' calls for more flexibility. Workplace employment relations systems should facilitate change, promote flexibility and prepare the workforce to be able, adaptive and responsive to the challenges of globalisation and related changes.

On the issue of flexibility in the labour market, we argue that while the formal and legal systems have not been changed since the economic reforms of the 1990s, employers and governments have made changes. Consequently, there has been enough flexibility for enterprises to be able to compete at home and abroad. There has been increased casualisation and more flexibility in employment relations through the widespread use of contract labour. The official data do not capture the extent of these changes. Even as unions opposed reform initiatives at a political level, they sought to expand their membership by organising hitherto neglected segments of workers. They demanded and received better terms and conditions of employment and limited employment security for flexi-workers. They also negotiated limited forms of flexibility and agreed to productivity bargaining under certain conditions. Some employers pursued flexibility practices to a great extent so that it resulted in serious conflict, setting back the process of negotiated settlements and of constructive social dialogue.

The reforms have not won wide acceptance from workers and unions because they have not resulted in robust job creation, even when there was more than 8 per cent annual economic growth. National Sample Survey Office (NSSO) surveys do show positive job creation, but its pace is modest. Although employers complain that labour market rigidity is a problem, the flexibility available to employers (through contract labour, casual labour, judicial decisions and so on) has been sufficient to give management the practical tools to be competitive. Thus, flexibility needs have been met in the short term, but more fundamental reforms are still needed in the long term.

For sustainable long-term growth, the employment relations actors should broaden the concept of flexibility in employment from a micro workplace level to the macro level of the labour market. At the macro level, the economy needs reforms in three key areas: improving the quality and level of skills of the workforce by upgrading its education and training infrastructure; investing in physical infrastructure such as transport, communication and energy, so that urbanisation can reach every citizen who seeks it; and creating a public safety net that would allow for greater flexibility at the workplace level. If substantial progress is made in all three areas, it is likely that the current narrowly focused debate over employers' right to fire workers could be recast within a more constructive set of policy options.

Given the clamour for more labour reforms, it seems likely that India's mix of market and state policies will begin to tilt in favour of the market in the longer run. However, it may not necessarily result in a complete shift from state intervention to an LME (see Chapter 1). As long as a significant part of the population is still poor and unable to escape the subsistence economy, there will be a role for the state to intervene. Perhaps in some ways China (see Chapter 12) is an indicator of how the mix between market and state policies may develop in India. Even after more than 20 years of high economic growth, China's policy-makers say the country is not yet ready for a completely liberalised economy. The precise mix of market and state policies in India will probably echo the pace at which the economy grows and social reforms take root. The right balance between regulation and deregulation will reflect the strategies and degree of sophistication of the policy-makers, institutions and actors.

We could see the Indian variety of capitalism as an Asian variant, which might represent a move from being a form of CME to being closer to a form of LME. But, given India's developmental needs, policy-makers would need to temper market reforms with social priorities to ensure inclusive growth. The shift from CME-style policies to LME-style policies would, of necessity, be gradual and constrained. For the foreseeable future, until relatively full employment has been achieved, the economy will include controls that try to achieve a balance between less regulation to ensure growth, and greater regulation (or re-regulation) to offer basic protections to employees, irrespective of the nature of the work, or the type of workplace or employer.

## FURTHER READING

Breman, J. (2010) *Outcast Labour in Asia: Circulation and Informalization of the Workforce at the Bottom of the Economy*. New Delhi: Oxford University Press.

Guha, R. (2007) *India after Gandhi: The History of the World's Largest Democracy*. London: Picador.

Hensman, R. (2011) *Workers, Unions and Global Capitalism: Lessons from India*. New Delhi: Tulika Books.

Sen, R. (2014) *Industrial Relations: Texts and Cases*. New Delhi: Trinity Press.

Srivastava, S.C. (2013) *Industrial Relations and Labour Laws*. New Delhi: Vikas.

## USEFUL WEBSITES

Labour Bureau: <http://labourbureau.nic.in>.

Labour Start India: <www.labourstart.org/india>.

Ministry of Labour and Employment: <http://labour.gov.in/content>.

Ministry of Statistics and Programme Implementation: <http://mospi.nic.in/Mospi_New/site/home.aspx>.

Planning Commission: <http://planningcommission.nic.in>.

## A CHRONOLOGY OF INDIAN EMPLOYMENT RELATIONS

| | |
|---|---|
| 1875 | First Factory Commission appointed by UK colonial government. |
| 1877 | First recorded strike on pay, Empress Mills, Nagpur. |
| 1881 | First *Factory Act*. |
| 1890 | Bombay Mill-Hands' Association (first organisation of workers) formed by N.M. Lokhanday. |
| 1908 | First political strike to protest six-years prison sentence to Lokmanya Tilak. |
| 1918 | First modern union formed, Madras Labour Union. |
| 1918 | Workers' protest led by Mahatma Gandhi in textile mills in Ahmedabad. |
| 1920 | Formation of Textile Labour Association in Ahmedabad. |
| 1920 | AITUC formed by Indian National Congress; later associated with CPI and affiliated to World Federation of Trade Unions. |
| 1926 | *Indian Trade Unions Act 1926* provides for registration of unions and extending immunity from civil suits and criminal conspiracy. |
| 1929 | *Trade Disputes Act 1929*: first law providing for state intervention in industrial disputes. |
| 1933 | Formation of EFI, affiliate of IOE. |
| 1940 | First large strike (40 days) in Bombay, demanding cost-of-living allowance. |
| 1940 | (22–23 January) First Indian Labour conference (tripartite, voluntary and national). |
| 1946 | *Bombay Industrial Relations Act 1946*, a provincial (state) law to govern unions and industrial disputes. |
| 1946 | *Industrial Employment Standing Orders Act 1946*, to regulate terms and conditions of work. |
| 1947 | (1 April) *Industrial Disputes Act 1947*. |
| 1947 | (May) The INC formed its labour wing, INTUC. |
| 1947 | (15 August) Independence from UK rule. |
| 1948 | HMS, allied with the Socialist Party, formed as a breakaway from AITUC (affiliated to ITUC). |
| 1948 | *Factories Act 1948* to regulate conditions of work. |
| 1948 | *Minimum Wages Act* to provide for extension and revision of minimum wages for scheduled employment including agriculture. |
| 1950 | (26 January) Constitution of India implemented. |
| 1953 | AIOE formed. |
| 1955 | BMS allied with BJP, affiliated with an international federation. |
| 1956 | CIE formed—constituents are EFI, AIOE and Standing Conference of Public Sector Enterprises. |

| | |
|---|---|
| 1964 | (31 October – 7 November) CPI(M) formed as a breakaway from CPI, during annual conference, Calcutta. |
| 1965 | *Payment of Bonus Act 1965*. |
| 1966 | National Commission on Labour (NCL) appointed; submitted its report in 1969. |
| 1969 | Split in Congress Party led by Indira Gandhi; later, she forms Congress Party. |
| 1970 | CITU formed, aligned with CPI(M) and affiliated with World Federation of Trade Unions. |
| 1972 | Formation of SEWA under the *Trade Unions Act 1926*. |
| 1973 | The *Contract Labour (Regulation & Abolition) Act 1970*; provides for the abolition of the old contract labour system and regulation of contract labour under new terms. |
| 1973 | Standing Conference of Public Enterprises formed as an apex of the Central Public Sector Enterprises. |
| 1974 | Some 1.7 million workers in the Indian Railways strike for 20 days. |
| 1975 (June) – 1977 (March) | Internal Emergency regime during which constitutional and democratic rights are frozen. |
| 1976 | Though adopted in 1956 by the Indian parliament, the term 'socialist' is added to the Preamble to the Indian Constitution by the 42nd Amendment. |
| 1976 | Chapter V-B inserted in the *Industrial Disputes Act 1947*, requiring prior permission to lay off or retrench workers and close establishments for employers with 300 or more workers in defined industrial establishments. |
| 1976 | *Equal Remuneration Act 1976, Bonded Labour (Abolition) Act 1976*. |
| 1977 | Defeat of Indira Gandhi and her Congress Party; restoration of democracy. |
| 1982–84 | Bombay textile strike, led by maverick union leader Dr Datta Samant. |
| 1982–84 | *Industrial Disputes Act* amended to reduce the scope of Chapter V-B to establishments employing more than 99 workers. |
| 1986 | *Child Labour (Prohibition & Regulation) Act 1986* prohibits employment of children under the age of fourteen in hazardous work. |
| 1990 | (May) Participation of Worker in Management Bill 1990 introduced in Rajya Sabha, but never passed. |
| 1991 | Congress government initiates the reform process by introducing the New Economic Policy. |
| 1999 | Second National Commission on Labour appointed; submits its report in 2002. |

| | |
|---|---|
| 2002 | The 86th Amendment to Constitution of India (A. 21-A) makes free and compulsory education for all children between the ages of six and fourteen a fundamental right. |
| 2003 | Supreme Court holds that government employees have no fundamental, statutory, moral or equitable right to strike. |
| 2004 | Government appoints NCEUS; submits reports in 2006, 2007 and 2011. |
| 2005 | *Mahatma Gandhi National Rural Employment Guarantee Act* entitles families in rural areas 100 days of unskilled work at the minimum wage prescribed by the government. |
| 2008 | *Unorganised Workers' Social Security Act*. |
| 2013 | *Sexual Harassment of Women at Workplace (Prevention, Prohibition & Redressal) Act*. |
| 2014 | Street Vendors (Protection of Livelihood and Regulation of Street Vending) Bill. |

# CHAPTER 14

# Conclusions: Beyond Varieties of Capitalism, towards convergence and internationalisation?

Chris F. Wright, Nick Wailes, Russell D. Lansbury and Greg J. Bamber

The preceding chapters have provided a review of key features of employment relations in twelve countries. In this chapter, we examine some of the similarities and differences in employment relations across these countries, and consider what the analysis tells us about the important factors shaping contemporary employment relations around the world.

Chapter 1 discussed the concept of Varieties of Capitalism, and argued that it provides a useful starting framework for thinking about how to compare national employment relations systems. In this chapter, we reassess the Varieties of Capitalism (VoC) framework in light of the evidence presented in the country-specific chapters. We argue that while these chapters provide evidence that supports aspects of the VoC approach, they also help to identify some of the limitations of this framework. The country chapters point to other key factors that need to be taken into account when seeking to explain similarities and differences in employment relations across countries. We focus in particular on the interplay between national institutional arrangements and sectoral variables—that is, features of industry sectors derived from technology, production and regulatory arrangements that shape employment relations outcomes. We argue that the combination of these two approaches offers a way for people to gain a greater understanding of contemporary employment relations developments. We also draw attention to the ways in which the international actors and institutions influence outcomes at the national level.

The next section gives a brief assessment of the extent to which the preceding chapters provide empirical support for some of the key aspects of the VoC approach. We then examine evidence of increased diversity within national patterns of employment relations, focusing in particular on some indicators of this trend: growth in non-standard employment, differences in employer preferences for coordination, and growth in the use of outsourcing and offshoring. Finally, we discuss some of the ways in which the international dimension impacts national patterns of employment relations.

## CONVERGENCE TOWARDS A LIBERAL MODEL?

At the beginning of this book, we asked whether, given the increasing interconnectedness of the global economy, we are witnessing the end of diversity in employment relations. One of the clearest trends emerging from the twelve country chapters is the tendency of each country to adopt increasingly liberal employment relations policies. As Baccaro and Howell (2011: 522) argue, it seems that national systems 'are being transformed in a common [liberal] direction'. However, this trend has not been uniform in either its speed or its scope. Rather, the evidence seems consistent with Thelen's (2014: p. xx) claim that 'common liberalizing pressures . . . are being channelled in different ways'.

Despite a broadly similar trajectory, national institutions still matter, and have a continuing impact on key employment relations issues such as the setting of pay and other working conditions, how the interests of employers and employees are represented and the form of employment. This is consistent with one of the core propositions of the VoC approach: rather than there being one best way of organising a market economy, similar levels of economic performance can be produced under different sets of institutional arrangements (Hall & Soskice 2001).

A key contribution of the VoC literature to understanding comparative employment relations is the distinction made between *coordinated market economies* (CMEs), where firms coordinate their activities through forms of non-market mechanisms such as multi-employer collective bargaining, and *liberal market economies* (LMEs), where firms rely primarily upon market forms of coordination, such as enterprise-level determination, to set wages and develop competencies (Hall & Soskice 2001; Hamann & Kelly 2008). The evidence from the twelve countries examined in this book suggests that these different modes of coordination continue to produce differences in employment relations practices and outcomes across countries, although the pattern is not simple.

Forms of non-market coordination remain a key feature of many CMEs—for example, through the persistence of strong cooperation among employers in Denmark and in the German manufacturing sector over pay determination and skill formation, as reflected in high levels of collective bargaining coverage. Non-market coordination also remains a feature of employment relations among some LMEs, and countries that fall somewhere in between the LME and CME categories. For example, Australia has an award system—pay 'safety nets' for each occupation and industry; France and Italy have their own distinctive forms of corporatism; and Korea has a business conglomerate (*chaebol*) system where production systems are vertically integrated between firms.

Notwithstanding the persistence of non-market coordination in such examples, a stronger pattern of market-based coordination has been developed in countries with distinct national systems. There has been a growth in workplace-level collective bargaining in France (largely due to the requirements for the parties to negotiate over working time arrangements following the introduction of the 35-hour week) and some minor sector-specific victories for unions—for example, in Australia, the United Kingdom and the United States. Aside from these examples, there have been no successful recent attempts to construct new forms of non-market coordination among the twelve countries examined in this book. Such attempts, where they have occurred, have been thwarted by actors seeking to defend current forms of market-based coordination. For instance, while unions in Korea have sought to strengthen bargaining coordination at the sector level, this has been attenuated by opposition from large enterprises and conservative governments. The Blair Labour government in the United Kingdom strengthened statutory rights for individual workers, but was unwilling to answer calls from unions for a return to multi-employer bargaining. It may have been expected that the post-2007 global financial crisis would generate renewed interest in non-market coordination as a preventative antidote to market failure. Instead, there has been a strengthening and extension of market forms of coordination among countries, including CMEs as well as LMEs.

Among LMEs, workplace-level bargaining has been reaffirmed as the main arena for determining pay and conditions, while managerial prerogative has been enhanced. This outcome, assisted by tribunal decisions (in Australia) and legislative reform (in the United Kingdom, the United States and Canada), can be interpreted as a consolidation of the prevailing logic of market coordination. Unions continue to be marginalised to a relatively greater degree in these countries, including through government intervention to curtail protections on collective bargaining and industrial action. Recent developments in employment relations among LMEs—as demonstrated in the chapters on Australia, Canada, the United Kingdom and the United States—lends some support to Colvin and Darbishire's (2013: 1049) claim that 'a common "Anglo-American" model is now emerging'. While distinct features continue to exist in each of these countries, there has been 'substantial convergence in the legal foundations of the industrial relations systems [among LMEs] as the voluntarist and award models have broken down and been replaced by new legal frameworks' (1049).

Turning to CMEs and other countries, the Danish and French employment relations systems have remained relatively stable. This is also true in Italy, although to a lesser extent, given the increased importance of enterprise-level bargaining since the post-2007 global financial crisis. However, there has been considerable change in the systems of Germany and other countries sharing elements of the CME model, such as Japan and Korea. While the German system of non-market coordination persists in the manufacturing sector, it is being replaced by employment relations arrangements exhibiting LME-type features among private services sector firms and small and medium-sized employers. These employers have opted out of sectoral bargaining in favour of enterprise-based determination—typically without unions. Lifetime employment, traditionally a hallmark of the Japanese system, has come under pressure from a more shareholder-driven model of corporate governance, and led to a notable growth in non-standard and precarious employment. Similar outcomes are identified in Korea.

As observed in Chapter 1, the traditional VoC approach, which contrasts only two major varieties of capitalism, appears too restrictive to analyse key features of the broad range of countries covered in this book. For example, neither France nor Italy can easily be accommodated in the CME framework. Perhaps more significantly, it is even more challenging to accommodate many of the rapidly developing economies in the VoC framework—particularly those in Asia that are playing an increasingly important role in the global economy.

Some have argued that we could identify additional varieties of capitalism, such as Mediterranean or even Asian market economies (Rhodes et al. 2007; Yeung 2000). An alternative view is that the focus solely on the institutional ensemble within which enterprises operate should be supplemented with consideration of a broader range of factors that can influence the employment relationship at a national level, such as the distinct features that often exist at a sector level (Bechter et al. 2012).

## INCREASING WITHIN-COUNTRY DIVERSITY

The country chapters also raise doubts about another aspect of the original VoC approach: the assumption that because enterprises operate within the same institutional ensemble, they will tend to resolve coordination problems in a similar fashion. The implication is that there is likely to be diversity between CMEs and LMEs, but strong similarities within particular national contexts. Contrary to this inference, the country chapters provide evidence that employment relations practices and outcomes are becoming increasingly diverse *within countries*. Over time, a greater range of employment relations practices and outcomes are emerging within each country—a pattern that is consistent with Katz and Darbishire's (2000) notion of 'converging divergences'. We focus here on three aspects of this broader trend: the rise of non-standard employment, the emergence of dual patterns of employer coordination and the growing use of outsourcing.

### The rise in non-standard work

Most of the country chapters point to the persistence or growth in 'non-standard' or atypical forms of employment. While the form that non-standard employment takes differs from country to country, in the majority of cases it is less secure and offers fewer protections than standard forms of employment, such as permanent full-time contracts. For this reason, it is often referred to as 'precarious employment' (Kalleberg 2009). Non-standard employment tends to be associated more strongly with the LME countries because it is generally underpinned by employment contracts of limited duration or uncertain status (e.g. in terms of the number of guaranteed weekly working hours), in contrast to standard open-ended and generally permanent employment relationships.

However, the growth of non-standard employment is becoming increasingly widespread. As several chapters show, the rising incidence of precarious work has contributed to growing income inequality and labour market segmentation and polarisation. Non-standard employment tends to be concentrated among women, younger and migrant workers—especially those employed in small and medium-sized enterprises (SMEs). Workers engaged on non-standard contracts often have lower pay and restricted upward labour mobility (McDowell & Christopherson 2009).

The weakening of collective forms of representation and regulation has exacerbated the spread of non-standard and precarious forms of employment. Across many countries, there is a trend for union membership and collective bargaining coverage to become increasingly concentrated in the public sector, in larger enterprises and in some sectors such as transport, mining and heavy industry. With few exceptions, unions have been less successful in organising workers in the private services sector and those employed by SMEs. In some cases, this contrast is especially stark. For example, in Japan unions remain reasonably strong in enterprises employing more than 1000 employees (45 per cent membership density), but have very weak coverage in firms with fewer than 100 employees (only 1 per cent density) (see Chapter 10). Similar trends have contributed to a fragmentation of the formerly strong system of sectoral collective bargaining in Germany, where employers in the non-unionised private services sector have been inclined to eschew sectoral agreements in favour of enterprise-specific arrangements. Similar outcomes are evident in emerging economies. For example, in India unions have hardly any members in the very large private 'informal' sector, thus limiting their capacity to extend collective bargaining and employment rights to the vast majority of the Indian workforce, who lack such protections.

Although the characteristics of non-standard work make it difficult to organise the growing number of workers on the periphery of the labour market, unions in some countries have not adapted their structures and strategies to confront this reality. The chapters on Japan, Korea and Germany show that unions in those countries have largely maintained a sectional focus on protecting the interests of their shrinking membership base of 'core' workers with permanent employment. However, in LME countries such as the United Kingdom, the United States and Australia, where the trend towards precarious and low-paid jobs has been evident since at least the late twentieth century, we see certain unions investing resources into innovative organising and campaigning activities to reach non-standard workers. The success of these and similar initiatives to strengthen collective regulation has been limited, but Stone and Arthurs (2013) suggest that they may provide some insight into the likely future responses by unions and other labour market actors to any further growth in precarious work, especially if conventional strategies continue to prove ineffective.

## Dual patterns of employer coordination

In many of the countries discussed in this book, there are growing differences in the coordination strategies adopted by various types of employers. This is having the effect of increasing the diversity in employment relations practices and outcomes within countries, and eroding national patterns. In some cases, these growing differences reflect a shift in industry composition. In Australia, for example, there has been a marked shift away from non-market coordination of skills development and pay determination, which were favoured by manufacturing employers, whose influence has waned. By contrast, there is a strong preference for market coordination among employers in the private services and resource sectors, which have experienced considerable growth in the twenty-first century. This shift in the dominant employer coordination preferences has served to embed the 'liberal' features of Australia's employment relations system, thereby affirming the country's status as an LME.

In other countries, there are differences between employers according to organisation size or the extent to which they are operating in 'tradable', or internationally exposed, sectors. The chapter on Italy suggests that there is a divergence in employer preferences between large enterprises favouring non-market coordination and smaller operations favouring market coordination. In Germany, there is a 'dualist' system where long-standing preferences for non-market coordination continues among industrial, finance and public sector employers, but market coordination preferences are becoming increasingly evident among private services sector and small business employers. This dualist trend illustrates the extent to which sectoral issues, such as the mix of industries within a particular national economy, can impact on employment relations patterns independently of national-level institutional arrangements.

Thelen (2014) argues that one of the most significant limitations of the VoC framework is that it equates the coordination preferences of all employers with the specific preferences of manufacturing employers. She notes that the structural shift from manufacturing to services that has occurred in nearly all developed economies 'has upset previous political dynamics because both firms and workers in these emerging sectors have interests that are very different from their counterparts in traditional manufacturing' (25). Whereas manufacturing employers might prefer CME-type arrangements, such as long-term employment relationships and skill regimes focused on the development of enterprise and industry-specific skills, service sector employers favour general and portable skill regimes and arrangements that facilitate flexible employment relationships (25–8).

Appelbaum et al. (2010), in their study of low-paid work in six developed economies, explore the interplay between national regulation and sectoral characteristics. They argue that high collective bargaining coverage across industrial sectors and 'inclusive' regimes of employment regulation have largely contained low-paid work in Denmark and, to a lesser extent, France. Conversely, low collective bargaining coverage has encouraged its growth in countries with 'market' regimes such as the the United Kingdom and the United States. However, they also note the emergence of a dualist regulatory regime in Germany, with a high incidence of low-paid work, the growing prevalence of 'low-road' employer strategies and 'institutional avoidance' of collective bargaining in some if not all contexts (Appelbaum et al. 2010: 20–7; see also Gallie 2007).

Yet this study also shows that, in some cases, sectoral characteristics are more important than national regulatory frameworks. Using the example of the hotel industry, Appelbaum et al. (2010) show that the type of work makes it very difficult for unions in all countries to organise workers, negotiate collective agreements and enforce labour laws compared with other industries, leading to similar outcomes in the hotel industry in countries with diverse employment relations systems.

However, this is not the case in other industries. In health and retail, for example, US workers in jobs that are low paid and low skilled and with routinised task requirements (such as nursing assistants and sales clerks) tend to have much worse working conditions and career advancement opportunities than their counterparts in Denmark, where protective institutions generally lead to better prospects for workers in these jobs (Appelbaum et al. 2010; see also Gautié & Schmitt 2010). Sector-based logics, then, may cut across national systems, thus enabling increased diversity in employment relations outcomes within countries. Without discounting the influence of national systems, we would argue that the role of sector-level variables—such as technology, the labour process, the organisation of production and product market regulations—needs to be given considerable weight as a potential influence on comparative employment relations outcomes (Locke 1992; Katz & Darbishire 2000; Batt et al. 2009; Bechter et al. 2012).

## Outsourcing and organisational fragmentation

A third aspect of the increased diversity within national patterns of employment relations relates to the outsourcing and offshoring of existing business activities. The growth in these forms of 'organisational fragmentation' has stark implications for employment relations practices and the resilience of national systems. The country chapters suggest that this trend is evident among LMEs, CMEs and emerging economies such as China and India.

The large number of enterprises engaging in outsourcing or subcontracting has contributed to labour market polarisation in several of the countries in this book. For example, in countries as diverse as the United Kingdom and Korea, large numbers of 'supplier firms' are using non-standard labour and adopting low-road employment relations practices in response to the commercial pressures imposed by 'lead enterprises' located further up the supply chain.

The common practice among many US enterprises to offshore parts of their activities to countries with lower pay represents a challenge for US unions seeking to protect the jobs and working conditions of their members. Since the 1980s, many Japanese manufacturers have created a large number of jobs in offshore subsidiaries situated in countries where the cost of labour is relatively cheap. This has coincided with a decline in manufacturing employment in Japan. In China, employment agencies engaging large numbers of low-paid workers have been the beneficiaries of widespread downsizing among state-owned enterprises (SOEs) and of significant migration of workers from rural to urban areas.

Even in Denmark—a country that has largely resisted the trend towards market-based coordination—the European Union (EU) Posted Workers Directive has enabled Danish firms to circumvent collective agreements by hiring workers through subcontractors registered in Central and Eastern European countries with lower pay rates. This process has allowed these firms to gain similar cost advantages to those that might otherwise have been achieved through offshoring. In Germany—another CME—Doellgast (2012) points to the close connections between the use of outsourcing and the 'de-verticalisation' being carried out by German enterprises, and the emergence of non-unionised bargaining and contingent employment practices.

While there are 'networked' forms of inter-organisational arrangements involving enduring and trust-based business relationships, which are associated with non-market coordination, outsourcing and offshoring often entail a shift to a more market-oriented relationship between a lead firm and a supplier firm governed by commercial imperatives (see Gereffi et al. 2005; Marchington et al. 2005). Therefore, even in CMEs, increased use of outsourcing and offshoring is likely to produce a greater incidence of more 'liberal' employment relations than we would expect to find in LMEs.

## THE INTERNATIONAL DIMENSION

Similarities in the trajectories of changes in national employment relations and evidence of increasing diversity within national systems suggest the need to go beyond some of the assumptions of the VoC approach and to examine a broader range of factors that can shape national patterns of employment relations. So far, we have argued for the need to pay greater attention to sectoral factors. In this section, we turn to the role of international actors and institutions as well as cross-border forms of business activity. It seems somewhat ironic that, in an era when national economies are becoming increasingly interconnected, the dominant theoretical frameworks for explaining similarities and differences between countries—like the VoC approach—tend to emphasise national-level variables and to downplay the role of international factors.

As noted in Chapter 1, we seek to adopt both a comparative *and* an international approach to employment relations. In this section, we argue that a focus on international actors and institutions helps to explain increased levels of diversity across national patterns of employment relations. Furthermore, there are important developments taking place across and beyond national borders that impact on employment relations in each of the countries under consideration. We suggest that there are good reasons for the VoC framework to be supplemented by a greater understanding of how nation states and national-level actors and institutions are integrated and enmeshed in a broader international system.

## Multinational enterprises and global supply chains

As this book demonstrates, globalisation has not created uniform market pressures in all countries, and has not completely eroded the differences that exist between countries. Nonetheless, we see evidence in each chapter that international pressures impact the employment relationship and how it is regulated in some sectors of each economy. Two important international trends influencing outcomes in each of the countries examined in this book are the increasing extent to which global economic activity in concentrated in multinational enterprises (MNEs) that operate across national borders, and the growing tendency for local enterprises to be incorporated into global supply chains (GSCs). These two factors are often—although not always—connected, and are both potential drivers of increased pressure for liberalisation and increased diversity within national employment relations systems.

It has been argued that MNEs have a tendency to adopt the employment relations policies and frameworks of the host countries in which they operate. This view largely assumes that MNEs operate as multi-domestic firms, servicing each national market separately and operating independently of subsidiaries in other countries. In this context, it makes sense for MNEs to adopt the employment relations practices of the host country (Katz & Wailes 2014).

Research on employment relations in MNEs has found that while host-country institutional constraints require at least some adaptation by MNEs, their employment relations practices generally reveal a strong country-of-origin or home-country effect. Studies of US MNEs operating in Europe, for example, have shown the tendency of these firms to adopt centralised human resources policies with an emphasis on performance management, workplace diversity and anti-unionism (e.g. Ferner et al. 2001). Thus, while the transfer of employment relations practices across US MNEs is in part shaped by institutional arrangements in the host country and power relations between corporate headquarters and the subsidiary, they are also influenced by distinctive features of the US national business system, including the structure of capital markets and the dominant form of corporate governance (Clark & Almond 2006). Related research into German MNEs suggests that 'the consensual thrust of German employment relations . . . has strongly coloured the internationalization process' (Ferner & Quintanilla 1998: 726). Thus, German MNEs tend to encourage employee cooperation, make relatively high investments in training and are less likely to use widespread downsizing than MNEs from other countries (Ferner et al. 2001). Ferner (1997) argues that this tendency of MNEs to diffuse key employment relations practices across their subsidiaries reflects the extent to which MNEs and their managers are embedded in the institutional context of their home countries.

More recently, it has been argued that, while the institutional context of the country of origin remains important, the firm's corporate strategy, its structure and the markets in which it operates also influence MNE employment relations strategies (Edwards et al. 2005; Pudelko & Harzing 2007; Hall & Wailes 2009). In many cases, these factors result in MNEs aiming to adopt common policies and practices across their subsidiaries, including in the areas relevant to employment relations (Katz & Wailes 2014). Whether the primary driver for MNEs is to reproduce the employment relations patterns of their home country or to adopt a global pattern of employment relations consistent with the firm's global strategic direction, MNEs are likely to be an important source of diversity in national patterns of employment relations as a result (Lane & Wood 2009).

GSCs—that is, buyer–supplier relationships between enterprises across national boundaries—have a similar potential impact on national patterns of employment relations. As is the case with MNEs, there is also evidence of a country-of-origin effect on the way GSCs operate and in their implications for employment relations among suppliers in other countries. Konzelmann et al. (2005), for example, argue that the 'transactional' arrangements that US MNE retailers like Wal-Mart typically establish with suppliers can be expected to produce more stringent cost pressures, which are likely to result in the transfer of LME-type employment relations practices further down the supply chain. In contrast, the supply chain practices of Swedish MNEs such as IKEA tend to be more long term and 'relational', thus producing CME-oriented employment relations practices at the supplier level (see also Lane 2008).

Lakhani et al. (2013) provide a useful framework for thinking about the impact of GSCs on patterns of employment relations. Noting that 'traditional employment relations theories that focus on individual firms embedded in distinct national contexts are no longer adequate for the analysis of employment relations in a globalised era' (440), they identify five different configurations that GSCs can take and the implications of each for employment relations. For instance, in market-based supply chains characterised by suppliers and buyers exchanging standard products, Lakhani and colleagues argue that the influence of the lead firm on the employment relations of the supplier firm is likely to be low and that the national institutions of the supplier will be most relevant. This contrasts with 'captive' supply chain arrangements, in which the lead firm has the ability to exert considerable influence on the employment relations of the supplier firm, while the national institutional context of both the lead company and the supplier firm is also likely to be significant. The key point is that differences in GSCs can produce differences in employment relations dynamics. As shown in some of the country chapters, the extent to which firms in a specific country are integrated into different types of GSCs can be an important source of diversity within and between national systems.

## International institutions

The VoC approach tends to assume that the institutional arrangements that affect how employers resolve coordination problems in a market economy are national in character, and separate from and independent of the institutional arrangements that exist in other countries. However, the research on MNEs and GSCs reveals that this is not always the case; rather, MNEs and GSCs have the potential to link different institutional domains together (Morgan & Kristensen 2006). This is an example of a more general point: in an increasing interconnected global economy, national economies tend to be *institutionally incomplete* (Deeg & Jackson 2007). That is, all of the institutional arrangements that are relevant to shaping the behaviour of employment relations actors in a particular national economy are not necessarily located in the *same* national economy (Wailes 2008).

There are formal institutions beyond the level of the nation state that can have both direct and indirect impacts on laws and regulations at a national level (Gumbrell-McCormick 2008). A good example is the extent to which employment relations in most European countries are shaped by developments at the EU level. In the United Kingdom, for example, the European Directive on Information and Consultation resulted in the introduction of—albeit limited—statutory consultation rights for UK workers for the first time. While EU regulations have improved working conditions for employees in some Member States, EU-level developments have tended to erode protective national-level institutions in others. The decisions of the European Court of Justice have placed limits on the ability of unions to enforce national regulations on employers engaging 'posted workers' from other countries, as outlined in Chapter 9, on Denmark. EU institutions such as the European Commission and the European Central Bank have influenced the decisions of governments (particularly in Southern Europe) to weaken provisions for sectoral bargaining as part of the package of austerity measures imposed in the wake of the post-2007 global financial crisis (Marginson 2014).

As these examples suggest, institutions beyond the level of the nation state can have complex and contradictory implications for employment relations in particular countries. The International Labour Organization (ILO) has been the main agency for developing and enforcing international labour standards (Engerman 2003). The ILO was founded in 1919 as part of the World War I peace treaty. In 1946, the ILO became the first specialist agency of the newly formed United Nations. Since its inception, the ILO has been involved in promoting international labour standards through the use of conventions and recommendations. Conventions, once ratified by member states, are meant to be legally binding, while recommendations are advisory standards that are designed to assist member states to apply a convention (whether ratified or not) to their local setting. These instruments deal with a wide range of issues, including fundamental human rights such as freedom of association, equality of treatment and the abolition of forced labour; occupational health and safety; working conditions; social security and workers' compensation; labour administration; migrant workers; and the specific needs or circumstances of particular occupational groups. Collectively, these standards are referred to as the International Labour Code.

Has the impact of the ILO been diluted by the influence of other international institutions tasked with promoting international trade liberalisation? International institutions played a key role in reforming the formal international trade rules, which relaxed trade barriers and gave firms increased access to foreign markets, driving both liberalisation and the growth of MNEs and GSCs. These changes have been introduced through bilateral and multinational free-trade agreements. Multilateral trade liberalisation began in the 1940s, with the negotiation of the General Agreement on Tariffs and Trade, and led to the formation in 1996 of the World Trade Organization (WTO), another United Nations agency. Its aim is to promote free trade and to provide mechanisms for the resolution of trade disputes between member countries (Wilkinson 2002a).

During the processes of trade liberalisation, there has been considerable debate as to whether these agreements should include reference to minimum labour standards. In the lead-up to the formation of the WTO, the United States (supported by France) sought the inclusion of minimum labour standards in the new rules of world trade (Wilkinson 2002a). This occurred because US policy-makers argued that without enforceable minimum labour standards, US (and French) workers would be faced with unfair competition from countries where there were no protections against child labour and other practices. So this would precipitate a 'race to the bottom' in relation to terms and conditions of employment. One of the main sources of opposition to this 'social clause' came from developing countries, which argued that minimum labour standards would be used as a form of non-tariff barrier, and would limit their access to the markets of developed economies. Despite a vigorous campaign by labour movements, ultimately there was no direct inclusion of labour standards in the rules of the WTO; nor were social items to be the grounds for trade disputes between countries (Hughes & Wilkinson 1998; Wilkinson 2002b, 2002c).

However, in rejecting the inclusion of labour standards in the rules of international trade, the WTO recognised the ILO as 'the competent body to set and deal with these standards and we affirm our support for its work in promoting them' (WTO Singapore Ministerial Declaration 1996, cited in Hughes 2005: 416). According to Hughes, this created the conditions for a significant change in the strategic direction of the ILO, as it sought to re-establish its relevance in an era of globalisation. The first sign of this new strategy was the 1998 Declaration on Fundamental Principles and Rights at Work and Its Follow-Up. This

**Table 14.1  ILO core labour standards**

| Fundamental principle | Relevant convention |
|---|---|
| Freedom of association and the effective recognition of the right to collective bargaining | 87 (Freedom of Association and Protection of the Right to Organise) and 98 (Right to Organise and Collective Bargaining) |
| The elimination of all forms of forced or compulsory labour | 29 (Forced Labour) and 105 (Abolition of Forced Labour) |
| The effective abolition of child labour | 138 (Minimum Age) and 182 (Worst Forms of Child Labour) |
| The elimination of discrimination in respect of employment and occupation | 100 (Equal Remuneration) and 111 (Discrimination, Occupation and Employment) |

*Source:* ILO (2009).

declaration summarises what the ILO regards as universal and core labour standards, and was binding on member states (see Table 14.1).

The ILO's Decent Work Agenda builds on these core labour standards. Its aim is the achievement of 'decent work for all by promoting social dialogue, social protection and employment creation, as well as respect for international labour standards' (ILO 2009). The principles of the Decent Work Agenda are contained in the Declaration on Social Justice for a Fair Globalization, which was adopted by the ILO's General Assembly in June 2008. The Decent Work Agenda represents an attempt to extend the ILO objectives in recognition of the growth of non-traditional forms of work, and to integrate its programs within a single conceptual framework.

Addressing the challenges facing the ILO as it nears a century since its foundation, the director general of the ILO, Guy Ryder (2015), has expressed his concern about the role of multilateral organisations within the United Nations system:

> There's a fundamental question about whether in this globalised environment in which we live, the multilateral system is seen as being fit for the purpose in addressing the global challenges that confront us all. I worry that we are seeing a retreat from multilateralism. One could easily see a process by which multilateral endeavour is basically abandoned in favour of regional cohesion and action.

## Global labour activism

Formal international institutions are not the only way in which the international dimension can impact on national patterns of employment relations. There is a long history of international cooperation between labour movements, or *labour internationalism*. Just as firms look for international opportunities, workers and their representatives can and do attempt to use the international dimension to support their interests.

Traditionally, one of the ways labour has sought to advance its interests is through collective bargaining with employers. Some have suggested that, with the increasing internationalisation of business, labour needs to pursue opportunities for transnational collective bargaining—that is, collective bargaining between multinationals and their workers (and perhaps also the workers of their suppliers) in more than one country. However, as Haworth (2005) notes, there are many inherent difficulties in and obstacles to transnational collective bargaining, which suggest that this goal is unlikely to be achieved. These include management hostility to the extension of collective bargaining, fear of loss of sovereignty by national unions, lack of membership support, differences within national employment relations systems that are hard to reconcile and the lack of an international regulatory framework. Even in the European context, where the conditions for the development of transnational collective bargaining appear to be the most favourable, the weakening of multi-employer bargaining at the national level is undermining the opportunities for cross-border agreements (Marginson 2014).

Wills (1998) argues that globalisation requires labour to rethink its modes of representation and action. Evans (2010) suggests that while globalisation is a potential source of weakness for organised labour, it also presents opportunities for counter-mobilisation using less traditional forms. He points to evidence that the spread of mass digital communication has helped to bridge cultural and geographical gaps, and created networks between local and national labour activists. Evans also claims that the renewed interest in international labour rights and the conditions of workers at the lower ends of GSCs provides a vehicle for unions to build a common agenda at a transnational level.

One of the ways in which organised labour has responded to intensified international market pressures is through reforming the structures of international unions. The international union federations representing the joint interests of national-level unions covering specific occupational groups began in the late nineteenth century. In recent years, there has been a series of mergers of these federations into ten global union federations (GUFs), which were created as industry or multi-industry organisations with more efficient organisational structures to enhance cross-border union activity (Croucher & Cotton 2011).

Some doubt whether a reform of the international structures of unions is enough to revitalise labour internationalism. According to Evans (2010: 367), this outcome depends 'not on the success of any single organisational form or strategy, but on the ability of the movement to interconnect different forms in strategically effective ways'. In identifying the strategies that can allow labour activists to mobilise across national boundaries effectively, Donaghey et al. (2014: 246) claim that 'managing consumption relations in global supply chains . . . has become central to managing employment relations'. They argue that the increasingly globalised and inter-organisational nature of production requires unions to forge alliances with non-government organisations (NGOs) in developing 'consumer-oriented' strategies—that is, by mobilising consumers to pressure MNEs to improve working conditions among their offshore suppliers and subcontractors. But there are limitations to the claim of these authors that 'a critical mass of consumers have started to include ethical issues in their evaluations of products and services, potentially making consumer power a counter-force to globalization's race to the bottom' (233). Hainmueller and Hiscox's (2012) study of consumer behaviour for clothing sold under the banner of 'fair labour standards' found that certain consumer groups are more willing to purchase high-price fashion items produced in accordance with ILO standards. However, this is not true for consumers purchasing lower priced goods, which are likely to account for more sales. More generally, targeting the vulnerability of large firms to reputational damage and their aversion to bad media publicity, rather than seeking to mobilise consumer pressure alone, has been identified as a way for unions and NGOs to pressure these firms to improve labour standards among suppliers (Wright 2015a).

## International framework agreements and private labour regulation

The development of international framework agreements (IFAs) is another interesting development that reflects a change in the way workers and their representatives have sought to engage with employers in the context of globalisation. IFAs are voluntary agreements providing a framework of minimum labour standards negotiated between GUFs and MNEs. Many IFAs apply to the signatory firm's suppliers and subsidiaries, giving unions the potential to obtain 'a grip on the global supply chain, thereby extending (core) labour rights beyond national borders' (Hammer 2005: 525).

At a minimum, IFAs contain a commitment to freedom of association and the right to collective bargaining, and typically incorporate other core ILO labour standards. They also provide unions with formal representation at the corporate level of the enterprise. As Riisgaard (2005) points out, this representation at the corporate level offers unions the potential to overcome hostile management at a local level. IFAs also give GUFs a role in monitoring compliance with the agreement across the enterprise's operations. But as Davies et al. (2011) found when they examined the implementation of the IFA signed by Hotchief, a German construction firm, enforcement at the enterprise level is contingent upon the strength of local unions and the effectiveness of national employment relations institutions. The existence of weak institutions and regulatory frameworks 'renders the enforcement of compliance notorious, and, in some cases, unfeasible', according to Niforou (2012: 370), who is sceptical about the capacity of IFAs to systematically strengthen the role of organised labour in MNEs and their supply chains.

While IFAs have become a way for MNEs and GUFs to jointly regulate labour standards across national boundaries, only a relatively small number of agreements have been established (for a list, see Papadakis 2011: 245–68). The use of 'private regulation'—referred to variously as 'civil regulation', 'private social standards', 'sustainable sourcing mechanisms' and 'ethical sourcing mechanisms'—is a much more common way for MNEs to oversee labour arrangements across their global operations and supply chains. Private regulation involves MNEs implementing and monitoring voluntary standards to evaluate working conditions and management practices in their subsidiaries and suppliers. These instruments are most often found among firms that are brand sensitive or averse to reputational risk. They use private regulation as an independent means of establishing or certifying the practices of their suppliers, as a way of placating or undermining NGO and union campaigns, or to send a 'market signal' to consumers who demand certain standards of MNEs (O'Rourke 2003; Vogel 2008).

Corporate codes of conduct are the most usual form of private regulation. These codes are generally formulated unilaterally by MNEs, although often with informal input from NGOs or consultants. The contents of these codes vary, often containing provisions relating to core ILO standards (see Table 14.1), but rarely covering more substantive issues such as pay, benefits, working conditions and workplace health and safety. Although suppliers may be expected to comply with codes of conduct, monitoring and enforcement mechanisms tend to be very weak. Consequently, codes of conduct have been criticised for being tokenistic instruments that are used opportunistically by MNEs to enhance their association with socially responsible practices.

By contrast, multi-stakeholder initiatives are generally seen to be more effective than codes of conduct for maintaining labour standards. This is because such initiatives involve some form of verification from an NGO or other independent agencies, although some are viewed as being influenced too heavily by business interests. Examples of multi-stakeholder initiatives include labelling systems from which MNEs can obtain certification if they implement specified practices in their supply chains that withstand the scrutiny of independent evaluation. For instance, the Fairtrade Certification Mark and the Social Account-ability International 8000 standard are based on ILO core conventions and are overseen jointly by NGOs. Other examples include the Ethical Trading Initiative and the Fair Labor Association, which consist of MNE member firms, NGOs and unions, with the aim of improving supply chain practices of member firms through internal audits. In addition, international governance mechanisms, such as the UN Global Compact, the Organisation for Economic Cooperation and Development (OECD) Guidelines for Multinational Enterprises, the Global Reporting Initia-tive and the Global Social Compliance Program, are becoming more influential. These provide a baseline of good practice that firms can incorporate into their codes of conduct (O'Rourke 2003; Vogel 2008; Wright & Brown 2013: 431–7; Donaghey et al. 2014: 233–7).

There are conflicting views about the effectiveness of such forms of private regulation in protecting labour standards. Hassel (2008) argues that, notwithstanding the lack of a legal framework of global regulation and enforceability, patterns of local self-regulation, norm-setting and international codes can lead to higher expectations of the behaviour of firms that operate transnationally. She suggests also that this can become an indirect form of regulation. In particular, Hassel claims that international firms with high labour standards have strong incentives to ensure that other firms—particularly their competi-tors—comply with the standards to which they have committed, and will therefore be more likely to enter into alliances with NGOs and governments and to advocate the adoption of higher standards and the improved monitoring of outcomes. Others have suggested that private regulatory initiatives are more flexible and responsive to the structure of contemporary employing organisations compared with legislated protections and collective bargaining, but can nevertheless comple-ment and enhance these traditional forms rather than replacing them (see O'Rourke 2003; Ruggie 2004).

However, many are sceptical about the effectiveness of private initiatives for regulating labour standards in global production systems and supply chains. Critics claim that they represent an attempt to free business from traditional forms of employment regulation, displace independent forms of worker protection provided by unions and the state, provide a false sense of security to consumers, and serve only to protect lead firms against legal liability and reputational damage (O'Rourke 2003; Vogel 2008; Locke et al. 2013). In assessing the extent to which private regulation acts as a 'complement or substitute' to public regulation, Locke et al. (2013) conclude that, in countries with active government enforcement of labour standards, private regulation complements public regulation, but generally serves as a substitute to public regulation in contexts where government labour standards are poorly enforced.

Several high-profile cases involving severe breaches of labour standards by the offshore suppliers of MNEs have highlighted the 'governance deficit' relating to the protection of labour standards within GSCs. For example, the poor management practices that led to a spate of worker suicides at the Chinese operations of electronics manufacturer Foxconn were partly attributed to the commercial pressure around price, production quality and delivery deadlines imposed by major brands based in developed economies, such as Apple (Pun & Chan 2012).

Following the collapse of the Rana Plaza factory complex that killed more than 1100 workers in Bangladesh in 2013, there has been substantial international pressure for MNEs to take more responsibility for the labour practices of their suppliers in emerging economies (Ter Haar & Keune 2014). Unless international institutions such as the ILO are able to address the governance deficit in regulating labour standards across national borders, MNEs averse to the reputational damage associated with these incidents may rely on private and multi-stakeholder initiatives to ensure that standards within their GSCs are upheld (Wright & Brown 2013).

## BEYOND VARIETIES OF CAPITALISM

This book has provided an introduction to international and comparative employment relations and an analysis of contemporary developments. In this chapter we have reassessed the VoC framework in light of the evidence in each of the chapters. The analysis suggests that examining the national institutional context within which employers and employees operate is still important. Nevertheless, there are other factors—including the inherent features of industry sectors, and the connections between national economies, such as MNEs and international institutions—that also shape employment relations patterns. The implication is that students of employment relations need to go beyond simple models to examine the complex political, economic and social factors that influence work and how it is regulated in a rapidly changing international economy. Each of the country chapters in this book provides a framework and overview for more detailed analysis of this complex interplay.

## FURTHER READING

Baccaro, L. & Howell, C. (2011) 'A common neoliberal trajectory: The transformation of industrial relations in advanced capitalism'. *Politics & Society*, 39(4): 521–63.

Bechter, B., Brandl, B. & Meardi, G. (2012) 'Sectors or countries? Typologies and levels of analysis in comparative industrial relations'. *European Journal of Industrial Relations*, 18(3): 185–202.

Gautié, J. & Schmitt, J. (eds) (2010) *Low-Wage Work in the Wealthy World*. New York: Russell Sage Foundation.

Lakhani, T., Kuruvilla, S. & Avgar, A. (2013) 'From the firm to the network: Global value chains and employment relations theory'. *British Journal of Industrial Relations*, 51(3): 440–72.

Stone, K.V.W. & Arthurs, H. (2013) *Rethinking Workplace Regulation: Beyond the Standard Contract of Employment*. New York: Russell Sage Foundation.

## USEFUL WEBSITES

Ethical Trading Initiative: <www.ethicaltrade.org>.

Fair Labor Association: <www.fairlabor.org>.

GUFs and IFAs: <www.global-unions.org>.

ILO Decent Work Agenda: <www.ilo.org/global/about-the-ilo/decent-work-agenda/lang--de/index.htm>.

ILO Declaration on Fundamental Principles and Rights at Work: <www.ilo.org/declaration/lang--en/index.htm>.

OECD Guidelines for Multinational Enterprises: <www.oecd.org/corporate/mne>.

United Nations Global Compact: <www.unglobalcompact.org>.

WTO: <www.wto.org>.

361

# Notes

## Chapter 1 Introduction: An internationally comparative approach to employment relations

1 The Gini coefficient is a measure of the deviation of the distribution of income among individuals or households in a country from a perfectly equal distribution. A value of 0 represents equality, a value of 100 a very high degree of inequality; see World Bank (2013).

2 Apart from the OECD and Eurofound (an agency of the EU), other sources of international data that can be helpful when conducting comparative employment relations analysis include the ILO, World Bank, Eurostat and US Bureau of Labor Statistics; see: <http://www.ilo.org/ilostat>; <http://data.worldbank.org>; <http://ec.europa.eu/Eurostat>; <www.bls.gov>.

3 Outsider forms of corporate governance typically prioritise the enterprise's outside investors, mainly those who own stocks or shares. They may have only a short-term interest in the success of the enterprise.

4 Insider forms of corporate governance typically involve stakeholders who have a longer term interest in the performance of the enterprise, including banks that loan funds to it, as well as executives and other employees of the enterprise.

## Chapter 2 Employment relations in the United Kingdom

1 Earlier editions of the chapter were co-authored variously by Greg Bamber, John Berridge, John Goodman, Mick Marchington, Ed Snape and Andrew Timming. Jeremy Waddington has sole responsibility for this edition.

2 The United Kingdom comprises England, Northern Ireland, Scotland and Wales. Many people use the terms United Kingdom and Britain interchangeably, but Britain comprises only England, Scotland and Wales. Where possible, this chapter uses UK data.

3   Unless otherwise stated, data in the opening section of this chapter is drawn from the *Statistical Bulletin* published by the ONS published in January 2014 (ONS 2014). The data refer to November 2013 in most cases. Percentages cited are rounded to the nearest whole number.

4   The figure of 100 includes 32 employers' associations that are classified as 'unlisted' by the Certification Officer (2013).

5   The living wage is calculated by reference to an acceptable low-cost budget that constitutes basic living costs.

6   Eight countries from Eastern Europe joined the EU in 2004: <www.migrationobservatory.ox.ac.uk/briefings/migration-flows-a8-and-other-eu-migrants-and-uk>, accessed 3 November 2014.

### Chapter 3   Employment relations in the United States

1   The authors thank Hoyt Wheeler for permission to draw on the chapter he co-authored in an earlier edition of this book, especially in the historical section.

2   Using an alternative measure, GDP in terms of PPP, the IMF estimates that the size of China's economy (see Chapter 12) has overtaken that of the United States to become world's largest. PPP is an (imperfect) attempt to account for varying price levels between countries. See <http://blogs.ft.com/ftdata/2014/10/08/chinas-leap-forward-overtaking-the-us-as-worlds-biggest-economy>, accessed 10 December 2014.

### Chapter 4   Employment relations in Canada

1   We are grateful for the contributions Mark Thompson made to this chapter, as an author of earlier editions.

### Chapter 5   Employment relations in Australia

1   Earlier editions of the chapter were co-authored variously by Russell D. Lansbury, Nick Wailes and Ed Davis.

2   The FWC was originally Fair Work Australia, prior to its name change in January 2013.

### Chapter 6   Employment relations in Italy

1   Earlier editions of the chapter were co-authored variously by Serafino Negrelli, Claudio Pellegrini and Peter Sheldon.

2   See Union Members and Employees database, OECD, annual updating (1999 onwards) (web access restricted).

3   The information cited in this section is based on calculations on unpublished 2008 survey data, courtesy of the IRES-CGIL.

4   The official data on union density in the public sector presented in the previous section are a result of this legal requirement.

5   Authors' calculations on data from <www.aranagenzia.it>, accessed 20 September 2014.

**Chapter 7    Employment relations in France**

1    Earlier editions of the chapter were co-authored variously by Janine Goetschy, Annette Jobert and Jacques Rojot.

**Chapter 9    Employment relations in Denmark**

1    The unemployment insurance funds and the unions have always been treated as formally separate in the legislation, but have never been perceived as such in practice, until recent years. To use a sociological paradigm, we might say that when a situation is defined as real, it becomes real in its consequences (Ritzer 1977).

2    We should add that regulation via legislation has also been practised in such important areas as the working environment. This is partly because the first factory laws were enacted before the labour market actors were fully developed. But the labour market actors have also played a significant role in the system via their participation in national councils and a special system of cooperation at enterprise level. The actors have also been involved in formulating regular amendments to the legislation. The trend has been for the labour market actors to be accorded greater responsibility.

3    The expression 'yellow' trade unions is of French origin. Some of the first such alternative organisations were established in France in 1887, where they acted as strike-breakers. In violent conflicts, striking workers smashed windows in buildings housing the strike-breakers, which were subsequently patched with yellow paper (Friis & Hegna 1974: 550–1).

**Chapter 10    Employment relations in Japan**

1    We are grateful that Yasuo Kuwahara (Emeritus Professor, Dokkyo University) wrote earlier editions of the chapter. We also thank Shozo Inoue (Ibaraki Christian University) for his helpful comments.

2    Estimates in this paragraph are based on 2013 data from the Ministry of Health, Labour and Welfare.

3    Such estimates are generally based on 2012 data from the Ministry of Internal Affairs and Communication Labour Force Survey.

4    See <www.jpc-net.jp/eng> (accessed 20 December 2014).

5    In 2012, the survey carried out by the Ministry of Economy, Trade and Industry covered around 5000 Japanese enterprises with at least one overseas subsidiary (all sectors except finance, insurance and real estate). A subsidiary is one in which Japanese enterprises hold more than 10 per cent of capital. The survey began in 1971.

6    These changes included the 1997 revision of the anti-monopoly law, the 1999 revision of the Commercial Code, the 2001 revision of the Commercial Code for Corporate Divesture, the 2001 tax system for enterprise reorganisation, the 2003 revision of the Commercial Code, the 2003 revision to the Law on Special Measures for Industrial Revitalisation, the 2000 Civil Rehabilitation Law, the 2003 revision of the Corporate Reorganisation Law and the 2006 Company Law.

7    Performance means individual performance, which is rated by assessment by managers, rather than enterprise performance.

8    It has sometimes been difficult to distinguish one type of non-regular worker from another type. Moreover, different surveys have used different definitions of non-regular workers.

9    Data are collected every month by the Ministry of Internal Affairs; every June, it considers special topics, such as non-regular workers, in more detail.

## Chapter 11    Employment relations in South Korea

1    It is acknowledged that earlier editions of this chapter were co-authored variously by Young-bum Park and Chris Leggett.

2    The FKTU was formed in 1946 as the anti-communist union organisation, which was patronised by right-wing political leaders to fight against the All-Korean Labour Union, led by socialists. The FKTU was a partner supporting the authoritarian regime's labour policy until 1987.

3    The share of male members in total union membership increased from about 64 per cent in 1980 to 78 per cent in 2006 (KLI 2014).

4    Australian Prime Minister Bob Hawke, who visited Korea in 1989, gave President Tae-woo Roh advice about the tripartite social dialogue model and its achievements for forging labour–management cooperation and over-coming economic difficulties in Australia. President Roh was impressed with that approach, and sent government officials and research fellows to study Australia's experiences in early 1990.

5    The government expanded the scope of the *Minimum Wage Act* to include all businesses from November 2000.

6    There has been much debate on the size of the non-regular workforce, drawing upon the Economic Active Population Supplementary Survey conducted by the National Statistics Office yearly since 2002. The Labour Circle insists that the number of people in the non-regular workforce includes workers under recurrent renewal of temporary employment contracts, who are excluded by the government's statistics. According to the Labour Circle's estimate, for instance, the non-regular workforce in 2013 was around 46 per cent of the working population, compared with the government's estimate of less than 33 per cent.

7    Figure 11.1 in the 2011 edition of this book illustrates the growing pay discrepancy between large and small enterprises. Definitions of workplace size changed after the 2007 survey; subsequent data are not comparable (KLI 2014). Hence, it is not practicable to offer an updated version of Figure 11.1 in this edition.

8    Multiple unions were allowed at the national and sector levels by the 1997 TULRAA revision.

## Chapter 12    Employment relations in China

1    For a long period, the US economy was the largest in the world according to the usual indicator: relative levels of GDP. But using an alternative indicator—GDP in terms of PPP—the IMF estimates that the size of China's economy has overtaken that of the United States to become the world's largest economy. PPP is an (imperfect) attempt to account for varying price levels between countries. See Fray (2014).

2    'Democratic management' (民主管理) is a CCP management ideology
     introduced in the late 1950s that emphasises mass participation in all
     kinds of political activities, including enterprise management. The idea is
     for the majority to manage the majority.

3    On the Gini coefficient, see Chapter 1, note 1.

**Chapter 13    Employment relations in India**

1    We acknowledge that an earlier edition of this chapter was co-authored by
     the late C.S. Venkata Ratnam. We also thank the three anonymous referees
     and the editors for their helpful comments.

2    The legal framework for employment relations is defined mainly by
     four labour laws: the *Trade Unions Act 1926*, the *Industrial Employ-*
     *ment (Standing Orders) Act 1946*; the *Industrial Disputes Act 1947* and
     the *Contract Labour (Regulation and Abolition) Act 1970* (the *Contract*
     *Labour Act*).

3    Some state laws, like the Maharashtra *Industrial Relations Act 1946*,
     provide for recognition of trade unions among other organisations (Shyam
     Sundar 2008).

4    <http://bms.org.in/pages/BMSATGlance.aspx> (accessed 1 April 2014).

5    The full names of such unions are included in the list of abbreviations at
     the front of the book.

6    <www.simamills.org> (accessed 2 April 2014).

7    <www.upasi.org> (accessed 2 April 2014).

8    <www.efionline.in>, <www.aioe.in/htm/about.html> (accessed 2 April
     2014); Venkata Ratnam & Verma (2011).

9    <www.cii.in/about_us_History.aspx?enc=ns9fJzmNKJnsoQCyKqU
     maQ==> (accessed 2 April 2014).

10   <www.cii.in/Sector_Landing.aspx> (accessed 2 April 2014).

11   <www.scopeonline.in/genesis.htm>, accessed 2 April 2014.

12   <http://dpe.nic.in/important_links/dpe_guidelines/wage_policies/
     glch4aindex/glch04a16> (accessed 2 April 2014).

13   For a discussion on industrial violence in India, see Shyam Sundar (2012).
     See also Shyam Sundar (2010b); <http://sanhati.com/articles/5121>
     (accessed 3 April 2014).

14   <www.rsby.gov.in/about_rsby.aspx> (accessed 3 April 2014).

15   This includes factories, mines and plantations.

16   <http://articles.economictimes.indiatimes.com/2014–11–26/news/
     56490286_1_apprenticeship-act-small-firms-labour-laws-act>    (accessed
     27 November 2014).

17   <http://timesofindia.indiatimes.com/india/New-advisory-to-end-inspector
     -raj/articleshow/38036699.cms> (accessed 15 July 2014).

18   See Venkata Ratnam (1996) for a regional perspective on employment
     relations in India.

19   For data on settlement of industrial disputes by these courts, see <http://
     labour.nic.in/content/division/lok-adalat-ir.php> (accessed 10 April 2014).

# References

ACAS (2013) *Annual Report and Accounts 2012/13*. London: ACAS.

ACFIC (2015) Website. Retrieved 17 August 2014 from <www.chinachamber. org.cn/publicfiles/business/htmlfiles/qleng/s2569/index.html>.

Ackers, P. (2002) 'Reframing employment relations: The case for neo-pluralism'. *Industrial Relations Journal*, 33(1): 2–19.

Adams, R.J. (1980) *Industrial Relations Systems in Europe and North America*. Hamilton, ON: McMaster University.

Ahsan, A. & Pagés, C. (2009) 'Are all labor regulations equal? Assessing the effects of job security, labor disputes and contract labor laws in India'. Retrieved 3 May 2015 from <http://siteresources.worldbank.org/SOCIALPROTECTION/ Resources/SP-Discussionpapers/Labor-Market-DP/0713.pdf>.

AIAS (Amsterdam Institute for Advanced Labour Studies) (2013) *ICTWSS database—version 4*. Retrieved 19 May 2015 from <www.uva-aias. net/208>.

Aleks, R. (2015) 'Estimating the effect of "Change to Win" on union organizing'. *Industrial and Labor Relations Review*, 68(3): 584–605.

Allen, M. (2004) 'The varieties of capitalism paradigm: Not enough variety?' *Socio-Economic Review*, 2(1): 87–108.

Amable, B. (2003) *The Diversity of Modern Capitalism*. Oxford: Oxford University Press.

Anderman, S. (1986) 'Unfair dismissal and redundancy', in R. Lewis (ed.), *Labour Law in Britain*. Oxford: Blackwell, pp. 415–47.

Andersen, S.K. (2001) *Mellem politik og marked: Interesseorganisering og lønregulering på de kommunale/regionale arbejdsmarkeder i EU*. Copenhagen: DJØF.

—— (2003) 'Danmark: Vejen mod en erga omnes model', in S.K. Andersen (ed.), *EU og det nordiske spil om lov og aftale: De nordiske lande og de europæiske aftaler/direktiver om deltid og tidsbegrænset ansættelse*. Stockholm: Institute for Working Life, pp. 41–72.

Andersen, S.K. & Felbo-Kolding, J. (2013) *Danske virksomheders brug af østeuropæisk arbejdskraft.* Copenhagen: FAOS, University of Copenhagen.

Andersen, S.K. & Hansen, J.A. (2008) 'Strong trade unions meet EEC workers: Locating, monitoring and organising EEC workers in the Danish construction sector'. *Bulletin of Comparative Labour Relations*, 67: 101–16.

Andersen, S.K. & Ibsen, C.L. (2013) *Forligsmuligheder på den smalle sti ud af krisen.* Research Paper No. 137. Copenhagen: FAOS, University of Copenhagen.

Andersen, S.K. & Mailand, M. (2005) 'Flexicurity og det danske arbejdsmarked: Et review med fokus på overenskomssystemet, FAO', in *Flexicurity: Udfordringer for den danske model.* Copenhagen: Ministry of Employment.

Andolfatto, D. & Labbé, D. (2007) *Sociologie des syndicates.* Paris: La Découverte.

Appelbaum, E. (2008) 'Fairness at work pays off'. Paper presented to the University of Manchester Fairness at Work Research Group Launch, Manchester, UK, October.

Appelbaum, E., Bailey, T., Berg, P. & Kalleberg, A. (2000) *Manufacturing Competitive Advantage: The Effects of High Performance Work Systems on Plant Performance and Company Outcomes.* New York: Cornell University Press.

Appelbaum, E., Bosch, G., Gautié, J., Mason, G., Mayhew, K., Salverda, W., Schmitt, J. & Westergaard-Nielsen, N. (2010) 'Introduction and overview', in J. Gautié & J. Schmitt (eds), *Low-Wage Work in the Wealthy World.* New York: Russell Sage Foundation, pp. 1–32.

Arkless, D. (2007) 'The China talent paradox'. *China-Britain Business Review*, June: 14–15.

Armstrong, M. (2002) *Employee Reward*, 3rd ed. London: Chartered Institute of Personnel and Development.

Artus, I., Böhm, S., Lücking, S. & Trinczek, R. (eds) (2006) *Betriebe ohne Betriebsrat: Informelle Interessenvertretung in Unternehmen.* Frankfurt: Campus.

Australian Bureau of Statistics (2014a) *Employee Earnings, Benefits and Trade Union Membership Australia.* Cat. No. 6310.0. Canberra: ABS.

—— (2014b) *Industrial Disputes, Australia.* Cat. No. 6321.0.55.001. Canberra: ABS.

*Australian Financial Review* (2012) '*Fair Work Act* blocks progress'. 21 February: 54.

Avdagic, S., Rhodes, M. & Visser, J. (eds) (2011) *Social Pacts in Europe.* Oxford: Oxford University Press.

Baccaro, L. (2001) 'Union democracy revisited: Decision-making procedures in the Italian labour movement'. *Economic and Industrial Democracy*, 22: 183–210.

—— (2007) 'Political economy *della concertazione sociale*'. *Stato e mercato*, 1: 47–77.

Baccaro, L., Carrieri, M. & Damiano, C. (2003) 'The resurgence of the Italian confederal unions: Will it last?' *European Journal of Industrial Relations*, 9(1): 43–59.

Baccaro, L. & Howell, C. (2011) 'A common neoliberal trajectory: The transformation of industrial relations in advanced capitalism'. *Politics & Society*, 39(4): 521–63.

Baccaro, L. & Simoni, M. (2004) 'Il referendum sull'articolo 18 e gli interventi per la flessibilità del mercato del lavoro', in V. Della Sala & M. Fabbrini (eds), *Politica in Italia*. Bologna: Il Mulino.

Bach, S., Bordogna, L., Della Rocca, G. & Winchester, D. (eds) (1999) *Public Service Employment Relations in Europe: Transformation, Modernization or Inertia*. London: Sage.

Bailey, J. & Peetz, D. (2014) 'Australian unions and collective bargaining in 2013'. *Journal of Industrial Relations*, 56(3): 415–32.

Baird, M. & Whitehouse, G. (2012) 'Paid parental leave: First birthday policy review'. *Australian Bulletin of Labour*, 38(3): 184–98.

Bamber, G.J., Pochet, P., Allan, C., Block, R., Burchill, F., Cuillerier, J., Fitzner, G., French, B., Hickox, S., Keller, B., Moore, M.L., Murhem, S., Murray, G., Nakamichi, A., Nienhauser, W. & Rasmussen, E. (2010) *Regulating Employment Relations, Work and Labour Laws: International comparisons between key countries*. Special issue of the *Bulletin of Comparative Labour Relations*, 74.

Bamber, G.J., Ryan, S. & Wailes, N. (2004) 'Globalisation, employment relations and human resource indicators in ten developed market economies: International data sets'. *International Journal of Human Resource Management*, 15(8): 1481–516.

Barbash, J. (1967) *American Unions: Structure, Government and Politics*. New York: Random House.

Barbash, J. & Barbash, K. (eds) (1989) *Theories and Concepts in Comparative Industrial Relations*. Columbia: University of South Carolina Press.

Barca, F. & Magnani, M. (1989) *L'industria tra capitale e lavoro: piccole e grandi imprese dall'autunno caldo alla ristrutturazione*. Bologna: Il Mulino.

Bardhan, P. (2002) 'The political economy of reforms in India', in R. Mohan (ed.), *Facets of the Indian Economy*. New Delhi: Oxford University Press.

Batt, R., Holman, D. & Holtgrewe, U. (2009) 'The globalization of service work: Comparative institutional perspectives on call centers'. *Industrial and Labor Relations Review*, 62(4): 453–88.

Bayer, W. (2009) *Drittelbeteiligung in Deutschland: Ermittlung von Gesellschaften, die dem DrittelbG unterliegen*. Düsseldorf: Hans-Böckler Stiftung.

BDA/BDI (Bundesvereinigung der Deutschen Arbeitgeberverbände/Bundesverband der Deutschen Industrie) (2004) *Bericht der Kommission Mitbestimmung: Mitbestimmung modernisieren*. Berlin: BDA/BDI.

Bean, R. (1994) *Comparative Industrial Relations: An Introduction to Cross-National Perspectives*, rev. ed. London: Routledge.

Beaumont, P. (1987) *The Decline of the Trade Union Organisation*. London: Croom Helm.

Bechter, B., Brandl, B. & Meardi, G. (2012) 'Sectors or countries? Typologies and levels of analysis in comparative industrial relations'. *European Journal of Industrial Relations*, 18(3): 185–202.

Behrens, M. (2011) *Das Paradox der Arbeitgeberverbände: Von der Schwierigkeit, durchsetzungsstarke Unternehmensinteressen kollektiv zu vertreten*. Berlin: Edition Sigma.

—— (2014) 'Conflict resolution in Germany', in W.K. Roche, P. Teague & A. Colvin (eds), *The Oxford Handbook of Conflict Management in Organizations*. Oxford: Oxford University Press, pp. 357–78.

Behrens, M., Fichter, M. & Frege, C. (2003) 'Unions in Germany: Regaining the initiative'. *European Journal of Industrial Relations*, 9(1): 25–42.

Bell, D. (1962) *The End of Ideology: On the Exhaustion of Political Ideas in the Fifties*. New York: The Free Press.

Bennett, L. (1995) 'Bargaining away the rights of the weak: Non-union agreements in the federal jurisdiction', in P. Ronfeldt & R. McCallum (eds), *Enterprise Bargaining, Trade Unions and the Law*. Sydney: Federation Press, pp. 129–53.

Berg, P. (2008) 'Working time flexibility in the German employment relations system'. *Industrielle Beziehungen*, 15(2): 133–50.

Berger, S. (1996) 'Introduction', in S. Berger & R. Dore (eds), *National Diversity and Global Capitalism*. Ithaca, NY: Cornell University Press, pp. 1–27.

Bernstein, I. (1970) *The Turbulent Years*. Boston: Houghton Mifflin.

Béroud, S., Denis, J.-M., Giraud, B., Pélisse, J., Desage, G. & Carlier, A. (2008) 'Une nouvelle donne? Regain et transformation des conflits au travail', in T. Amossé, C. Bloch-London & L. Wolff (eds), *Les relations professionnelles en enterprise: Un portrait à partir des enquêtes 'Relations professionnelles et négociations d'entreprise'*. Paris: La Découverte, pp. 223–55.

Besley, T. & Burgess, R. (2004) 'Can regulation hinder economic performance? Evidence from India'. *Quarterly Journal of Economics*, 119(1): 91–134.

Bévort, A. & Jobert, A. (2008) *Sociologie du travail: Les relations professionnelles*. Paris: Armand Colin.

Bhattacharya, A. (2009) 'The effects of employment protection legislation on Indian manufacturing'. *Economic and Political Weekly*, 30 May: 55–62.

Bhattacherjee, D. (1999) *Organized Labour and Economic Liberalisation: India Past, Present and Future*. Geneva: International Institute for Labour Studies.

Bhowmik, S.K. (2005) 'Street vendors in Asia: A review'. *Economic and Political Weekly*, 28 May: 2256–64.

Biagi, M., Sacconi, M., Dell'Aringa, C., Forlani, N., Reboani, P. & Sestito, P. (2002) 'White paper on the labour market in Italy: The quality of European industrial relations and changing industrial relations'. *Bulletin of Comparative Labour Relations Series*, 44:1–117.

BIS (2013) *Trade Union Membership 2012*. Statistical Bulletin, May. London: Department for Business, Innovation and Skills.

Bishop, V., Korczynski, M. & Cohen, L. (2005) 'The invisibility of violence: Constructing violence out of the job centre workplace'. *Work, Employment and Society*, 19(3): 583–602.

Bispinck, R. & WSI-Tarifarchiv (2013) *Statistisches Taschenbuch 2013*. Düsseldorf: Hans-Böckler-Stiftung.

Blanchflower, D., Saleheen, J. & Shadforth, C. (2007) *The Impact of the Recent Migration from Eastern Europe on the United Kingdom Economy*. Discussion Paper No. 2615. Bonn: Institute for the Study of Labor (IZA).

Blanden, J., Machin, S. & Van Reenen, J. (2006) 'Have unions turned the corner? New evidence on recent trends in union recognition in UK firms'. *British Journal of Industrial Relations*, 44(2): 169–90.

Blanpain, R. (ed.) (2014) *Comparative Labour Law and Industrial Relations in Industrialized Market Economies*, 11th ed. Dordrecht: Wolters Kluwer.

Blau, F.D. & Kahn, L.M. (1996) 'International differences in male wage inequality: Institutions versus market forces'. *Journal of Political Economy*, 106: 791–837.

Block, R.N., Friedman, S., Kaminski, M. & Levin, A. (eds) (2006) *Justice on the Job: Perspectives on the Erosion of Collective Bargaining in the United States*. Kalamazoo, MI: W.E. UpJohn.

Bordogna, L. (1994) *Pluralismo senza mercato: Rappresentanza e conflitto nel settore pubblico*. Milan: Angeli.

—— (1997) 'Un decennio di contrattazione aziendale nell'industria', in L. Bellardi & L. Bordogna (eds), *Relazioni industriali e contrattazione aziendale. Continuità e riforma nell'esperienza Italiana recente*. Milan: Angeli.

—— (1999) 'Il fattore dimensionale nelle relazioni industriali e nella contrattazione collettiva in azienda', in F. Trau (ed.), *La 'questione dimensionale' nell'industria Italiana*. Bologna: Il Mulino.

—— (2008) *Industrial Relations in the Public Sector*, Dublin: Eurofound. Retrieved 19 May 2015 from <www.eurofound.europa.eu/observatories/eurwork/comparative-information/industrial-relations-in-the-public-sector>.

Bordogna, L. & Provasi, G.C. (1989) 'La conflittualita', in G.P. Cella & T. Treu (eds), *Relazioni industriali: Manuale per l'analisi dell'esperienza Italiana*. Bologna: Il Mulino.

Borland, J. (2012) 'Industrial relations reform: Chasing a pot of gold at the end of the rainbow?' *Australian Economic Review*, 45(3): 269–89.

Bosch, G. & Charest, J. (2008) 'Vocational training and the labour market in liberal and coordinated economies'. *Industrial Relations Journal*, 39(5): 428–47.

Bosch, G. & Weinkopf, C. (eds) (2008) *Low-Wage Work in Germany*. New York: Russell Sage Foundation.

Brandl, B. (2013) 'Die Repräsentativität von Arbeitgeberverbänden in Europa: Eine Standortbestimmung des "deutschen Modells"'. *WSI-Mitteilungen*, 66(7): 510–18.

Bray, M. & Macneil, J. (2011) 'Individualism, collectivism, and the case of awards in Australia'. *Journal of Industrial Relations*, 53(2): 149–67.

Brewer, M., Goodman, A., Muriel, A. & Sibieta, L. (2007) *Poverty and Inequality in the United Kingdom: 2007*. London: Institute for Fiscal Studies.

Bronfenbrenner, K. (1997) 'The role of union strategies in NLRB certification elections'. *Industrial and Labor Relations Review*, 50(2): 195–212.

Brown, R. (2006) 'China's Collective Contract provisions: Can collective negotiations embody collective bargaining?' *Duke Journal of Comparative and International Law*, 16(35): 35–77.

Brox, H., Rüthers, B. & Henssler, M. (2007) *Arbeitsrecht*, 17th rev. ed. Stuttgart: Kohlhammer.

Bryson, A. (2004) 'Managerial responsiveness to union and non-union worker voice in Britain'. *Industrial Relations*, 43(1): 213–41.

Bryson, A. & Gomez, R. (2005) 'Why have workers stopped joining unions? The rise in never-membership in Britain'. *British Journal of Industrial Relations*, 43(1): 67–116.

Bureau of Economic Analysis (2014) 'National income and product accounts: Gross domestic product, 4th quarter and annual 2013 (third estimate)'. Media release, 27 March. Retrieved 22 April 2014 from <www.bea.gov/newsreleases/national/gdp/2014/gdp4q13_3rd.htm>.

Bureau of Labor Statistics (2014a) 'Union members 2013'. Media release, 24 January. Retrieved 22 April 2014 from <www.bls.gov/news.release/pdf/union2.pdf>.

—— (2014b) 'Employment situation: March 2014'. Media release, 4 April. Retrieved 22 April 2014 from <www.bls.gov/news.release/pdf/empsit.pdf>.

—— (2015) 'Union Members 2014'. Washington, DC: US Department of Labor.

Bureau of National Affairs (2007) 'Groundbreaking UAW-GM contract receives 66 percent union membership approval vote'. *Daily Labor Report*, 29 August, 168: A–7.

Busemeyer, M.R. (2009) 'Die Sozialpartner und der Wandel in der Politik der beruflichen Bildung seit 1970'. *Industrielle Beziehungen*, 16(3): 273–94.

Calmfors, L. & Driffill, J. (1988) 'Bargaining structure, corporatism and macro-economic performance'. *Economic Policy*, 3(6): 13–61.

Campbell, I. & Tham, J.-C. (2013) 'Labour market deregulation and temporary migrant labour schemes: An analysis of the 457 visa program'. *Australian Journal of Labour Law*, 26(3): 239–72.

Carrieri, M. (1985) 'Accordi non conclusi, accordi non efficaci, accordi non voluti', in M. Carrieri & P. Perulli (eds), *Il teorema sindacale*. Bologna: Il Mulino.

—— (1995) *L'incerta rappresentanza*. Bologna: Il Mulino.

—— (1996) 'Le RSU nel sistema italiano di relazioni industriali'. *Lavoro e diritto*, 10(1): 153–85.

—— (1997) *Seconda Repubblica: Senza sindacati?* Rome: Ediesse.

—— (2008) *L'altalena della concertazione*. Rome: Donzelli.

Cella, G.P. (2012) 'L'arte della comparazione nelle relazioni industriali'. *Quaderni di rassegna sindacale*, 13(1): 75–80.

Cella, G.P. & Treu, T. (1989) 'La contrattazione collettiva', in G.P. Cella & T. Treu (eds), *Relazioni industriali: Manuale per l'analisi dell'esperienza Italiana*. Bologna: Il Mulino.

—— (2009) *Relazioni industriali e contrattazione collettiva*. Milan: Il Mulino.

Certification Officer (2013) *Annual Report of the Certification Officer 2012–2013*. London: Certification Office for Trade Unions and Employers' Associations.

Chan, A. (2001) *China's Workers under Assault: The Exploitation of Labour in a Globalising Economy*. New York: M.E. Sharpe.

Chan, A. & Unger, J. (2008) 'Is China's core industry closer to the Japanese-German or the Anglo-American model? Management–employee relations at a Chinese state enterprise'. Paper presented to the International Conference on Breaking down Chinese Walls: The Changing Faces of Labor and Employment in China, Cornell University, Ithaca, NY, September.

Charlesworth, S. & Macdonald, F. (2014) 'Women, work and industrial relations in Australia in 2013'. *Journal of Industrial Relations*, 56(3): 381–96.

Chen, F. (2003) 'Between the state and labour: The conflict of Chinese trade unions' double identity in market reform'. *China Quarterly*, 176: 1006–28.

—— (2007) 'Individual rights and collective rights: Labour's predicament in China'. *Communist and Post-Communist Studies*, 40(1): 59–79.

Chertier, D.-J. (2006) *Pour une modernisation du dialogue social: Rapport au premier ministre*. Paris: La Documentation Française.

China Education Online (2013) 'China's recent university graduates'. Retrieved 1 March 2014 from <www.eol.cn/html/c/2014xbys/index.shtml>.

China Labor News Translations (2008) 'Promising Wal-Mart trade union chair resigns over collective contract negotiations'. 22 September. Retrieved 24 September 2008 from <www.clntranslations.org/article/34/promising-wal -mart-trade-union-chair-resigns-over-collective-contract-negotiations>.

—— (2010) 'The Nanhai Honda strike and the union'. 18 July. Retrieved 21 April 2014 from <www.clntranslations.org/article/56/Honda>.

*China Labour Bulletin* (2014) 'Searching for the union: The workers' movement in China 2011–13'. Retrieved 21 April 2014 from <www.clb. org.hk/en/sites/default/files/File/research_reports/searching%20for%20 the%20union%201.pdf>.

Clark, I. & Almond, P. (2006) 'Overview of the US business system', in P. Almond & A. Ferner (eds), *American Multinationals in Europe: Managing Employment Relations across National Borders*. London: Oxford University Press, pp. 37–56.

Clark, T., Gospel, H. & Montgomery, J. (1999) 'Running on the spot? A review of twenty years of research on the management of human resources in comparative and international perspective'. *International Journal of Human Resource Management*, 10(3): 520–44.

Clarke, S. (2005) 'Post-socialist trade unions: China and Russia'. *Industrial Relations Journal*, 36(1): 2–18.

Clarke, S., Lee, C. & Li, Q. (2004) 'Collective consultation and industrial relations in China'. *British Journal of Industrial Relations*, 42(2): 235–54.

Clarke, S. & Pringle, T. (2009) 'Can party-led trade unions represent their members?' *Post-Communist Economics*, 21(1): 85–101.

CNEL (Consiglio Nazionale dell'Economia e del Lavoro) (2007) *Lineamenti della contrattazione aziendale nel periodo 1998–2006*. Rome: CNEL.

Cochrane, J.L. (1976) 'Industrialism and industrial man in retrospect: A preliminary analysis', in J.L. Stern & B.D. Dennis (eds), *Proceedings of the Twenty-Ninth Annual Winter Meetings, Industrial Relations Research Association Series*. Madison, WI: Industrial Relations Research Association (IRRA), pp. 274–87.

Colvin, A.J.S. (2006) 'Flexibility and fairness in liberal market economies: The comparative impact of the legal environment and high performance work systems'. *British Journal of Industrial Relations*, 44(1): 73–97.

—— (2007) 'Empirical research on employment arbitration: Clarity amidst the sound and fury?' *Employee Rights and Employment Policy Journal*, 11: 405–47.

Colvin, A.J.S. & Darbishire, O. (2013) 'Convergence in industrial relations institutions: The emerging Anglo-American model?' *ILR Review*, 66(5): 1047–77.

Commission on the Future of Worker–Management Relations (1994) 'Report and Recommendations'. Washington, DC: US Departments of Labor and Commerce.

Commons, J.R. (1909) 'American shoemakers'. *Quarterly Journal of Economics*, 24: 39–81.

Cooke, F.L. (2008) 'The dynamics of employment relations in China: An evaluation of the rising level of labour disputes'. *Journal of Industrial Relations*, 50(1): 111–38.

—— (2011) 'Labour market regulations and informal employment in China: To what extent are workers protected?' *Journal of Chinese Human Resource Management*, 2(2): 100–16.

—— (2012) *Human Resource Management in China: New Trends and Practices*. London: Routledge.

—— (2013) 'New dynamics of industrial conflicts in China: Causes, expressions and resolution alternatives', in G. Gall (ed.), *New Forms and Expressions of Conflict at Work*. Basingstoke: Palgrave Macmillan, pp. 108–29.

—— (2014) 'Chinese industrial relations research: In search of a broader analytical framework and representation'. *Asia Pacific Journal of Management*, 31(3): 875–98.

Cooke, F.L., Saini, D. & Wang, J. (2014) 'Talent management in China and India: A comparison of management perceptions and human resource practices'. *Journal of World Business*, 49(2): 225–35.

Cooney, R. (2010) 'Workplace training in a deregulated training system: Experiences from Australia's automotive industry'. *Economic and Industrial Democracy*, 31(3): 389–403.

Cooney, S. (2007) 'China's labour law, compliance and flaws in implementing institutions'. *Journal of Industrial Relations*, 49(5): 673–86.

Cooper, R. (2000) 'Organise, organise, organise! The 2000 ACTU Congress'. *Journal of Industrial Relations*, 42(4): 582–94.

Cooper, R. & Ellem, B. (2008) 'The neoliberal state, trade unions and collective bargaining in Australia'. *British Journal of Industrial Relations*, 46(3): 532–54.

Cooper, R., Ellem, C., Briggs, C. & van den Broek, D. (2009) 'Anti-unionism, employer strategy and the Australian state, 1996–2005'. *Labour Studies Journal*, 34(3): 339–62.

Cortis, N. & Meagher, G. (2012) 'Recognition at last: Care work and the equal remuneration case'. *Journal of Industrial Relations*, 54(3): 377–85.

Cowie, J. (1999) *Capital Moves: RCA's Seventy-Year Quest for Cheap Labor*. Ithaca, NY: Cornell University Press.

Crouch, C. (1993) *Industrial Relations and European State Traditions*. Oxford: Clarendon Press.

—— (2005) *Capitalist Diversity and Change: Recombinant Governance and Institutional Entrepreneurs*. Oxford: Oxford University Press.

Croucher, R. & Cotton, E. (2011) *Global Unions, Global Business: Global Union Federations and International Business*, 2nd ed. London: Libri.

Cully, M., Woodland, S., O'Reilly, A. & Dix, G. (1999) *Britain at Work: As Depicted by the 1998 Workplace Employee Relations Survey*. London: Routledge.

DA (1998) *Arbejdsmarkedsrapport 1998*. Copenhagen: DA.

—— (2007) *Arbejdsmarkedsrapport 2007*. Copenhagen: DA.

—— (2009) *Arbejdsmarkedsrapport 2008*. Copenhagen: DA.

—— (2014) *Arbejdsmarkedsrapport 2013*. Copenhagen: DA.

Davala, S. (1996) *Enterprise Unionism in India*. New Delhi: Fredrich Ebert Stiftung.

Davies, P. & Kilpatrick, C. (2004) 'UK worker representation after single channel'. *Industrial Law Journal*, 33(2): 121–51.

Davies, S., Hammer, N., Williams, G., Raman, R., Ruppert, C.S. & Volynets, L. (2011) 'Labour standards and capacity in global subcontracting chains: Evidence from a construction MNC'. *Industrial Relations Journal*, 42(2): 124–38.

Deakin, S. & Morris, G. (2005) *Labour Law*, 4th ed. Oxford: Hart.

Deakin, S. & Sarkar, P. (2011) *Indian Labour Law and Its Impact on Unemployment, 1973–2006: A Leximetric Study*. Working Paper No. 428. Cambridge: Centre for Business Research.

Dean, D. & Liff, S. (2010) 'Equality and diversity: The ultimate industrial relations concern', in T. Colling & M. Terry (eds), *Industrial Relations: Theory and Practice*. Chichester: Wiley, pp. 422–46.

Deeg, R. & Jackson, G. (2007) 'Towards a more dynamic theory of capitalist diversity'. *Socio-Economic Review*, 5(1): 149–79.

Dell'Aringa, C., Della Rocca, G. & Keller, B. (eds) (2001) *Strategic Choices in Reforming Public Service Employment*. London: Macmillan.

Deshpande, L.K., Sharma, A.N., Karan, A.K. & Sarkar, S. (2004) *Liberalization and Labour: Labour Flexibility in Indian Manufacturing*. New Delhi: Institute for Human Development.

Deshpande, S., Standing, G. & Deshpande, L. (1998) *Labour Flexibility in a Third World Metropolis*. New Delhi: Indian Society of Labour Economics/ Commonwealth Publishers.

DI (2013) *The New Nordic Approach*. Copenhagen: DI.

Dickens, L. & Hall, M. (2010) 'The changing legal framework of employment relations', in T. Colling & M. Terry (eds), *Industrial Relations: Theory and Practice*. Chichester: Wiley, pp. 298–322.

Dilger, A. (2002) *Ökonomik betrieblicher Mitbestimmung: Die wirtschaftlichen Folgen von Betriebsräten*. Munich: Hampp.

Doellgast, V. (2008) 'National industrial relations and local bargaining power in the US and German telecommunications industries'. *European Journal of Industrial Relations*, 14(3): 265–87.

—— (2009) 'Still a coordinated model? Market liberalization and the transformation of employment relations in the German telecommunications industry'. *Industrial and Labor Relations Review*, 63(1): 2–23.

—— (2012) *Disintegrating Democracy at Work: Labor Unions and the Future of Good Jobs in the Service Economy*. Ithaca, NY: Cornell University Press.

Doeringer, P. (1981) 'Industrial relations research in international perspective', in P.B. Doeringer, P. Gourevitch, P. Lange & A. Martin (eds), *Industrial Relations in International Perspective: Essays on Research and Policy*. London: Macmillan, pp. 1–21.

Doeringer, P. & Piore, M. (1971) *Internal Labor Markets and Manpower Analysis*. Lexington, MA: D.C. Heath.

Dølvik, J.E. & Eldring, L. (2008) *Mobility of Labour from New EU States to the Nordic Region: Development Trends and Consequences*. Copenhagen: Nordic Council of Ministers.

Dølvik, J.E. & Waddington, J. (2005) 'Can trade unions meet the challenge? Unionisation in the marketised services', in G. Bosch & S. Lehndorff (eds), *Working in the Service Sector*. London: Routledge, pp. 316–41.

Donaghey, J., Reinecke, J., Niforou, C. & Lawson, B. (2014) 'From employment relations to consumption relations: Balancing labor governance in global supply chains'. *Human Resource Management*, 53(2): 229–52.

Donovan, T.N. (1968) *Royal Commission on Trade Unions and Employers' Associations: Report*. Command Paper No. 3623. London: Her Majesty's Stationery Office.

Dore, R.E. (1979) *British Factory–Japanese Factory: The Origin of National Diversity in Industrial Relations*. London: Allen & Unwin.

Drolet, M. & Mumford, K. (2012) 'The gender pay gap for private sector employees in Canada and Britain'. *British Journal of Industrial Relations*, 50(3): 529–53.

Due, J. & Madsen, J.S. (2005) 'Denmark: The survival of small trade unions in the context of centralised bargaining', in J. Waddington (ed.), *Restructuring Representation: The Merger Process and Trade Union Structural Development in Ten Countries*. Brussels: PIE/Peter Lang, pp. 87–112.

—— (2006) *Fra storkonflikt til barselsfond: Den danske model under afvikling eller fornyelse*. Copenhagen: DJØF.

—— (2008) *OK 2007 og OK 2008: Perspektiver og konsekvenser*. Research Paper No. 100. Copenhagen: FAOS, University of Copenhagen.

—— (2009) *Forligsmagere og forumshoppere: Analyse af OK 2008 i den offentlige sektor*. Copenhagen: DJØF.

—— (2013) '20 år med den danske model'. *Tidsskrift for arbejdsliv*, 15(1): 95–103.

Due, J., Madsen, J.S. & Strøby Jensen, C. (1993) *Den danske model. En historisk sociologisk analyse af det kollektive aftalesystem*. Copenhagen: DJØF.

Due, J., Madsen, J.S., Strøby Jensen, C. & Petersen, L.K. (1994) *The Survival of the Danish Model: A Historical Sociological Analysis of the Danish System of Collective Bargaining*. Copenhagen: DJØF.

Dunlop, J.T. (1958) *Industrial Relations Systems*. New York: Henry Holt.

Dustmann, C., Fitzenberger, B., Schönberg, U. & Spitz-Oener, A. (2014) 'From sick man of Europe to economic superstar: Germany's resurgent economy'. *Journal of Economic Perspectives*, 28(1): 167–88.

Dustmann, C. & Weiss, Y. (2007) 'Return migration: Theory and empirical evidence from the United Kingdom'. *British Journal of Industrial Relations*, 45(2): 236–56.

Ebbinghaus, B. (2003) 'Ever larger unions: Organisational restructuring and its impact on union confederations'. *Industrial Relations Journal*, 34(5): 446–60.

Ebbinghaus, B. & Göbel, C. (2014) 'Mitgliederrückgang und Organisationsstrategien deutscher Gewerkschaften', in W. Schroeder (ed.), *Handbuch Gewerkschaften in Deutschland*, 2nd ed. Wiesbaden: Springer, pp. 207–39.

*Economic Report of the President* (2001). Washington, DC: US Government Printing Office.

*The Economist* (2013) 'Gini out of the bottle'. 26 January. Retrieved 3 March 2014 from <www.economist.com/news/china/21570749-gini-out-bottle>.

*The Economist* (2014) 'The world's biggest economies: China's back'. 11 October. Retrieved 6 May 2015 from <www.economist.com/news/finance-and-economics/21623758-chinas-back>.

Edwards, P. & Ram, M. (2006) 'Surviving on the margins of the economy: Working relationships in small, low-wage firms'. *Journal of Management Studies*, 43(4): 895–916.

Edwards, T., Almond, P., Clark, I., Colling, T. & Ferner, A. (2005) 'Reverse diffusion in US multi-nationals: Barriers from the American business system'. *Journal of Management Studies*, 42(6): 1261–86.

Elfstrom, M. & Kuruvilla, S. (2014) 'The changing nature of labor unrest in China'. *Industrial and Labor Relations Review*, 67(2): 453–80.

Elgar, J. & Simpson, B. (1993) 'The impact of the law on industrial disputes in the 1980s', in D. Metcalf & S. Milner (eds), *New Perspectives in Industrial Relations*. London: Routledge, pp. 70–114.

Ellguth, P. (2009) 'Betriebsspezifische Formen der Mitarbeitervertretung: Welche Betriebe, welche personalpolitischen Wirkungen?' *Industrielle Beziehungen*, 16(2): 109–35.

Ellguth, P. & Kohaut, S. (2010) 'Tarifbindung und betriebliche Interessenvertretung: Aktuelle Ergebnisse aus dem IAB-Betriebspanel 2009'. *WSI-Mitteilungen*, 63(4): 204–9.

—— (2013) 'Tarifbindung und betriebliche Interessenvertretung: Ergebnisse aus dem IAB-Betriebspanel 2012'. *WSI-Mitteilungen*, 66(4): 281–8.

Engerman, S. (2003) 'The history and political economy of international labour standards', in K. Basu, H. Horn, L. Roman & J. Shapiro (eds), *International Labour Standards: History Theory, Policy Options*. London: Blackwell, pp. 9–45.

Esping-Andersen, G. (1990) *The Three Worlds of Welfare Capitalism*. Princeton, NJ: Princeton University Press.

Estevez-Abe, M. (2006) 'Gendering the varieties of capitalism: A study of occupational segregation by sex in advanced industrial societies'. *World Politics*, 59(1): 142–75.

Eurofound (2014) *Industrial relations country profiles*. Retrieved 15 December 2014 from <http://eurofound.europa.eu/observatories/eurwork/comparativeinformation/industrial-relations-country-profiles>.

Eurostat (2014) 'February 2014: Euro area unemployment rate at 11.9%'. News release: Euroindicators, 1 April, 52.

Evans, P. (1997) 'The eclipse of the state? Reflections on stateness in an era of globalisation'. *World Politics*, 50(1): 62–87.

—— (2010) 'Is it labor's turn to globalize? Twenty-first century opportunities and strategic responses'. *Global Labour Journal*, 1(3): 352–79.

Ewing, K. & Hendy, J. (2013) *Reconstruction after the Crisis: A Manifesto for Collective Bargaining*. Liverpool: Institute of Employment Rights.

Ewing, K., Moore, S. & Wood, S. (2003) *Unfair Labour Practices: Trade Union Recognition and Employer Resistance*. London: Institute of Employment Rights.

Faini, R. & Sapir, A. (2005) 'Un modello obsoleto? Crescita e specializzazione dell'economia Italiana', in T. Boeri, R. Faini, A. Ichino, G. Pisauro & C. Scarpa (eds), *Oltre il declino*. Bologna: Il Mulino, pp. 19–65.

Fairbrother, P. (2002) 'Unions in Britain: Towards a new unionism?' in P. Fairbrother & G. Griffin (eds), *Changing Prospects for Trade Unionism: Comparisons between Six Countries*. London: Continuum, pp. 56–92.

Farrell, D. & Grant, A. (2005) 'China's looming talent shortage'. *McKinsey Quarterly*, 4. Retrieved 3 March 2007 from <www.mckinseyquarterly.com/article_page.aspx?ar=1685>.

Ferner, A. (1997) 'Country of origin effects and HRM in multinational companies'. *Human Resource Management Journal*, 7(1): 19–37.

Ferner, A. & Hyman, R. (1998) 'Introduction: Towards European industrial relations?' in A. Ferner & R. Hyman (eds), *Changing Industrial Relations in Europe*, 2nd ed. Oxford: Blackwell, pp. xi–xxvi.

Ferner, A. & Quintanilla, J. (1998) 'Multinationals, national business systems and HRM: The enduring influence of national identity or a process of "Anglo-Saxonisation"?' *International Journal of Human Resource Management*, 9(7): 710–31.

Ferner, A., Quintanilla, J. & Varul, M. (2001) 'Country of origin effects, host country effects and the management of HR in multinationals: German companies in Britain and Spain'. *Journal of World Business*, 36(2): 107–27.

Feuille, P. & Wheeler, H.N. (1981) 'Will the real industrial conflict please stand up?' in J. Stieber, R.B. McKersie & D.Q. Mills (eds), *US Industrial Relations 1950–1080: A Critical Assessment*. Madison, WI: Industrial Relations Research Association (IRRA), pp. 255–95.

Fine, J. (2006) *Worker Centers: Organizing Communities at the Edge of the Dream*. Ithaca, NY: Cornell University Press.

Fleisher, B. & Yang, D. (2003) 'Labour laws and regulations in China'. *China Economic Review*, 14: 426–33.

Foreign Affairs, Trade and Development (Canada) (2013) 'International commerce by indicator/rank'. Retrieved 20 July 2014 from <http://w03.international.gc.ca/Commerce_International/Commerce_Indicator-Indicateur.aspx?lang=eng>.

Forth, J. & Millward, N. (2000) *The Determinants of Pay Levels and Fringe Benefit Provision in Britain*. Discussion Paper No. 171. London: National Institute of Economic and Social Research.

Fray, Keith (2014) 'China's leap forward: Overtaking the US as the world's biggest economy'. 8 October. Retrieved 10 December 2014 from <http://blogs.ft.com/ftdata/2014/10/08/chinas-leap-forward-overtaking-the-us-as-worlds-biggest-economy>.

Freeman, R.B. (2008) 'Labour market institutions around the world', in P. Blyton, N. Bacon, J. Fiorito & E. Heery (eds), *Sage Handbook of Industrial Relations*. London: Sage, pp. 640–58.

Frege, C. & Godard, J. (2014) 'Varieties of capitalism and job quality: The attainment of civic principles at work in the United States and Germany'. *American Sociological Review*, 79(5): 942–65.

Frege, C. & Kelly, J. (eds) (2004) *Varieties of Unionism: Strategies for Union Revitalisation in a Globalising Economy*. Oxford: Oxford University Press.

Frick, B. (ed.) (2003) 'Symposium: "The economics of mandated codetermination"'. *Schmollers Jahrbuch. Journal of Applied Social Science Studies*, 123(3).

Friedman, T.L. (2006) *The World Is Flat: The Globalized World in the Twenty-First Century*. Harmondsworth: Penguin.

Friis, J. & Hegna, T. (1974) *Arbeidernes leksikon: Bind I–III*. Oslo: Pax.

Fukuyama, F. (1992) *The End of History and the Last Man*. New York: Simon and Schuster.

Gabriel, S. (2006) *Chinese Capitalism and the Modernist Vision*. London: Routledge.

Galenson, W. (1952) *The Danish System of Labor Relations: A Study of Industrial Peace*. Cambridge, MA: Harvard University Press.

Gall, G. (2004a) 'British employer resistance to trade union recognition'. *Human Resource Management Journal*, 14(2): 36–53.

—— (2004b) 'Trade union recognition in Britain, 1995–2002: Turning a corner?' *Industrial Relations Journal*, 35(3): 249–70.

—— (2007) 'Trade union recognition in Britain: An emerging crisis for trade unions?' *Economic and Industrial Democracy*, 28(1): 78–109.

Gallagher, M. (2005) *Contagious Capitalism: Globalisation and the Politics of Labor in China*. Princeton, NJ: Princeton University Press.

Gallie, D. (2007) *Employment Regimes and the Quality of Work*. Oxford: Oxford University Press.

Garnaut, R. & Huang, Y.P. (2001) *Growth Without Miracles: Readings on the Chinese Economy in the Era of Reform*. Oxford: Oxford University Press.

Garrett, G. (1998) 'Global markets and national policies: Collision course or virtuous circle?' *International Organization*, 52(4): 787–824.

Gautié, J. & Schmitt, J. (eds) (2010) *Low-Wage Work in the Wealthy World*. New York: Russell Sage Foundation.

Gereffi, G., Humphrey, J. & Sturgeon, T. (2005) 'The governance of global value chains'. *Review of International Political Economy*, 12(1): 78–104.

Gerum, E. (2007) *Das deutsche Corporate-Governance-System: Eine empirische Untersuchung*. Stuttgart: Schäffer-Poeschel.

Getman, J.G. (1998) *The Betrayal of Local 14*. Ithaca, NY: Cornell University Press.

Ghailani, D. (2009) 'The Rüffert and Luxembourg cases: Is the European social dimension in retreat?' in C. Degryse (ed.), *Social Developments in the European Union, 2008*. Brussels: European Trade Union Institute, pp. 205–22.

Giudice, G. (2014) 'Industrial relations law reform: What value should be given to stability?' *Journal of Industrial Relations*, 56(3): 433–41.

Godard, J. (2004) 'The new institutionalism, capitalist diversity, and industrial relations', in B.E. Kaufman (ed.), *Theoretical Perspectives on Work and the Employment Relationship: Annual Research Volume*. Champaign, IL: Industrial Relations Research Association, pp. 229–64.

Goergen, M., Brewster, C., Wood, G. & Wilkinson, A. (2012) 'Varieties of capitalism and investments in human capital'. *Industrial Relations*, 51(1): 501–27.

Goldar, B. & Aggarwal, S.C. (2012) 'Informalization of industrial labour in India: Are labour market rigidities and growing import competition to blame?' *Journal of Developing Economies*, 50(2): 141–69.

Golden, M. (1988) *Labor Divided: Austerity and Working-Class Politics in Contemporary Italy*. Ithaca, NY: Cornell University Press.

Goldthorpe, J.H. (1984) 'The end of convergence: Corporatist and dualist tendencies in modern Western societies', in J.H. Goldthorpe (ed.), *Order and Conflict in Contemporary Capitalism: Studies in the Political Economy of Western European Nations*. Oxford: Clarendon Press, pp. 315–43.

Gomez-Mejia, L.R., Balkin, D.B. & Cardy, R.L. (1995) *Managing Human Resources*. Englewood Cliffs, NJ: Prentice Hall.

Goodman, J. (1994) 'The United Kingdom', in A. Trebilcock et al., *Towards Social Dialogue: Tripartite Cooperation in National Economic and Social Policy-Making*. Geneva: ILO, pp. 273–96.

—— (2000) 'Building bridges and settling differences: Collective conciliation and arbitration under ACAS', in B. Towers & W. Brown (eds), *Employment Relations in Britain: 25 Years of the Advisory, Conciliation and Arbitration Service*. Oxford: Blackwell, pp. 31–65.

Gopalakrishnan, R. (2009) 'MRF United Workers' Union case'. Retrieved 2 April 2014 from <http://kafi la.org/2009/09/24/mrf-united-workers%E2%80%99-union-case-ramapriya-gopalakrishnan>.

Gospel, H. & Pendleton, A. (2005) *Corporate Governance and Labour Management: An International Comparison*. Oxford: Oxford University Press.

Government of India (2006) 'Economic survey 2005–06'. Retrieved 3 May 2015 from <http://indiabudget.nic.in/es2005-06/esmain.htm>.

—— (2008) 'Eleventh plan'. Vol. 1. 2007. Retrieved 3 May 2015 from <http://planningcommission.nic.in/plans/planrel/fiveyr/11th/11_v1/11th_vol1.pdf>.

Green, R., Toner, P. & Agarwal, R. (2012) *Understanding Productivity: Australia's Choice*. Sydney: McKell Institute/University of Technology Sydney.

Grimshaw, D. (2009) 'The United Kingdom: A progressive statutory minimum wage in a liberal market economy context', in D. Vaughan-Whitehead (ed.), *Minimum Wage Systems in an Extended Europe*. Geneva: ILO.

Grimshaw, D. & Rubery, J. (2010) 'Pay and working time: Shifting contours of the employment relationship', in T. Colling & M. Terry (eds), *Industrial Relations: Theory and Practice*. Chichester: Wiley, pp. 349–77.

Grimshaw, D., Willmott, H. & Vincent, S. (2002) 'Going privately: Practices of partnership in the outsourcing of services in the public sector'. *Public Administration*, 80(3): 475–502.

Guillot, J.P. & Rubia, C. (2009) *Osez le dialogue social dans l'entreprise*. Paris: Les Editions de l'Atelier.

Gumbrell-McCormick, R. (2008) 'International actors and international regulation', in P. Blyton, N. Bacon, J. Foirito & E. Heery (eds), *Sage Handbook of Industrial Relations*. London: Sage, pp. 325–45.

Gumbrell-McCormick, R. & Hyman R. (2013) *Trade Unions in Western Europe: Hard Times, Hard Choices*. Oxford: Oxford University Press.

Guthrie, D. (1999) *Dragon in a Three-Piece Suit: The Emergence of Capitalism in China*. Princeton, NJ: Princeton University Press.

Hainmueller, J. & Hiscox, M.J. (2012) *The Socially Conscious Consumer? Field Experimental Tests of Consumer Support for Fair Labor Standards*. Research Paper No. 2012–15. Cambridge, MA: Political Science Department, Massachusetts Institute of Technology.

Hall, M. & Purcell, J. (2012) *Consultation at Work: Regulation and Practice*. Oxford: Oxford University Press.

Hall, P.A. & Gingerich, D.W. (2009) 'Varieties of capitalism and institutional complementarities in the political economy: An empirical analysis'. *British Journal of Political Science*, 39(3): 449–82.

Hall, P.A. & Soskice, D. (eds) (2001) *Varieties of Capitalism: The institutional foundations of comparative advantage*. New York: Oxford University Press.

Hall, R. (2008) 'The politics of industrial relations in Australia in 2007'. *Journal of Industrial Relations*, 50(3): 371–82.

Hall, R. & Wailes, N. (2009) 'International and comparative human resource management', in A. Wilkinson, N. Bacon, T. Redman & S. Snell (eds), *Sage Handbook of Human Resource Management*. London: Sage, pp. 115–32.

Hamann, K. & Kelly, J. (2008) 'Varieties of Capitalism and industrial relations', in P. Blyton, E. Heery, N. Bacon & J. Fiorito (eds), *Sage Handbook of Industrial Relations*. New York: Sage, pp. 129–48.

Hammer, N. (2005) 'International framework agreements: Global industrial relations between rights and bargaining'. *Transfer: European Review of Labour and Research*, 11(4): 511–30.

Han, J. & Jang, J. (2000) 'Job history and career in the transition between regular and non-regular jobs' [in Korean]. *Korean Journal of Labor Economics*, 23(2): 33–53.

Hancock, K. (1984) 'The first half century of wage policy', in B. Chapman, J. Isaac & J. Niland (eds), *Australian Labour Relations Readings*. Melbourne: Macmillan, pp. 44–99.

—— (2012) 'Enterprise bargaining and productivity'. *Labour and Industry*, 22(3): 289–301.

Harcourt, M. & Wood, G. (2007) 'The importance of employment protection for skill development in coordinated market economies'. *European Journal of Industrial Relations*, 13(2): 141–59.

Hassel, A. (1999) 'The erosion of the German system of industrial relations'. *British Journal of Industrial Relations*, 37(3): 483–505.

—— (2008) 'The evolution of a global labour governance regime'. *Governance*, 21(2): 231–51.

Hauser-Ditz, A., Hertwig, M. & Pries, L. (2009) 'Kollektive Interessenvertretung in der "betriebsratsfreien Zone": Typische Formen "Anderer Vertretungsorgane"'. *Industrielle Beziehungen*, 16(2): 136–53.

Haworth, N. (2005) '"You've got to admit it's getting better . . .": Organised labour and internationalisation', in B. Harley, J. Hyman & P. Thompson (eds), *Participation and Democracy at Work*. London: Palgrave, pp. 186–203.

Healy, J. (2014) 'The Australian labour market in 2013'. *Journal of Industrial Relations*, 56(3): 345–64.

Heery, E. (1998) 'The relaunch of the Trades Union Congress'. *British Journal of Industrial Relations*, 36(3): 339–60.

—— (2002) 'Partnership versus organising: Alternative futures for British trade unionism'. *Industrial Relations Journal*, 33(1): 20–35.

Heery, E., Bacon, N., Blyton, P. & Fiorito, J. (2008) 'Introduction: The field of industrial relations', in P. Blyton, N. Bacon, J. Fiorito & E. Heery (eds), *Sage Handbook of Industrial Relations*. London: Sage, pp. 1–32.

Heery, E., Delbridge, R. & Simms, M. (2003) *The Organising Academy*. London: Trades Union Congress.

Hession, C.H. & Sardy, H. (1969) *Ascent to Affluence: A History of American Economic Development*. Boston: Allyn & Bacon.

High Pay Commission (2011) *More for Less*. London: HPC.

Hill, E. (2009) 'The Indian industrial relations system: Struggling to address the dynamics of a globalizing economy'. *Journal of Industrial Relations*, 51(3): 395–410.

Hirst, P. & Thompson, G. (1996) *Globalisation in Question: The International Economy and the Possibilities of Governance*. Cambridge: Polity Press.

Hodson, R. (2001) *Dignity at Work*. Cambridge: Cambridge University Press.

Hoel, H. & Beale, D. (2006) 'Workplace bullying, psychological perspectives and industrial relations: Towards a contextualized and interdisciplinary approach'. *British Journal of Industrial Relations*, 44(2): 239–62.

Hoffman, C. (1981) 'People's Republic of China', in A. Albert (ed.), *International Handbook of Industrial Relations*. Westport, CT: Greenwood Press.

Holgate, J., Hebson, G. & McBride, A. (2006) 'Why gender and "difference" matter: A critical appraisal of industrial relations research'. *Industrial Relations Journal*, 37(4): 310–28.

Home Office/BIS (2014) *Impacts of Migration on UK Native Employment: An Analytical Review of the Evidence*. Occasional Paper No. 109. London: Home Office/BIS.

Höpner, M. (2005) 'What connects industrial relations and corporate governance? Explaining institutional complementarity'. *Socio-Economic Review*, 3(2): 331–58.

Howell, C. (2003) 'Varieties of Capitalism: And then there was one?' *Comparative Politics*, 36(1): 103–24.

—— (2005) *Trade Unions and the State: The Construction of Industrial Relations Institutions in Britain, 1890–2000*. Princeton, NJ: Princeton University Press.

Hu, X.J. (2004) 'On the legal system of China's labour market'. *Journal of Anhui University of Technology* (Social Sciences Edition), 21(5): 19–20.

Huang, Y. (2008) *Capitalism with Chinese Characteristics: Entrepreneurship and the State*. Cambridge: Cambridge University Press.

Hughes, S. (2005) 'The International Labour Organization'. *New Political Economy*, 10(3): 413–25.

Hughes, S. & Wilkinson, R. (1998) 'International labour standards and world trade: No role for the World Trade Organization'. *New Political Economy*, 3(3): 375–89.

Human Resources and Skills Development Canada (2008) 'A profile of federal labour workplace jurisdictions: Results from the 2008 Federal Workplace Jurisdiction Survey'. June. Cat. No. HS24–89/2011E-PDF. Retrieved 20 July 2014 from <www.labour.gc.ca/eng/standards_equity/st/pubs_st/pdf/fjws.pdf>.

Hyman, R. (1999) 'Imagined solidarities: Can trade unions resist globalization?' in P. Leisink (ed.), *Globalization and Labour Relations*. Cheltenham: Edward Elgar, pp. 94–115.

—— (2005) 'Trade unions and the politics of the European social model'. *Economic and Industrial Democracy*, 26(1): 9–40.

Hyman, R. & Brough, I. (1975) *Social Values and Industrial Relations*. Oxford: Blackwell.

Ibsen, C.L. (2013) 'Consensus or coercion: Collective bargaining coordination and third party intervention'. Unpublished PhD thesis. FAOS, University of Copenhagen.

IHD/ISLE (Institute for Human Development/Indian Society of Labour Economics) (2014) *India Labour and Employment Report*. New Delhi: IHD/Academic Foundation.

ILO (2008) *Global Wage Report, 2008/09*. Geneva: ILO.

—— (2009) *Rules of the Game: A Brief Introduction to International Labour Standards*, rev. ed. Geneva: ILO.

Ilsøe, A. (2008). *Tillidsrepræsentanter i industrien: Udbredelsen af tillidsrepræsentanter på overenskomstdækkede danske produktionsvirksomheder*. Research Paper No. 93. Copenhagen: FAOS, University of Copenhagen.

Ilsøe, A., Due, J. & Madsen, J.S. (2007). 'Impacts of decentralisation: Erosion or renewal? The decisive link between work place representation and company size in German and Danish industrial relations'. *Industrielle Beziehungen*, 14(3): 201–22.

IMF (International Monetary Fund) (2015) *World Economic Outlook Database*. Retrieved 12 December 2014 from <www.imf.org/external/pubs/ft/weo/2015/01/weodata/index.aspx>.

Industry Canada (2013) 'Canadian trade balances'. Retrieved 20 September 2014 from <www.ic.gc.ca/app/scr/tdst/tdo/crtr.html%3bjsessionid=0003bjdp54KOQ9ZMI5c0-cJgOIK:-1OO0GVI:-S11FKP?naArea=9999&toFrom Country=CDN&grouped=GROUPED&runReport=true&countryList=ALL &currency=CDN&productType=NAICS&searchType=All&reportType= TB&timePeriod=5%7cComplete+Years>.

Institut Montaigne (2011) *Reconstruire le dialogue social*. Paris: Rapport.

Isaac, J. (2012) 'Keynes versus the classics in the 1970s'. *Australian Bulletin of Labour*, 38(2): 96–110.

ISTAT (2002) *La flessibilità del mercato del lavoro nel periodo 1995–96*. Rome: ISTAT.

Iversen, T. (1999) *Contested Economic Institution: The Politics of Macroeconomics and Wage Bargaining in Advanced Democracies*. Cambridge: Cambridge University Press.

Jackson, G. (2001) 'The origins of non-liberal corporate governance in Germany and Japan', in W. Streek & K. Yamamura (eds), *The Origins of Nonliberal Capitalism: Germany and Japan in Comparison*. Ithaca, NY: Cornell University Press, pp. 121–70.

Jackson, G. & Kirsch, A. (2014) 'Employment relations in liberal market economies', in A. Wilkinson, G. Wood & R. Deeg (eds), *The Oxford Handbook of Employment Relations*. Oxford: Oxford University Press, pp. 263–91.

Jackson, G. & Sorge, A. (2012) 'The trajectory of institutional change in Germany, 1979–2009'. *Journal of European Public Policy*, 19(8): 1146–67.

Jacobi, O., Keller, B. & Müller-Jentsch, W. (1998) 'Germany: Facing new challenges', in A. Ferner & R. Hyman (eds), *Changing Industrial Relations in Europe*, 2nd ed. Oxford: Blackwell, pp. 190–238.

Jacobs, D. & Myers, L. (2014) 'Union strength, neoliberalism, and inequality: Contingent political analyses of US income differences since 1950'. *American Sociological Review*, 79(4): 752–74.

Jacoby, S.M. (1985) *Employing Bureaucracies*. New York: Columbia University Press.

Jefferson, T. & Preston, A. (2013) 'Labour markets and wages in Australia in 2012'. *Journal of Industrial Relations*, 55(3): 338–55.

JILPT (Japan Institute for Labour Policy and Training) (2003) *Kigyo no jinji senryaku to rodosha no syugyo ishiki ni kansuru chosa* [Survey on Enterprises' Human Resource Management Strategy and Sentiment of Workers]. Tokyo: JILPT.

—— (2005) *Nihon no chojikan rodo fubarairodojikan no jittai to jisshobunseki* [Facts and an Empirical Analysis Concerning Long Working Hours and Unpaid Working Hours in Japan]. Tokyo: JILPT.

—— (2006) *Gendai nihon kigyo no jinzai manejimento* [Human Resource Management of Modern Japanese Firm]. Tokyo: JILPT.

—— (2013) Projection of Labour Supply and Demand. Document series No. 129.

Jirjahn, U. (2011) 'Ökonomische Wirkungen der Mitbestimmung in Deutschland: Ein Update'. *Schmollers Jahrbuch* (*Journal of Applied Social Science Studies*), 131(1): 3–57.

John, J. (2007) 'Overall increase and sectoral setbacks: Lessons from trade union verification 2002 data (provisional)'. *Labour File*, January–April: 1325.

Jung, E. (2006) *Political Economics of Modern Labor Markets* [in Korean]. Seoul: Humanitas.

Juravich, T. & Bronfenbrenner, K. (1999) *Ravenswood: The Steelworkers' Victory and the Revival of the American Labor Movement*. Ithaca, NY: Cornell University Press.

Kaine, S. & Wright, C.F. (2013) 'Conceptualising CSR in the context of the shifting contours of Australian employment regulation'. *Labour and Industry*, 23(1): 54–68.

Kalleberg, A.L. (2009) 'Precarious work, insecure workers: Employment relations in transition'. *American Sociological Review*, 74(1): 1–22.

—— (2011) *Good Jobs, Bad Jobs: The Rise of Polarized and Precarious Employment Systems in the United States, 1970s to 2000s*. New York: Russell Sage Foundation.

Kambayashi, R. & Kato, T. (2011) *Long-Term Employment and Job Security over Twenty-Five Years: A Comparative Study of Japan and the US*. Discussion Paper No. 6183. Bonn: Institute for the Study of Labor (IZA).

Kassalow, E.M. (1974) 'The development of Western labor movements: Some comparative considerations', in L.G. Reynolds, S.A. Masters & C. Moser (eds), *Readings in Labor Economics and Labor Relations*. Englewood Cliffs, NJ: Prentice-Hall.

Kato, T. & Morishima M. (2002) 'The productivity effects of participatory employment practices: Evidence from new Japanese panel data'. *Industrial Relations*, 41: 487–520.

Katz, H.C. (1985) *Shifting Gears*. Cambridge, MA: MIT Press.

—— (1993) 'The decentralization of collective bargaining: A literature review and comparative analysis'. *Industrial and Labor Relations Review*, 47(1): 3–22.

—— (2005) 'Industrial relations and work', in S. Ackroyd, R. Bart, P. Thompson & P. Tolbert (eds), *The Oxford Handbook of Work and Organisations*. Oxford: Oxford University Press, pp. 263–82.

—— (2013) 'Is US public sector labor relations in the midst of a transformation?' *Industrial and Labor Relations Review*, 66(5): 1031–46.

Katz, H.C., Batt, R. & Keefe, J.H. (2003) 'The revitalization of the CWA: Integrating political action, organizing, and collective bargaining'. *Industrial and Labor Relations Review*, 56(4): 573–89.

Katz, H.C. & Darbishire, O. (2000) *Converging Divergences: Worldwide Changes in Employment Systems*. Ithaca, NY: ILR Press.

Katz, H.C., Kochan, T.A. & Colvin, A.J.S. (2007) *An Introduction to Collective Bargaining and Industrial Relations*, 4th ed. New York: Irwin-McGraw Hill.

Katz, H.C. & Wailes, N. (2014) 'Convergence and divergence in employment relations', in A. Wilkinson, G. Wood & R. Deeg (eds), *The Oxford Handbook of Employment Relations: Comparative Employment Systems*. Oxford: Oxford University Press, pp. 42–61.

Katzenstein, P. (1985) *Small States in World Markets: Industrial Policy in Europe*. Ithaca, NY: Cornell University Press.

Keller, B. (2010) *Arbeitspolitik im öffentlichen Dienst: Ein Überblick über Arbeitsmärkte und Arbeitsbeziehungen*. Berlin: Edition Sigma.

—— (2013a) 'The public sector in the United States and Germany: Comparative aspects in an employment relations perspective'. *Comparative Labor Law and Policy Journal*, 34(10–12): 415–41.

—— (2013b) 'Germany: The public sector in the financial and debt crisis'. *European Journal of Industrial Relations*, 19(4): 359–74.

Keller, B. & Seifert, H. (2013) *Atypische Beschäftigung zwischen Prekarität und Normalität: Entwicklung, Strukturen und Bestimmungsgründe im Überblick*. Berlin: Edition Sigma.

Kelly, J. (1982) *Scientific Management, Job Redesign and Work Performance*. London: Academic Press.

—— (1990) 'British trade unionism 1979–1989: Change, continuity and contradictions'. *Work, Employment and Society*, 4 (Special Issue): 29–65.

—— (1998) *Rethinking Industrial Relations: Mobilization, Collectivism and Long Waves*. London: Routledge.

Kennedy, S. (ed.) (2011) *Beyond the Middle Kingdom: Comparative Perspectives on China's Capitalist Transformation*. Stanford, CT: Stanford University Press.

Kerr, C., Dunlop, J.T., Harbison, F.H. & Myers, C.A. (1960) *Industrialism and Industrial Man: The problems of labour and management in economic growth*. Harmondsworth: Penguin.

Kersley, B., Alpin, C., Forth, J., Bewley, H. & Oxenbridge S. (2006) *Inside the Workplace: Findings from the 2004 Workplace Employment Relations Survey*. London: Routledge.

Kessler, I. & Purcell, J. (1994) 'Joint problem solving and the role of third parties: An evaluation of ACAS advisory work'. *Human Resource Management Journal*, 4(2): 1–21.

Khoo, S.E., McDonald, P., Voigt Graf, C. & Hugo, G. (2007) 'A global labor market: Factors motivating the sponsorship and temporary migration of skilled workers to Australia'. *International Migration Review*, 41(2): 480–510.

Kim, S., Han, J. & Zhao, L.K. (2014) 'Union recognition by multinational companies in China: A dual institutional pressure perspective'. *Industrial and Labor Relations Review*, 67(1): 33–59.

Kim, S. & Sung, J. (2005) *Employment Policy in Korea* [in Korean]. Seoul: KLI.

Kim, Y. (2005) *Wage Policy for Korean Workers* [in Korean]. Seoul: Humanitas.

Kirsch, A. & Blaschke, S. (2014) 'Women's quotas and their effects: A comparison of Austrian and German trade unions'. *European Journal of Industrial Relations*, 20(3): 201–17.

KLI (Korean Labour Institute) (2014) *2014 KLI Labor Statistics* [in Korean]. Seoul: KLI.

Kochan, T.A. (1998) 'What is distinctive about industrial relations research?', in K. Whitfield & G. Strauss (eds), *Researching the World of Work: Strategies and Methods in Studying Industrial Relations*. Ithaca, NY: Cornell University Press, pp. 31–49.

—— (2013) 'The American jobs crisis and its implication for the future of employment policy: A call for a new jobs compact'. *ILR Review*, 66(2): 291–314.

Konzelmann, S.J., Wilkinson, F., Craypo, C. & Aridi, R. (2005) *The Export of National Varieties of Capitalism: The Cases of Wal-Mart and IKEA*. Working Paper No. 314. Cambridge: Centre for Business Research, University of Cambridge.

Kristiansen, J. (2013) *Aftalemodellen og dens europæiske udfordringer: Om rollefordelingen mellem overenskomstparterne, Folketinget og domstolene*. Copenhagen: DJØF/Jurist-og Økonomforfundet.

Krugman, P. (2012) *End This Depression Now!* New York: W.W. Norton.

Lakhani, T., Kuruvilla, S. & Avgar, A. (2013) 'From the firm to the network: Global value chains and employment relations theory'. *British Journal of Industrial Relations*, 51(3): 440–72.

Lama, L. (1976) *Intervista sul sindacato*. Bari: Laterza.

Lane, C. (2008) 'National capitalisms and global production networks: An analysis of their interaction in two global industries'. *Socio-Economic Review*, 6(2): 227–60.

Lane, C. & Wood, G. (2009) 'Capitalist diversity and diversity within capitalism'. *Economy and Society*, 38(4): 531–51.

Lange, P. & Vannicelli, M. (1982) 'Strategy under stress: The Italian union movement and the Italian crisis in developmental perspective', in P. Lange,

G. Ross & M. Vannicelli (eds), *Unions, Change, and Crisis*. Boston: Unwin Hyman, pp. 95–206.

Lansbury, R.D., Kitay, J. & Wailes, N. (2006) 'Globalisation and working life: A comparative analysis of the automobile and banking sectors in Australia and Korea', in G. Wood & P. James (eds), *Institutions, Production and Working Life*. Oxford: Oxford University Press, pp. 83–103.

Lansbury, R.D. & Wailes, N. (2008) 'Employee involvement and direct participation', in P. Blyton, N. Bacon, J. Fiorito & E. Heery (eds), *Sage Handbook of Industrial Relations*. London: Sage, pp. 434–46.

Laroche, P. (2009) *Les relations sociales en entreprise*. Paris: Dunod.

Lebergott, S. (1984) *The Americans: An Economic Record*. New York: W.W. Norton.

Ledvinka, J. & Scarpello, V.G. (1991) *Federal Regulation of Personnel and Human Resource Management*, 2nd ed. Belmont, CA: Kent.

Lee, B. (2003) 'Industrial relations system', in J. Kim (ed.), *Employment and Industrial Relations in Korea*. Seoul: KOILAF, pp. 171–213.

—— (2005) 'Solidarity crisis of Korean labor movement'. *Korea Focus*, 13(1): 86–106.

Lee, B. & Kim, J. (2013) *Revitalizing Strategies for Industry Union Movement* [in Korean]. Seoul: KCTU.

Lee, C.K. (2007) *Against the Law: Labor Protests in China's Rustbelt and Sunbelt*. Berkeley, CA: University of California Press.

Lee, C.K. & Shen, Y. (2011) 'The anti-solidarity machine? Labor nongovernmental organizations in China', in S. Kuruvilla, C.K. Lee & M. Gallagher (eds), *From Iron Rice Bowl to Informalization*. Ithaca, NY: ILR Press, pp. 173–87.

Lee, J. (2002) 'Industrial unionization and change of bargaining structure'. Paper presented to the International Conference of International Labor Standards and Korean Industrial Relations, Seoul.

Lee, M. & Peetz, D. (1998) 'Trade unions and the *Workplace Relations Act*'. *Labour and Industry*, 9(2): 5–22.

Lee, W. & Lee, B. (2003) 'Industrial relations and labor standards in Korea', in O. Kwon (ed.), *Korea's New Economy Strategy in the Globalization Era*. Cheltenham: Edward Elgar, pp. 173–91.

Leibfried, S. & Wagschal, U. (eds) (2000) *Der deutsche Sozialstaat: Bilanzen—Reformen—Perspektiven*. Frankfurt: Campus.

Levine, S.B. (1984) 'Employers' associations in Japan', in J.P. Windmuller & A. Gladstone (eds), *Employers' Associations and Industrial Relations: A Comparative Study*. Oxford: Clarendon Press, pp. 318–56.

Levy, F. & Murname, R.J. (1992) 'US earnings levels and earnings inequality: A review of recent trends and proposed explanations'. *Journal of Economic Literature*, 30: 1333–81.

Lewin, D. (2008) 'Employee voice and mutual gains', in *Proceedings of the 60th Annual Meeting*. Champaign, IL: Labor and Employment Relations Association.

Lewin, D., Keefe, J.H. & Kochan, T.A. (2012) 'The new great debate about unionism and collective bargaining in US state and local governments'. *Industrial and Labor Relations Review*, 65(4): 747–75.

Li, H. (2000) 'An analysis of the situation of China's labour market'. *Journal of Beijing College of Management of Planning and Labour*, 3: 14, 57.

Li, J., Cooke, F.L. & Mu, J.L. (2014) 'The measurement and determinants of underpayment of wages in China: An empirical assessment of the 2003–2008 period'. Unpublished working paper.

Li, X.J., Xu, Y.D. & Zhu, J.X. (2006) 'Employment relationship under the form of employment leasing' [in Chinese]. *Labor Economy and Labor Relations*, 1: 5–8.

Li, Y.B. (2003) 'The progress and forecast of the Chinese labour market'. *Contemporary Finance and Economics*, 3: 15–19.

Linden, M. (1998) 'Doing comparative labour history: Some essential preliminaries', in J. Hagan & A. Wells (eds), *Australian Labour and Regional Change: Essays in Honour of R.A. Gollan*. Sydney: University of Wollongong in association with Halstead Press, pp. 75–92.

Liu, M.W. (2010) 'Union organizing in China: Still a monolithic labor movement?' *Industrial and Labor Relations Review*, 64(1): 30–52.

Liu, X. & Yuan S. (2005) 'Labour disputes in privately owned enterprises: An analysis of forms and causes'. *Journal of Jiaxing University*, 17(4): 62–5.

Locke, R.M. (1992) 'The decline of the national union in Italy: Lessons for comparative industrial relations'. *Industrial and Labor Relations Review*, 45: 229–49.

—— (1995) *Remaking the Italian Economy*. Ithaca, NY: Cornell University Press.

Locke, R.M., Rissing, B.A. & Pal, T. (2013) 'Complements or substitutes? Private codes, state regulation and the enforcement of labour standards in global supply chains'. *British Journal of Industrial Relations*, 51(3): 519–52.

Locke, R.M. & Thelen, K. (1995) 'Apples and oranges compared: Contextualized comparisons and the study of comparative politics'. *Politics & Society*, 23(3): 337–67.

Low Pay Commission (2011) *National Minimum Wage Report 2011*. London: Her Majesty's Stationery Office.

Lu, F. (2010) 'Characteristics of labour relations related mass incidences during global financial crisis and solutions'. *Journal of Hunan Public Security College*, 22(4): 22–4.

Lyons, M. & Smith, M. (2007) '2020 vision or 1920s myopia? Recent developments in gender pay equity in Australia'. *International Employment Relations Review*, 13(2): 27–39.

Machin, S. (2011) 'Changes in UK wage inequality over the last forty years', in P. Gregg & J. Wadsworth (eds), *The Labour Market in Winter*. Oxford: Oxford University Press, pp. 155–69.

Macintyre, S. & Mitchell, R. (eds) (1989) *Foundations of Arbitration: The Origins and Effects of State Compulsory Arbitration, 1890–1914*. Melbourne: Oxford University Press.

Mailand, M. (2008) *Regulering af arbejde og velfærd: Mod nye arbejdsdelinger mellem staten og arbejdsmarkedets parter*. Copenhagen: DJØF.

—— (2011a) *Trepartssamarbejde gennem tiderne: Hvordan, hvornår og hvilke udfordringer*. Paper. Copenhagen: FAOS, University of Copenhagen.

—— (2011b) *Overenskomstfornyelsen 2011: Den kommunale sektor perspektiveret.* Research Paper No. 127. Copenhagen: FAOS, University of Copenhagen.

—— (2013) *Når man går foran: Gymnasieskolernes Lærerforenings delta-gelse i OK13.* Research Paper No. 136. Copenhagen: FAOS, University of Copenhagen.

Malila, J. (2007) 'The great look forward: China's HR evolution'. *China Business Review*, 34(4): 16–19.

Marchington, M. & Cox, A. (2007) 'Employee involvement and participation: Structures, processes and outcomes', in J. Storey (ed.), *Human Resource Management: A Critical Text*, 3rd ed. London: Thomson.

Marchington, M., Grimshaw, D., Rubery, J. & Willmott, H. (2005) (eds) *Frag-menting Work: Blurring Organizational Boundaries and Disordering Hierarchies.* Oxford: Oxford University Press.

Marchington, M. & Parker, P. (1990) *Changing Patterns of Employee Relations.* Hemel Hempstead: Harvester Wheatsheaf.

Marchington, M. & Wilkinson, A. (2012) *Human Resource Management at Work*, 5th ed. London: Chartered Institute of Personnel and Development.

Marginson, P. (2014) 'Coordinated bargaining in Europe: From incremental corrosion to frontal assault?' *European Journal of Industrial Relations*, April. doi: 10.1177/0959680114530241.

Martin, J. (2010) 'China: Honda workers' strike; The beginning of a new labour movement?' *Marxism*, 1 June. Retrieved 21 April 2014 from <www.marxist.com/china-honda-workers-strike.htm>.

Martin, R. (1989) *Trade Unionism: Purposes and Forms.* Oxford: Clarendon Press.

Martin, R. & Bamber, G.J. (2004) 'International comparative employment relations theory: Developing the political economy perspective', in B.E. Kaufman (ed.), *Theoretical Perspectives on Work and the Employ-ment Relationship.* Pittsburgh, PA: Industrial Relations Research Associa-tion (LERA), pp. 293–320.

Martinez Lucio, M. & Perrett, R. (2009) 'The diversity and politics of trade union responses to minority ethnic and migrant workers: The context of the United Kingdom'. *Economic and Industrial Democracy*, 30(3): 324–47.

Martinez Lucio, M. & Stuart, M. (2005) 'Partnership and new industrial rela-tions in a risk society: An age of shotgun weddings and marriages of conve-nience'. *Work, Employment and Society*, 19(4): 797–818.

Mascini, M. (2000) *Profitti e salari.* Bologna: Il Mulino.

Mason, B. & Bain, P. (1993) 'The determinants of trade union membership in Britain: A survey of the literature'. *Industrial and Labor Relations Review*, 46(2): 332–51.

Massa-Wirth, H. (2007) *Zugeständnisse für Arbeitsplätze? Konzessionäre Beschäftigungsvereinbarungen im Vergleich Deutschland—USA.* Berlin: Edition Sigma.

McCallum, R. (1997) 'Australian workplace agreements: An analysis'. *Austra-lian Journal of Labour Law*, 10(1): 50–61.

McCallum, R., Moore, M. & Edwards, J. (2012) *Towards More Produc-tive and Equitable Workplaces: An Evaluation of the Fair Work*

*Legislation*. Canberra: Department of Education, Employment and Workplace Relations.

McClendon, J.A., Kriesky, J. & Eaton, A. (1995) 'Member support for union mergers: An analysis of an affiliation referendum'. *Journal of Labor Research*, 16(1): 9–23.

McCrystal, S. (2014) 'Industrial legislation in Australia in 2013'. *Journal of Industrial Relations*, 56(3): 331–45.

McDowell, L. & Christopherson, S. (2009) 'Transforming work: New forms of employment and their regulation'. *Cambridge Journal of Regions, Economy and Society*, 2(3): 335–42.

McLaughlin, C. (2009) 'The productivity-enhancing impacts of the minimum wage: Lessons from Denmark and New Zealand'. *British Journal of Industrial Relations*, 47(2): 327–48.

Meager, N. & Speckesser (2011) *Wages, productivity and employment: A review of theory and international data*. Retrieved from <www.eu-employment-observatory.net/resources/reports/WagesProductivity andEmploymentpdf>.

Mehrotra, S., Gandhi, A., Saha, P. & Sahoo, B.K. (2012) *Joblessness and Informalization: Challenges to Inclusive Growth in India*. Occasional Paper No. 9/2012. New Delhi: Institute of Applied Manpower Research, Planning Commission, Government of India.

Meng, X. (2000) *Labour Market Reform in China*. Cambridge: Cambridge University Press.

Metcalf, D. (1991) 'British unions: Dissolution or resurgence?' *Oxford Review of Economic Policy*, 7(1): 18–32.

—— (2005) 'Trade unions: Resurgence or perdition? An economic analysis', in S. Fernie & D. Metcalf (eds), *Trade Unions: Resurgence or Demise?* London: Routledge.

Millward, N., Bryson, A. & Forth, J. (2000) *All Change at Work? British Employment Relations 1980–1998, as Portrayed by the Workplace Industrial Relations Survey Series*. London: Routledge.

Millward, N., Stevens, M., Smart, D. & Hawes, W. (1992) *Workplace Industrial Relations in Transition*. Aldershot: Dartmouth.

Ministry of Economy, Trade and Industry (Japan) *Kaigaijigyo katsudo chosa* (Annual Survey on Overseas Activities of Japanese Enterprises).

Ministry of Health, Labour and Welfare (Japan) (each year) Monthly Labour Survey.

—— (2010) Survey on the Diversification of the Forms of Employment.

Ministry of Internal Affairs and Communications (Japan) (1992) Employment Status Survey.

—— (2012) Employment Status Survey.

Ministry of Labour (Japan) (1975) *Rodo hakusho* (White Paper on Labour). Tokyo: Ministry of Finance Printing Office.

Minkin, L. (1991) *The Contentious Alliance: Trade Unions and the Labour Party*. Edinburgh: Edinburgh University Press.

Miyajima, H. & Nitta, K. (2011) 'Kabushiki shijono tayokato sono kiketsu' (Diversification of ownership structure and its effect on performance) in H. Miyajima (ed.), *Nihon no kigyo tochi* (Corporate Governance in Japan). Tokyo: Toyokeizai Shimposha.

MoEL (Ministry of Employment and Labour) (2014) *2013 Report on Organizational Status of Trade Unions* [in Korean]. Seoul: MoEL.

Molina, O. & Rhodes, M. (2002) 'Corporatism: The past, present, and future of a concept'. *Annual Review of Political Science*, 5: 305–31.

Möller, J. (2010) 'The German labor market response in the world recession: Demystifying a miracle'. *Zeitschrift für Arbeitsmarktforschung*, 42(4): 325–36.

—— (2012) 'Minimum wages in German industries: What does the evidence tell us so far?' *Journal of Labour Market Research*, 45(3–4): 187–99.

Moore, S. (2013) 'Ten years of statutory recognition: A changed landscape for UK industrial relations?' *Centre for Employment Studies Research Review*, January. (Bristol: Centre for Employment Studies Research, University of the West of England.)

Morgan, G. & Kristensen, P.H. (2006) 'The contested space of multinationals: Varieties of institutionalism, varieties of capitalism'. *Human Relations*, 59(11): 1467–90.

Morishima, M. (1991) 'Information sharing and firm performance in Japan'. *Industrial Relations*, 30(1): 37–62.

Mu, J. (2003) 'Building a unified urban–rural labour market is an inevitable trend'. *Journal of Kunming University*, 2: 11–14.

Müller-Jentsch, W. & Ittermann, P. (2000) *Industrielle Beziehungen: Daten, Zeitreihen, Trends 1950–1999*. Frankfurt: Campus.

Nam, J. & Kim, T. (2000) 'Are non-standard jobs a bridge or a trap?' [in Korean]. *Korean Journal of Labor Economics*, 23(2): 85–105.

Nankervis, A., Compton, R., Baird, M. & Coffey, J. (2011) *Human Resource Management: Strategies and Practice*, 7th ed. Melbourne: Cengage.

Navrbjerg, S.E., Larsen, T. & Johansen, M.M. (2010) *Fokus på tillidsrepræsentanterne 2010*. Five reports. Copenhagen: Confederation of Danish Trade Unions.

NBSC (National Bureau of Statistics of China) (2002–13) *China Labour Statistical Yearbook*. Beijing: China Statistics Press.

Nienhüser, W. & Hoßfeld, H. (2004) *Bewertung von Betriebsvereinbarungen durch Personalmanager: Eine empirische Studie*. Frankfurt: Bund-Verlag.

Niforou, C. (2012) 'International framework agreements and industrial relations governance: Global rhetoric versus local realities'. *British Journal of Industrial Relations*, 50(2): 352–73.

Nolan, P. (2001) *China and the Global Economy*. London: Palgrave.

OECD (2008) *Employment Outlook 2008*. Paris: OECD.

—— (2011) *Divided We Stand: Why Inequality Keeps Rising*. Geneva: OECD.

—— (2013) *OECD Factbook 2013: Economic, Environmental, and Social Statistics*. Paris: OECD.

—— (2014a) *Union Members and Employees database*. Annual updating (1999 onwards). Retrieved 20 November 2014 from <http://stats.oecd.org/Index.aspx?DatasetCode=U_D_D>.

—— (2014b) *OECD StatExtracts. Gross domestic products: Germany*. Retrieved 21 May 2015 from <https://stats.oecd.org/index.aspx?queryid=60702>.

ONS (2014) *Labour Market Statistics, January 2014*. Statistical Bulletin, January. London: ONS.

O'Rourke, D. (2003) 'Outsourcing regulation: Analyzing nongovernmental systems of labor standards and monitoring'. *Policy Studies Journal*, 31(1): 1–29.

Orth, J.V. (1991) *Combination and Conspiracy: A Legal History of Trade Unionism, 1721–1906*. New York: Oxford University Press.

Page, R. (2006) *Co-determination in Germany: A Beginners' Guide*. Düsseldorf: Hans-Böckler-Stiftung.

Pagés, C. & Roy, T. (2006) 'Regulation, enforcement and adjudication in Indian labor markets: Historical perspective, recent changes and the way forward', in *India: Meeting the Employment Challenge; Conference on Labour and Employment Issues in India*. New Delhi: Institute for Human Development/World Bank.

Palier, B. & Thelen, K. (2010) 'Institutionalizing dualism: Complementarities and change in France and Germany'. *Politics & Society*, 38(1): 119–48.

Papadakis, K. (ed.) (2011) *Shaping Global Industrial Relations: The Impact of International Framework Agreements*. New York: Palgrave Macmillan.

Papola, T.S., Pais, J. & Sahu, P.P. (2008) *Labour Regulation in Indian Industry: Towards a Rational and Equitable Framework*. New Delhi: Institute for Studies for Industrial Development/EU/International Institute for Labour Studies/Bookwell.

Park, J. (1992) *A Study on the Industrial Relations at Korean Large Firm* [in Korean]. Seoul: Baeksanseodang.

Park, W. & Roh, Y. (2001) *Changes in Human Resource Management and Industrial Relations in the Period of Post-Crisis*. Seoul: KLI.

Pedersen, O.K. (2006) 'Corporatism and beyond: The negotiated economy', in J.L. Campbell, J.A. Hall & O.K. Pedersen (eds), *National Identity and the Varieties of Capitalism: The Danish Experience*. Toronto: McGill-Queens University Press, pp. 245–70.

Pedersini, R. (2012a) 'Italy: Impact of the crisis on industrial relations'. Retrieved 20 September 2014 from <www.eurofound.europa.eu/eiro/studies/tn1301019s/it1301019q.htm>.

—— (2012b) 'Recent developments in Fiat's industrial relations'. Retrieved 20 September 2014 from <http://eurofound.europa.eu/observatories/eurwork/articles/industrial-relations/recent-developments-in-fiats-industrial-relations>.

Pedersini, R. & Regini, M. (2013) *Coping with the crisis in Italy: Employment Relations and Social Dialogue Amidst Recession*. Working Paper No. 50. Geneva: ILO.

Peetz, D. (1998) *Unions in a Contrary World: The Future of the Australian Trade Union Movement*. Melbourne: Cambridge University Press.

—— (2012) 'Does industrial relations policy affect productivity?' *Australian Bulletin of Labour*, 38(4): 268–92.

Pendleton, A., Whitfield, K. & Bryson, A. (2009) 'The changing use of contingent pay in the modern British workplace', in W. Brown, A. Bryson, J. Forth & K. Whitfield (eds), *The Evolution of the Modern Workplace*. Cambridge: Cambridge University Press.

Pernot, J.-M. (2005) *Syndicats: Lendemains de crise?* Paris: Gallimard.

Perraton, J., Goldblatt, D., Held, D. & McGrew, A. (1997) 'The globalisation of economic activity'. *New Political Economy*, 2(2): 257–77.

Piketty, T. (2014) *Capital in the Twenty-First Century*. Cambridge, MA: The Belknap Press of Harvard University Press.

Piketty T. & Saez, E. (2003) 'Income inequality in the United States, 1913–1998'. *Quarterly Journal of Economics*, 118: 1–39.

Piore, M.J. (1981) *Convergence in Industrial Relations? The Case of France and the United States*. Working Paper No. 286. Cambridge, MA: Department of Economics, Massachusetts Institute of Technology.

Pittard, M. (1997) 'Collective employment relationships: Reform of arbitrated awards and certified agreements'. *Australian Journal of Labour Law*, 10(1): 62–88.

Pizzorno, A., Regalia, I., Regini, M. & Reyneri, E. (1978) *Lotte operaie e sindacato in Italia: 1968–1972*. Bologna: Il Mulino.

Plowman, D. (1989) 'Forced march: The employers and arbitration', in S. Macintyre & R. Mitchell (eds), *Foundations of Arbitration: The Origins and Effects of State Compulsory Arbitration, 1890–1914*. Melbourne: Oxford University Press, pp. 135–55.

Pocock, B., Elton, J., Preston, A., Charlesworth, S., MacDonald, F., Baird, M., Cooper, R. & Ellem, B. (2008) 'The impact of Work Choices on women in low paid employment in Australia'. *Journal of Industrial Relations*, 50(3): 475–88.

Potter, P. (1999) 'The Chinese legal system: Continuing commitment to the primacy of state power'. *China Quarterly*, 159: 673–83.

Price, R. & Bain, G. (1983) 'Union growth in Britain: Retrospect and prospect'. *British Journal of Industrial Relations*, 11(1): 46–68.

Przeworski, A. & Teune, H. (1970) *The Logic of Comparative Social Inquiry*. New York: Wiley.

Pudelko, M. & Harzing, A.W. (2007) 'Country-of-Origin, Localization or Dominance Effect? An empirical investigation of HRM practices in foreign subsidiaries', *Human Resource Management*, 46(4): 535–59.

Pulignano, V. (2006) 'The diffusion of employment practices of US-based multinationals in Europe: A case study comparison of British- and Italian-based subsidiaries between two sectors'. *British Journal of Industrial Relations*, 44(3): 497–518.

—— (2007) 'Going national or European? Local trade union politics within transnational business contexts in Europe', in K. Bronfenbrenner (ed.), *Global Unions: Challenging Global Capita through Cross-Border Campaigns*. Ithaca, NY: Cornell University Press, pp. 137–54.

Pun, N. & Chan, J. (2012) 'Global capital, the state, and Chinese workers: The Foxconn experience'. *Modern China*, 38(4): 383–410.

Pun, N. & Smith, C. (2007) 'Putting transnational labour process in its place: The dormitory labour regime in post-socialist China'. *Work, Employment and Society*, 21(1): 47–65.

Purcell, J. & Georgiades, K. (2007) 'Why should employees bother with worker voice?' in R. Freeman, P. Boxall & P. Haynes (eds), *What Workers Say: Employee Voice in the Anglo-American Workplace*. Ithaca: ILR Press, pp. 181–97.

Purcell, J. & Hutchinson, S. (2007) *Bringing Policies to Life: The Vital Role of*

*Front Line Managers in People Management*. London: Chartered Institute of Personnel and Development.

Purcell, J. & Sisson, K. (1983) 'Strategies and practice in the management of industrial relations', in G. Bain (ed.), *Industrial Relations in Britain*. Oxford: Blackwell, pp. 95–120.

Ramaswamy, E.A. (1977) *The Worker and His Union: A Study in South India*. New Delhi: Allied Publishers.

—— (1984) *Power and Justice: The State in Industrial Relations*. New Delhi: Oxford University Press.

—— (1988) *Worker Consciousness and Trade Union Response*. New Delhi: Oxford University Press.

Ramsay, H. (1977) 'Cycles of control: Worker participation in sociological and historical perspective'. *Sociology*, 11: 481–506.

Redding, G. & Witt, M. (2007) *The Future of Chinese Capitalism: Choices and Chances*. New York: Oxford University Press.

Regalia, I. & Regini, M. (1998) 'Italy: The dual character of industrial relations', in A. Ferner & R. Hyman (eds), *Changing Industrial Relations in Europe*, 2nd ed. Malden, MA: Blackwell, pp. 459–503.

Regini, M. (1985) 'Relazioni industriali e sistema politico: L'evoluzione recente e le prospettive degli anni '80', in M. Carrieri & P. Perulli (eds), *Il teorema sindacale*. Bologna: Il Mulino.

Rehder, B. (2014) 'Vom Korporatismus zur Kampagne? Organizing als Strategie der gewerkschaftlichen Erneuerung', in W. Schroeder (ed.), *Handbuch Gewerkschaften in Deutschland*, 2nd ed. Wiesbaden: Springer, pp. 241–64.

Reilly, P., Tamkin, P. & Broughton, A. (2007) *The Changing HR Function: Transforming HR?* London: Chartered Institute of Personnel and Development.

Rhodes, M. (1996) *Globalisation, Labour Markets and Welfare States: A Future of 'Competitive Corporatism'?* Florence: European University Institute.

—— (2001) 'The political economy of social pacts: "Competitive corporatism" and European welfare reform', in P. Pierson (ed.), *The New Politics of the Welfare State*. Oxford: Oxford University Press, pp. 165–94.

Rhodes, M., Hancké, B. & Thatcher, M. (2007) 'Introduction: Beyond varieties of capitalism' in M. Rhodes, B. Hancké & M. Thatcher (eds), *Beyond Varieties of Capitalism: Conflict, contradictions and complementarities in the European economy*. Oxford: Oxford University Press, pp. 1–32.

Richardson, S. & Law, V. (2009) 'Changing forms of employment and their implications for the development of skills'. *Australian Bulletin of Labour*, 35(2): 355–92.

Richardson, S., Lester, L. & Zhang, G. (2012) 'Are casual and contract terms of employment hazardous for mental health in Australia?' *Journal of Industrial Relations*, 54(5): 557–78.

Rideout, R.W. (1971) 'The *Industrial Relations Act 1971*'. *Modern Law Review*, 34(6): 655–75.

Riisgaard, L. (2005) 'International framework agreements: A new model for securing workers' rights?' *Industrial Relations*, 44(4): 707–37.

Ritzer, G. (1977) *Working, Conflict and Change*. Englewood Cliffs, NJ: Prentice Hall.

Rollinson, D. & Dundon, T. (2007) *Understanding Employment Relations*. London: Addison-Wesley.

Romagnoli, U. & Treu, T. (1981) *I sindacati in Italia dal '45 ad oggi: Storia di una strategia*. Bologna: Il Mulino.

Rose, J. & Chaison, G. (2001) 'Unionism in Canada and the United States in the 21st century'. *Relations Industrielles/Industrial Relations*, 56(1): 34–65.

Rosenblum, J. (1995) *Copper Crucible*. Ithaca, NY: Cornell University Press.

Ross, C. (2013) 'New unions and the United Kingdom: The vanguard or the rearguard of the union movement?' *Industrial Relations Journal*, 44(1): 78–94.

Rossi, F. & Sestito, P. (2000) 'Contrattazione aziendale, struttura negoziale e determinazione del salario'. *Rivista di politica economica*, 90(10–11): 129–83.

Rostow, W.W. (1960) *The Stages of Economic Growth: A Non-Communist Manifesto*. Cambridge: Cambridge University Press.

Rothstein, J. (2012) 'The labor market four years into the crisis: Assessing structural explanations'. *Industrial and Labor Relations Review*, 65(3): 467–500.

Roy, S.D. (2002) 'Job security regulations and worker turnover: A study of the Indian manufacturing sector'. *Indian Economic Review*, 37: 141–62.

Rubery, J., Earnshaw, J., Marchington, M., Cooke, F.L. & Vincent, S. (2002) 'Changing organizational forms and the employment relationship'. *Journal of Management Studies*, 39(5): 645–72.

Ruggie, J.G. (2004) 'Reconstituting the global public domain: Issues, actors, and practices'. *European Journal of International Relations*, 10(4): 499–531.

Ryder, G. (2015) 'The ILO: The next 100 years'. *Journal of Industrial Relations*, 57(5): forthcoming.

Sabel, C. (1982) *Work and Politics*. New York: Cambridge University Press.

Saich, T. (2001) *Governance and Politics of China*. Basingstoke: Palgrave.

Saini, D. (1991) 'Compulsory adjudication of industrial disputes: Juridification of industrial disputes'. *Indian Journal of Industrial Relations*, 27(1): 1–18.

—— (2005) 'Management case: Honda Motorcycles and Scooters India Limited'. *Vision*, 9(4): 71–81.

Salisbury, D. (2001) 'The state of private pensions', in S. Friedman & D.C. Jacobs (eds), *The Future of the Safety Net: Social Insurance and Employee Benefits*. Champaign, IL: Industrial Relations Research Association.

Salvati, M. (1984) *Economia e politica in Italia dal dopoguerra ad oggi*. Milan: Garzanti.

Sanz, S. (2011) 'Intersectoral agreement on representativeness heals rift'. Retrieved 20 September 2014 from <www.eurofound.europa.eu/eiro/2011/08/articles/it1108029i.htm>.

Savage, L. (2011) *Low Pay in Britain*. London: Resolution.

Schettkat, R. (2006) *Lohnspreizung: Mythen und Fakten; Eine Literaturübersicht zu Ausmaß und ökonomischen Wirkungen von Lohngleichheit*. Düsseldorf: Hans-Böckler-Stiftung.

Schmidt, V. (2002) *The Futures of European Capitalism*. Oxford: Oxford University Press.

Schroeder, W. (ed.) (2014) *Handbuch Gewerkschaften in Deutschland*. 2nd ed. Wiesbaden: Springer.

Schroeder, W. & Greef, S. (2014) 'Struktur und Entwicklung des deutschen Gewerkschaftsmodells: Herausforderung durch Sparten- und Berufsgewerkschaften', in W. Schroeder (ed.), *Handbuch Gewerkschaften in Deutschland*, 2nd ed. Wiesbaden: Springer, pp. 123–45.

Schroeder, W., Kalass, V. & Greef, S. (2011) *Berufsgewerkschaften in der Offensive: Vom Wandel des deutschen Gewerkschaftsmodells*. Wiesbaden: VS Verlag.

Schroeder, W. & Silvia, S. (2014) 'Gewerkschaften und Arbeitgeberverbände', in W. Schroeder (ed.), *Handbuch Gewerkschaften in Deutschland*, 2nd ed. Wiesbaden: Springer, pp. 337–65.

Schroeder, W. & Weßels, B. (eds) (2010) *Handbuch Arbeitgeber- und Wirtschaftsverbände in Deutschland*. Wiesbaden: VS Verlag.

Shrouti, A. & Nandkumar, A.V. (1995) *New Economic Policy Changing Management Strategies: Impact on workers and unions*. New Delhi/Mumbai: Friedrich EbertStiftung/Maniben Kara Institute.

Schuler, R., Budhwar, P. & Florkowski, G. (2002) 'International human resource management: Review and critique'. *International Journal of Management Reviews*, 4(1): 41–70.

Sefton, T. & Sutherland, H. (2005) 'Inequality and poverty under New Labour', in J. Hills & K. Stewart (eds), *A More Equal Society? New Labour, Poverty, Inequality and Exclusion*. Bristol: Policy Press, pp. 231–50.

Seifert, H. (ed.) (2005) *Flexible Zeiten in der Arbeitswelt*. Frankfurt: Campus.

—— (2008) 'Regulated flexibility: Flexible working time patterns in Germany and the role of works councils'. *International Journal of Comparative Labour Law and Industrial Relations*, 24(2): 227–40.

Sengupta, A.K. (1993) *Trends in Industrial Conflict in India, 1961–87*. New Delhi: Friedrich Ebert Stiftung.

Sexton, P.C. (1991) *The War against Labor and the Left*. Boulder, CO: Westview Press.

Shalev, M. (1980) 'Industrial relations theory and the comparative study of industrial relations and industrial conflict'. *British Journal of Industrial Relations*, 18(1): 26–43.

Sharma, G.K. (1982) *Labour Movement in India (Its Past and Present: From 1885 to 1980)*. New Delhi: Sterling.

Sheehan, J. (1999) *Chinese Workers: A New History*. London: Routledge.

Sheldon, P., Gan, B. & Bamber, G.J. (2014) 'Collective bargaining: Globalizing economies and diverse outcomes', in R.I. Blanpain (ed.), *Comparative Labour Law and Industrial Relations in Industrialized Market Economies*, 11th ed. Dordrecht: Wolters Kluwer, pp. 681–730.

Sheldon, P. & Thornthwaite, L. (1999) *Employer Associations and Industrial Relations Change: Catalysts or Captives?* Sydney: Allen & Unwin.

Shirai, T. (ed.) (1983) *Contemporary Industrial Relations in Japan*. Madison, WI: University of Wisconsin.

Shyam Sundar, K.R. (2008) *Impact of Labour Regulation on Growth, Investment, and Employment: A study of Maharashtra*. New Delhi: Institute for Studies for Industrial Development (ISID)/European Union (EU)/International Institute for Labour Studies (IILS)/Bookwell.

—— (2009a) *Current Status and Evolution of Industrial Relations in Maharashtra*. New Delhi: ILO.

—— (2009b) *Labour Institutions and Labour Reforms in Contemporary India*. Vol. 1: *Trade Unions and Industrial Conflict*. Hyderabad: Icfai Press.

—— (2009c) *Labour Institutions and Labour Reforms in Contemporary India*. Vol. 2: *The State and the Labour Reforms Debate*. Hyderabad: Icfai Press.

—— (2010a) *Labour Reforms and Decent Work in India: A Study of Labour Inspection in India*. New Delhi: Bookwell.

—— (2010b) *Industrial Conflict in India: Is the Sleeping Giant Waking Up?* New Delhi: Bookwell.

—— (2010c) *The Current State of Industrial Relations in Tamil Nadu*. Project report submitted to the ILO office, New Delhi.

—— (2011) *Non-regular Workers in India: Social Dialogue and Organizational and Bargaining Strategies and Practices*. Geneva: Social Dialogue, ILO.

—— (2012) 'Industrial violence and labour reforms'. *Economic and Political Weekly*, 13 October: 35–40.

—— (2014) 'Some aspects of productivity bargaining in India in the recent period'. Paper presented to the International Seminar on Development from the Perspective of Labour Experiences, Challenges and Options, Giri Institute of Development Studies, Lucknow, February.

Shyam Sundar, K.R. & Venkata Ratnam, C.S. (2007) 'Labour reforms in China and India: Reform aggression (China) versus reform allergy (India)!' *Indian Journal of Labour Economics*, 50(3): 497–512.

Si, S.X., Wei, F. & Li, Y. (2008) 'The effect of organizational psychological contract violation on managers' exit, voice, loyalty and neglect in the Chinese context'. *International Journal of Human Resource Management*, 19(5): 932–44.

Siaroff, A. (1999) 'Corporatism in 24 industrial democracies: Meaning and measurement'. *European Journal of Political Research*, 36(2): 175–205.

Simms, M., Holgate, J. & Heery, E. (2013) *Union Voices: Tactics and Tensions in UK Organising*. Ithaca, NY: Cornell University Press.

Simpson, B. (2000) 'Trade union recognition and the law: A new approach'. *Industrial Law Journal*, 29(3): 193–222.

Sisson, K. (1987) *The Management of Collective Bargaining*. Oxford: Blackwell.

—— (ed.) (1994) *Personnel Management*. Oxford: Blackwell.

Sisson, K. & Purcell, J. (2010) 'Management: Caught between competing views of the organisation', in T. Colling & M. Terry (eds), *Industrial Relations: Theory and Practice*. Chichester: Wiley, pp. 83–105.

Skopcol, T. & Somers, M. (1980) 'The uses of comparative history in macro-social inquiry'. *Comparative Studies in History and Society*, 228(2): 174–92.

SNCL (Second National Commission on Labour) (2002) *Report of the National Commission on Labour*. Vol. 1, Part 1. New Delhi: Ministry of Labour, Government of India.

Solinger, D. (1999) *Contesting Citizenship in Urban China: Peasant Migrants, the State, and the Logic of the Market*. Berkeley, CA: University of California Press.

Statistics Canada (2011) 'Projected trends to 2031 for the Canadian labour force'. Retrieved 20 September 2014 from <www.statcan.gc.ca/pub/11 -010-x/2011008/part-partie3-eng.htm>.

—— (2014) 'Gross domestic product at basic prices, construction and manufacturing industries'. Retrieved 20 September 2014 from <www.statcan. gc.ca/tables-tableaux/sum-som/l01/cst01/manuf10-eng.htm>.

Statistics Denmark (2010) *External Trade of Denmark 2009*. Copenhagen: Statistics Denmark.

—— (2014) *External Trade of Denmark 2013*. Copenhagen: Statistics Denmark.

Stewart, A. (2011) 'Fair Work Australia: The commission reborn?' *Journal of Industrial Relations*, 53(5): 563–77.

Stewart, J. & Walsh, K. (1992) 'Change in the management of public services'. *Public Administration*, 70(4): 499–518.

Stiglitz, J. (2013) *The Rise of Inequality*. New York: W.W. Norton.

Stone, K.V.W. (1996) 'Mandatory arbitration of individual employment rights: The yellow dog contract of the 1990s'. *Denver Law Review*, 73: 1017–34.

Stone, K.V.W. & Arthurs, H. (2013) *Rethinking Workplace Regulation: Beyond the Standard Contract of Employment*. New York: Russell Sage Foundation.

Strauss, G. (1998) 'Comparative international industrial relations', in K. Whitfield & G. Strauss (eds), *Researching the World of Work: Strategies and Methods in Studying Industrial Relations*. Ithaca: Cornell University Press, pp. 175–92.

Streeck, W. (1987) 'The uncertainty of management in the management of uncertainty: Employers, labour relations and industrial adjustments in the 1980s'. *Work, Employment and Society*, 1(3): 281–308.

—— (1997) 'Beneficial constraints: On the economic limits of rational voluntarism', in J.R. Hollingsworth & R. Boyer (eds), *Contemporary Capitalism: The Embeddedness of Institutions*. Cambridge: Cambridge University Press, pp. 197–219.

—— (2000) 'Competitive solidarity: Rethinking the "European social model"', in K. Hinrichs, H. Kitschelt & H. Wiesenthal (eds), *Kontingenz und Krise: Institutionenpolitik in kapitalistischen und postsozialistischen Gesellschaften*. Frankfurt: Campus Verlag, pp. 245–62.

Streeck, W. & Yamamura, K. (eds) (2001) *The Origins of Nonliberal Capitalism: Germany and Japan in Comparison*. Ithaca, NY: Cornell University Press.

—— (2003) *The End of Diversity? Prospects for German and Japanese Capitalism*. Ithaca, NY: Cornell University Press.

Sturmthal, A. (1973) 'Industrial relations strategies', in A. Sturmthal & J. Scoville (eds), *The International Labor Movement in Transition*. Urbana, IL: University of Illinois Press.

Stuvøy, I. & Andersen, S.K. (2013) 'Temporary staffing and labour migration to Denmark', in J.H. Friberg & L. Eldring (eds), *Labour Migrants from Central and Eastern Europe in the Nordic Countries*. Oslo: Nordic Council of Ministers, TemaNord, pp. 231–72.

Taft, P. (1964) *Organized Labor in American History*. New York: Harper & Row.

Tarantelli, E. (1986) *Economia politica del lavoro*. Turin: UTET.

Taylor, B., Chang, K. & Li, Q. (2003) *Industrial Relations in China*. Cheltenham: Edward Elgar.

Taylor, B. & Li, Q. (2007) 'Is the ACFTU a union and does it matter?' *Journal of Industrial Relations*, 49(5): 701–15.

—— (2010) 'China's creative approach to "union" organizing'. *Labor History*, 51(3): 411–28.

Tchobanian, R. (1996) 'La représentation des salariés dans l'entreprise: Entre participation et action syndicale', in G. Murray, M.-L. Morin & I. Da Costa (eds), *L'état des relations professionnelles: Traditions et perspectives de recherché*. Toulouse: Octarès, pp. 259–83.

Ter Haar, B.P. & Keune, M.J. (2014) 'One step forward or more window-dressing? A legal analysis of the recent CSR initiatives in the garment industry in Bangladesh'. *International Journal of Comparative Labour Law and Industrial Relations*, 30(1): 4–25.

Thelen, K.A. (1991) *Labor Politics in Postwar Germany*. Ithaca, NY: Cornell University Press.

—— (2001) 'Varieties of labor politics in the developed democracies', in P.A. Hall & D. Soskice (eds), *Varieties of Capitalism: The Institutional Foundations of Comparative Advantage*. New York: Oxford University Press, pp. 71–103.

—— (2014) *Varieties of Liberalization and the New Politics of Social Solidarity*. New York: Cambridge University Press.

Thireau, I. & Hua, L.S. (2003) 'The moral universe of aggrieved Chinese workers: Workers' appeals to arbitration committees and letters and visits offices'. *China Journal*, 50: 83–103.

Thornthwaite, L. & Sheldon, P. (2014) 'Employer and employer association matters in Australia in 2013'. *Journal of Industrial Relations*, 56(3): 397–415.

Tilly, C. (1995) 'Globalization threatens labor's rights'. *International Labor and Working-Class History*, 47 (Spring): 1–23.

Todd, P. & Preston, A. (2012) 'Gender pay equity in Australia: Where are we now and where are we heading?' *Australian Bulletin of Labour*, 38(3): 251–67.

Towers, B. (1997) *The Representation Gap: Change and Reform in the British and American Workplace*. Oxford: Oxford University Press.

Toynbee, P. & Walker, D. (2008) *Unjust Reward: Exposing Greed and Inequality in Britain Today*. London: Granta Books.

Traxler, F. (1995) 'Farewell to labor market associations? Organized versus disorganized decentralization as a map for industrial relations', in C. Crouch & F. Traxler (eds), *Organized Industrial Relations in Europe: What Future?* Aldershot: Avebury, pp. 3–19.

—— (2003) 'Bargaining (de)centralization, macroeconomic performance and control over the employment relationship'. *British Journal of Industrial Relations*, 41(1): 1–27.

—— (2004) 'The metamorphosis of corporatism: From classical to lean patterns'. *European Journal of Political Research*, 43(4): 571–98.

Traxler, F., Blaschke, S. & Kittel, B. (2001) *National Labour Relations in Inter-nationalized Markets: A Comparative Study of Institutions, Change and Performance*. Oxford: Oxford University Press.

Tripathy, S. (2014) 'President nod to Rajasthan labour law amendments'. 9 November. Retrieved 2 December 2014 from <http://timesofindia.india-times.com/india/President-nod-to-Rajasthan-labour-law-amendments/articleshow/45084160.cms>.

TUC (2013) *Workers on the Board: The Case for Workers' Voice in Corporate Governance*. London: TUC.

Tuck, R., Criddle, B. & Brittenden, S. (2013) *Labour Law Highlights 2013*. Liverpool: Institute of Employment Rights.

Tulpule, B. (1978) 'Industrial relations legislation: An alternative model'. *Economic and Political Weekly*, 9 December: 2017–20.

Turner, L., Katz, H.C. & Hurd, R.W. (2001) *Rekindling the Movement*. Ithaca, NY: Cornell University Press.

Turone, S. (1992) *Storia del sindacato in Italia*. Bari: Laterza.

Undy, R., Ellis, V., McCarthy, W. & Halmos, A. (1981) *Change in Trade Unions*. London: Hutchinson.

Unger, J. (ed.) (2008) *Associations and the Chinese State: Contested Spaces*. Armonk, NY: M.E. Sharpe

Vaciago, G. (1993) 'Exchange rate stability and market expectations: The crisis of the EMS'. *Review of Economic Conditions in Italy*, 1: 11–29.

Vanhercke, B. (2011) 'Is the social dimension of Europe 2020 an oxymoron?' in C. Degryse & D. Natali (eds), *Social Developments in the European Union, 2010*. Brussels: European Trade Union Institute, pp. 141–74.

Van Ruysseveldt, J. & Visser, J. (1996) *Industrial Relations in Europe*. London: Sage.

Van Wanrooy, B., Bewley, H., Bryson, A., Forth, J., Freeth, S., Stokes, L. & Wood, S. (2013) *Employment Relations in the Shadow of the Recession*. Houndsmills: Palgrave Macmillan.

Varshney, A. (1999) 'Mass politics or elite politics? India's economic reforms in comparative perspective', in J. Sachs, A. Varshney & N. Bajpai (eds), *India in the Era of Economic Reforms*. New Delhi: Oxford University Press.

Vartia, M. & Hyyti, J. (2002) 'Gender differences in workplace bullying among prison officers'. *European Journal of Work and Organizational Psychology*, 11(1): 113–26.

Vatta, A. (2007) 'Italy', in F. Traxler & G. Huemer (eds), *Handbook of Business Interest Associations, Firm Size and Governance*. London: Routledge, pp. 204–39.

Venkata Ratnam, C.S. (1996) 'Industrial relations in Indian states: An overview', in C.S. Venkata Ratnam (ed.), *Industrial Relations in Indian States*. New Delhi: Global Business Press/Indian Industrial Relations Association.

—— (2003) *Negotiated Change: Collective Bargaining, Liberalization and Restructuring in India*. New Delhi: Response.

—— (2006) *Industrial Relations*. New Delhi: Oxford University Press.

Venkata Ratnam, C.S. & Verma, A. (2011) 'Employment relations in India', in G.J. Bamber, R.D. Lansbury & N. Wailes (eds), *International and Comparative Employment Relations: Globalisation and Change*, 5th ed. Sydney/London: Allen & Unwin/Sage.

Venkatesan, J. (2012) 'Supreme Court orders states to implement workers' welfare plans'. *Hindu*, 10 February. Retrieved 1 April 2014 from <www.thehindu.com/todays-paper/tp-national/tp-newdelhi/supreme-court-orders-states-to-implement-workers-welfare-plans/article2877209.ece>.

Verma, A. & Yan, Z.M. (1995) 'The changing face of human resource management in China: Opportunities, problems and strategies', in A. Verma, T. Kochan & R. Lansbury (eds), *Employment Relations in the Growing Asian Economies*. London: Routledge, pp. 315–35.

Visser, J. (2006) 'Union membership statistics in 24 countries', *Monthly Labor Review*, 129(1): 38–49.

Visser, J. & Van Ruysseveldt, J. (1996) 'Robust corporatism, still? Industrial relations in Germany', in J. Van Ruysseveldt & J. Visser (eds), *Industrial Relations in Europe: Traditions and Transitions.* London: Sage, pp. 124–74.

Voelkl, M. (2002) *Der Mittelstand und die Tarifautonomie: Arbeitgeberverbände zwischen Sozialpartnerschaft und Dienstleistung*. Munich: Hampp.

Vogel, D. (2008) 'Private global business regulation'. *Annual Review of Political Science*, 11: 261–82.

Voos, P. (1984) 'Trends in union organizing expenditures: 1953–1977'. *Industrial and Labor Relations Review*, 38(1): 52–63.

Vosko, L. (2010) *Managing the Margins: Gender, Citizenship and the International Regulation of Precarious Employment*. Oxford: Oxford University Press.

Wacjman, J. & Edwards, P. (2005) *The Politics of the Workplace*. Oxford: Oxford University Press.

Waddington, J. (1992) 'Trade union membership in Britain, 1980–1987: Unemployment and restructuring'. *British Journal of Industrial Relations*, 30(2): 287–324.

—— (2003) 'Heightening tension in relations between trade unions and the Labour government'. *British Journal of Industrial Relations*, 41(2): 335–58.

—— (ed.) (2005) *Restructuring Representation: The Merger Process and Trade Union Structural Development in Ten Countries.* Brussels: Lang.

Waddington, J. & Hoffmann, J. (2000) 'The German union movement in structural transition: Defensive adjustment or setting a new agenda?' in R. Hoffmann, O. Jacobi, B. Keller & M. Weiss (eds), *Transnational Industrial Relations in Europe*. Düsseldorf: Hans-Böckler-Stiftung, pp. 113–37.

Wade, R. (1996) 'Globalisation and its limits: Reports of the death of the national economy are greatly exaggerated', in S. Berger & R. Dore (eds), *National Diversity and Global Capitalism*. Ithaca, NY: Cornell University Press, pp. 60–88.

Wailes, N. (2007) 'Globalization, varieties of capitalism and employment relations in retail banking'. *Bulletin of Comparative Labour Relations*, 64: 1–14.

—— (2008) 'Are national industrial relations regimes becoming institutionally incomplete?' in M. Ronnmar (ed.), *EU Industrial Relations v National*

*Industrial Relations: Comparative and Interdisciplinary Perspectives.*
Alphen aan den Rijn: Wolters Kluwer, pp. 3–14.

Wang, X., Bruning, N. & Peng, S.Q. (2007) 'Western high performance HR practices in China: A comparison among public-owned, private and foreign-invested enterprises'. *International Journal of Human Resource Management*, 18(4): 684–701.

Warner, M. & Ng, S.H. (1999) 'Collective contracts in Chinese enterprises: A new brand of collective bargaining under "market socialism"?' *British Journal of Industrial Relations*, 37(2): 295–314.

Warner, M. & Zhu, Y. (2010) 'Labour–management relations in the People's Republic of China: Seeking the "harmonious society"'. *Asia Pacific Business Review*, 16(3): 285–98.

Watts, J. (2010) 'Chinese workers strike at Honda Lock parts supplier'. *Guardian*, 11 June. Retrieved 28 August 2010 from <www.guardian.co.uk/business/2010/jun/11/honda-china>.

Wedderburn, K. (1986) *The Worker and the Law*, 3rd ed. Harmondsworth: Penguin.

Weiss, M. (2013) 'Die Entwicklung der Arbeitsbeziehungen aus arbeitsrechtlicher Sicht'. *Industrielle Beziehungen*, 20(4): 393–417.

Weiss, M. & Schmidt, M. (2008) *Labour Law and Industrial Relations in Germany*, 4th ed. Deventer: Wolters Kluwer.

Wheeler, H.N. (1985) *Industrial Conflict: An Integrative Theory*. Columbia, SC: University of South Carolina Press.

Whitfield, K. & Strauss, G. (1998) 'Research methods in industrial relations', in K. Whitfield & G. Strauss (eds), *Researching the World of Work: Strategies and Methods in Studying Industrial Relations.* Ithaca, NY: Cornell University Press, pp. 5–31.

Wilkinson, R. (2002a) 'The World Trade Organization'. *New Political Economy*, 7(1): 129–41.

—— (2002b) 'Peripheralising labour: The ILO, the WTO and the completion of the Bretton Woods project', in J. Harrod & R. O'Brien (eds), *Global Unions? Theory and Strategy of Organised Labour in the Global Political Economy*. London: Routledge, pp. 204–20.

—— (2002c) 'Locked out, shut down: Worker rights and the World Trade Organization'. Paper presented to the *British Journal of Industrial Relations* Conference on Politics and Industrial Relations, Windsor, September.

Wills, J. (1998) 'Taking on the Cosmo-Corps? Experiments in trans-national labour organization'. *Economic Geography*, 74(2): 111–31.

Winchester, D. & Bach, S. (1995) 'The state: The public sector', in P. Edwards (ed.), *Industrial Relations: Theory and Practice in Britain*. Oxford: Blackwell, pp. 304–36.

Witt, M. & Redding, G. (2014) 'China: Authoritarian capitalism', in M. Witt & G. Redding (eds), *Asian Business Systems*. Oxford: Oxford University Press, pp. 11–32.

Women and Work Commission (2006) *Shaping a Fairer Future*. London: Women and Work Equality Unit.

Wood, S. & Bryson, A. (2009) 'High involvement management', in W. Brown, A. Bryson, J. Forth & K. Whitfield (eds), *The Evolution of the Modern Workplace*. Cambridge: Cambridge University Press.

World Bank (2013) 'World development indicators 2013'. Retrieved 29 November 2014 from <http://data.worldbank.org/data-catalog/world-development-indicators>.

Wright, C.F. (2012) 'Immigration policy and market institutions in liberal market economies'. *Industrial Relations Journal*, 43(2): 110–36.

—— (2015a) 'Leveraging reputational risk: Sustainable sourcing campaigns for improving labour standards in production networks'. *Journal of Business Ethics*, January. doi: 10.1007/s10551-015-2552-1.

—— (2015b) 'Why do states adopt liberal immigration policies? The policy-making dynamics of skilled visa reform in Australia'. *Journal of Ethnic and Migration Studies*, 41(2): 306–28.

Wright, C.F. & Brown, W. (2013) 'The emergence of socially sustainable sourcing: A mechanism for protecting labour standards in the context of collective bargaining decline' in M. Freedland & N. Countouris (eds), *Resocialising Europe in a Time of Crisis*. Cambridge: Cambridge University Press, pp. 426–46.

Wright, C.F. & Lansbury, R.D. (2014) 'Trade unions and economic reform in Australia: 1983–2013'. *Singapore Economic Review*, 59(4): 1–22.

Xie, Y.H. (2011) 'Collective wage negotiation: Can "a third way" be found in coordinating labour relations?' *Socialist Studies*, 3: 99–102.

Xu, F. (2009) 'The emergence of temporary staffing agencies in China'. *Comparative Labor Law and Policy Journal*, 30(2): 431–62.

Yamashita, N. & Fukao, K. (2010) 'Expansion abroad and jobs at home: Evidence from Japanese multinational enterprises'. *Japan and the World Economy*, 22: 88–97.

Yao, Y. & Zhong, N.H. (2013) 'Unions and workers' welfare in Chinese firms'. *Journal of Labor Economics*, 31(3): 633–67.

Yeung, H.W.C. (2000) 'The dynamics of Asian business systems in a globalizing era'. *Review of International Political Economy*, 7(3): 399–433.

Yoshimori, M. (1995) 'Whose company is it? The concept of the corporation in Japan and the West'. *Long Range Planning*, 28: 33–44.

You, J. (1998) *China's Enterprise Reform: Changing State/Society Relations after Mao*. London: Routledge.

Zhang, J.G. (2006) 'Chinese trade unions actively promoting development of tripartite consultation and collective contract mechanism'. Retrieved 25 October 2008 from <www.acftu.org.cn/template/10002/file.jsp?cid=70&aid=125>.

# Index